CU00919968

Greek and Roman Sexualities:
A Sourcebook

Greek and Roman Sexualities

A Sourcebook

JENNIFER LARSON

BLOOMSBURY
LONDON • NEW DELHI • NEW YORK • SYDNEY

Bloomsbury Academic

An imprint of Bloomsbury Publishing Plc

50 Bedford Square
London
WC1B 3DP
UK

175 Fifth Avenue
New York
NY 10010
USA

www.bloomsbury.com

First published 2012

© Jennifer Larson, 2012

All rights reserved. No part of this publication may be reproduced or transmitted in any form or by any means, electronic or mechanical, including photocopying, recording, or any information storage or retrieval system, without prior permission in writing from the publishers.

Jennifer Larson has asserted her right under the Copyright, Designs and Patents Act, 1988, to be identified as Author of this work.

No responsibility for loss caused to any individual or organization acting on or refraining from action as a result of the material in this publication can be accepted by Bloomsbury Academic or the author.

British Library Cataloguing-in-Publication Data
A catalogue record for this book is available from the British Library.

ISBN: HB: 978-1-4411-5889-5
PB: 978-1-4411-9685-9

Library of Congress Cataloging-in-Publication Data
A catalog record for this book is available from the Library of Congress.

Typeset by Fakenham Prepress Solutions, Fakenham, Norfolk NR21 8NN
Printed and bound in India

For Christina A. Clark

Table of Contents

Introduction

In this volume, readers will find a broad variety of texts illustrating attitudes toward sexuality and gender in the cultures of ancient Greece and Rome. Some of the selections are familiar to any student of Classics, while others will be new to most readers. Chronologically, they stretch from the eighth century BCE, when the Homeric epics were composed, through the fifth century CE, when the Christian father Augustine reflected on the sexual mores of paganism in a Mediterranean world that was rapidly turning toward Christianity. Poets, historians, scholars, philosophers, lawgivers, physicians, sorcerers, and inscribers of graffiti are represented. That these voices are almost exclusively male is something all readers should keep in mind when using this book. Unlike the written culture of our modern world, ancient writings were typically products of a male perspective on life, and for the most part, the authors of the texts that follow were men of education and privilege. Therefore, as varied as the texts here appear to be, for the most part they represent the thought of a relatively small (though influential) slice of society.

How much of a difference does this make? It depends on our concept of history. If we approach history as a narrative of outstanding cultural achievements, great thinkers, and pivotal events, then what has been preserved to the modern day is a trove of valuable information (with the caveat that what ends up being recognised as 'great' has been decided in part by this same small group of people). If, on the other hand, we wish to learn more about the everyday experiences of ordinary people, or even influential and famous people who happened to be female, the sources available to us can be misleading. We are forced to examine them more carefully and critically, in the hope of uncovering precious insights into all that has been lost. I hope that this book will be helpful to readers pursuing both these types of history.

In the United States, most of us live in a defiantly monolingual culture, and it is easy to forget that a translation is just that – not the original text, but a creative and scholarly product that seeks to accurately convey the thought and aesthetic of the original. Because I have chosen and translated all the texts in this book myself, the process of translation and its implications for the experience of students have been uppermost in my mind throughout its preparation. Sourcebooks are typically compiled by licensing selections from existing works by a number of translators. Where the translations are all relatively recent (which is not always the case), this method works reasonably well, because the editor is able to draw upon the specialised expertise of translators working in various fields. However, even under ideal conditions, this approach has drawbacks, because every translator is faced with a myriad of choices when approaching a text. Should poetic originals be rendered as verse in English? Should the final product reflect stylistic features of the original even at the expense of readability in English? Do hints of the original syntax and sentence structure, and the literal translation of idioms help the reader grasp the 'otherness' of the culture under study, or do they amount to clumsy 'translationese'? To what degree should cultural references unfamiliar to the reader be clarified in the translated text itself, and when should they be relegated to notes? In texts dealing with sexuality, how should colloquial, explicit, and obscene terms be rendered in English? These are just a few of the choices facing each translator, and each translator inevitably makes different choices based on personal preference and the perceived needs of the audience for the translation. These varied choices can result in compilations that are wildly inconsistent in the vocabulary used for key terms, as well as accessibility to general readers, and the aesthetics of the final product.

Only in the twenty-first century has Translation Studies been fully established as a distinct discipline, and the complexities involved in the translation of Classical texts are receiving increased scholarly attention.[1] Critical attention has long been lavished on major new translations, particularly of epic poetry, and this has revealed a chasm between literary critics, who evaluate translations primarily as creative works using aesthetic criteria, and scholars, who tend to come down on the side of 'fidelity' to the content and even the syntax of the original text. Classicists often favour Richmond Lattimore's translation of the *Iliad*, for example, because it takes a 'line by line' approach and adheres very closely to the content of the original. Critics, on the other hand, have enthusiastically welcomed the Homeric translations of Robert Fagles, who exercises greater metrical freedom and jettisons stylistic features of the original, including the repetitions characteristic of poetry derived from an oral tradition. Because the goals of this book are primarily pedagogical, my general strategy is closer to that of Lattimore than Fagles. I adopt a 'sense for sense' approach, and a line of poetry in this book, more often than not, closely approximates the content in the original line. I avoid bold creative liberties and the use of anachronistic modern equivalents. On the other hand, there is sometimes a surprisingly inverse relationship between so-called 'fidelity' to the wording or stylistic features of an original, and the degree to which a translation achieves 'equivalence' to the source text. For example, in Lattimore's *Iliad*, the six-beat English line represents the six-footed Greek hexameter, but feels heavy and slow in comparison to the original. While the translation of classical texts is a scholarly process, the aesthetic choices are as essential to the final product as the philological ones.

Crucial to the translator are the intended audience for and purpose of a given work. For example, translation of Greek comedy for presentation on the stage leads to a product quite different from a translation for study purposes, where it is possible to provide explanatory notes on the text. I have translated the texts in this sourcebook for people engaged in serious formal or informal study of the ancient world. Because a student's knowledge of ancient genres and literary styles is blurred when poetry is presented as prose, I offer verse translations where appropriate. It seems important to me, for example, that students experience the work of the philosophers Empedocles and Lucretius as poetry. While I make no attempt to reproduce the metrical systems of the originals, I use a variety of rhythms, line-lengths, and other techniques in order to convey differences in genre. In place of the dactylic hexameter in epic selections, for example, I use a five-beat English line; elegiacs are represented by the alternation of five- and four-beat lines. In order to help acquaint students with the cultures in question, I avoid anachronistic 'equivalents', even in comic texts where the jokes may not translate well. Endnotes explain unfamiliar names and features of the text when the translation alone is not sufficient. Throughout, I have attempted to make the texts as accessible and readable as possible without sacrificing essential features of the originals.

One of the more dismaying discoveries I made while consulting existing translations of the texts in this volume was the frequency with which sexual terms and ideas are elided or translated with euphemisms in English. Students often rely on translations freely available via the internet for reasons of cost and convenience, but because of copyright issues, these are likely to be older versions and to reflect the prudish sensibilities of the late nineteenth and early twentieth centuries. In some cases, sections that contain sexual content are simply omitted from these translations. For coursework on ancient concepts of gender and sexuality, students need access to unexpurgated translations that accurately convey whether the diction in the original is vulgar, clinical, or euphemistic. It is essential that translators make no attempt to conceal the role of pederasty and other homosexual behaviours in ancient cultures (for example, the assumption in many of Plato's texts that *erōs* is operating between two males). Finally, the translator must accurately convey ancient cultural attitudes (for example, concerning rape or sexual relations with slaves) that are offensive to modern ethical standards.

Throughout this book, I have aimed at consistency in the use of key terminology, without falling into rigid one-for-one correspondences that could damage the integrity of the individual translations. A few observations about the vocabulary of the texts in this book, and how I have translated key terms, are in order.

Love, Desire and Affection

The Greeks distinguished between *erōs*, which they personified as a god, and *philia*. *Erōs* (or *eros* with a short o, depending on the dialect) is the feeling we describe as 'falling in love', the restless and passionate desire to draw near to and to touch another person. We can feel *erōs* for someone we hardly know. To the Greek way of thinking, a person we find physically beautiful inspires *erōs* in us, yet this emotion has a dark side; the effect of *erōs* is 'limb-loosening' and often destructive. In this book, I most often use 'love', 'to love', and 'fall in love' to translate *erōs,* the verb *eramai* and related words. When Zeus suddenly feels a strong desire for his wife Hera, he exclaims:

For never has such *love* [*eros*] for goddess or woman
Mastered my heart so overwhelmingly…(1.1; Homer *Iliad* 14.315–16)

Philia and its relatives in Greek have a much broader application, encompassing both non-sexual and sexual forms of love. *Philia* is friendship, but also tender concern and the emotion one feels for family members. We would be unlikely to feel *philia* for someone we hardly know. *Erōs* tends to be focused on the needs of the person who feels it, and is not completely incompatible with hate, whereas *philia* involves a feeling of goodwill and affection for its object. In order to convey a distinction between these two concepts in my translations, I render *philia* and its relatives by terms such as 'care', 'affection', or 'friendship', except in cases where it is clearly non-sexual: a king may feel a 'love of music' and a woman may mourn her 'loved ones'. Thus two women discussing their friendship say:

'See, *you don't care for me* [*ou phileis me*] or you would not hide such things.'
'*I care for you* [*philō men se*] as much as I do any other woman.' (5.16; Lucian *Dialogues of the Courtesans* 5.1)

In relationships that involve sexual attraction, of course, it is often the case that both *erōs* and *philia* are present, and one may speak of the *philia* that the partners feel. In a performance by two actors portraying a loving encounter between Dionysus and his bride Ariadne as they prepare for bed, the verb *philein* is emphasised:

For they heard Dionysus asking her *if she loved him* [*ei philei auton*], and she vowed that she did, in such a way that not only Dionysus, but all those present would have sworn that this boy and girl truly *cared for* [*phileisthai*] one another. (8.9; Xenophon *Symposium* 9.6)

In poetry, moreover, and particularly in Homeric texts, the related term *philotēs* often refers to sexual love. In the *Iliad*, Hera protests at Zeus' desire to have sex out in the open:

If you want *to make love* [*eunēthēnai en philotēti*] right now on Ida's peak
Where everything is visible to anyone... (1.1; Homer *Iliad* 14.331–2)

The verb *kataphilein* means 'to kiss', an act that is associated with loving affection as much as (or even more than) erotic love. Thus Plutarch notes that the Athenian statesman Pericles felt both desire and affection for Aspasia:

They say that *he kissed her* [*kataphilein*] every day as he left for the city centre, and he greeted her the same way when he returned home. (10.14; Plutarch *Pericles* 24.6)

The terms *pothos* and *himeros* are often used, especially in poetry, for the feelings that accompany *erōs*. I usually translate *pothos* as 'yearning' and *himeros* as 'longing', although both can also be rendered 'desire', depending on the context. The word I most often translate as 'desire' is *epithumia*, which is used to refer to physical desires and lustfulness. It is the term used when the speaker is thinking of desire in a neutral way, as physicians do, or as something to be avoided, as philosophers often do:

Yet surely no one considers men inferior to women, or less able to *school their own desires* [*epithumias paidagōgein*]... (6.11; Musonius Rufus 12 *Concerning Sexual Pleasures*)

When criminal or deviant lust is at issue, Greek texts may use *pathos*, 'passion', or the word *hubris,* which emphasises failure to restrain the baser urges toward violence and sex. In Latin texts, *cupīdo* is a close counterpart to *epithumia*, and I generally translate it as 'desire'. The word *libīdo* ('lust'), meanwhile, has a still more negative connotation:

For people *blinded by desire* [*cupidine caecī*] often do thus...(6.9; Lucretius *On the Nature of Things* 4.1154)

At this terrifying prospect, his *savage lust* [*trux libīdo*] prevailed as if by force over her resolute chastity. (9.12; Livy *History of Rome* 1.58)

The Latin noun *amor* and the verb *amāre* are used analogously to English 'love', encompassing sexual love, family feeling, and friendly affection. Like Greek *philia, amor* can refer to a sexual attachment and loving devotion at the same time, as in Livy's story of a prostitute who risked her life for her the young man she loved:

For she *loved and sought him out* [*amātus adpetītusque erat*] of her own accord, and since his own relatives were very stingy, the prostitute generously supported him. (1.11; Livy *History of Rome* 39.9.6)

Yet as a sexually charged emotion *amor*, like Greek *erōs*, was viewed in a more negative light in Roman culture than 'love' is in ours, and often refers to sexual passion in the absence of caring or even goodwill. Livy sees no contradiction in describing as *amor* the emotion felt by the rapist Sextus Tarquinius:

Burning with passion [*amōre ardens*], he waited until everyone seemed to be asleep and it was safe to move about. (9.12; Livy *History of Rome* 1.58.2)

The ambivalence with which the ancients viewed *amor* and *erōs*, and their conviction that it often led to disastrous and fatal outcomes, is a key difference between their culture and ours.

Sexual Relations and Partners

Greek texts exhibit a broad variety of terms for sexual relations, but the most common are *sunousia* 'being together', *homilia* 'intercourse', and *mixis* or *summixis* 'mingling, mingling together'. These nouns and their related verbs may be used in poetry as well as philosophical or medical writings:

Some people suppose that it is a good thing for the female to continue in a state of virginity as long as there is not yet *an urge for intercourse* [*hormēn pros tēn mixin*]. (6.13; Soranus *Gynecology* 1.8 [33])

Circumlocutions involving the words for 'bed' (*eunē*, *lechos*) are common, especially in poetic texts. In the *Bacchae*, Pentheus expresses his suspicion that the women of his family are engaging in illicit sex:

And they slink off here and there in secret,
To *serve the beds* [*eunais hupēretein*] of men. (3.6; Euripides *Bacchae* 222–3)

A more prosaic verb is *plēsiazein*, which literally means 'draw near to' and is similar in tone to our phrase 'have relations with' where the context is understood to be sexual. In Latin we find *coitus* 'sexual intercourse' and *concubitus* 'lying together' used as positive or neutral terms for sexual relations, while *stuprum* is used instead if the act is perceived negatively:

And the Spartans themselves, while they grant every freedom in the love of youths except *actual fornication* [*stuprum*]... (4.14; Cicero *On the Republic* 4.4)

In both Greek and Latin, the goddesses of love give their names to parts of speech denoting sexual intercourse; in these cases the emphasis is on the pleasurable aspects of sex. Therefore I typically translate *ta aphrodisia* (literally 'the things of Aphrodite') as 'sexual pleasures' and the verb *aphrodisiazein* as 'to enjoy sex' or the like. In Latin too, particularly in poetic texts, the name of Venus herself is used by metonymy for sexual love:

Near tears, she asks 'Where will it end for me,
Gripped by a strange new love [*novae...Veneris*], unknown to any?' (5.7; Ovid *Metamorphoses* 9.726–8)

Modern scholarship on ancient sexualities has shown that for the ancients, the gender of a sexual partner was less important than the roles played by the respective partners in the sexual act. The 'active' role of the penetrator was assigned to the masculine, dominant, and powerful partner, while the supposedly 'passive' role of one who is penetrated belonged to the weaker, submissive, and/or feminine partner. When sexual relations are described, the cognate verbs *paschein* in Greek and *patī* in Latin often refer to the role of the 'passive' partner. For example, the Julian law says that any male who willingly 'submits' (*patitur*) is guilty of criminal behaviour (9.18; Julius Paulus, *Opinions*, 2.26.13), while Lucian's prostitutes gossip about women who 'won't do it' (*ouk ethelousas auto paschein*) with men (5.16; Lucian *Dialogues of the Courtesans* 5.2). The historian Theopompus uses this terminology when he expresses shock at Etruscan men's sexual habits:

The Etruscans feel no shame if they are seen having sex in the open, and they do not even feel ashamed *to be the passive partner* [*paschontas*], for this too is the custom in their country. (7.6; Theopompus of Chios *FGrHist* 115 F 204)

In more vulgar and colloquial contexts, the verbs *binein* in Greek and *futuere* in Latin are very close to English 'fuck' and are so translated in this book. The active and passive roles are reflected in the grammatical voice chosen for the verb. Thus in Martial's advice to the woman he calls Lesbia, he refers to the fact that she is penetrated by her partner, and the words have the same insulting tone as in English:

Don't get caught, but do get fucked [*futuī*]. (10.15; Martial *Epigrams* 1.34.10)

Another Greek term that can be used to refer to the different roles of partners in sex is the verb *charizesthai*, which has the basic meaning of 'grant a favour for' or 'gratify'. Xenophon's character Ischomachus uses this verb to indicate his own dominant status in relation to his wife and female slaves:

And whenever her looks are compared with those of a female servant, she will be cleaner and better dressed, and altogether more stimulating, especially since she is *willing to gratify me* [*hekousan charizesthai*], whereas a female servant is compelled to do so. (8.10; Xenophon *Economics* 10.12)

Just as sex acts were assumed to require an active and a passive partic-ipant, the partners in a love affair could themselves be assigned active and passive labels. I use the English noun 'lover' to translate Greek *erastēs*. Conventionally, the *erastēs*, an older male partner in a pederastic relationship (or the male partner in a heterosexual relationship) actively pursued the satis-faction of his desire, while the 'beloved', *erōmenos* (or if female, *erōmenē*) was perceived as a relatively passive object of desire. Another word used to denote the beloved (typically in the case of younger males) was *paidika*, which I translate 'boyfriend', 'darling', or 'favourite'. Thus in his speech on pederasty in the *Symposium*, Pausanias says:

For example, if a man in pursuit of someone's money, or political office, or any other type of power were to behave the way *lovers* [*erastai*] do with their *boyfriends* [*paidika*], begging and pleading in a needy fashion... (4.6; Plato *Symposium* 183a)

There was debate in antiquity over what the beloved felt, or ought to feel, toward the lover. According to pederastic ideals, the beloved felt affection rather than desire. Thus differing emotions are ascribed to the lovers Harmodius and Aristogiton:

The tyrants here certainly learned this by experience, for the love [*erōs*] of Aristogiton and the affection [*philia*] of Harmodius were strong enough to destroy their power. (4.6; Plato *Symposium* 182c)

When the love object is female, a different vocabulary seems to apply. In Greek, a female lover (as opposed to a spouse or prostitute) was often called a *pallakē* or *pallakis*. I translate 'mistress' when the context makes clear that the woman with this title is a slave or a person of low status, and 'concubine' when the context indicates that she cohabits with her partner as a spouse would, but has a status lower than that of a wife. The Latin equivalents, *paelex* and *concubīnus/a*, are used to denote dependent male or female sex partners who have relatively low status. Suetonius uses the latter term to refer to a sexual partner of the emperor Galba, a freed slave:

Icelus, *one of his old lovers* [*e veteribus concubīnīs*], brought him news in Spain of Nero's death. (4.20; Suetonius *The Twelve Caesars* 7.22.1)

Sexual Virtues and Vices

In Classical antiquity, at least insofar as it is conveyed to us through the written sources, the most admired virtue when it came to sexual behaviour was not abstinence, but self-control and moderation. Particularly for men who were free citizens and possessed economic and political privileges, the ability to control one's bodily urges and to enjoy physical pleasures in moderation demonstrated one's worthiness to exercise power. In Greek thought *enkrateia* ('self-control') was highly prized. In his praise of archaic Spartan marriage customs that required spouses to meet clandestinely, Plutarch approvingly observes:

Not only were such meetings good practice in *self-control* [*enkrateias*] and *moderation* [*sōphrosynēs*], they also brought together the spouses in sexual union when their bodies were ready for procreation. (8.16; Plutarch *Lycurgus* 15.5)

The opposite of *enkrateia* is *akrateia*, which literally means 'lack of control'. This vice encompasses overindulgence and self-indulgence. The related term *akolasia* refers to a lack of discipline or restraint that may be either internal or external. I translate the adjective *akolastos* variously as 'undisciplined', 'unbridled', and 'unrestrained':

...the tactile pleasure of *the undisciplined person* [*akolastoi*] has to do not with the whole body, but with certain parts. (6.7; Aristotle *Nichomachean Ethics* 1118a 9)

The virtue of moderation is not as highly valued in modern times as it was in antiquity, and the English word does not fully convey the prestige attached to Greek *sōphrosynē*. In Latin, the equivalent virtue is *temperantia* and the vice *intemperantia*. While *sōphrosynē* and related parts of speech have to do with moderation in every aspect of life, they are often used specifically in reference to sexual behaviour, and in such cases I translate them as 'chastity', 'chaste', etc. When the misogynist character Hippolytus complains about women's lack of moderation, he is thinking of sexual transgressions:

Either *let them be taught chastity* [*sōphronein didaxatō*],
Or let me trample them down forever. (3.4; Euripides *Hippolytus* 667–8)

This type of chastity did not mean total abstinence from sex, but the restriction of sexual activity to the appropriate amount and type for the individual concerned. Thus, for a virgin daughter chastity meant no sex, for a wife it meant sex only with her husband, and for a husband it meant sex in moderation, and only with partners sanctioned by society. The Latin noun *castitas* and adjective *castus* (which give us our words 'chastity' and 'chaste') refer to this same virtue and are often found in poetry as synonyms of Latin *pudicitia*, which I also translate as 'chastity'. The virtue of *pudicitia* had a special prestige in Roman culture, similar to that of *sōphrosynē* in Greek, and the Romans personified Pudicitia as a goddess. *Pudicitia* was desirable for both men and women and the possession of this virtue meant that a person had self-control. The Elder Seneca deplored the apparent lack of *pudicitia* as a manly virtue in the youth of his day:

They are born spineless weaklings, and remain like that for life, assaulting the *chastity* [*pudicitiae*] of others, and careless of their own. (3.16; Seneca *Controversiae* 1 Pref. 9)

As this passage from Seneca suggests, *pudicitia* could be forcibly taken from a man and especially from a woman. Livy reports that after Lucretia's rape,

When her husband asked whether all was well with her, she replied, 'Not at all. For how can a woman be well when *she has lost her chastity* [*āmissā pudicitiā*]?' (9.12; Livy *History of Rome* 1.58.7)

Thus *pudicitia* was not only a virtue, but also a physical state subject to violation and irretrievable loss.

Modesty, Shame, and Disgrace

In antiquity, the concepts of modesty and shame were often invoked in texts touching on sexuality. The Latin noun *pudor* and verb *pudēre* share the same root as *pudicitia* and refer to the sense of modesty, shame, or respect that causes people to make the 'right', socially approved choice in a given situation. Thus Ovid's self-consciously naughty manual of seduction ridicules men who hesitate to force themselves on their dates:

Such a short path from kisses to your heart's desire –
Blunders, *not scruples* [*nōn pudor*], hold you back! (9.13; Ovid *The Art of Love* 1.671–2)

Latin *verēcundia* is similar to *pudor*, with stronger connotations of shyness and physical modesty. Augustine uses both terms when he professes that strenuous effort is required to convey the shameful facts about pagan religion without offending his readers:

Let human *modesty* [*verēcundiae*] be spared; let the tale of lustful flesh and blood go forward in a way that preserves *respect* [*pudōris*]. (1.17; Augustine *City of God* 6.9)

In Greek, the person who possesses a sense of modesty or shame has *aidōs* or *aischunē*. *Aidōs* is often personified as a virtue. In a Euripidean tragedy, the title character sings a song of praise to the virgin goddess Artemis, personifying *aidōs* as a keeper of an inviolate garden:

The spring bee roams this untouched meadow
And *Reverence* [*Aidōs*] tends the plants with river dew (7.4; Euripides *Hippolytus* 77–8)

Things about which one ought to feel shame or modesty, on the other hand, are *aischra* or *aidoia*. The phrase *ta aidoia* is often used euphemistically to refer to the genitals. In medical writings, it is used as a neutral word for the genitals without connotations of shame:

As to the outgrowths of skin at the ends of *the genitals* [*ta aidoia*] of both sexes, in women they are present for the sake of ornament... (6.14; Galen *On the Usefulness of Parts of the Body* 15.3)

Greek generally uses words formed from one of these roots to describe sexual acts considered shameful or disgraceful. For example, Herodotus disapprovingly refers to the alleged practice of sacred prostitution in Babylonia:

This is the most shameful [*aischistos*] of the Babylonian customs...(10.2; Herodotus *Histories* 1.99.1)

In Latin, the adjective *impudīcus/a* describes people who exhibit a shameless lack of *pudor*, and the noun *stuprum* is the favoured term for virtually any kind of transgressive sexual activity. In this book, *stuprum* is often translated as 'fornication' in order to capture the sense of moral condemnation it carries, but also in other ways depending on the context. Livy's account of the Bacchanalian scandal illustrates some of the possibilities:

The harm they did was not limited to the *promiscuous coupling* [*prōmiscua stupra*] of freeborn men and women...(1.11; Livy *History of Rome* 39.8.7)

The men practiced more *sexual immorality* [*stupra*] with one another than with the women. (1.11; Livy *History of Rome* 39.13.10)

These were the ones who were unwilling to join the conspiracy, to participate in crimes, or *to suffer sexual abuse* [*stupra patī*]...(1.11; Livy *History of Rome* 39.13.13)

I translate the term *flāgitium* as 'disgraceful act'. It encompasses almost any type of disgrace but is often employed to describe sexual misconduct:

At first you were a common whore; you performed *disgraceful acts* [*flāgitiī*] at a fixed price, and it was not cheap. (3.14; Cicero *Philippics* 2.44)

Both Greeks and Romans associated ideas of purity and pollution with sexual activity. The gods often required that worshipers approach them in a 'pure' state, having abstained from sexual relations for a specified period of time. Abstention from sex resulted in a state of 'purity' known in Greek as *hagneia* and in Latin as *castimōnia*. This is the state Plutarch ascribes to the Vestal Virgins at Rome:

The king ordained thirty years of *purity* [*hagneia*] for the sacred virgins. (7.13; Plutarch *Life of Numa* 10.1)

Particularly in Roman culture, there was a strong element of disgust and moral condemnation tied to the concept of physical impurity, especially when it came to anything touched by the mouth. Both Greek and Latin texts reveal a particular aversion to touching another person's genitals with the mouth. Providing oral sex was considered demeaning to those who practiced it, and a source of defilement to anyone they might kiss. In Roman poetic invective and in brothel graffiti we find the frank use of the obscene verb *fellāre*:

Fortuna *sucks* [*fellāt*]. (10.13; CIL 4.2259)

In other types of texts, euphemisms or circumlocution are used when referring to oral sex:

He *laboured over my groin* [*sūper inguinā meā...moluit*] for a long time, but in vain. (9.14; Petronius *Satyrica* 23)

But if a man dreams that he himself *performs the unmentionable act* [*arrhētopoiein*] on someone he knows, either a man or a woman, he will grow to hate that person because it is no longer possible for their mouths to be joined together. (9.16; Artemidorus of Daldis *Interpretation of Dreams* 1.79)

The concern with potential defilement caused by contact with someone who has engaged in 'impure' acts of any kind is echoed in other sources such as Valerius Maximus (7.12) and Tertullian (5.18).

Transgression and Deviance

The Greeks and Romans lacked an exact equivalent to our word 'rape'. The Latin verb *rapere* and the Greek verb *harpazein* mean 'to abduct, carry off' and these terms may imply rape. More often, however, rape is described through a circumlocution using the words for 'force', especially *vīs* (Latin) and *bia* (Greek). Thus in Valerius Maximus' account of the rape of Lucretia, she is literally 'compelled to suffer fornication by force':

Lucretia... was *forcibly subjected to rape* [*per vim stupra patī coacta*] by Sextus Tarquinius, the son of the king Superbus. (7.12; Valerius Maximus *Memorable Deeds and Sayings* 6.1.1)

In a speech on an adultery case, the Greek orator Lysias distinguishes 'those who use force' from 'those who use persuasion' to achieve transgressive liaisons:

Rapists [*tous biazomenous*] are hated by the people they forcibly ruin, but *seducers* [*tous peithontas*] function by corrupting the souls of their victims. (9.8; Lysias *On the Murder of Eratosthenes* 1.32–3)

The Greeks included rape within the broader category of *hubris*, physical assault or unjustified violence. An Athenian law cited by Aeschines lays out the penalties for this offense:

If any Athenian *commits physical violation* [*hubrisēi*] against a freeborn child, the guardian of the child shall bring an accusation to the Thesmothetae, specifying a penalty. (9.9; Aeschines *Against Timarchus* 16)

Definitions of rape are culturally determined, and in the slave-owning cultures of the Greeks and Romans, different rules often applied depending on the status of the person who suffered the assault. A slave-owner's rape of his or her slave, for example, was not normally considered a criminal offense.

For both Greeks and Romans, the crime of adultery was the seduction or rape of another man's wife, and the male *moichos* (Greek) or *adulter* (Latin) bore the primary responsibility for the crime, although straying wives were usually divorced or otherwise punished as well, and there are feminine forms of these terms. Depending on the context, I translate *moicheia/adulterium* as 'adultery' and *moichos/adulter* as 'adulterer' or 'lover' (the latter only where it is clear that the activity is illicit). For example, adultery is an important theme in Cicero's speech in defense of Caelius:

The accusers speak of lustful desire, love affairs, adultery [*libidinēs, amorēs, adulteria*]; of Baiae and beaches and banquets; of revelry, songs, musical entertainments and sailing. (3.12; Cicero *For Caelius* 15.35)

The adulterer was related in Roman thought to the *cinaedus*, a stock villain with no exact equivalent in our culture. The Latin term is a loan word from Greek, and the word originally referred to a type of male dancer who effeminately wiggled his backside. It came to refer to a man who compromised his masculinity by paying too much attention to his grooming, who was perceived as effeminate by other men, and who was suspected of a secret desire to be anally penetrated. Aulus Gellius reports on the general Scipio Aemilianus' suspicion of such gender-deviant men:

The kind of perfumed man who primps every day in front of a mirror, who shaves his eyebrows, who walks around with plucked beard and thighs…who would doubt that he has done the same things that *perverts* [*cinaedī*] do? (3.19; Aulus Gellius *Attic Nights* 6.12)

To Roman men of power, whose prestige depended in large part on their perceived masculinity, the label of *cinaedus* was a serious insult. Translators often render this term as 'faggot' or use other words that echo modern insults against homosexuals. These terms may be misleading, however, because the *cinaedus* could also be attractive to women (who were thought to have a decided preference for sweet-smelling, fashionable men of androgynous appearance), and he was practiced at seducing other men's wives or daughters. In this book, I have chosen to translate *cinaedus* as 'pervert', which lacks the visceral impact of a slang term like 'faggot', yet expresses the ideas of sexual deviance and failure to conform to gender expectations. I have reserved the term 'faggot' as an equivalent for words that specifically refer to men or boys who are anally penetrated. Thus Catullus writes of Caesar and Mamurra (who were notorious for seducing women):

Those nasty *perverts* (*cinaedī*) get along well,
Mamurra and that *faggot* (*pathicus*) Caesar. (3.13; Catullus *Songs* 57.1–2)

It was an insult to suggest that a man was effeminate or enjoyed being penetrated (though a desire to penetrate youthful males was accepted as a normal masculine trait). A gender-deviant man might be described as *mollis* or *dēlicātus* in Latin and *malakos* in Greek, words that refer to softness, weakness, and fragility. In most cases, I translate these words as 'effeminate'. In the comedy *Clouds*, the pederast character Just Argument pines for the old days when boys adopted a properly masculine demeanor:

Nor did any boy greet his lover with a *high, effeminate voice* [*malakēn… phonēn*],
Fluttering his eyelashes and going about like a prostitute. (4.4; Aristophanes *Clouds* 979)

A more extreme word is Greek *androgunos*, literally 'man-woman', which Justin uses in reference to 'effeminate' male prostitutes:

In all the nations, a great number of females as well as *effeminate males* [*androgunōn*] who do unspeakable things are set up to practice this defilement… (10.19; Justin Martyr *Apology* 1.27.2)

There is no Greek or Latin equivalent for the English word 'homosexual', although the ancients did not fail to notice that some individuals preferred same-sex partners. For a woman who preferred female partners, we find in Plato (*Symposium* 191e) the term *hetairistria*, which seems to refer to 'prostitutes who enjoy other women'. Where this term appears in Lucian's dialogue between prostitutes, I translate 'woman-lover'. The awkwardness of this term conveys the uncertainty of the speaker about this category of women:

I don't understand what you mean, unless perhaps she is a *woman-lover* [*hetairistria*]. They say that there are women like that in Lesbos, who look like men… (5.16; Lucian *Dialogues of the Courtesans* 5.2)

Later texts sometimes use Greek *tribas* (also a loan word in Latin) and its Latin equivalent *frictrix*, both of which literally mean 'woman who rubs'. For Martial's poem describing a masculine woman, I have used a modern slang term as an equivalent:

Philainis the *dyke* [*tribas*] screws boys,
And bruises eleven girls a day. (5.11; Martial *Epigrams* 7.67.1–2)

Elsewhere, however, I translate these terms 'women who love women' or 'women who have sex with each other'.

Prostitution

In Greek and Roman culture, prostitution was an industry practiced at many economic and social levels, with corresponding vocabulary used to denote higher- and lower-prestige sex workers. At the top of the economic and social ladder were the Greek *hetaira* and (with a rather lower level of prestige) the Roman *meretrix*. When a Greek orator wants to prove that a woman called Neaera was a prostitute, he presents testimony that she attended dinner parties in the company of men:

Nicarete accompanied her, and they stayed with Ctesippus son of Glauconides of Cydantidae, and Neaera drank and dined in front of them all, *just like a courtesan* [*hōs an hetaira ousa*]. (10.4; Pseudo-Demosthenes *Against Neaera* 59.24)

Whereas I always translate *hetaira* as 'courtesan', the best translation of *meretrix* depends on the context. In Juvenal's portrait of the empress Messalina as a prostitute, I use the word 'whore' in order to deepen the contrast between Messalina's exalted social rank and the poet's revelation of her nightly activities:

That *imperial whore* [*Augusta meretrix*] would don her hooded cloak,
Spurning the palace for a cheap mat in a stall. (10.16; Juvenal *Satires* 6.117–18)

Prostitutes who sold their bodies for lower prices were called *pornos/ pornē* in Greek and *scortum* in Latin; the terms could be applied to both males and females. In order to convey the low status of these individuals, I translate 'whore'. Another Latin term for a low-paid prostitute was *lupa*, 'wolf'. In an epigram, Martial shows how different classes of prostitutes seek privacy for their activities, in contrast to the woman he is lampooning:

Courtesans [meretrīces] repel onlookers with a curtain or bolt...
Even *dirty hookers [spurcās lupās]* take cover in tombs. (1–15; Martial *Epigrams* 1.34.5, 8)

In more formal contexts, authors used circumlocution and euphemism when speaking of prostitution; a typical example occurs in the speech *Against Neaera*, where the Greek literally means 'to work with the body':

They were accompanied by this Neaera, who had already begun *to work as a prostitute [ergazomenē...tōi sōmati]* although she was younger and had not reached adolescence. (10.4; Pseudo-Demosthenes *Against Neaera* 59.22)

The vocabulary of prostitution alludes to the fact that pimps and panders expose prostitutes to public view as merchandise. Greek *proagōgeuein* (literally 'lead forth') and Latin *prostituēre* ('cause to stand in front') refer to the activities of these entrepreneurs:

There are those who *prostitute [proagōgeuontai]* even their own children or wives... (10.20; Justin Martyr *Apology* 1.27)

In Greek, a 'brothel' was a *porneion*, while Latin used a number of colourful words including *stabulum* (an inn), *fornix* ('arch', referring to the arches of the circus where prostitutes found customers), and *lupānar* (literally a 'wolf-den'). Because these words do not appear often in this book, I have not attempted to differentiate among them.

Over the past two decades, the discipline of Classics has seen the coursework and research focus on 'Women in Antiquity' that prevailed in the 1980s expanded to include gender, masculinity, the body, and now sexuality. I would like to express my appreciation to one of the pioneers in this field, Marilyn Skinner, for her constructive comments on the proposal for this volume, which is intended to complement her fine introduction (Skinner 2005). I also thank my editor Michael Greenwood for allowing me the additional time I needed in order to complete the project. This book is dedicated to my longtime friend Christina A. Clark, who has faithfully offered valuable encouragement and support, both professional and personal, for many years.

Further Reading

Essay collections and surveys of sexuality in Greek and Roman culture include Halperin, Winkler and Zeitlin 1990, Hallett and Skinner 1997, McClure 2002, and Skinner 2005. For sexual symbols in art and visual representations of sex and lovemaking in the ancient Greek and Roman worlds, see Johns 1982, Clarke 1998, Clarke 2003. On sexual vocabulary in Greek, see Henderson 1991; on sexual vocabulary in Latin see Adams 1982. For a survey of the evidence for same-sex love in the Greek and Roman worlds, see Cantarella 1992. For assessment of the influence of Foucault on the scholarship of sexuality in antiquity, see Larmour, Miller and Platter 1998.

Using This Book

This book consists of ten topical chapters, each of which is arranged chronologically. The range and variety of possible text selections for a volume like this is very great, and I make no claim to have achieved complete coverage of the subject. I have attempted to balance the selections in order to provide appropriate coverage of time periods, genres, text types, and so on. Because of the fundamental role of Greek thought in establishing many of the Classical world's cultural assumptions about sexuality, and the predominance of Greek authors in the philosophical and medical texts, there is a slightly heavier emphasis on Greek selections. Each chapter includes a brief introduction to the texts included, with references to selections by chapter and number within the chapter (for example, 3.5 is selection five in Chapter Three), and suggestions for further reading; these focus mainly on recent works accessible in English. The spellings of Greek words are Latinised except where the words appear in italics, and Latinised forms of familiar Greek names are used (Plato, Oedipus).

Abbreviations of journal names in the bibliography follow those in *L'Année Philologique*. Source texts cited according to specific editions use the following abbreviations and conventions:

CIL	*Corpus Inscriptionum Latinarum*. 1862–. Berlin: G. Reimer. [Various editors; the abbreviation *CIL* is followed by the volume number and inscription number.]
Diggle	*Euripidis fabulae*. 1981. Edited by James Diggle. Oxford: Clarendon Press.
Diels-Kranz	*Die Fragmente der Vorsokratiker*. 1957. Edited by Hermann Diels and Walter Kranz. Zurich: Weidmann.
FGrHist	*Die Fragmente der griechischen Historiker*. 1954–. Edited by Felix Jacoby. Leiden: Brill. [The abbreviation *FGrHist* is followed by the author number and fragment number.]
IG	*Inscriptiones Graecae*. 1915–. Berlin: De Gruyter. [Various editors; the abbreviation *IG* is followed by the volume number and inscription number.]

Joly	Hippocrate. *De la génération; De la nature de l'enfant; Des maladies IV; Du foetus de huit mois.* 1970. Volume 11. Edited by R. Joly. Paris: Belles Lettres.
Lee	Lee, Guy with Maltby, Robert. *Tibullus: Elegies. Introduction, Text, Translation and Notes.* 1990. Third Edition. Leeds: Francis Cairns.
Littré	Hippocrates. *Oeuvres complètes.* 1961–1978 [reprint of 1839 edition]. Edited and translated by E. Littré. 10 Volumes. Amsterdam: M. Hakkert.
Lobel-Page	*Poetarum Lesbiorum Fragmenta.* 1955, repr. 1997. Edited by Edgar Lobel and Denys Page. Oxford: Clarendon Press.
LSCG	Sokolowski, Franciszek. *Lois sacrées des cités grecques.* 1969. Paris: Boccard.
LSCG Supp.	Sokolowski, Franciszek. *Lois sacrées des cités grecques. Supplément.* 1962. Paris: Boccard.
Lutz	Lutz, Cora. *Musonius Rufus, 'The Roman Socrates'.* 1947. New Haven: Yale University Press.
Muehll	*Epicuri epistulae tres et ratae sententiae.* 1982. Edited by P. von der Muehll. Stuttgart: B. G. Teubner.
PCG	*Poetae Comici Graeci.* 1983–. Edited by R. Kassel and C. Austin. Berlin and New York: De Gruyter. [The abbreviation *PCG* is followed by the volume number and fragment number for the specified author.]
PGM	*Papyri Graecae Magicae.* 1973–. Edited by Karl Preisendanz. 2 Vols. Stuttgart: B. G. Teubner.
PMG	*Poetae Melici Graeci.* 1962. Edited by Denys Page. Oxford: Clarendon Press.
Rabe	*Scholia in Lucianum.* 1906, repr. 1971. Edited by Hugo Rabe. Stuttgart: B. G. Teubner.
Snell-Maehler	*Pindari Carmina cum fragmentis.* 1975–80. Edited by Herwig Maehler based on the editions by Bruno Snell. Leipzig: B. G. Teubner.
Suppl. Mag.	*Supplementum Magicum.* 1990–92. 2 Vols. Edited by Robert W. Daniel and Franco Maltomini. Opladen: Westdeutscher Verlag.

TrGF   *Tragicorum Graecorum Fragmenta.* 1986–. Göttingen: Vandenhoeck & Ruprecht. [The abbreviation *TrGF* is followed by the volume number and fragment number.]

West   *Iambi et elegi Graeci ante Alexandrum cantati.* 1989–92. Second edition. 2 Vols. Edited by M. L. West. Oxford and New York: Oxford University Press.

1

Sexuality and the Gods

Myths and rituals in both Greek and Roman culture attest belief in a dynamic relationship between human sexuality and natural fertility. In Archaic Greek thought, creation is established and maintained through reproductive processes analogous to human sexual relations and birth. Although the primordial beings in the universe arise spontaneously and asexually, Eros (Sexual Desire) is among the first of these (2.2). Ge or Gaea (Earth) comes together with her son and partner Uranus (Heaven) in a union that ensures the earth's fertility, for the rain from the heavens impregnates the land (1.5). This concept of the 'sacred marriage' between deities is recapitulated in the union of Zeus and Hera, which produces lush greenery and flowers from the earth (1.1). The sacred marriage was also enacted in ritual, as in the Athenian ceremony uniting the wife of the King Archon with the god Dionysus (1.8). We do not know how this 'marriage' was consummated: did the King Archon play the role of the god, wearing his mask, or was the bride shut into a chamber alone to await the god's visit?

A similar ritual is probably reflected in the myth that Demeter had sexual intercourse with the mortal man Iasion in a thrice-ploughed field (1.3). Ploughing and sowing are common metaphors for sexual intercourse, and many sexual elements are present in the rituals of the cult of Demeter and Persephone, which was concerned with both grain agriculture and afterlife hopes. Performed primarily by women, these rituals include *aischrologia* (sex-talk, often in the form of bantering insults) and the handling of sacred objects in the shape of male and female genitals. The scholiast on Lucian (1.18) provides two key descriptions of these types of rites, although questions surround the accuracy of this late source. Another figure in the Demeter cult was the woman Baubo or Iambe, who seems to personify this type of salacious, insult-laden ritual banter. Baubo's scurrilous exposure of her genitals to Demeter (1.16) does not provoke divine wrath; instead, the sight of the human organs of generation cheers the goddess of agriculture. This myth pertained to the Eleusinian Mysteries, one of the most prestigious cults in the ancient Mediterranean world, whose initiates held hopes for a better afterlife. Pagan mystery religions competed directly with Christianity, which also required initiation rites and promised a life after death. Christian authors such as Clement of Alexandria and Augustine vigorously attacked pagan practices and beliefs they deemed indecent (1.16, 1.17), making the mysteries special targets of ridicule. While they must be read with care, these authors often provide the most detailed evidence (and in some cases the only evidence) for specific myths or rituals.

Evoking Archaic Greek practices of bride capture, the myth of Persephone's abduction and sexual conquest by Hades has many layers of meaning. Familiar in Greek thought is the idea that for a girl, marriage is a kind of death, requiring the extinction of the girl's former life in favour of her new identity as wife. Premature death, meanwhile, can be visualised as a marriage to Hades (8.3). In the Homeric *Hymn to Demeter*, the rape of Persephone planned by Zeus and his brother without the consent of her mother Demeter provides the waiting cosmos with its Queen of the underworld (1.4). Persephone's union with Hades, however, is also a kind of sacred marriage, because her descent to the underworld recapitulates the planting of the seed grain and its germination, while her annual ascension to the earth and the embrace of her mother represents the emergence of the crops.

Archetypal masculine and feminine sexual qualities are embodied in the goddesses and gods (beauty, chastity, seductiveness, sexual jealousy, sexual prowess, and so on). Zeus, the 'father of gods and men', embodies a male fantasy of supreme power and unlimited access to sexual partners (1.1, 1.2); his sexual potency is closely tied to his identity as progenitor and king. Zeus helps to populate the cosmos with deities and humans through his activities as husband, lover, seducer, and rapist. So great is his procreative power that he usurps in part the reproductive prerogative by birthing Athena from his head, while Hera, angry at this infringement, produces the lame Hephaestus without a male partner (1.2). The myth reflects cultural views, later enshrined in scientific writings by Aristotle (6.6), Galen (6.14, 6.15), and others, about the superior instrumentality of the male role in reproduction. As the divine exemplar of wifely deceit, jealousy, and attraction, Hera uses sexual wiles to draw Zeus' attention from the events at Troy; her elaborate grooming in preparation for the seduction is parallel to a warrior's arming scene. Such emphasis on rich dress and ornament (also evident in the description of Aphrodite's preparations to meet Anchises [2.3] and in the Maiden Song of Alcman [5.1]) characterises the Archaic Greek ideal of feminine beauty.

In the Homeric *Hymn to Aphrodite*, the goddess of sexual desire must disguise herself as a mortal in order to overcome Anchises' scruples and fire his passions, enabling him to undertake an active, masculine role in their lovemaking (2.3). Once their union is consummated, she reveals her true identity to her terrified suitor, who anticipates punishment for his presumption in touching a goddess. Unlike Zeus, whose affairs with mortals are brief, Aphrodite longs to make Anchises her permanent companion and spouse, but the example of Tithonus' fate shows why this is impossible. In the *Odyssey*, Calypso offers Odysseus immortality as her consort, but he proves unwilling to relinquish his human identity (and vitiate his masculinity) as the price of avoiding death. When she is ultimately forced to release the captive Odysseus, Calypso complains bitterly about the divine double standard (1.3): while the male gods have as many mortal lovers as they wish, they disapprove of unions between goddess and man. Indeed, they often take steps to end such episodes by destroying a goddess' favourite. Through such 'case studies' of sex between mortals and deities, the myths explore the boundaries of traditional ideas about gender and power. In relationships between gods and mortal women or boys, the standard hierarchies are preserved, but when goddesses desire mortal men, these hierarchies are thrown into chaos.

The cult of Dionysus was another major venue for ritual involving sexual elements. In contrast to the focus on the female generative role in the worship of Demeter and Persephone, Dionysiac cult was permeated by images of the penis, a symbol of natural vigour and procreative energy. The god himself is virtually never shown with an erection and, unlike the other male Olympians, is usually clothed – often in feminine dress. Dionysus was not perceived as a promiscuous lover in the style of his father Zeus. His rituals involve gender-deviant behaviours, and in a few myths he appears to accept penetration by another male (1.16), but he is also represented as the loving husband of Ariadne (8.9). His exuberant mythic entourage of satyrs, on the other hand, is comically preoccupied with sex; satyrs existed in a nearly permanent state of sexual excitement and/or frustration. One of the most characteristic Dionysiac rituals was the procession with model phalluses on poles or carts (1.6); the phallus was also a sacred object, revealed in Dionysiac mystery rituals. The penis could be perceived as a willful part of the body, which often functioned independently of its owner's wishes and seized control of the proceedings (6.4). Thus the phallus is an appropriate symbol of the loss of control experienced in Dionysiac ecstasy and the god's power to impose his will on the minds and bodies of any who refused to worship him. This aspect of Dionysus, as well as his challenge to gender roles, was already problematic in Classical Greece, as Euripides' dark portrait of the god in the *Bacchae* illustrates (9.7). The focus on the iconic phallus does not imply an androcentric cult, for Dionysus was a deity notably attractive to women, and the ecstatic Bacchants of myth had their counterparts in real life *thiasoi*, or bands of female celebrants.

Worship of Dionysus/Bacchus included secret mystery rites that promised afterlife benefits to initiates. Greek colonists brought this cult to Italy, and its popularity, as well as innovations in ritual practice that conflicted with traditional Roman ideas of sexual modesty and decent behaviour, alarmed the Senate. As depicted in Livy's account (1.11), the Bacchic worshipers were murderous, criminal monsters in pursuit of sexual debauchery, led by domineering women who decreed that the sexes would worship together, rather than in the gender-segregated groups of the past. The report that large numbers of people were involved in the Bacchic mysteries may well be correct, and the pervasiveness of this movement, which 'almost amounted to a second state', goes far to explain the hostility of the Senate. Whether these groups actually engaged in systematic criminal behaviour is unknown, but the account reflects entrenched suspicion of a cult that emphasised ecstatic experience and blurring of gender roles.

In spite of the Roman Senate's concerns about the lack of modesty in Bacchic rites, what concerned it was certainly not the display of the phallus itself, for in the early Italian context, too, the penis was symbolic of generative powers. A number of traditional tales attribute the birth of various heroes to the appearance of a phallus from the hearth, which then impregnates a woman (1.12). The worship of the phallic god Priapus, imported to Italy from the Greek city of Lampsacus, became extremely popular in Roman Italy. Priapus was essentially a protector of gardens who threatened anal rape to any would-be thieves (1.14). His phallicism is here tied to the popular Italian concept of the penis as a talisman to ward off evil. As every visitor to Pompeii knows, the phallus was a familiar neighbourhood image, carved on walls and streets. During the early empire, poets amused themselves by composing brief, comic poems about Priapus and his monstrous penis; later, Petronius played on the suspect associations between religious mysteries and sexuality when he made supposed 'mystery rites of Priapus' an important motif in his *Satyrica* (9.14).

The early Romans had fused Priapus' worship with that of a native phallic deity, Mutinus Titinus, and employed his statue in a ritual meant to ensure a bride's fertility. Another distinctive practice of the early Romans was the enumeration of individual *nūmina* or deities assigned to specific functions, including those to be performed on the wedding night. Long after these beliefs were no longer current among the Romans and had faded to the realm of antiquarian scholarship, the Christian father Augustine used them in a polemical attack on paganism (1.17).

As we have seen, ecstatic forms of religion, which often include sexual elements, were problematic in Greek and especially in Roman culture because of the challenge they posed to gender norms. The cult of Adonis, Aphrodite's consort, involved passionate laments for the death of the youthful and handsome god. Athenian men associated this worship with licentious and disruptive behaviour (1.7). In Hellenistic Alexandria, by contrast, the Adonis cult was adopted as a state festival and lavishly celebrated with elaborate effigies of Aphrodite and her consort. Theocritus' depiction of the women at the Adonia (1.9) emphasises Adonis' physical attractiveness to his female worshipers.

The self-castrated devotees of Cybele known as the Galli were objects of fascination, suspicion, and disgust in Rome, even as the Senate imported the goddess' cult from Hellenised Asia Minor. The myth of Agdistis (another name for Cybele) appears in several versions that contradict each other in various specifics, but in each case they evoke disturbing images of castration, madness, androgyny, and rejection of heterosexual and marital relationships (1.13, 1.15). Cybele's beloved consort was a priestly figure called Attis, whose example the Galli followed when they castrated themselves. Catullus created a vivid portrait (1.10) of Attis leading the chaotic, fast-moving swarm of Cybele's devotees through the Phrygian countryside to the sound of hypnotic drumming. Although Catullus states that Attis, the archetypal Gallus, and his fellows renounce 'Venus' (i.e. sex), the dancing, gender-ambiguous Galli were nevertheless associated in Roman thought with the sexually deviant figure of the *cinaedus*.[2]

1.1 Homer *Iliad* 14.159–86, 214–21, 312–51. Eighth century BCE. Hera seduces her husband Zeus in order to draw his attention away from events on the Trojan battlefield.

Then the ox-eyed Lady Hera pondered
A way to deceive the aegis-bearer Zeus.[3]
And in her heart this counsel seemed the best,
To adorn herself well and visit the peak of Ida.
In case he wished to lie with her, loving her body,
She could shed a harmless, gentle sleep
Over his eyelids and his cunning mind.
She went to the chamber, built by her own son,
Hephaestus, who fitted strong doors to the posts
With a secret bolt no other god could open.
Entering, she closed the shining doors.
With ambrosia she cleansed her desirable body
From all impurities and anointed herself
With immortal oil, sweet and fragrant;
Sprinkled about the bronze-floored house of Zeus,

Its aroma would reach all earth and heaven.
With this she anointed her lovely body, and combed
Her hair, braiding the shining, immortal tresses
That graced with beauty her undying head.
She slipped into an immortal robe, fine work
Smoothed by Athena and stitched with clever patterns,
Fastening it at the breast with golden clasps.
The belt at her waist was trimmed with a hundred tassels.
From her pierced ears swung artful pendants,
Triple drops, which sparkled attractively.
Over all the bright goddess spread a lovely veil,
Newly made, white, and brilliant as the sun;
On her shining feet she tied lovely sandals.

[On a pretext, Hera convinces Aphrodite to lend her a garment with magical powers of allure.]

She spoke, and from her breast she loosed the band,
Embroidered with colours, and full of bewitchments;
Within are love, longing and whisperings,
Lures to beguile even the minds of deep thinkers.
She laid this in Hera's hands and spoke to her:
Place on your breast this colourful band, wherein
All things have been wrought, and I say
You shall return successful, whatever your plan.

[Hera bribes Sleep, brother of Death, to lull Zeus once her seduction is complete, then visits Zeus on Mt. Ida.]

Then Zeus who gathers the clouds spoke in answer:
'Hera, you may start that journey later.
But let us both delight in lying together
For never has such love for goddess or woman
Mastered my heart so overwhelmingly,
Not even when I loved the wife of Ixion,
Who bore Pirithous,[4] equal in counsel to gods,
Nor Danaë Acrisius' daughter with pretty ankles,
Who bore Perseus, most glorious of men,
Nor the daughter of famous Phoenix,[5] who bore
Minos and godlike Rhadamanthys to me.
Nor yet Semele or Alcmene in Thebes;
One brought forth stout-hearted Heracles;

The other Dionysus, delight of mortals.
Not with queenly Demeter of the beautiful hair,
Nor splendid Leto,[6] nor even you yourself
Did sweet desire seize me as it does now.'
And the scheming Lady Hera said to him,
'Dread son of Cronus, what a thing you are saying!
If you wish to make love here on Ida's peak
Where everything is visible to anyone,
What if one of the everlasting gods
Saw us lying together, and showed the others?
Then I could not leave my couch to visit your house,
For that would be a very scandalous thing.
But if you wish, and if it pleases your heart,
You have a chamber, which your own son built,
Hephaestus, and fitted stout doors to the posts.
Let us lie there, since the bed is your desire'.
Then Zeus who gathers the clouds spoke in answer,
'Hera, have no fear that god or mortal
Will see a thing. With such a golden cloud
Shall I enfold you, not even bright Helius
Could spy us, though his vision is most keen.'
Then Cronus' son took his wife in his arms.
Beneath the pair, divine earth sprouted grass,
Dewy lotus, crocus and hyacinths,
Thick and soft, which held them off the ground.
Here they lay, wrapped in a lovely cloud
Of gold, as the sparkling dewdrops fell.

1.2 Hesiod *Theogony* 886–929. Eighth century BCE. Zeus' amorous and reproductive capacities are described through a catalogue of his most important consorts.

Zeus, the king of the gods, first took as wife
Wisdom, who knows more than gods or mortals.
But when she was soon to bear grey-eyed Athena,
Deceiving the wits of Wisdom by a trick,
With wheedling words he placed her in his belly
Through the cunning of Earth and starry Heaven.
Thus they advised him, in order that Zeus and no other
Might be king of the everlasting gods.
For she was fated to bear wise children indeed:
First the maiden, grey-eyed Tritogenia,[7]

Mighty like her father and wise in counsel.
But next she was fated to bear a son, a king
Of gods and men, possessing a lawless heart.
But Zeus instead placed Wisdom in his belly,
That the goddess might show him good and evil.
Second he took sleek Themis, who bore the Hours,[8]
Good Order, Justice and blossoming Peace,
Who attend to the works of humans subject to death,
And the Fates, whom Counselor Zeus honoured most:
Clotho, Lachesis and Atropus, who give
Both good and evil to mortals for their own.
Three Graces with lovely cheeks Eurynome[9] bore,
Aglaea, Euphrosyne and charming Thalia.
From their eyes darts Love, the loosener
Of limbs, and their glances are alluring.
Zeus then came to bountiful Demeter's bed.
She bore white-armed Persephone, whom Hades
Snatched from her mother; Counselor Zeus approved.
Again, he desired lovely-haired Mnemosyne;[10]
She bore the nine Muses with their golden tiaras
Who delight in good cheer and the pleasures of song.
Leto bore Apollo and the archer Artemis,
Offspring more lovely than all the Heavenly Ones,
Mingling in love with Zeus who bears the aegis.
Blossoming Hera he made the last of his wives,
And she bore Hebe and Ares and Ilithyia[11]
United in love with the father of gods and men.
He himself from his head bore grey-eyed Athena
Terrible host-leader, stirrer of strife, the Untiring
Lady, whom tumult, wars and battles delight.
But Hera in great anger quarreled with her mate,
And because of this strife she bore a shining son
Apart from aegis-bearing Zeus: Hephaestus,
Who surpasses all the Heavenly Ones in crafts.

1.3 Homer *Odyssey* 5.118–29. Late eighth century BCE. Zeus sends Hermes to free Odysseus, who is being held unwillingly as Calypso's lover on her remote island.

As he spoke, divine Calypso winced.
Addressing him, she spoke with winged words:
'You gods stop at nothing, and overly jealous

You resent that goddesses sleep with men
Openly, if one makes a man her bedmate.
When rosy-fingered Dawn captured Orion,[12]
You easy-living gods harboured a grudge,
Till gold-throned holy Artemis in Ortygia
Stalked and slew him with her gentle arrows.
So lovely-haired Demeter, when she gave
Her heart to Iasion[13] in the thrice-ploughed field:
Soon their loving came to the ears of Zeus,
Who killed him, throwing the dazzling thunderbolt.
Now I too face your anger over a mortal.
Him I rescued, sitting alone on the keel,
When Zeus' bolt had cleaved his swift ship,
Leaving him in the midst of the wine-dark sea.
There all his noble comrades perished,
But wind and wave carried him here to me.
I loved and cared for him, and gave my word
To make him immortal and ageless for all his days.
But since it is impossible for other gods
To evade the will of aegis-bearing Zeus,
If Zeus compels and commands it, let him go
Over the restless sea.'

1.4 Homeric *Hymn to Demeter* 4–20. Early seventh century BCE. Hades
abducts Demeter's daughter Cora/Persephone in order to make her his bride.

Apart from bountiful Demeter of the golden sword,
She danced with Ocean's full-breasted daughters,
Plucking the rose, the crocus and pretty violets
In the soft meadow, with iris and hyacinth,
And a narcissus, which by Zeus' will Earth grew
As a snare for the girl with a face like a flower,
Pleasing the Host of All:[14] a glowing treasure,
A thing of awe to mortals and to gods.
Its root produced a hundred flower-heads,
With scent so sweet that wide heaven above
Smiled, and earth and the salt-swell of the sea.
The girl in wonder reached out with both hands
For this fine plaything, but the wide earth gaped
Over Nysa's plain, and the lordly Host of All,
Cronus' son of many names, rushed forth

With a team of undying horses. The golden car
Swept her away, lamenting.

1.5 Aeschylus *Danaids TrGF* 3 Fr. 44.1–7. Ca. 460 BCE. In this fragment of a lost tragedy, Aphrodite describes how her power to induce sexual desire brings about the fertility of the land through the sacred marriage of Earth and Heaven.

Pure Heaven feels sexual desire for the Land;
Earth is gripped by love for marital union.
Rain pouring down in streams from Heaven
Quickens Earth and she bears for mortals
The pasture for herds and Demeter's bounty;
From this moist marriage the tree's ripe fruit
Is made perfect. Of these things I am the cause.

1.6 Aristophanes *Acharnians* 259–78. 426 BCE. Dicaeopolis organises the family celebration of Dionysus, which involves a procession with model penises on poles. The slave Xanthias is included in the festivities.

Xanthias! Walk behind the basket-bearer and
Hold that phallus erect!
I will follow singing the phallus-song.
And you, wife, observe from the roof. Forward!

Phales,[15] friend of Bacchus,
Fellow-reveler, Roamer-about in the night,
Adulterer, Boy-lover,
In the sixth year I greet you
As I joyfully return to the village,
Having made my own peace treaty
Freed from cares and battles
And Lamachuses.[16]
Sweeter by far, Phales O Phales,
To catch pretty Thratta the wood-bearer,
Strymodorus' slave, stealing from Phelleus,
And grabbing her up about the middle,
Throw her down, and pop her pip!
O Phales, Phales, if you'll drink with me
We'll drain a cup at dawn in honour of Peace.

1.7 Aristophanes *Lysistrata* 387–98. 411 BCE. As choruses of old men and women threaten each other with fire and water during the women's sex strike (see 8.7), the magistrate enters with a general comment on women's bad behaviour.

Have the women indulged themselves with lamps,
Drumming, and the crowded Sabazian rites?[17]
Have they mourned Adonis on the roofs,
As I heard in the Assembly lately?
For Demostratus, damn him,
Was saying we should invade Sicily,[18]
While a woman kept leaping about
Crying, 'Woe for Adonis!' And Demostratus
Was saying we should muster men in Zacynthus,
While the tipsy woman on the roof yelled
'Beat your breast for Adonis!' He was shut down,
That goddamned, foul bile-driver,
By the song of women run amok.

[The magistrate follows this speech with another in which he airs his suspicions that the citizen wives are regularly cheating on their husbands.]

1.8 Aristotle *The Constitution of Athens* 3.5. Mid fourth century BCE. This description of Athenian political institutions contains one of the few references to the ritual marriage of the Basilinna, the wife of a magistrate known as the King Archon.

The nine Archons were not all located together, but the King Archon had what is now called the Herdsman's House near the city hall. Evidence of this is the fact that even now this is where the union of the King Archon's wife with Dionysus takes place, and the marriage. The Archon had the City Hall, the Warlord had the Epilyceum (which before was called the Warlord's House, but after Epilycus rebuilt and furnished it when he was Warlord, they called it the Epilyceum), and the Lawgivers had the Lawgivers' Court.

1.9 Theocritus *Idylls* 15.65–149. Third century BCE. Theocritus' collection of *Idylls* includes three 'mimes', sketches of daily life in the city. In this excerpt, a pair of affluent women with their maidservants brave crowds to view effigies of Adonis and Aphrodite during their festival.

Gorgo:
Praxinoa, look what a crowd is gathered at the door!

Praxinoa:
Unspeakable. Gorgo, give me your hand. Eunoa,
See to Eutychis. Hold on tight or you'll be lost.
We'll all go in together. Eunoa, stick close to us!
Oh no, my summer dress has already been torn!
Sir, if you don't mind, be careful of my gown.

Stranger:
I can't help it, but even so, I'll try my best.

Praxinoa:
The crowds are pushing and shoving like pigs!

Stranger:
Ma'am, don't fear. We've come through now.

Praxinoa:
May good luck go with you now and ever more,
For protecting us. What a kind and decent man!
Oh! We're crushing Eunoa. Be brave, now, push!
'We're all in', as the man said and shut out his wife.[19]

Gorgo:
Praxinoa, come and see this embroidered cloth,
How fine and lovely! A robe truly fit for a god.
Lady Athena! What sort of weavers did this work?
What artisans painted these scenes so true to life?
They look real, not embroidered. How clever
Is the human race. And He, lying on his silver couch,
With the soft down on his cheek! Dearest Adonis,
Thrice beloved, who even in death is cherished!

Another Stranger:
You women, stop cooing like pigeons and shut up!
That accent of theirs is trying my nerves to the limit.

Gorgo:
Where did he come from? What business of yours
Is it if we talk? Confine your orders to your slaves,
And don't tell ladies from Syracuse how to behave.
We are of Corinthian stock, I'll have you know,

Like Bellerophon, and our speech is Peloponnesian.
I think a Dorian woman is allowed to speak Doric!

Praxinoa:
By the Honey-sweet goddess,[20] only one man on earth
Can order us about. Who cares what this one thinks?

Gorgo:
Hush, Praxinoa. That skillful singer, Argeia's daughter
Is starting the dirge for Adonis. Last year she won!
A clear, fine voice she has, with a touch of vibrato.

Singer:
My Lady, you who delight in Golgi and Idalium
And Eryx,[21] Lady Aphrodite playful in gold,
The gentle feet of the Hours brought you Adonis
From the ever-flowing Acheron,[22] after a year.
The longed-for Hours travel slowest of the gods,
Yet when they come they bring delights to all.
Oh Cypris child of Dione,[23] you made mortal
Berenice[24] a goddess, so the stories say,
Letting fall drops of ambrosia in her breast.
Lady of many names and shrines, to please you
Arsinoë her daughter, a queen lovely as Helen
Decks Adonis with every exquisite ornament.
Beside him are fruits in season borne by the trees,
Delicate gardens grown in baskets of silver,
Golden flasks filled with finest Syrian perfumes
And molded cakes, the pastry-cook's labours,
Of flour mingled with every kind of blossom.
Each cake filled with honey and moist with oil
Takes the shape of a flying or stepping creature.
The green canopy overhead is weighted with dill,
And through it youthful Loves flutter upward.
Like nightingales in the lush foliage they fly,
Testing their wings as they flit from branch to branch.
See the ebony, the gold, the eagles of bright ivory,
As they carry to Cronian Zeus his youthful cupbearer.
Hangings of purple, softer than sleep, are above.
Miletus and Samian pastures[25] proudly proclaim:
'We have spread the couch for the fair Adonis.'
One bed holds Aphrodite and one the bridegroom,

A boy of eighteen or nineteen with pink arms
And red lips still soft and smooth for her kisses.
Let Cypris rejoice now in her spouse restored,
And with the dew of tomorrow's dawn, together
We'll carry him down to the wave-splashed shore.
We'll let down our hair and loosen our gowns,
Baring our breasts as we sing the clear-toned song:
Of the heroes, you alone, Adonis, walk both below
And here on earth. This Agamemnon never did,
Nor great Ajax, the hero whose wrath was heavy,
Nor Hector, eldest of Hecabe's twenty children.
Not Patroclus, or Pyrrhus who returned from Troy,
Nor even older, the Lapiths or Deucalion's sons,
The line of Pelops, or the ancient Pelasgian race.[26]
Be gracious, Adonis, and smile on the coming year,
Each time you return, your advent is dear to us.

Gorgo:
Praxinoa, what a clever thing that woman is!
How lovely to know so much and sing so sweetly.
But it's time to go! Diocleides has no dinner,
No vinegar is more sour than a hungry husband.
Farewell, dear Adonis, be near to those who love you.

1.10 Catullus *Songs* 63.1–26. Ca. 55 BCE. In this portrait of Attis, the archetypal priest of Cybele, Attis' self-castration results in an immediate shift of gender from male to female.

Sailing the deep seas in his swift ship,
And reaching the Phrygian grove with hasty foot,
Attis came to the shady wood of the goddess,
And spurred by madness and disordered wits,
He lopped the weight of his loins with sharp flint.
Feeling her limbs released from the manly state,
Still spotting the earth with fresh blood, she
Quickly took the drum in her snowy hands
The drum, source of your rites, mother Cybele,
And beating the hollow bullskin with soft fingers,
She rose quivering to sing to her companions:
'Gather here, Gallae,[27] in Cybele's deep grove,
Come, wandering herd of Dindymus' mistress,[28]
You exiles who go in search of foreign lands,

Follow where I lead, my own companions.
You braved salt surges and the savage sea
And became un-men through deep hate of Venus.
You gladden Cybele's heart as you swiftly stray!
Banish dull delay, together follow
To Cybele's Phrygian house and Phrygian grove
Where the cymbals speak and the drums resound,
The piper draws deep notes from the curved reed,
Ivy-bearing madwomen toss their heads,
Holy objects are brandished amid sharp cries
As the goddess' disordered band flits about:
There we must speed the solemn steps of our dance'.

1.11 Livy *History of Rome* 39.8.3–39.13.14. Ca. 25 BCE. Livy's work covered the history of Rome from its foundation to the reign of the emperor Augustus. Here he describes events leading to the Senate's crackdown on Bacchic mystery cults in 186 BCE.

First of all, a low-born Greek came into Etruria, bringing none of the arts that this most cultivated of peoples has introduced for the care of our minds and bodies. He was a sacrificer and seer, not one of those who leads people into error by professing his religion openly and making clear that his expertise is to be had for a price, but instead one who supervised secret, nocturnal rituals. There were initiations, administered at first only to a few, but then the common men and women took them up. The pleasures of wine and feasting were added to religion, in order that more people might be enticed to participate. When wine had inflamed their minds, and the night together with the mingling of men and women, old and young, had vanquished all traces of modesty, then every type of corruption began, for each person had ready to hand the kind of pleasure to which he was most naturally inclined. The harm they did was not limited to the promiscuous coupling of freeborn men and women; from this same workshop there came perjured witnesses, forged seals, falsified wills and other evidence. From here too came poisonings and secret murders, so that indeed sometimes there were no bodies to be found for burial. They dared much by deceit, but even more by violence. The violence was hidden because the screams of people being debauched and murdered could not be heard amid the ritual howling and the clash of drums and cymbals.

The stain of this evil spread from Etruria into Rome like a contagious plague. At first it was not apparent, for the city's size allows it to contain and tolerate such ills; but finally it came to the notice of the consul Postumius in the following manner. Publius Aebutius, whose father received a public allowance for his military service, was left a ward, and then when his guardians died, he was placed in the care of his mother Duronia and his stepfather Titus Sempronius Rutilus. His mother was devoted to this man, and the stepfather, who had managed the stepson's finances in such a way that he could not answer for them, wanted his ward either to be done away with, or compromised and bound to him by some chains of guilt. The Bacchanalia were the one way to corrupt him. His mother spoke to him and said that while she was sick, she had vowed that as soon as she gained her strength, she would initiate him into the Bacchic mysteries; since she was obligated to the gods by their kindness, she now wished to fulfill her vow. For ten days he must practice sexual abstinence; on the tenth day she would bring him to the banquet, and then, once he was bathed and purified, into the shrine. There was a well-known prostitute named Hispala Faecenia, a freedwoman who deserved better than the occupation to which she had become accustomed while still a young slave. But even after she was manumitted, she still supported herself by that trade. Because they were neighbours, Hispala and Aebutius developed an intimacy, though not one that harmed either the youth's fortune or his reputation. For she loved and sought him out of her own accord, and since his own relatives were very stingy, the prostitute generously supported him. And more than that, because of her feelings for him, once her patron died and she was legally her own woman, she petitioned the tribunes for approval and made a will establishing Aebutius as her sole heir.

Because they had these assurances of love, and they kept no secrets from one another, the young man teasingly told her not to be surprised, if he slept apart from her for several nights. He said that he wished to be initiated into the Bacchic mysteries as a matter of religious duty, in order to free himself from a vow made for the sake of his health. When the woman heard this, she cried out in distress 'Gods forbid!' and said that it would be better for them both to die than for him to do that; she called down vengeance and punishment on the heads of those who had persuaded him to this. Wondering at her language as well as her evident distress, he told her to spare the curses, for it was his mother who bade him do this, with the approval of his stepfather. 'Perhaps it is not right to accuse your mother,' she said, 'but in that case it is your stepfather who hastens to destroy your virtue, your reputation, your hopes, and your life.' He was even more astonished, and asked her what she meant. Praying to the gods and goddesses for peace and forgiveness if, impelled by her affection for him, she said anything that ought to remain unspoken, she explained that as a slave girl she had accompanied her mistress to the shrine, but had never gone near it once she was free. She knew that it was a laboratory for every form of corruption, and it was certain that for the past two years, nobody over the age of twenty had been initiated. As each person was brought in, he was handed over to the priests like a sacrificial victim, and they led him to a place resounding with ritual howling, songs sung in unison, and the banging of cymbals and drums. This was done so that the voices of those screaming could not be heard as they were violently raped. Then she begged and implored him to put a stop to this in any way he could, and not to throw himself into a situation where he would first be made to suffer every unspeakable horror, and then forced to perform them himself. Nor would she let him go until the young man promised her that he would abstain from those mysteries.

When he came home, and his mother began to suggest what he ought to do on that day and the following days in order to prepare for the mysteries, he informed her that he was not going to do any of them, nor did he plan to be initiated; his stepfather was present during this conversation. Immediately the woman exclaimed that Aebutius was unable to forego sleeping with Hispala for ten nights; he was so drunk on the poisonous allure of that serpent, she said, that he had no respect for his parents, his stepfather, or the gods. And while his mother reviled him on one side and his stepfather on the other, they drove him from the house with the assistance of four slaves. The young man consulted with his aunt Aebutia, telling her why he had been thrown out of the house by his mother, and at her suggestion, he reported the matter on the next day to the consul in a private interview. The consul dismissed him, bidding him return in three days, and in the meantime he asked his own mother-in-law Sulpicia, a wise and venerable woman, whether she knew of an Aebutia living in the Aventine neighbourhood. When she replied that she knew Aebutia was a woman of virtuous character who conducted herself according to old-fashioned morals, the consul said that he must meet with her; Sulpicia should send her a message to come. Aebutia was summoned and visited Sulpicia. A little later the consul dropped in on them as if by chance, and steered the conversation around to Aebutius, her brother's son. Tears sprang to her eyes and she began to lament the youth's bad luck, for he had been robbed of his fortune by the ones who should have been last to harm him. 'He is at my house,' she said, 'for his mother threw him out because – may the gods forgive me – he refused to be initiated into mysteries which are abominations, according to what we have heard.'

Considering that his investigation of Aebutius was sufficient and that his story was trustworthy, the consul dismissed Aebutia and asked his mother-in-law to summon Hispala the freedwoman, also a resident of the Aventine neighbourhood and well-known there. He wished to put to her certain questions as well. When Hispala received the message she was distressed, because she did not know why she was being summoned to the house of such a venerable and respected woman. When she saw the lictors[29] in the hallway and the consul's entourage and the consul himself, she nearly fainted. Bringing her into the inner part of the house and keeping his mother-in-law present, the consul told her that if she could bring herself to tell the truth, she had no cause for alarm. For this she could accept the pledge either of Sulpicia, who was so highly respected, or his own. She must disclose to him what things were normally done during the nocturnal mysteries of the Bacchanalia, held in the grove of Stimula.[30] When she heard this, such a shaking and trembling of all her limbs seized the woman, that she could not open her mouth for a long time. At last, gathering her courage, she stated that as a young slave she had been fully initiated with her mistress, but that for several years now, since the time of her manumission, she had known nothing of what went on there. The consul praised her because she had not denied the fact of her initiation, but he said that she must disclose the rest under the same pledge as before. When she denied that she knew anything else, he said that she would not receive the same pardon or consideration if she were convicted on someone else's evidence as if she confessed of her own accord; the man who heard it from her had told him the whole story.

Thinking that surely (as was in fact the case) it was Aebutius who revealed the secret, the woman fell at Sulpicia's feet and first begged her not to turn a freedwoman's chatter with her lover into something that was not only serious but a life and death matter. She had spoken in order to frighten him, not because she knew anything. At this point Postumius became angry and declared that even now she believed that she was having a joke with her lover Aebutius, and not speaking with a consul in the home of a highly respectable woman. Sulpicia raised the terrified woman to her feet, and encouraged her even as she calmed her son-in-law's anger. At last she took heart, and with many complaints about the treachery of Aebutius, who repaid her in this way when she deserved far better from him, she said that she was in great fear of the gods, whose secret initiations she was revealing. But even more, she feared those people who would tear her limb from limb if they knew she was the informer, and so she begged both Sulpicia and the consul to banish her to someplace outside Italy, where she could spend the rest of her life in safety. The consul told her to be of good cheer, for he would see to it that she could safely live in Rome. Then Hispala explained the origin of the mysteries. At first, she said, it was a ritual for women, and it was the custom that no men were admitted. There were three dates appointed each year when the initiations took place during the daytime; the custom was to choose matrons as the priestesses by turns. Paculla Annia, a woman of Campania, had changed all this when she was priestess, as if in response to divine commands. She had been the first to initiate men, her own sons Minius and Herennius Cerrinius, and had changed the time of the rites from day to night, and instead of holding initiations three days a year, she changed them to five times a month. From the time that mixed rites were performed, men mingled with women and the freedom of darkness was added, no crime or disgraceful deed was left undone. The men practiced more sexual immorality with one another than with the women. If they were unwilling to suffer abuse or reluctant to commit crimes themselves, they were sacrificed as victims. To consider no deed impious was the highest form of piety for them.

Men uttered prophecies as though they had lost their minds, while frantically tossing their bodies about. Matrons with their hair loose and dressed in the costumes of Bacchants ran to the Tiber carrying burning torches; they plunged the torches into the water and, because they were made with live sulfur and calcium, drew them out still burning. They said that people were carried off by the gods, who in fact had been bound to machines, which whisked them out of sight to hidden caves. These were the ones who were unwilling to join the conspiracy, to participate in crimes, or to suffer sexual abuse. The number of participants was huge, almost amounting to a second state now, and among them were certain distinguished men and women. Within the last two years it was ordained that nobody older than twenty years should be initiated, for they wished to get hold of those whose age made them vulnerable to both moral error and sexual corruption.

1.12 Dionysius of Halicarnassus *Roman Antiquities* 4.2–3. Ca. 7 BCE. The historian relates a popular tale about the conception of the Roman king Servius Tullius, whose mother was a slave in the house of the reigning king Tarquinius.

In the local records there is another story about his birth, which raises the circumstances surrounding it to the realm of myth; we have found it in many Roman histories. The story – provided it is pleasing to the greater and lesser gods that I tell it – goes something like this. They say that in the palace hearth, on which the Romans consecrate first portions from their meals, and offer up other sacrifices, there arose from the fire a man's private part. Ocrisia was the first to see it, as she was carrying the customary offering of cakes to the fire, and she immediately went to the royal couple to inform them. When Tarquinius heard this and afterward saw the prodigy, he was astonished. Tanaquil,[31] however, who was in no way inferior to the Tyrrhenians[32] in her knowledge of divination, and also wise in other matters, told him that as a result of a union between this phantom and a woman, an offspring superior to the human race would be born from the royal hearth. And with the agreement of the other examiners of prodigies, the king thought it was best for Ocrisia, to whom the prodigy had first appeared, to have intercourse with it. Accordingly this woman, dressed in the manner customary for brides, was shut up alone in the room where the prodigy had been seen. One of the gods, whether Vulcan, as some think, or the guardian spirit of the household, had sex with her and then disappeared, and she conceived, giving birth to Tullius after the normal period of time.

1.13 Ovid *Fasti* 4.224–44. Ca. 10 CE. In the fourth book of Ovid's unfinished poem about the festivals of the Roman calendar, Erato, the Muse of love poetry, describes the love affair of Attis and the goddess Cybele.

A handsome Phrygian boy in the forest, Attis,
Won the tower-crowned goddess with chaste love.
She asked him to be her servant and guard her temple,
And asked for his pledge to stay a boy forever.
He promised to obey, and added, 'If I lie,
May the love I disappoint be the last I feel.'
He failed: in loving the nymph Sagaritis he ceased
To be a boy. The goddess took her revenge:
She angrily killed the Naiad by wounding her tree:
The nymph died, for her life was bound to the tree.
Attis raved, and fearing his roof would collapse,
Escaped and fled to Mount Dindymus' peak,
Shouting, 'Take away the torches and the whips!'
For he swore he felt the Furies near at hand.
He mangled his body too with a sharp stone
And dragged his long hair in the dust and dirt, and cried,
'I deserve to pay the price for my deeds in blood!
Let the parts that have harmed me be destroyed!
Let them perish!' as he lopped the weight of his groin.
And now all marks of manhood were utterly gone.
His effeminate servants feel his madness too;
Flinging their hair, they remove the parts they call worthless.

1.14 *Priapea* 10–17, 25–31, 67–70. Uncertain date, possibly the second half of the first century CE. Numerous authors penned this collection of ninety-five poems pertaining to the phallic god Priapus. Poems like these were written on signs attached to rustic statues of the god.

10–17
Why do you laugh, O silly girl?
No fine sculptor fashioned me,
Nor was I polished by Phidias'[33] hand;
A farmer chopped some gnarly wood,
And said to me, 'You be Priapus.'
Yet you giggle as soon as you look:
Surely for you it's a joke to savor,
This pillar standing erect at my groin.

25–31

This scepter, once cut from a tree,
Now shall thrive without a leaf.
The scepter dear to pathic girls,
That certain kings desire to hold,
And pervert nobles love to kiss,
Will probe the innards of the thief
As far as the hairy hilt of my balls.

67–70
Let the first syllable of 'Dido' follow 'Penelope',
And the first of 'Remus' follow 'Canus'.[34]
When I catch you in the garden, that's what you'll get,
Thief–the penalty due for your crime.

1.15 Pausanias *Description of Greece* 7.17.9–12. Second century CE. Pausanias wrote a travel guide for visitors to Greece. In this selection, his description of the sanctuaries at the Achaean city of Dyme leads to discussion of the myths of Attis.

The people of Dyme have a temple of Athena with a very ancient statue; they also have another sanctuary, built for Mother Dindymene[35] and for Attis. As to Attis, I was unable to learn the secret traditions about him, but Hermesianax the elegiac poet says in a poem that he was the son of Calaus the Phrygian, and that he was born without the ability to father children. Hermesianax says that when he grew up, he moved to Lydia and celebrated with the Lydians the ecstatic rites of the Mother, and that he achieved such great honour with her that Zeus became resentful and sent a boar to destroy the fields of the Lydians. Then Attis himself and some of the Lydians were killed by the boar, and this explains why the Gauls of Pessinus abstain from pork. But they have different views on Attis, and the local legend goes like this. While Zeus was sleeping, he released semen onto the earth, which in the course of time sent up a supernatural creature with double sexual organs, those of a man as well as a woman. They call this creature Agdistis. But the gods bound Agdistis and cut off its male organ. From this there grew an almond tree with ripe fruit, and they say that a daughter of the river Sangarius took hold of the fruit and placed it in her lap. It immediately disappeared, and she became pregnant. When the boy was born, he was abandoned, but watched over by a billy goat. As he grew up, his beauty was more than human, and Agdistis fell in love with him. Once he was grown, his relatives sent Attis to Pessinus to marry the king's daughter. The wedding song was being sung when Agdistis appeared. Attis went mad and cut off his genitals and so did the king who was giving his daughter in marriage.

But Agdistis felt regret at the harm done to Attis, and petitioned Zeus to grant that his body would neither rot nor decay in any way. These are the best-known stories about Attis.

1.16 Clement of Alexandria *Exhortation to the Greeks* 2.17–18, 29–30. Ca. 200 CE. Clement's *Exhortation* is an attack on traditional religion from a Christian perspective. Here he deplores sexual elements in the worship of Demeter (Deo) in the Eleusinian Mysteries and quotes ancient lines attributed to the hero Orpheus. In the second selection, he recounts the story of Dionysus' bargain with Prosymnus, which is said to explain the use of the phallus in his rituals.

2.17–18
Receiving Deo as a guest, Baubo[36] offers her a drink of wine mixed with flour. She refuses to accept it and to drink, for she is in mourning, but because of this Baubo is deeply hurt, and thinks she is being insulted. Therefore she uncovers her genitals and shows them to the goddess. Deo is pleased at the sight, and at length receives the drink, delighted with the spectacle. These are the secret mysteries of the Athenians! Orpheus also writes about this. I will quote you the actual lines of the epic, in order that you may have the man who originated the mysteries as a witness of their shamelessness:

She spoke, and drew up her gown, revealing all
Her improper parts. The child Iacchus[37] was there,
And laughing, thrust his hand below her breasts.
Then the goddess smiled, as did her heart;
She took the gleaming cup that held the drink.

2.29–30
Dionysus was anxious to go down into Hades[38] but did not know the way. A certain man named Prosymnus promised to tell him this, but not without payment. The payment was an evil thing, though Dionysus liked it well. It was a sexual favour, this reward that Dionysus was asked to pay. The god was willing, and he promised to grant the request if he should return, sealing his promise with an oath. He learned the way, set out, and returned, but he did not find Prosymnus, who had died in the meantime. In order to fulfill the oath to his lover, Dionysus hastened to the tomb, experiencing a desire to be penetrated. He cut off a branch from a fig tree that happened to be there, gave it the shape of a man's part, and then sat on the branch, fulfilling his promise to the dead man. As a mystic memorial of this passion, phalluses are set up in the cities. 'For if they were not holding processions and singing the phallus-songs

for Dionysus, what they do would be most shameful,' says Heraclitus, 'and Hades is the same as Dionysus, the god for whom they go mad and celebrate the Lenaea.'[39]

1.17 Augustine *City of God* 6.9. Fifth century CE. Writing after the sack of Rome by the Visigoths, Augustine was concerned to justify the Roman empire's adoption of Christianity and its rejection of traditional paganism. Here he ridicules the 'functional gods' of archaic Roman religion, drawing largely on a lost account by Varro (first century BCE).

As to the roles of the divine powers, defined with such stinginess and exactness, on account of which they say that each one ought to be supplicated according to its own special domain, we have already had much to say, though we have not told the whole story. Are they not more fitted to the ridiculous clowning of a mime show than to divine majesty? If anyone gave a baby two nurses, one to provide nothing but solid food, and one to provide nothing but drink, as these people employ two goddesses, Educa and Potina,[40] would he not seem to be a fool, enacting something like a comic show in his own house? They think that Liber[41] gets his name from the word for liberation, because through his care males are 'liberated' when their semen is released. Libera (who they think is the same as Venus) does the same thing for women, for they ascribe to her the release of the woman's seed, and for these reasons male body parts are placed in the temple of Liber, and female parts in the temple of Libera. In addition to this there are the women devoted to Liber, and wine drunk in order to incite lust. This is how the Bacchanalia used to be celebrated, in the grip of complete insanity. On this subject Varro himself admits that such things would not have been done at the Bacchanalia had their minds not been disturbed. Later on, these behaviours displeased the Senate, which was saner, and it commanded that they cease. At least in this case, perhaps, they finally realised what effect unclean spirits have on people's minds, when they are mistaken for gods. These things are not done in the theaters, for there in fact they are playacting, not raving, although having gods who are delighted by such plays is very much like madness.

But what sort of distinction is this he makes between the superstitious and the religious person? He says that the superstitious person fears the gods, whereas the religious one honours them like his parents and does not fear them like enemies; also that the gods are all so good, that they will more readily spare the guilty than harm the innocent. Yet he records that three gods are assigned as guardians to a woman who has just given birth, in order to prevent the god Silvanus[42] from entering at night and molesting her, and that in order to indicate that these guardians are present, three men make a circuit of the house at night and first strike the threshold with an axe, then with a pestle, and thirdly, they sweep it with brushes, so that Silvanus will be prevented from entering by means of these symbols of farming. For trees are not cut or pruned without iron blades, and grain is not ground without a pestle, nor heaped up without brushes. Now from these three things gods have been named: Intercidona from the cut made by the hatchet, Pilumnus from the pestle, and Deverra from the brushes, and these guardian gods protect the woman who has just given birth against the power of the god Silvanus. Therefore the protection of the good gods would not be effective against the malice of the harmful one, unless they outnumbered him and fought against his roughness and uncivilised harshness, as an inhabitant of the woods, with the opposing symbols of culture. Is this then the harmlessness of the gods, and their harmonious nature? Are these the health-bringing gods of the cities, more laughable than the ludicrous shows at the theaters?

When the male and female are joined, the god Jugatinus presides; let us accept this for now. But the new bride must be brought home, so the god Domiducus is assigned. In order that the bride may live in the home, the god Domitius is assigned, and in order for her to remain with her husband, they add the goddess Manturna. What more is needed? Let human modesty be spared; let the tale of lustful flesh and blood go forward in a way that preserves respect. Why is the bedroom filled with a crowd of deities, when even the groomsmen have departed? It is crowded not in order to encourage chastity as a result of their presence, but in order that women, as the weaker sex, frightened by that which is new and strange, may with the help of these gods more easily give up their virginity. For those present include the goddess Virginiensis, the god Father Subigus, the goddess Mother Prema, the goddess Pertunda, and Venus, and Priapus. What is this? If a man doing this work must at all costs have assistance from the gods, would not one goddess or one god be sufficient? Would not Venus alone be sufficient, the goddess who they say is named from the fact that without her power, no woman ceases to be a virgin? If people have any shame at all, a thing that the gods lack, will the newlyweds not feel bashful, he less eager and she more reluctant, at the idea that so many gods of both sexes are present and assisting with the matter at hand? Indeed, the goddess Virginiensis is there so that the virgin's belt may be loosened, and Subigus is there to put her beneath the husband, and the goddess Prema is there so that once she is under him, she does not move, and submits to the embrace. What does the goddess Pertunda do? Let her blush and go outdoors. Leave something for the husband to do! It is disgraceful that anyone other than he himself should perform the role from which she takes her name. But perhaps she is tolerated because she is said to be a goddess rather than a god, for if a masculine god called Pertundus were thought to exist, the husband would have to seek out more protection against him for his wife's chastity than the new mother does against Silvanus. But why am I saying this, since Priapus[43] is there too, he who is overly masculine, and upon whose incredibly huge and disgusting member new brides were told to sit, according to a most respectable and pious custom of Roman matrons?

1.18 Scholiast on Lucian *Dialogues of the Courtesans* 2.1, 7.4. Fifth to ninth century CE, drawing upon earlier sources. Scholia are marginal explanatory notes added to ancient manuscripts. The scholia on Lucian are one of the most important sources for the rituals of Demeter.

2.1 The Thesmophoria is a Greek festival that includes mysteries, and the same festival is also called the Scirophoria. According to the more mythic explanation, it was held because when Cora was abducted by Pluto[44] while picking flowers, a certain swineherd Eubuleus was present at the spot, grazing his pigs. They were swallowed up in Cora's chasm, and therefore in honour of Eubuleus, piglets are thrown into the 'chasms of Demeter and Cora'. The rotted remains of what was thrown into the chambers below are brought up by women called Bailers, who have spent three days in ritual purity. They go down into the interior spaces and when they have recovered the remains, they place them on the altars. They believe that if someone takes some of this and sows it with the seed grain, he will have a good crop. They say that there are also snakes down in the chasms, which eat much of the material thrown in. For this reason they make a rattling noise when the women are bailing, and whenever they put back those models,[45] so that the snakes, which they believe are the guardians of the interior spaces, will withdraw. The same thing is also called the Arrhetophoria,[46] and it is conducted according to the same reasoning about the genesis of the earth's fruits, and the procreation of humans. At that festival too they deposit sacred objects, which cannot be named, made of wheat-dough, and these are copies of snakes and male members. And they take hold of pine branches because this plant produces many offspring. These things as well as piglets are thrown into the chambers (for so they call the interior spaces), as I said. The piglets are used on account of their fecundity, as a symbol of the genesis of the earth's fruits and of humans, and are a thanksgiving offering to Demeter, because in providing her fruits she civilised the human race. Thus the reason formerly given for the festival is a mythological one, but the one set forth here is physical. It is called the Thesmophoria because Demeter is given the epithet Thesmophoros[47] as a result of setting the laws or Thesmoi according to which human beings must work to provide themselves with nourishment.

7.4 Haloa: a festival at Athens, including mysteries of Demeter, Cora and Dionysus, held by the Athenians when the vines are cut and the wine that has been laid down is tasted. At this time, they set out objects in the shape of male private parts, and they explain them as tokens of the seed by which humans come to be, because when Dionysus made the gift of wine, he provided it as a stimulating drug for sexual intercourse. He gave it to Icarius, who was killed by the shepherds because they did not understand how wine affects those who drink it. Because of their disrespectful rebellion against Dionysus, they were driven mad and placed in a continual state of shameful arousal. An oracle directed them to end their madness by making clay genitals and dedicating them. Once they did this, they were released from the curse, and the festival is a reminder of their suffering. As part of the festival a secret women's rite also takes place at Eleusis, with a great deal of joking and banter. The women go in alone and are free to say whatever they wish. And indeed then they say the most shameful things to each other, and the priestesses go up to the women stealthily and speak into their ears, advising them to cheat on their husbands as though telling some holy secret. All the women shout shameful and unholy things at each other, while handling objects that are indecent, images of bodies male and female. And a great deal of wine is set out for them, and tables filled with all the foods of land and sea, except for those forbidden in the mysteries, namely pomegranates, quinces, domestic birds and eggs, and among sea creatures the red mullet, pandora, black-tail, crayfish and dogfish. The chief magistrates prepare the tables and leave them inside for the women, while they themselves withdraw and remain outside, pointing out to all the visitors that cultivated foods originated with them and were shared with humankind by them. Also set out on the tables are the genitals of both sexes molded from cake. It is called the Haloa because of the fruit of Dionysus, for *halōai* are plantings of vines.

Further Reading

On liaisons between goddesses and mortals, see Stehle 1990. For gender and sexuality in the cults of Demeter and Persephone, see Lincoln 1979, Zeitlin 1982, Brumfield 1996, and Chlup 2007. On using the scholia to Lucian as a source for the Thesmophoria, see Lowe 1998. For Cybele and Attis, see Roller 1999 and Borgeaud 2004; for Aphrodite and Adonis, see Detienne 1994 and Reed 1995. More generally on Greek religion, gender, and sexuality, see Goff 2004 and Pirenne Delforge 2007. For the Bona Dea or 'Good Goddess' at Rome, see Brouwer 1989 and Staples 1998. On Baubo and Priapus, see respectively Olender 1990, 2001; for phallicism in Dionysiac cult, see Csapo 1997, and for the phallus in Roman religion, see Palmer 1975, pp. 87–206. On the Bacchanalian scandal in Roman Italy, see Flower 2002. On Jewish and Christian reception of Greco-Roman culture in the context of sexuality, see Gaca 2003.

2

Deities of Desire: Their Nature and Effects

For the ancients, sexual desire was perceived as a cosmic principle and personified in deities of primordial power (Aphrodite, Venus, Eros, Amor) who cast their spell over helpless mortals. According to Hesiod's *Theogony* (2.2), which possessed great authority as an account of the origins of the cosmos and the gods, Eros was one of the first four primordial beings who arose spontaneously from nothingness. Once Eros appeared, the primary mode of generation became sexual reproduction. The 'Orphic' cosmogonies, alternatives to Hesiod's Panhellenic account, are thought to have included the birth of Eros from a cosmic egg, which gave the comic poet Aristophanes fodder for his parody in the *Birds* (2.9). In later poetry, however, Eros was often simply the son of Aphrodite (2.13). He was worshiped from at least the fifth century BCE, and in later times had an important sanctuary and festival in Boeotia (2.22).

Aphrodite, meanwhile, was born from the genitals of the castrated Heaven according to Hesiod (2.2), or was daughter of Zeus and Dione (Homer *Iliad* 5.370–71). The poets call her Cypris and Cytherea because of her connections with the islands of Cyprus and Cythera (2.2). The Homeric *Hymn to Aphrodite* (2.3) describes how this goddess is responsible for sexual desire not only in human beings, but also in the rest of the natural world; therefore she is a cosmic force to be reckoned with. In the mythic universe, only the goddesses Hestia, Athena, and Artemis are eternally virgin, free from her influence, and virtually all male deities are presumed to have sexual needs. Even Zeus falls victim to her powers, though he takes steps to turn the tables on her, humiliating her by causing her to desire the mortal Anchises. The love affair of Aphrodite and Anchises illustrates both the Greek belief in the semi-divine lineage of great heroes (such as their son Aeneas) and the equally powerful conviction that the incommensurability of human and divine natures makes successful long-term relationships impossible.

Homer presents Aphrodite as a goddess whose nature is to encourage sexual activity and sometimes to compel it (2.1). Her favourites, Paris and Helen, are distinguished by their physical attractiveness. Whereas they experience human feelings of doubt and shame at their love affair, which has caused a war, Aphrodite allows no such scruples to stand in the way of her simple goal – to bring the two together in bed. Homer's portrayal highlights the imperiousness of the goddess and her fickle disposition, but can also be interpreted on another level as an illustration of the unrelenting power of desire, which retains its potency even as circumstances change, and whether it benefits or harms the one who feels it. In Archaic and Classical thought, Aphrodite's attendants are the Charites or Graces, who represent personal beauty and charm (1.2, 2.3, 9.2), and Peitho, persuasion. While the Charites are always welcomed, Peitho is an ambiguous goddess, for persuasion may point to the delights of mutual consent on the one hand, or the harm of deceptive seduction on the other (3.2, 4.9, 10.1). The Roman Venus differed in many ways from Greek Aphrodite, especially in her role as a kind of Lady Luck and in her adoption as patroness by certain leading men of the state. Most notable among these were Julius Caesar, who claimed descent from Venus, and his heir, the emperor Augustus. Well before the Caesars boasted of their relationship to Venus, Lucretius (2.16) had already blended Greek ideas of Aphrodite as a cosmic deity of generation with a distinctively Roman emphasis on her maternal aspect and her pivotal role in the fortunes of the state.

The Greeks often speak of sexual desire as an overwhelming external force that physically and mentally wears out its victims. To experience desire is to be lashed by storm winds (2.6), melted like wax (2.13), stunned with a hammer (2.5), or in a metaphor that was to become a cliché, shot with an arrow of fire (2.13). Eros was at worst cruel and at best 'bittersweet' (2.4), while Aphrodite could be both ally (5.2) and persecutor (2.14). Illness was one of the most common metaphors for love. Sappho's classic description of the physical manifestations of *erōs* (2.4) reads like the description of a fever or a stroke. In Euripides' *Hippolytus*, Phaedra's attendants are initially unaware that the cause of her debilitating illness (2.8) is a forbidden desire for her stepson. In this play, Phaedra is the unwitting instrument of Aphrodite's vengeance on Hippolytus for his willful rejection of the goddess. Her desire causes Phaedra to grow pale, physically weak, and feverishly restless. The chorus, meanwhile, note the misery that can come about through the influence of Eros and pray that he never afflicts them with 'misplaced' love that manifests itself at the wrong time or with the wrong person.

The Roman love elegists drew on Hellenistic literary models to examine desire from a more topical, interpersonal, and situational perspective, exploring the thrill of pursuit, the joys of requited love and sexual gratification, the pain of separation, and the agonies of rejection. Propertius used the genre of elegy to play with gender expectations and to depict himself dominated by his mistress and subjected to the overwhelming might of Amor (2.19). Sulpicia, a patrician woman of the circle of Valerius Messala and the elegiac poet Tibullus, is the only Roman woman whose poetry has been preserved for posterity. Her love elegies (2.21) are similar in style to those the male elegists, but the shift in gender perspective raises many interpretative questions about the way female desire was perceived in her social circle. Ovid, meanwhile, creates for himself the persona of a sophisticated man of the world, who sees the art of love as his vocation (2.20, 9.13).

Philosophers had much to say about Eros and Aphrodite. Like the archaic poets, many interpreted these deities as impersonal cosmic forces. For Empedocles, 'Love' along with 'Strife' was one of two forces in the universe that drive all change (2.7); he identified the force of attraction (*philotēs*) with Aphrodite. In Plato's *Symposium*, the participants at a party take turns praising Eros. Pausanias' speech makes a distinction between two Aphrodites, one representing earthly, 'common', and heterosexual love, and the other representing 'heavenly' pederastic love, which ideally did not involve sexual contact (2.10). In the speech attributed to Aristophanes, Plato creates a profound yet comic fable explaining the human need for intimacy, and the apparent orientation of some individuals toward opposite-sex or same-sex partners. Eros, we learn, is the yearning for wholeness to be found in union with another person. While many philosophers held that *erōs* had its origins in the perception of beauty, Aristotle asserted that the enjoyment of beauty was only a precondition: *erōs* was not present unless a person experienced longing for the absent beloved (2.11, 2.12). Unlike friendship, *erōs* did not require feelings and acts of goodwill toward its object.

Eros was initially depicted in art as a beautiful youth. Just as Aphrodite's physical form represented the sexually desirable female, that of Eros represented a male object of desire. Although this concept of Eros' appearance never completely faded (2.23), Hellenistic poets and artists began to portray him as a mischievous young child (2.13) who used his bow to strike painful desire into the hearts of his hapless victims. The passage from the *Argonautica* recounts Medea's initial sight of Jason and her immediate confusion and pain at the force of her feelings for him (2.15). Aphrodite helps to drive the divine machinery of this epic by sending Eros to Medea, just as Venus would later send Amor to Dido in Vergil's Roman epic, the *Aeneid*. When Aeneas leaves

Dido to fulfill his destiny, her passion for him is transformed into hatred (2.18), with lasting significance for the futures of both Carthage and Rome. Already in his *Georgics*, Vergil (2.17) had explored the dark side of *amor* and its potential for destruction as a natural force that rules humans and animals alike, and over which humans have limited control.

In later antiquity, Eros/Amor continued to reign as a powerful deity in the new Greco-Roman genre of the novel, where love and the tribulations of lovers were paramount themes, but happy endings were the rule. In Apuleius' lush description of the love god's physical beauty (2.23), the reader experiences desire for Desire through the eyes of the protagonist Psyche.

2.1 Homer *Iliad* 3.380–420. Eighth century BCE. Aphrodite goads her favourites, Helen and Paris, to have sex.

> Him Aphrodite snatched,
> With the ease of the gods, folding him in thick mist,
> And set him down in his fragrant, scented chamber.
> She herself went to call Helen; she found her
> On a high turret, with a throng of Trojan women.
> Plucking Helen's nectar-sweet robe with her hand,
> She appeared like an aged woman, a carder of wool,
> A beloved servant, who produced fine work in wool
> For Helen, back home in Lacedaemon.[48] She said,
> 'Come with me; Alexander calls you home.
> He waits in your chamber on the turned-wood bed,
> Handsome in his bright robes. No one would think
> Him fresh from battle, but rather about to dance--
> Or that he had just sat down, his dance completed.'
> So she spoke, and Helen's heart was troubled.
> She noted the goddess' surpassingly lovely neck,
> Her desirable breasts, and the bright gleam of her eye.
> And marveling, she spoke a word to her and said,
> 'Uncanny one, why do you wish to deceive me?
> You will lead me into the well-placed cities
> Either of Phrygia or desirable Maeonia[49]
> If one of your favourite mortal men dwells there.
> Because Menelaus has bested bright Alexander,
> And wishes to lead my hateful self back home,
> This is why you approach me now with deceit.
> Go sit with him, withdrawing from the ways of gods,
> Let not your feet bear you again to Olympus,
> But forever worry over that man and guard him,

Until he makes you his wife or indeed his slave.
I shall not go there, for a shameful thing it would be
To share his bed. All Trojan women after this
Will blame me, while my heart holds endless grief.'
But Aphrodite growing enraged at her said,
'Wretch, do not anger me, lest I desert you.
Then I would hate you, as now I love you – utterly.
I would scheme dire hatred between the Danaans[50]
And Trojans, and you would suffer an evil fate.'
She spoke, and Helen who sprang from Zeus was afraid.
Wrapping herself in her brilliant cloak she went,
In silence, unseen by the Trojans, and the goddess led.

2.2 Hesiod *Theogony* 114–22, 173–206. Eighth century BCE. In Hesiod's account of the origins of the gods, Eros is described as one of the primordial beings who arose from Chaos. Later, Earth convinces her son Cronus to attack his father Uranus (Heaven) so that he and his siblings can be born, but his actions also lead to the genesis of other deities, including Aphrodite.

114–22
Muses who inhabit the Olympian mansions,
Tell me what came to be in the beginning.
First was Chaos, and then broad-chested Earth,
Secure seat forever of the undying ones
Who possess the peak of snowy Olympus.
Then dark Tartarus below the wide-pathed ground
And Eros, loveliest of the undying gods,
Limb-loosener, who overcomes the mind
And careful plans of gods and humans alike.
From Chaos there came Erebus[51] and black Night,
But Aether and Day sprang forth from Night,
Conceived and born of her mating with Erebus.

173–206
He spoke, and the mind of vast Earth was glad;
She sat him in a secret ambush and in his hands
Placed a jagged sickle, and laid out the plan.
Great Heaven led in the night, and longing for love
He spread and weighed down Earth in all directions.
But from his lair the son stretched his left hand,
And with his right he grasped the monstrous sickle,
Long and jagged. And his own father's genitals

He eagerly lopped, tossing them behind him.
But they did not fall uselessly from his hand,
For every bloody droplet that flowed away
Earth received, and as the seasons revolved
She bore the strong Erinyes[52] and huge Giants,
Shining in their armor and clutching long spears,
And Melian nymphs[53] over all the boundless earth.
But as soon as he cropped the genitals with steel,
He cast them from land into the surging sea.
So they travelled the waves for a time, as white
Foam rose from the undying flesh, and within
There grew a girl. First to holy Cythera,
And then to Cyprus, surrounded by sea, she came.
As she, revered and lovely, stepped ashore,
Grass appeared beneath her slender feet.
To men and gods she is known as Aphrodite,
The goddess born from foam; and lovely-crowned
Cytherea from the island where she touched;
Cyprogenes, for her wave-swept birthplace,
And Philommedes,[54] from the genitals.

2.3 Homeric *Hymn to Aphrodite* 45–246. Seventh century BCE. In this hymn, the goddess of sexual desire gets a taste of her own medicine, falling in love with the Trojan hero Anchises.

Zeus put sweet longing in Aphrodite's heart
To sleep with a man doomed to die, so that soon
She would not hold herself aloof from a mortal bed.
Then laughter-loving Aphrodite would not boast,
Smiling, how she paired the gods with women
Who bore the immortals sons doomed to die,
And how she paired the goddesses with men.
In her heart he put sweet longing for Anchises,
Built like a god, who at that time herded cattle
On the high peaks of Ida with its many springs.
Catching sight of him, Aphrodite fell in love,
And terrible longing seized hold of her mind.
Coming to Cyprus, she entered her fragrant temple,
Her Paphian precinct[55] with its fragrant altar.
Coming there, she closed the shining doors.
The Graces bathed and anointed her with oil,
Such as the gods who live forever use,

An ambrosial, sweet-scented balm she had on hand.
Wrapping her body in all her lovely robes,
And adorned with gold, laughter-loving Aphrodite
Hurried to Troy from sweet-smelling Cyprus,
Swiftly traveling through the highest clouds.
Once at well-watered Ida, mother of beasts,
She strode to his dwelling straight over the hills.
After her walked grey wolves wagging their tails,
Fierce-eyed lions, bears, and nimble leopards,
Ravenous for roe deer. The sight delighted her,
And into their breasts she cast desire. Together
They lay down in pairs, each in a shady den.
But she arrived at the well-constructed cabin,
And found him, left quite alone in the dwelling,
The hero Anchises, whose beauty was divine.
All of the others were following with the herds
Along the grassy pastures, but in that place
He walked to and fro, playing the lyre thrillingly.
Aphrodite Zeus's daughter stood before him,
Resembling a virgin maiden in height and looks,
Lest he be alarmed and awed at the sight of her.
And Anchises saw, and gazed in admiration
At her height and looks and all her shining garments.
For she wore a robe brighter than fire's gleam,
Lovely, golden, richly worked, like the moon
It shone upon her soft breast, a wonder to see.
She wore spiral-shaped armlets and brilliant earrings
And about her soft throat, exquisite chains.
Love seized Anchises, and he spoke to her:
'Greetings, Lady, whichever of the immortals you are
Who come to this house, whether Artemis or Leto,
Aphrodite, well-born Themis or grey-eyed Athena
Or perhaps you are one of the Graces, coming here,
Who attend all the gods and are called immortals,
Or one of the Nymphs who hold the lovely groves,
Or those who live around this lovely mountain
And the springs of rivers, and the grassy meadows.
For you I shall build an altar high on a peak,
Visible from all directions, and for you
I shall sacrifice well, in all seasons. But you,
Kindly make me eminent among the Trojans;
Grant me many hardy offspring hereafter,

And let me long enjoy the sunlight, blessed
Among the people, approaching the threshold of age.'
Aphrodite Zeus's daughter then answered him:
'Anchises, most glorious of humans born on earth,
Why liken me to immortals? I am no goddess,
But a mortal and my mother a mortal woman.
My father Otreus is famous – perhaps you know
His name? He rules over strong-walled Phrygia.
I know your speech as well as my native tongue,
For a Trojan nurse reared me in the hall, an infant
Apart from my mother, yet she cherished me.
This was how I learned your tongue. Just now,
Argus-Slayer[56] with his golden wand snatched me
From the dance for raucous Artemis of golden arrows.
We much-courted maidens and nymphs were dancing,
And a massive crowd surrounded us. Then it was
That Argus-Slayer with his golden wand snatched me.
He brought me past many fields of mortal men,
And vacant, untilled lands, inhabited
By ravenous beasts in shady dens. I feared
My feet would never touch the life-giving ground!
He told me that Anchises would wed and bed me,
That as your wife I would bear you splendid children.
Once he had said this, mighty Argus-Slayer
Returned once more to the tribes of the immortals.
But I come to you in the grip of powerful necessity.
I implore you, by Zeus and your noble parents,
For no base ones produced such a son as you:
Take me, virgin and untested in love as I am;
Show me to your father and capable mother
And to your brothers who were born from them.
No ill-favoured daughter shall I be, but suitable.
Quickly send word to the nimbly-mounted Phrygians
And tell my father and deeply grieving mother,
Who will send gold in plenty and woven cloth;
Receive all these splendid gifts as your reward.
This done, present the charming wedding feast
That wins respect from men and immortal gods.'
She spoke, and cast sweet longing on his heart.
Love seized Anchises and he spoke to her:
'If you are mortal, your mother a mortal woman,
And your father is famous Otreus, as you say,

And you are here by the will of the deathless Guide
Hermes, you shall be called my wife henceforth.
None among gods or mortals shall restrain me
From making love to you here and now, no,
Not even if Apollo the Far-Shooter himself
Sends grievous missiles from his silver bow.
Goddess-like woman, once I take you to bed
I would not mind if I sink to the house of Hades.'
So he spoke, and took her hand. Aphrodite,
The laughter loving, cast her eyes down and stepped
Toward the comfortable bed, already well spread
With soft cloaks for the prince, and over these
Lay bearskins and pelts of deep-roaring lions
Which he himself had slain on the mountain heights.
And when they were together in the sturdy bed,
First he took the bright jewels from her body,
Pins, twisted armlets, earrings and chains.
He unfastened her belt, and her glittering dress
He stripped off and placed on a silver-studded seat.
Then mortal Anchises bedded an undying goddess
By the will of the gods, not knowing what he did.
At the hour the herdsmen guide the cattle back
And the fat sheep homeward from the flowering fields
She poured on Anchises sweet, delightful sleep,
But dressed her body again in lovely clothing.
And once she was fully arrayed, the bright goddess
Stood by the couch, her head reaching the sturdy
Roof-beam. Divine beauty shone from her face
As is fitting for blossom-crowned Cytherea.
She spoke a word and woke him from his sleep:
'Dardanus' son! Why do you sleep so soundly?
Rise and tell me if my appearance now
Is the same as when you first laid eyes on me.'
She spoke, and he heard, waking with a start.
Seeing the goddess' lovely face and neck,
He was struck with awe and averted his eyes,
Hiding his handsome face away in his cloak.
Then he begged her, speaking with winged words:
'From the moment my eyes first saw you, goddess,
I knew you were a god, but you did not speak truth.
I implore you now by Zeus who bears the aegis –
Render me not a weakling among my fellows;

But pity me, for one who beds an immortal
Goddess does not remain a healthy man.'
Aphrodite Zeus's daughter answered him,
'Anchises, most honoured of humans doomed to die,
Cheer your heart and do not be too fearful.
No harm will come to you from me, or the other
Blessed ones, since you are dear to the gods.
A son shall be yours, a ruler among the Trojans
And his descendants will multiply forever.
His name shall be Aeneas,[57] for the dire distress
That gripped me when I bedded with a mortal.
Still, among all human men who are doomed to die,
Those of your race are especially close to the gods
In looks as well as height. Yes, Counselor Zeus
Snatched away blond Ganymede for his beauty,
To live among the undying and pour their wine,
A wonder to see, honoured by all the immortals,
As he draws ruby nectar from the golden bowl.
But unending grief seized Tros, nor did he know
Where the wondrous wind had swept his son;
He used to weep unceasingly day after day.
But Zeus pitied him, and in exchange for his son
Gave high-stepping horses like those of the gods.
These were his gift, and at the command of Zeus
Hermes the Guide informed him of everything,
How his son, like a god, would neither age nor die.
But when Tros heard the message of Zeus, at last
He wept no more but began to rejoice in his heart,
And gladly rode the horses with whirlwind feet.
Dawn of the golden throne snatched up Tithonus,
One of your race who closely resembled the gods.
She entreated the dark-clouded son of Cronus
To make him immortal and able to live forever,
And Zeus approved, giving her wish fulfillment.
Yet it slipped the mind of Lady Dawn, that fool,
To ask that Youth slough off his deadly age.
So long as desirable Youth remained with him,
He lived in delight with the early-born goddess Dawn,
Beside at river Ocean at the ends of the earth.
But when the first white strands flowed out
Over his handsome head and noble chin,
The Lady Dawn retreated from his bed.

Still she cherished him within her rooms,
Supplying immortal food and lovely robes,
But after hateful age had weighed him down,
And he could neither move nor lift his limbs,
This counsel seemed to her the best: to place
Him in a room and close the shining doors.
There indeed his voice flows on unceasing;
His supple limbs have lost their former strength.
Such a fate I would not choose for you,
Immortal and ageing forever among the gods.
Yet if your bodily form could remain unchanged
And if you could abide and be called my spouse,
Then grief would not enfold my troubled heart.
But pitiless Age soon will arrive to enfold you,
Just as it visits all humans – wearying Age,
Accursed and hateful, even to the gods.'

2.4 Sappho Frs. 31, 47, 130 Lobel-Page. Ca. 600 BCE. Sappho's love poems are among the most famous ever written, in spite of their fragmentary state.

Fr. 31
He seems like one of the gods to me,
That man who sits facing you
And hears the sweetness of your speech,

The charm of your laughter. Truly,
This flutters the heart within me.

One look at you, and I can no longer speak,
My tongue breaks, and suddenly
A fine flame races beneath my skin,
I am blinded and noise fills my ears.

Sweat pours from me, and trembling
Seizes my whole body. I am greener
Than grass, and feel myself close to death.

But I must endure it all...

Fr. 47
Eros shook my
Spirit like wind falling on the mountain oaks.

Fr. 130

Once again Eros, loosener of limbs, whirls me about.
A bittersweet god: no use fighting his stealthy approach.

2.5 Anacreon *PMG* 413. Mid to late 6ᵗʰ century BCE. Anacreon was an Ionian poet celebrated around the Aegean for his lyrics on drinking, love, and other topics.

Like a blacksmith Eros once again struck me with his great
Hammer, and plunged me into the wintry stream.

2.6 Ibycus *PMG* 286. Mid to late 6ᵗʰ century BCE. A citizen of Rhegium, a Greek colony in Italy, Ibycus was famed for his love poetry.

In spring the quince trees of Cydonia⁵⁸
Are watered from flowing streams
Where grows the untouched garden
Of the Maidens,⁵⁹ and the tender vines
Blossom under shaded boughs.

But for me, Eros sleeps in no season.

Like the Thracian North Wind
Darting with fire and lightning
From the Cyprian, with scorching madness
Dark-hued and relentlessly forceful,
He devours my heart utterly.

2.7 Empedocles Fr. 17.15–29 Diels-Kranz. Mid-fifth century. In the poetry of this Presocratic philosopher, Aphrodite was another name for the unifying principle of the cosmos, which he calls *philotēs*, Love.

As I said, declaring the enterprise of my words,
My tale will be twofold. One thing grew from many;
Another time many things diverged from one:
Fire, earth, water, and boundless height of air,
And deadly Strife apart, but wholly comparable,
And Love among them, equal in length and breadth.
See, but let not your eyes be amazed at her,
Whom mortal men deem inborn in their joints.
They achieve kindness and harmonious deeds
Through her, and name her Joy or Aphrodite.

No mortal man has seen her whirl among them,
But hear the guileless voyage of my words:
Though all of these are equal in birth and age,
Yet each rules its realm and has its ways.
They dominate by turns as time rolls on.

2.8 Euripides *Hippolytus* 170–222, 525–64. 428 BCE. One of the three great
Athenian tragedians, Euripides is noted for his interest in sexuality and female
psychology.

170–222
Chorus:
But here is the ancient nurse at the doors;
Bringing her outside the palace.
The gloomy cloud on her brow is growing.
My soul yearns to know what is happening,
What bodily mischief the queen, so pale,
Has suffered.

Nurse:
What ills and miserable diseases we mortals have.
What shall I do, or not do for you?
Here is your light, this bright sky,
And your sick-bed is now outdoors.
For all your talk was to come out here,
But soon you will hurry back to your room,
For you falter quickly, and there is no pleasing you.
What is at hand you dislike, and think better of
Whatever is distant.
Better to be the sick woman than to tend her:
The one lot is a single sorrow, but the other
Joins heartache with tiresome tasks.
The whole life of human beings is painful
And there is no rest from labours.
That which is dearer than life
Darkness hides away in the clouds;
Clearly we desperately love
What part of this shines through to earth.
In our ignorance of other modes of life,
Since that beneath the earth is not revealed,
We are carried along aimlessly by tales.

Phaedra:
Lift my body, hold my head up!
The bond that knits my limbs is loosened.
Take my delicate forearms, servants.
This cap weighs heavily on my head.
Take it off! Spread my curls on my shoulders.

Nurse:
Take heart, my child, and do not
Throw yourself about so roughly.
You will bear your sickness more easily
In a state of calm and genteel resolution.
Mortals must endure suffering.

Phaedra:
Oh! If only I could draw pure water,
And drink from a spring of dew.
I would take my rest reclining
Beneath poplars in a lush meadow.

Nurse:
Child, why do you speak so?
Will you utter such things before the crowds,
Flinging words borne upon madness?

Phaedra:
Send me to the mountain! I will go to the woods,
To the pine trees, where the beast-killing
Hounds tread, pressing close upon
The dappled deer.
By the gods! I want to cry out to the dogs,
Heft a Thessalian javelin beside my blonde hair,
And hold barbed arrows in my hand.

525–64
Eros, O Eros, you who drip desire
Into lovers' eyes, bringing sweet charm
To the souls of those you battle,
May you never show your harmful side to me,
Nor arrive in misplaced time.
For neither fire nor starlight burns brighter

Than Aphrodite's arrow, shot from the hand
Of Eros, Zeus' son.

Foolishly does Hellas[60] increase
The slaughter of cattle beside the Alpheus[61]
And in the Pythian house of Apollo,[62]
Yet Eros, who lords it over men
And holds the keys to the most intimate
Chambers of Aphrodite, we fail to revere.
He ravages mortals and sends them into peril
Wherever he goes.
The girl of Oechalia,[63]
A filly still unjoined to a mate,
As yet without a husband and unwed,
Aphrodite took from Eurytion's house
Like a running Naiad or Bacchant,
And yoked her, handing her over amid
Blood and smoke and nuptial slaughter
To Heracles. Unhappy bride!

O sacred fortress of Thebes,
And fount of Dirce's spring,[64]
You too could tell how Cypris comes.
For she gave as bride
To the thunderbolt ringed with fire
The mother of twice-born Bacchus[65]
And laid her in a gory bed of doom.
Her breath touches every living thing,
As she flits now to this one, now to that.

2.9 Aristophanes *Birds* 673–702. 414 BCE. In this parody of cosmogonic myth, the birds claim the winged god Eros as one of their own race.

In the beginning was Chaos and Night, and black Erebus and wide Tartarus,
But no earth or air or heaven. First of all in Erebus' boundless bosom
Black-winged Night laid a wind-egg,[66] and therefrom
As the rolling seasons ran, Eros the Desirable grew, his back glistening
With two golden wings, swift as a whirling cyclone. And he mated
With nightlike Chaos, also winged, in wide Tartarus, and hatched
Our race, which first came forth into light.

The race of immortals did not exist, until Eros mingled everything,
And from the mating of one with another came heaven, ocean, earth
And indeed all the deathless race of the blessed gods.

Thus we are far older than all the blessed ones; as many proofs make clear, we are Eros' children, for we fly and we accompany those who love.

Thanks to us, many a lover has divided the thighs of a beauteous boy in his prime, who swore he would not yield.
What a powerful gift is a quail, a water-hen, a goose or a cock!

2.10 Plato *Symposium* 180c–181c, 189c–193d. 385–80 BCE. In this dialogue, the guests at a drinking party take turns making speeches about the nature of love. In the course of his speech, Pausanias provides an educated man's perspective on popular cult titles of Aphrodite ('Common' and 'Heavenly') and their relationship to Eros. Later, the comic poet Aristophanes tells a fantastic tale about the origins of gender and sexual preference.

180c–181c
I don't think we have planned our discussion well, Phaedrus, if the idea is merely to trade praises of Eros. If there were only one Eros, it would be all right, but Eros is not only one, and since this is the case, it would be better to state in advance what sort of Eros we ought to praise. Now, I will try to set us straight again, first by saying which sort of Eros we ought to praise, and then by praising this god as he deserves. We all know that there is no Aphrodite without Eros; and if that goddess were one, there would also be one Eros. But since there are two of her, two Erotes must also exist. That there are two Aphrodites is certain. For one of them is the elder and has no mother; she is the daughter of Uranus, whom we name 'Heavenly'. The younger one, whom we call Pandemus or 'Common', is the daughter of Zeus and Dione. It must be the case, then, that the Eros who shares the work of Common Aphrodite is called Common Eros, and the other, Heavenly Eros. Of course we ought to praise every god, but we must try to describe the role of each of these two.

Now, an action in and of itself is neither good nor bad. For example, in the case of the things we are doing now, whether drinking or singing or having a conversation, none of these things is good in and of itself, but depending on how a thing is carried out, it may turn out to be good. For when a thing is done well and correctly, it becomes good, but when a thing is not done correctly, it becomes bad. The same is true of loving, and not every Eros is good or worthy of praise; only the one who urges us to love well. Now, the Eros associated with Common Aphrodite is truly 'of the common folk' and works by happenstance. This is the type of love we see among men of the lower classes. To begin with, they are as likely to love women as boys; secondly, they focus on the body rather than the soul, and lastly, they are attracted to the stupidest people they can find, since they have in view only the achievement of their desires, and they don't care whether their actions are good or bad. So they proceed in a random fashion, and the results are sometimes good, and sometimes the opposite. This type of love comes from the Aphrodite who is by far the younger of the two, and in her origins she partakes of both female and male.

189c–193d

Eryximachus, said Aristophanes, I have in mind to speak in a rather different way from you and Pausanias. It seems to me that people entirely fail to perceive the power of Eros, for if they grasped this, they would establish great temples and altars for him, and sacrifice lavishly, but none of these things is currently done for him although he is owed them most of all. For he is the god who most loves the human race and brings us help. He is the doctor of those ills whose cure would bring the greatest happiness to humanity. Therefore I shall try to bring you to an understanding of his power, and you shall teach others.

First you must learn about human nature and its tribulations. Formerly our nature was not as it is now, but quite different. In the beginning there were three kinds of human being, not two as we have now, male and female, but also a third kind with a share of both the other types. Its name remains, but the thing itself has vanished. The 'manwoman' at that time was a unity in both physical form and in name, possessing a share of both male and female, but now the name is not used except as a reproach. Next, the form of each person was spherical, with back and sides forming a round. Everyone had four arms, and the same number of legs, and two identical faces on a round neck. There was one head with the two faces turned in opposite directions, four ears, and two sets of genitals, and all the rest was arranged just as you might guess. They walked upright as we do now, and went in whichever direction they wished, but when they began to run fast, they stuck their legs out straight and turned cartwheels as tumblers do now, only then they had eight arms and legs to support and speed them on their way around.

There were three kinds and they were these particular types, because the male was the original offspring of the sun, the female of the earth, and the kind partaking of both was born of the moon. For the moon too has a share of both sun and earth. They were rounded in bodily shape as well as their mode of travel, because they took after their parents.

Now they were amazingly strong and powerful, and they were very ambitious, even challenging the gods. Homer speaks of them when he recounts the story of Ephialtes and Otus, how they tried to mount to heaven in order to assault the gods. Zeus and the other gods met to discuss what they should do, and they were at a loss. For they did not see how they could destroy them as they had the giants, exterminating their race with the thunderbolt--for the honours and sacrifices they had from humans would also vanish – nor could they allow such outrageous behaviour.

Having reflected at length, Zeus said, 'I believe that I have hit on a plan, whereby the humans may continue to exist, yet be made weaker and cease their undisciplined behaviour. I shall slice each one of them in two, and thereby they will be both weaker and of more use to us through the multiplication of their numbers. They will walk upright on two legs. And if they still behave badly and choose not to keep quiet, why then I shall slice them in two again so that they go around hopping on one leg.' After he had spoken, he cut the human beings in two, just as one splits a sorb-apple[67] to pickle it, or as eggs are split with hairs. And as each human being was cut, he had Apollo turn its face and half-neck to the cut side, so that by seeing the evidence of its cutting, it might behave in a more orderly way; he ordered the god to heal them once this was done. So Apollo turned their faces about, and pulling the skin around what is now called the belly, he made a hole and tied it off in the middle just like a drawstring bag. And this we call the navel. Then he smoothed most of the folds of skin and defined the chest, just as a shoemaker smoothes the folds of a shoe on a wooden form; he left a few, the ones around the belly itself and the navel, as a reminder of their former state.

But when the creatures had been divided, each one longed to be joined with its other half, and throwing their arms about one another they embraced, yearning to grow together again, and they died from hunger and self-neglect, for they would do nothing separately. And whenever one of the halves died, and one was left behind, the survivor searched for another and embraced it, whether it was half of a female (which we now call a woman) or of a male. So they were dying out. But taking pity on them, Zeus came up with another plan, and turned their genitals to the front, for previously they were on the outside, and they did not reproduce with one another but deposited seed in the ground like cicadas. So he transformed them and henceforth they reproduced with one another, the male within the female, so that a man met a woman in a mutual embrace to breed, and the race was multiplied. Or if a male came together with a male, they derived satisfaction and rest from their companionship, and turned to their labours and the business of daily life. And so it is that ever since then, desire for one another has been innate in humans, and Eros brings us together in our original state, trying to make one from two, and to heal the human wound.

Thus, each of us is only half of a token, since we are cut in half like flatfish, two parts from one. And each one is always searching for the other half of the token. All the men who come from the original creature, which was then called the 'manwoman', are lovers of women, and from this group arose many seducers. And women who love men as well as adulteresses arose from this group. But those who were cut from the all-female creature have no great interest in men, and they are attracted instead to other women. The prostitutes who enjoy other women come from this group. And those who were cut from the all-male creature seek out whatever is masculine. As long as they are boys, seeing as they are slices from the male, they love men and they delight in lying intertwined with men. And these are the best of the boys and youths, since they are most manly in their nature.

Some say they are shameless, but falsely, for they do these things not from lack of shame, but from confidence, virility, and a manly spirit, welcoming their own kind with pleasure. And there is strong evidence of this fact, for once they mature, such men alone are the ones who succeed in politics. And when they become adults, they are boy-lovers and by nature have little interest in marriage and begetting children, but the force of custom compels them. They are content to live with one another unmarried. Such a one, at any rate, both accepts lovers when he is a boy, and loves boys when he is a man, always welcoming his own kind.

Whenever one of the boy-lovers or any of the others we spoke of happens to meet his other half, each of them is wondrously stricken with feelings of affection, kinship and desire, so much so that they are unwilling to be separated from one another for a single moment. These are the couples who remain together their whole lives, though they could not say just what it is that they see in one another. Nobody could suppose that their union was grounded in mere sexual pleasure, nor could it explain why each takes such eager delight in the other's company. Clearly the soul of each desires something that it is unable to express, except through a kind of prophecy and vague foreboding. Suppose that Hephaestus with his tools came to the pair as they lay together and asked, 'What do you want from each other, humans?' And seeing them in doubt, suppose that he again asked, 'Do you wish most of all to be joined into one, so that day and night you are never apart? If this is your desire, I am willing to fuse and weld you together, so that from two parts you become one as long as you live, sharing your life in common, and so that when you end your lives, you shall again be one instead of two, having died together. But consider whether this is your desire, and whether you would be content with this outcome.' We are certain that upon hearing this, nobody would deny it, or wish for anything else, but each would simply consider this the very thing his heart had long desired, to join and be fused with his beloved until the two became one.

The cause of it all is that this was our original nature, and we were whole. What we call Eros is the craving and pursuit of wholeness. Formerly, as I said, we were one, but now because of our wrongdoing the god has caused us to live apart, just as the Arcadians were forced to live apart by the Lacedaemonians.[68] And there is cause for fear, unless we behave properly toward the gods, that we may once again be parted, and have to go about like those relief carvings on tombstones, sawn in two right through the nose, like two halves of a token. Therefore we all should exhort every man to honour the gods, so that we may escape that fate, and enjoy those benefits which our leader and general Eros provides. Let no man act in opposition to him – and whoever incurs the hatred of the gods does act in opposition to Eros – for it is by our friendliness and reconciliation with the god that we shall discover and meet our very own beloved ones, which few people today ever do. And in case Eryximachus interrupts me with comic mocking, saying that I speak of Pausanias and Agathon – for they may perhaps belong to this group, and are both of the manly nature – I mean to say that this applies to everyone, both male and female, so that the human race will be happy if we bring Eros to fulfillment, and each finds his or her own darling love, reverting to the ancient state. If this is the best state, then we must get as close to it as we can by finding beloveds who match our own dispositions. And it is right to sing hymns to Eros, the god who brings this about. In the present he benefits us exceedingly by leading us to our own, and for the future he brings us great hopes, that if we offer reverence to the gods, they will restore us to our ancient state, and through healing make us blessed and happy.

2.11 Aristotle *Rhetoric* 1370b. Mid to late fourth century BCE. In his extant works, Aristotle comments only rarely on the psychological and emotional components of sexuality, but this brief passage reveals a keen insight into the experience of lovers.

Those who love always enjoy speaking and writing and doing anything that pertains to the one they love, for by means of all these rememberings, they feel that they are able to perceive the loved one. The beginning of love is the same for everyone: when a person rejoices not only in the presence of his beloved, but also when calling to mind the absent loved one. And while there is pain when the loved one is absent, there is also a certain pleasure in mourning and laments, and there is pleasure in recalling how he looks and his actions and personal qualities. This is why the poet was right in saying 'Thus he spoke, and aroused in them a desire to weep.'[69]

2.12 Aristotle, *Nichomachean Ethics* 1167a3–8. Ca. 330 BCE. Aristotle expresses the common philosophic view that love has its origins in the admiration of beauty.

Wishing someone well seems to be the beginning of friendship, just as pleasure in seeing someone is the beginning of love, for nobody falls in love without first taking pleasure in beauty. But rejoicing in beauty does not always mean one loves; this is the case only when someone longs for the absent beloved, and eagerly desires his presence. Similarly, it is not possible for people to be friends unless they wish one another well, but well-wishers are not necessarily friends. For by merely wanting good things for others, one becomes a well-wisher, but need not provide assistance nor be troubled for them. Thus interpreting the term 'well-wishing', one might say that it is an inactive form of friendship, which may over time and with regular contact become true friendship, but not the type whose purpose is usefulness or pleasure, for well-wishing does not follow from these.

2.13 Asclepiades *Greek Anthology* 5.210, 5.189, 12.105. Early third century BCE. The *Greek Anthology* is a collection of poetry ranging in date from the Classical through the Byzantine period. Many of the poems are erotic epigrams, a genre mastered by Asclepiades.

5.210
Tempting Didyme has carried me off, alas! And I
Melt when I see her, like wax in the fire.
So what if her skin is black? So are coals, and they
Shine like the petals of roses when lit.

5.189
It is night, in the middle of winter; the Pleiades have set.
I walk in the rain by her front door.
I bear a wound of desire for that cheating girl. Cypris
Sent me not love, but a dart of fire.

12.105
I, a small Eros, and easy to catch, escaped my mother
But I don't soar away from Damis.
Here I care and am cared for without a jealous thought,
Forsaking the many, one with one.

2.14 Posidippus *Greek Anthology* 5.211. Early 3rd century BCE. Born in Macedon, Posidippus became a court poet of the Ptolemies in Egypt.

Tears and revels, why do you urge me, before my feet
Are free of the flame, to tread new embers
Of Cypris? I never rest from love, and Aphrodite
Always brings new pain and desire.

2.15 Apollonius of Rhodes *Argonautica* 3.275–98. Mid-third century BCE. The third book of Apollonius' epic poem about the voyage of the Argonauts to win the Golden Fleece tells how Medea fell in love with Jason through the machinations of Aphrodite and her son Eros.

Now Eros arrived unseen in a grayish mist,
Like the stinging fly that troubles the grazing cows,
And herdsmen call it the cattle-goading gadfly.
Quickly stringing his bow at the door to the porch,
He drew from its quiver a fresh and grievous arrow.
Invisible on swift feet he crossed the threshold,
Darting quick glances about. Crouched beneath
Aeson's son,[70] he fitted the notch to the string
And pulling wide with both of his hands, he shot
Straight at Medea. Struck to the heart, she was speechless.
He himself flew out from the high-roofed chamber
Laughing, but the arrow burned within the girl,
Beneath her heart, like a flame. Opposite her,
Jason drew her constant, sparkling gaze,
As the toiling heart in her breast was tossed about;
A flood of sweet pain overwhelmed the thoughts in her mind.
As a poor woman piles up twigs about a brand,
A spinster, with wretched labours for her lot,
To prepare a fire in the dark beneath her roof
When she has risen early, and the wondrous flame
Rising from the brand, wholly engulfs the twigs--
Just so, coiled under her heart, cruel Eros burned
Secretly. By turns her cheeks flushed red,
Then blanched pale, in the anguish of her mind.

2.16 Lucretius *On the Nature of Things* 1–43. Ca. 60 BCE. The poet-philosopher Lucretius was a follower of Epicurus and hostile toward 'superstition' in religious belief, but he drew on Roman tradition as well as philosophical ideas for his invocation to Venus.

Mother of Romans, delight of gods and mortals,
Fruitful Venus, beneath the gliding stars
You cause the ship-bearing seas to multiply
And the bountiful lands, and it is through you
That all are born and see the light of the sun.
The winds flee at your coming, O Goddess; for you
The clouds of the sky disappear; the skillful Earth
Sculpts sweet blooms, and a calm sea smiles,

As the heavens glow with tranquil spreading light.
For soon as the dawn of Spring unfolds itself,
And fertile breezes blow freely from the west,
Birds on the wing are stricken to the heart with love
And herald your approach with song, Lady Divine,
The herds grow wild, frisking in happy fields,
And swimming swollen streams. Under your spell,
All are quick to follow where you lead.
Thus over seas and hills, through furious floods,
In lush-leaved homes of birds and verdant fields
You impress love's lure on every heart
That through desire, each kind may reproduce.
Now since you alone are Nature's guide,
And nothing reaches the shining shores of light
Without you, nor attains to joy and love,
May you be my ally as I undertake this task,
And set down verses on the Nature of Things
For Memmius,[71] my friend who is, thanks to you,
Splendid at every time, and in every way.
Therefore lend my words immortal charm:
And lull all savage works of war meanwhile
To restful sleep over all the lands and seas.
For you alone can aid the human race
With tranquil peace, since valiant Mars, who rules
Those savage works, is Love's eternal prey
And flings himself defeated on your breast.
He gazes upward with his head thrown back,
And feasts his eager eyes with mouth agape
At you, catching his breath at the sight, O Goddess.
Enfold the reclining god with your sacred body;
Pour from your lips soft speech, O glorious one,
And bring to the people of Rome your gentle peace.
For the task of the poet is hindered by troubled times,
And the brilliant scion of Memmius' clan cannot
In time of war neglect the public good.

2.17 Vergil *Georgics* 3.242–263. Ca. 37–29 BCE. Vergil's poetic manual on farming emphasises the ways in which both people and animals are driven by sexual desire. The word here translated as 'love' is *amor*, which Vergil calls 'harsh' (*dūrus*).

Every race on earth, human and beast,
Sea-life, flocks, and painted birds: all rush

Madly into the flame, and all feel Love.
Never more fiercely does the lioness prowl
The fields, heedless of her cubs, nor the bear
Rampaging in the woods deal such carnage.
Then the boar is fierce, the tigress at her worst,
Then it is death to roam the deserts of Libya.
Do you see how the horse trembles head to toe
When it catches the familiar scent in the air?
Then neither bits and savage whips will slow them,
Nor craggy hollows, and opposing rivers,
Nor waves that rend and wash away the hills.
Then the Sabellian[72] boar rushes to sharpen
His tusks, paws the earth and rubs on trees,
Toughening his frame against the wounds of battle.
What of the youth within whose bones harsh Love
Rolls and turns the great flame? Late at night
He blindly swims the strait, tossed by sudden
Storm clouds; on high the huge gate of heaven
Thunders, and breakers loudly crash on cliffs;
His grieving parents cannot call him back,
Nor the girl–soon to die on his funeral pyre.

2.18 Vergil *Aeneid* 4.296–330. 29–19 BCE. The fourth book of this Roman epic tells how the love of Aeneas and queen Dido of Carthage was doomed because Aeneas was fated to found a new Troy in Italy. Fearing her reaction, Aeneas delayed telling her of his preparations for departure.

But who can deceive a lover? The queen knew
His deceit, and guessing what was to come,
Dreaded each moment. As she raged, evil Rumour
Told of the fleet, armed and ready to depart.
Inflamed by helpless wrath, she raves throughout
The town, like a Thyiad[73] stirred by wild rites,
When the three-years' festival is spurred toward
Mount Cithaeron[74] at Bacchus' midnight call.
At last she confronts Aeneas, and suddenly says:
'Faithless man, you thought to hide such criminal
Intent, and leave my realm without a word?
Does our love mean nothing, nor your hand,
Once pledged, nor Dido at the brink of cruel death?
Why cruelly rouse the fleet under a wintry star,
And hasten to the deep amid the north wind's storms?

If the Troy of old remained, with no need to seek
Unknown lands and foreign shores, would Troy
Be your fleet's goal? Is it myself you are fleeing?
By these tears and by your word once given--
For in my misery I have nothing else left--
By our union, and our marriage rites begun,
If ever I helped you, if ever I pleased you at all,
I beg you! If there is still room for prayers,
Pity my fading fortunes and change your mind.
Because of you the Libyans and nomad leaders
Hate me, and my Tyrians[75] are hostile. To you
I yielded my modesty, and my reputation,
Which was the only guide of my ambition.
To whom shall I turn in this dire peril, guest?
(For now I must name you "guest," and no longer "husband")
How shall I die? Shall Pygmalion my brother
Raze my walls, or Iarbas[76] lead me in chains?
Oh, if only I had conceived a child before
Your flight, that in my hall some tiny Aeneas
Might play, and his face remind me of yours.
Then I would not be utterly lost and undone.'

2.19 Propertius *Elegies* 1.1. 25 BCE. Propertius wrote four books of elegies during the reign of Augustus. The first book was devoted to poems about his love for his mistress, whom he calls Cynthia.

Cynthia was the first to capture me with her eyes,
To my sorrow – Before, I was free from desire.
Then Love cast down my face with steadfast contempt
And planted a firm foot on my neck.
He taught me to hate chaste girls, that vile god,
And to live without a thought for tomorrow.
Alas, I have suffered this madness now for year
And yet, the gods persist in their grudge.
It wasn't by running away, Tullus, that Milanion
Bruised harsh Atalanta's savage heart.[77]
For he wandered mad in Parthenian caves,[78]
And faced down shaggy wild beasts.
He even groaned upon the Arcadian rocks,
Stricken by a wound from Hylaeus' branch.[79]
Thus he was able to master the fleet-footed girl.
In love, prayers and action prevail.

But sluggish Love inspires no skills in me,
Nor remembers his old familiar ways.
You, whose trick it is to draw down the moon,
And soothe the gods on magic altars,
Come now, and give my lady a change of heart.
Let her face grow even paler than mine!
Then I would believe that you lead the stars,
And alter Cytae's streams[80] with your songs.
You friends who called me from the brink too late,
Seek some help for my languishing heart.
I'll bravely face both blade and savage flame,
If my fury is free to speak its mind.
Take me to far-off peoples and over the waves,
Where no woman could know the way.
But you to whom the god has lent an ear,
Stay here, safe and equal in love.
My Venus lies awake through bitter nights;
My Love can never come to rest.
I warn you, flee this evil, and take care
Not to risk a familiar love.
And if anyone is slow to heed my warnings,
How sadly he will recall them later!

2.20 Ovid *Amores* 1.5. Ca. 15 BCE. Among Ovid's early works was a collection of love elegies, most focusing on a lover he calls Corinna.

It was a hot summer, and the middle of the day;
I took my ease stretched on the couch.
The windows were half open and half shut;
Just such light one sees in the woods,
Like the rays of the sun as it fades at dusk,
Or the space between night and day.
Bashful girls must have that type of light
To shield their modesty in shadows.
Here came Corinna, her flowing dress loose,
Hair parted to reveal her white neck –
Semiramis[81] looked this way as she went to bed,
They say, and Laïs[82] of many lovers.
I tore off her thin tunic with no great effort;
Still she struggled to draw it about her.
Fighting with no will to win, at last she yielded,
And gave herself up to my victory.

As she stood before me, her body revealed,
Not a single flaw met my eyes.
What shoulders, what arms I saw and touched;
Her breasts the perfect fit for my palms,
Her stomach flat beneath her slender waist;
What shapely hips, and long legs!
Why describe each part? All was ideal,
And I pressed her naked body close.
Who doesn't know the rest? We lay at peace.
May more afternoons like this be mine!

2.21 Sulpicia [Tib.] 3.18. Late first century BCE. Sulpicia is the only Roman woman poet whose work has survived to the present; her poems are included in the manuscripts of the love elegist Tibullus. She composed elegies similar to those of Propertius, Tibullus, and Ovid.

My light, may you not feel the same fire for me
As I think you did just days ago
If I have ever in my few years done a thing as stupid
And more to be regretted, I know,
Than I did when I left you alone last night
Pretending that I didn't care.

2.22 Pausanias *Description of Greece* 1.27.1–4. Second century CE. In his travel guide to Greece, Pausanias describes the shrine of Eros in the Boeotian town of Thespiae.

From the beginning, the Thespians have honoured Eros most of all the gods, and they possess a very ancient image of him, an unworked stone. Who it was that established among the Thespians the practice of worshiping Eros most of all, I do not know. He is equally worshiped by the Parians of the Hellespont, who were originally colonists from Erythrae in Ionia, but today pay taxes to the Romans. Most men believe that Eros is the youngest of the gods, the son of Aphrodite. But Olen the Lycian, who composed the oldest hymns of the Greeks, says in a hymn to Ilithyia that she was the mother of Eros. Later than Olen, both Pamphos[83] and Orpheus composed epics, and they both made verses about Eros for the Lycomidae[84] to sing when the rituals are performed. I read them after a conversation with the Torch Bearer, but of these matters I will speak no more. Hesiod, or the man who wrote the *Theogony* attributed to Hesiod, says that Chaos was first, and after it Ge and Tartarus and Eros were born. Sappho of Lesbos sang many poems about Eros, but they do not all agree on details. Later, Lysippus made a bronze Eros for the Thespians, and before that, Praxiteles made one of Pentelic marble. I have already related elsewhere the story of Phryne,[85] and the trick that this woman played on Praxiteles. They say that the first to move the statue of Eros was Gaius the Roman emperor,[86] but that Claudius sent it back to the Thespians and Nero carried it off a second time, and there at Rome a fire destroyed it.

2.23 Apuleius *Metamorphoses* 5.22–3. Ca. 170 CE. Apuleius' Latin novel is also known as *The Golden Ass* and tells of a man who is magically transformed into a donkey. In a digression, an old woman relates the story of Psyche and Cupid, which is a variation on the folktale of Beauty and the Beast. In this scene, Psyche discovers the true identity of her husband.

But as soon as the light of the lamp revealed what was hidden on the couch, she saw the most gentle and sweetest beast of all, handsome Cupid himself reclining in beauty, at the sight of whom the lamp burned brighter for joy, and the razor repented its sacrilegious edge. But Psyche, terrified and shocked at the sight, fell pale and trembling to her knees, and her first thought was to hide the razor, indeed to plunge it into her own heart, and indeed in fact she would have done so, if the steel, in fear of such a shameful deed, had not slipped and fallen from her rash hands. As she gazed at length on the beauty of his divine face, the exhaustion and illness of her spirit were relieved and she was refreshed. She saw his delightful golden head, which smelled of intoxicating ambrosia; his milk-white neck, his rosy cheeks, the way his elegant hair, dressed with some locks falling over his shoulders and some behind, glowed so brightly that it made the lamplight seem to waver; she saw the flying god's dewy wings sparkling like white flowers on his shoulders, and though they were at rest, the delicate down feathers at their edges quivered as if at play, back and forth. The other parts of his body were so smooth and bright as to cause Venus no regrets at bearing such a child. At the foot of the bed lay his bow and quiver and his arrows, the auspicious missiles of the great god. Psyche, whose curiosity was insatiable, handled and examined these, marveling at her husband's weapons. Drawing an arrow from the quiver, she tested the sharpness of its point with her thumb, and by this pressure she inflicted such a deep wound on that trembling finger that small drops of red blood flowed over her skin. Thus unknowingly Psyche through her own actions spurred her love for Love. Then, burning more and more with a desire for Desire, she leaned over, gazing at him with desperate longing, and quickly covered him with a multitude of wanton kisses, fearing all the while that he might awake. But while she wavered, her mind both wounded and excited by this great joy, the lamp spat out a drop of bubbling oil from its flame onto the right shoulder of the god, whether from vile treachery, from a jealous wish to harm, or simply because the lamp itself wished for the joy of touching that beautiful body with a light kiss. O bold and impulsive lamp, paltry minister of love, how could you burn the god of all flames, when surely some lover first invented you so that he could spend night as well as day satisfying his desires! Burned in this way, the god leaped up, and perceiving that her promise was worthless and tainted, he flew away without a word, forsaking the hands and kisses of his most unhappy spouse.

Further Reading

On the goddess Aphrodite, see Pirenne Delforge 1993 (in French), Budin 2003, and Rosenzweig 2004. Breitenberger 2007 covers Aphrodite, Eros, and related deities. For the role of Eros in Greek culture, see Carson 1986, Calame 1999, and Zeitlin 1999; on Eros at Thespiae, see Gutzwiller 2004. For the goddess Venus in Roman religion, see Staples 1998, pp. 97–128, and for Lucretius' Venus, Clayton 1999. For the effects of Eros as depicted in early Greek poetry, see Cyrino 1995 and Williamson 1998. For erotic relationships in Latin love poetry, see Greene 1998, and Ancona and Greene (eds) 2005. For Venus and erotic love in Vergil's *Aeneid*, see Gutting 2006.

3

Anxiety, Suspicion and Blame

In antiquity, deviation from gender roles and sexual norms was at best a cause for reproach, and at worst a criminal transgression. Both Greek and Roman men used charges of sexual misbehaviour to discredit enemies, and encouraged traditional beliefs about the sexuality of women in order to justify their social and political subordination. A recurrent motif in Greek and Roman texts is the need to control female sexuality (hence female mobility, dress, education, etc.) both before and during marriage. Beliefs about the inferiority of female moral and intellectual capacities contributed to anxieties about female sexual infidelity.

A deep-rooted distrust of women and a number of stereotypes about female sexuality and its effects can be traced in men's writings from earliest times. Pandora, the first woman, is a symbol of this distrust in the poems of Hesiod (3.1). While her seductive beauty makes her difficult to resist, her deceitful nature results in a host of evils for mankind when she opens a mysterious jar (3.2), releasing all the evils of the world. In similar fashion, the book of Genesis blames the fall from Paradise on the actions of Eve, and links sexual awareness to the advent of life's hardships. Under the Roman empire, Christians such as Tertullian took these teachings further (3.21), insisting that by bringing sin and death into the world, Eve was also responsible for Christ's sufferings, and that all women, as descendants of Eve, shared her guilt. Like Hesiod, Tertullian identified female beauty as a dangerous and fearsome attribute because of its potential to draw men into ruin. These ideas stand in contrast to the Classical Greek idealisation of male beauty, which was associated with the cultivation of moral and spiritual ideals in both the viewer and the object of his gaze.

A strain of misogynist suspicion surfaces throughout antiquity with predictable regularity. Arguing at Rome against the repeal of the Oppian law limiting women's access to luxuries, the Elder Cato (3.15) insisted that it would encourage women to greater audacity and over-empower them: 'The moment they begin to be your equals, they will be your superiors.'[87] Cato particularly disapproved of Roman women's action in taking to the streets to protest the law, because accosting 'other women's husbands' in the street suggested sexual licence on their part. In the end, Lucius Valerius' defense of the women's patriotism won the day and the law was repealed. The relative relaxation of social strictures on the behaviour of elite women in late Republican Rome did not protect the notorious Clodia from a vicious and detailed critique of her personal life by Cicero (3.12), who invoked stereotypes about women's extravagance, lust, and deceitfulness in order to attack her credibility. He missed no opportunity to point out that Clodia failed to meet traditional Roman standards of female modesty, and went so far as to suggest incest between Clodia and her brother. The Oppian law was not the first example of legislation intended to control women's behaviour and dress; laws addressing such matters were common in Archaic and Classical Greece. From the fourth century BCE to the second century CE, officials known as *gunaikonomoi* ('supervisors of women') functioned in many Greek cities to control the behaviour of women in public and private contexts (3.10). They are most often mentioned in connection with the need to regulate female dress and behaviour at funerals, weddings, and religious rituals.

Certain ancient authors display nuance in their treatment of this subject matter, and thus it would be a mistake to consider the misogynist perspective a cultural absolute. When the misogynist youth Hippolytus learns in Euripides' tragedy *Hippolytus* that his stepmother Phaedra has fallen in love with him, he bitterly derides women as deceitful, covetous, sex-crazed plotters (3.4). This speech occurs in the context of a broader opposition in the play between the goddesses Artemis and Aphrodite. While treating the stepmother Phaedra sympathetically (2.8), Euripides shows how Hippolytus himself deviates from societal norms by refusing the adult roles of husband and father. Hippolytus' total rejection of women and sexuality ultimately leads to his destruction.

The suspicion that women's rituals concealed nefarious behaviour surfaced often in the comedies of Aristophanes and was a staple of masculine culture. In the *Women at the Thesmophoria* (3.5) the spy Mnesilochus 'confesses' to the gathered women a catalog of sins that reveals the worst fears of Athenian husbands – wives will find ways to meet lovers, will pass off others' infants as their own, and will encourage other women to follow their example. Because of its ecstatic elements and gender reversals, the ancient cult of Dionysus was another source of anxiety, even in its homeland. The ambivalent attitude toward Dionysus resulted from the paradox that only through a willing (but temporary) surrender of self-control could men and women safely navigate the madness sent by the god. While the mythic maenads, or 'madwomen' who worshiped Dionysus remained chaste according to Tiresias in Euripides' *Bacchae* (3.6), King Pentheus insisted that the women's unorthodox behaviour was merely a cover for sexual licence. This attitude resurfaced among elite Romans when the Bacchic cult was exported to Italy. In spite of its popularity, the Roman Senate saw it as a threat to the stability of society and associated nocturnal meetings of men and women not only with deviance from approved conduct, but with outright conspiracy and crime (1.11). Centuries later, Juvenal's sixth *Satire* (3.18), a harsh indictment of women's vices, includes a detailed description of imaginary debaucheries at the decorous festival of Bona Dea ('Good Goddess'), which had a ritual requirement that men be excluded.

Greek mythology includes many stories of seductive but dangerous female monsters and witches, such as Circe, whose sexuality plays an important role in her relations with Odysseus. Before he can safely bed her, she must be physically mastered and forced to swear an oath not to harm him (3.3). Throughout antiquity, females were suspected of turning to drugs, poisons, and magic in order to achieve their ends, and women were considered especially likely to use nefarious methods where sex was involved. *Against the Stepmother for Poisoning* by the Athenian orator Antiphon (3.7) plays upon the suspicions of the male jury about the deceitful ways of women, as well as their affinity for dangerous drugs and potions. A similar line of thought is attributed to the early Romans by the author of *To Herennius on Rhetoric* (3.11). He writes that women found to be unchaste were automatically suspected of poisoning, and vice versa (compare the way in which Herod's suspicions of Mariame's infidelity [8.20] were stoked by accusations that she slipped him a love potion). In fact, both men and women made ample use of drugs and magic in antiquity. One branch of magic was the so-called curse tablet (3.20, 5.14), an inscription on lead usually purchased from a sorcerer and written out according to a fixed formula, with the appropriate names filled in. These tablets often targeted enemies in lawsuits or suspected thieves, and they were placed in wells or tombs in order to facilitate access to the underworld gods and spirits of the dead, whom the petitioner asked to assist him or her by 'binding' the victim. Many examples involve erotic magic, in which the petitioner seeks the gods' help in coercing the object of desire to engage in sex with him or her. Although the first tablets appear in the late fifth and early fourth centuries BCE, erotic magic was far older, as we see in the *Iliad* when Hera borrows the magical breast-band of Aphrodite in order to seduce Zeus (1.1).

The Greeks and Romans made masculinity a prerequisite for citizen status and privilege, and constructed elaborate codes of conduct and appearance that could be used to attack and exclude any male who did not conform. Among the most damaging of accusations, often employed in political attacks, was the suggestion that an opponent had allowed himself to be anally penetrated, thus taking a submissive, 'feminine' role in sex and disqualifying himself from the privileges of citizenship (3.8, 3.9, 3.14). Although the culture of Classical Greece accepted and even idealised pederasty, it also recognised that boy-love conflicted in serious ways with the ideals of masculinity. Any boy who accepted gifts too readily from a lover could later be accused of prostituting himself. Roman men's scrutiny of their colleagues for 'effeminate' behaviour was unrelenting; as Juvenal's second *Satire* demonstrates (3.18), even supposedly austere philosophers and rugged soldiers did not escape criticism. Seneca's complaint about the younger generation's adoption of gender-bending habits is typical of the hostility directed against men who deviated from the constraints of masculinity (3.16, 3.19). While such men were often described as soft, lazy, and languorous, they were also labeled *cinaedī* ('perverts') and suspected of energetic sexual debauchery, particularly adultery (3.13, 3.17).

3.1 Hesiod *Theogony* 565–612. Eighth century BCE. To punish Prometheus' theft of fire, which benefited mortal men, Zeus conceives a punishment for men: the first woman. Integral to the woman's danger is her beauty and sexual appeal.

But Iapetus' son[88] cheated him of the blessing,
Stealing the far-seen brilliance of steady fire
In a hollow stalk. This stung the innermost
Spirit of Zeus who thunders on high, and angered
His heart, that men had possession of far-seen fire.
Quickly he made them an evil in exchange:
At his command the famous Limping God[89]
Sculpted from earth the shape of a modest girl.
Grey-eyed Athena gowned her all in silver,
And veiled her head, spreading with her hands
The intricate garment, a wondrous thing to see;
And Pallas Athena crowned her with lovely garlands
Made from the blossoms of fresh-budding greenery.
She added a golden crown, which the famous
Limping God had crafted as a favour to Zeus,
His father. On the crown were intricate wonders,
Wild creatures nourished by land and sea,
Marvels as real as living beings with voices,
And it gleamed with a great power of attraction.
As the price of good he made this lovely evil,
And led her out, reveling in her ornaments,

Gifts from the grey-eyed child of mighty Zeus.
Wonder seized both gods and mortal men,
When first they saw this irresistible bait.
From her is the race of feminine women,
That deadly tribe, a great calamity,
They who dwell with mortal men, sharing
Not in accursed poverty, but only in riches.
As within vaulted hives the bees feed drones,
Partners in mischief, while they until sundown
Every day hasten to pack the white wax,
And the drones remain within the roofed hives,
Gathering the toil of others into their bellies –
Thus high-thundering Zeus created women,
As troublemakers, evils for mortal men.
A second evil he gave for the good of fire:
He who flees the sorrowful works of women
And refuses to wed, comes to hateful old age
With no one to care for him; and if he thrives,
After he dies his kin will divide all he owns.
Even if a man accepts the lot of marriage
And has a good wife, well suited to his taste,
Evil strives against good throughout his life;
For whoever happens to raise ungrateful children
Lives with unending pain in mind and heart,
And this is an evil for which there is no cure.

3.2 Hesiod *Works and Days* 53–105. Eighth century BCE. In this version of the Pandora myth, the first woman opens a jar in which the evils of the world are contained.

Angrily, Zeus who gathers the clouds addressed him:
'Son of Iapetus, excelling in strategy,
You take delight in thieving and deception.
But misery awaits both you and men still unborn.
As the price of fire, I shall give them an evil,
To cheer them as they embrace their utter ruin.'
So spoke the father of gods and men, and laughed.
Famous Hephaestus at his command made haste
To moisten clay and place within it speech
And vigour, forming a face like that of a goddess,
And a girl's desirable shape. Athena
Taught her the skill of intricate weaving, and golden

Aphrodite poured attraction over her head,
With painful yearning, and cares that gnaw the limbs.
Hermes, the Slayer of Argus, gave to her
The mind of a bitch and the morals of a thief.
Thus Zeus decreed, and all obeyed their lord.
At his command the famous Limping God
Sculpted from earth the shape of a modest girl.
Grey-eyed Athena gave her a gown and belt;
Lady Persuasion and the Graces supplied
Gold chains for her body, while the Hours,
Whose hair is lovely, crowned her with spring blooms.
Pallas Athena perfected the fit of each ornament.
Into her breast Hermes the Slayer of Argus
Put wheedling lies and the morals of a thief.
Obedient to the will of loud-thundering Zeus,
The Messenger gave her speech, and named the woman
Pandora, for all the gods who hold Olympus
Gave gifts to her, a misery to hardworking men.
But when the irresistible bait was complete,
The Father sent the gift with Argus-Slayer
The gods' swift messenger, to Epimetheus.[90]
He did not heed the warning of Prometheus,
Never to take a gift from Olympian Zeus,
But to send it back, lest it cause harm to mortals.
But once he possessed the evil, he understood.
Before this, the tribes of men lived on the earth
Free from troubles and free from difficult labour
And painful illness that carries death to men.
For age comes fast to mortals in misery.
All these ills the hand of the woman scattered
When she removed the great lid of the jar:
Her plan brought mournful grief to humankind.
Only Hope remained in her unbroken home
Beneath the rim of the jar, and did not fly out,
For the lid prevented her, by the will of Zeus
The bearer of the aegis, who gathers the clouds.
But countless miseries haunt the human race;
The earth is full of evils, and the sea is full.
Of their own will diseases visit mortals,
Bringing pain both day and night in silence.
For Counselor Zeus removed their power of speech.
Thus there is no escape from the will of Zeus.

3.3 Homer *Odyssey* 10.326–47. Late eighth century BCE. After turning his men into pigs, the witch Circe attempts to seduce Odysseus, even as he holds her at sword-point. Odysseus is not indifferent to her charms but takes precautions against any further traps.

'Who are you, and from what parents and city?
I marvel that the drink did not enchant you,
For no other man is able to resist these drugs,
Once he allows them past the wall of his teeth.
You have a spell-proof heart within your chest.
You must be that man Odysseus of many travels
Who Argus-Slayer with his golden wand
Said would come from Troy in a swift black ship.
But come now, sheathe your sword and let us two
Climb into my bed, and in the act of love
Learn to place intimate trust in one another.'
That is what she said, but I replied:
'Circe, how can you ask me to treat you gently,
When you turned my men to swine within your house,
And now, by keeping me here, you plot some trick,
Calling me into your room and bed, with intent
Once I am naked, to render me unmanly?
I have no wish to visit your bed, goddess,
Unless you undertake a solemn oath
To hatch no further plans to cause me harm.'
So I spoke, and the goddess swore as I bade.
But once she had undertaken and sworn the oath,
Then I went up to Circe's beautiful bed.

3.4 Euripides *Hippolytus* 616–68. 428 BCE. When the ascetic youth Hippolytus learns that his young stepmother Phaedra is in love with him, he delivers an impassioned speech condemning women. The speech includes some lines (indicated by square brackets) that editors suspect were not part of the original text, or are misplaced.

O Zeus, why did you settle under the sun
Womankind as a deceitful wrong for men?
For if you wished to sow the mortal race,
It should not have been through women.
By deposit of bronze, iron or gold,
Each according to an assessed value,
Mortals should have purchased the seed

Of their offspring in temples, and lived
In their homes utterly free of the female.
[But now we trade domestic happiness
For the privilege of leading home an evil.]
It is obvious that a woman is a great evil:
For once he sires and rears her, the father
Hands over a dowry to be rid of the ill.
But he who receives this ruinous creature
Delights in adorning the object of worship,
Decking out this worthless thing in gowns,
Poor man, and draining his wealth by degrees.
[It is inevitable: one has good in-laws
And a bitter marriage, or if the marriage
Is good, the relatives are a useless pain,
And the blessing is combined with a curse.]
It is easiest if the wife is a simpleton, though
An idiot wife in the house is of no use.
I hate a clever woman: may I never harbour
A woman who thinks more than she should.
For Cypris spawns more wickedness
In the smart ones; the incapable woman
Is saved from folly by her limited wit.
Slaves should be kept away from wives.
Instead give them voiceless and brute
Beasts for companions, so that they neither
Speak to them nor receive replies.
For the wives hatch their plots indoors,
And slaves carry their evils abroad.
So you, wretched woman, come to bargain
Over my father's inviolate bed.
I will wash this filth from my ears
With cleansing streams. How could I be so vile,
I who feel soiled at the very thought?
Know that my piety saves you, woman.
Had I not been trapped unawares by holy
Oaths, I would tell the whole to my father.
As it is, Theseus is out of the country,
And I shall leave the house in silence.
But when my father returns, I shall observe
How you and your mistress face him,
And recognise your boldness, now I have
Tasted it. Be damned to you both!

I'll never have my fill of hating women,
Not even if they say I talk of nothing else,
For their stock of evils is endless too.
Either let them be taught chastity,
Or let me trample them down forever.

3.5 Aristophanes *Women at the Thesmophoria* 466–519. 411 BCE. In this comedy, the women of Athens are angry with the tragic playwright Euripides for depicting women as sex-starved murderesses. Alarmed that they might plot against him, Euripides dresses a spy, Mnesilochus, in female attire and sends him to infiltrate the women's festival of Thesmophoria. Mnesilochus advocates for Euripides by declaring that women's sins are in fact far worse than the poet ever portrayed.

It is no wonder, ladies, that your anger at Euripides
Is so very sharp, and your bile is boiling,
Given the things you've heard about yourselves.
I myself hate the man – bless my children – I'd be crazy not to.
Yet let's have a cosy talk among ourselves.
It's just us ladies here, and nobody will blab a word.
Why do we accuse him so harshly,
For knowing and showing two or three of our faults,
When we have done thousands of naughty things?
I'll tell you about myself, not to speak of anyone else.
I have a lot to feel guilty about, but here's the very worst:
When I was married just three days,
And my husband lay beside me in bed, I had a friend,
Who first seduced me at age seven. Full of yearning
For me, he came scratching at the door,
And right away I knew who it was, so I crept down secretly.
My husband asked, 'Where are you going?'
'Ah me!' I said, 'I have the colic, husband, and cramps,
I've got to go to the crapper!' 'Go ahead,' he replied,
And began to grind juniper, anise and sage.
So, pouring water on the door-hinge, I went
Out to my lover. He gave it to me bending head-down
Over Apollo's altar, holding on to the laurel for support.
Well, do you see? Euripides never talked about *that*!
And when we bang slaves and mule-drivers,
If nobody better is around, does he speak of that?
And indeed, when we get it on all night,
And then chew garlic in the morning, so the husband,

Who has been on the city-wall, smells it and suspects nothing –
You see, Euripides has never mentioned that.
If he rails at Phaedra,[91] well, what is it to us?
He never tells how a woman shows her husband a cloak
To admire in the light, all the while concealing a lover's escape.
I know another wife who said she had labour pains
For ten days, till she bought herself a baby;
The husband bustled around buying medicine
To ease her pangs while an old woman brought the baby
In a pot, stuffing its mouth with honeycomb so it wouldn't cry.
She nodded toward the pot and the wife straightaway cried,
'Go away, go away, husband, I think the baby's coming!'
For it was kicking the 'pot-belly'. He went off delighted;
She cleared the baby's mouth and it screeched.
Then the nasty old woman who brought the baby
Runs smiling to the husband and says,
'A lion is born to you, in your exact image,
Everything about him is like you, even his little willy,
Curved like the heavens.' Don't we do these bad things?
By Artemis we do! And we are angry with Euripides,
When we get no more than our just deserts from him!

3.6 Euripides *Bacchae* 215–262, 314–27. 405 BCE. King Pentheus of Thebes expresses his determination to root out the new religion of Dionysus from his land, declaring that it is merely a pretext for women to engage in licentious behaviour. For more of the *Bacchae*, see 9.7.

Pentheus:
Traveling outside our land, I learned
Of fresh evils throughout the city,
That the women have left our homes
For counterfeit Bacchic revels, and dart
Through the shady mountains, dancing
For this new god Dionysus, whoever he is.
At their meetings the wine-bowls are full,
And they slink off here and there in secret,
To serve the beds of men. They pretend
To be maenads[92] performing sacrifices,
But follow Aphrodite before Bacchus.
I bound the hands of all those I captured;
Servants guard them in the civic chambers.
The rest I shall hunt from the mountains,

Ino, and Agave who bore me to Echion,
And Autonoë mother of Actaeon.[93]
I shall bind them in nets of iron, and soon
Put a stop to this criminal revelry.
They say that some stranger has come,
A spell-singing sorcerer from Lydia
With fragrant hair falling in blond waves,
And sexy, wine-dark eyes. Beside
The young girls he spends day and night,
Offering his mysteries of Bacchus.
If I catch him beneath my roof,
I'll stop his thyrsus-thumping[94] and
Hair-tossing, by chopping his head off.
That man says Dionysus is a god,
Says he was sewn into Zeus's thigh,
But him the torch of thunder consumed
With his mother, who pretended marriage
To Zeus. Whoever this stranger is,
Doesn't he deserve summary hanging
For hurling these outrageous insults?
But here is another wonder, the seer
Tiresias wearing dappled fawnskins,
And my grandfather – what a joke! –
Hoisting the Bacchic staff. I refuse,
Father, to watch this senile display.
Won't you shake off the ivy, Grandfather,
And free your hand from the thyrsus?
This is your doing, Tiresias. You wish
To profit from this new god, scrying
Birds and presiding at sacrifices.
If grey old age did not protect you,
I would bind and jail you with the Bacchae,
For importing their useless rites.
Whenever women possess the joyful grape
At a feast, I declare their revels corrupt.

[The chorus expresses disapproval of Pentheus' impiety, and the seer Tiresias responds to his speech, explaining that Dionysus is a great god, who has given mortals wine as a release from pain and cares. He describes Dionysus' birth and 'rebirth' from the thigh of Zeus, warns Pentheus to accept his worship, and then returns to the subject of women's behaviour under the god's influence.]

Tiresias:
Dionysus will not compel a woman
To chastity where Cypris is concerned,
But where chastity is in her nature,
You may rely on it. For a modest woman
Will not be corrupted by Bacchic rites.
Do you see? You are glad when crowds
Stand at the gates and magnify your name;
He too, I think, delights in honours.
Cadmus, whom you mock, and I will dance
And crown our heads with ivy. We make
A grey team, but still we must dance.
I will not battle the gods at your bidding.
For your madness is grievous. No drugs
Could cure the spell under which you suffer.

3.7 Antiphon *Against the Stepmother for Poisoning* 1.14–20. Ca. 400. In this excerpt from a speech for the prosecution in Athens, the accuser claims that his stepmother plotted to poison his father with a fake 'love potion' administered by a slave, the mistress of the father's friend Philoneos.

There was an upper room in our house, and our father's friend Philoneos, a man of good background, used to stay there whenever he spent time in the city. He had a slave mistress, whom he was about to place in a brothel. My brother's mother befriended this girl, and learning that Philoneos planned to do her wrong, she summoned the girl, and upon her arrival said that she herself was being wronged by my father. If the girl was willing to obey her, she stated that she could restore Philoneos' love for the girl, and the love of my father for herself. She knew the remedy, but the girl must carry it out. When the girl was asked whether she was willing to perform this service, I believe she lost no time in promising to do it.

Some time later, Philoneos had a sacrifice to perform for Zeus Ctesius in Piraeus,[95] while my father was about to sail to Naxus. Philoneos thought it would be an excellent idea to accompany my father to Piraeus, so that he could make his sacrifice and entertain his friend at the same time. The slave girl followed Philoneos in order to serve at the sacrifice. And once they were in Piraeus, of course he carried it out. When it was complete, this person then began to plan whether she should give them the drug before or after the meal. She decided it would be better to give it after the meal, following the suggestion of this Clytemnestra[96] here. To describe the meal would be too long a tale for me to recount and for you to hear, but I shall attempt to describe as briefly as possible the aftermath and how the drug was administered.

Once they had dined, they naturally made libations and burned incense, for Philoneos was sacrificing to Zeus and entertaining, while my father was about to make a sea journey and was enjoying a meal with his friend. But as Philoneos' mistress poured the libation for their prayers – prayers, gentlemen, which would never be fulfilled – she added the drug. She thought it was a clever idea to give Philoneos more, since then he might love her all the more, for not until the evil was accomplished did she understand that my stepmother had deceived her. She poured less for my father. So they completed the libation, and supervised their own killer as they drained their very last drink. Philoneos died quickly on the spot, but my father fell ill and died on the twentieth day. In return the one who followed orders and carried out the deed has received the punishment she deserved, although she did not bear the principal responsibility for the crime. She was tortured on the wheel and then handed over to the public executioner. But the woman who was truly guilty and carefully planned this deed shall also be punished, if you and the gods wish it.

3.8 Demosthenes *Against Androtion* 22.30–32. 355 BCE. In one of his earliest political speeches, Demosthenes explains why, in his view, the Athenian lawgiver Solon decided to penalise citizens who sold sexual favours.

Now it is worthwhile, men of Athens, to make a careful study of Solon, who instituted this law, and to observe what forethought he had for the constitution of the state in all the laws he instituted. Indeed, he was far more concerned for the constitution than for the specific topic on which he was legislating. One may draw this conclusion from many sources, but most especially from this law, which forbids those who have prostituted themselves from making speeches or proposing laws. For he saw that most of you who have the right to speak do not employ it, so this prohibition did not seem unduly harsh. He could have instituted much more severe penalties, if his goal was to punish such persons. But punishment was not his concern; he refused them the right to speak for your sake, and for the sake of the state. For he knew – he knew, I say – that for men who live in a shameful fashion, the most hostile state of all is that in which everyone is free to speak words of reproach to them. And what state is that? A democracy. For he thought that the state would not be secure, if ever there turned out to be a group of men, all active at the same time, who were gifted and bold speakers, but full of such disgraceful evil. They may lead the people to make many mistakes, and they may attempt to abolish the democracy altogether. (For in an oligarchy, even if there are people who live a more vile life than Androtion, criticism of leaders is not permitted.) Or such men may lead the people into moral failings, in order to make them as much like themselves as possible. Therefore he made it a basic principle to forbid such men from having any share in the counsels of the state, in order to prevent them from drawing the people into error by trickery. In disregard of all these considerations, this fine gentleman here not only found it necessary to make speeches and propose laws, in spite of the fact that he was ineligible; he also made proposals that are illegal.

3.9 Aeschines *Against Timarchus* 1.21. 346 BCE. As part of Aeschines' successful prosecution of his political enemy Timarchus, the Athenian law penalising citizens found to have sold their sexual favours was read out to the jury. Timarchus was excluded from public office, but the decision was reversed three years later.

If an Athenian man prostitutes himself, let him not be permitted to become one of the nine archons, nor be consecrated to a priesthood, nor act as a public advocate. Nor shall he hold any office whatsoever, either at home or abroad, either filled by lot or elected. Let him not be sent as a herald, nor take part in public debate, nor participate in public sacrifices. When the citizens wear garlands, let him not be crowned with a garland, and let him not enter into the marketplace when it has been purified with water for the assembly. If any man who is known to have prostituted himself acts contrary to this law, let him pay the penalty of death.

3.10 Ritual law from Methymna. *IG* XII, 2.499 (= *LSCG* 127). Fourth century BCE. In this fragmentary inscription regulating a mystery cult in Methymna on Lesbos, an official called a *gunaikonomos* ('supervisor of women') is appointed to prevent men from participating in the rites, thus guarding the chastity of the women.

...around the altar...Let them not hinder one another...those serving at the altar...Let this decree be fulfilled. Let there be a supervisor of women for Methymna, a citizen no younger than forty years. Let him stay outside the two doors of the temple during the all-night festival and let him take care that he alone and no other man goes in, and that no other impious thing happens. Let the sacrifices in Methymna to the ancestral gods be completed as is the requirement, and the Mysteries. The thyrsus-bearers...

3.11 *To Herennius on Rhetoric* 4.16.23. Ca. 85 BCE. This book by an unknown author is the oldest surviving work on Latin rhetoric and remained influential through the Renaissance.

Through the rhetorical figure of 'Reasoning by Question and Answer', we ask ourselves the reason why we say something, and we successively seek out the explanation of each thing we have proposed, like so: When our ancestors condemned a woman for one crime, they thought that through this single judgement, she was convicted of many evil deeds. How so? A woman whom they judged to be unchaste was also considered guilty of poisoning. Why? Because a woman who has given over her body to the foulest of desires must necessarily live in fear of many people. Who are these? Her husband, her parents, and the others whom she knows are affected by the infamy of her disgrace. What then? Those whom she fears so greatly, she must inevitably wish to kill. Why is that necessary? Because no considerations of decency can restrain a woman who is terrified by the magnitude of her crime, made bold by her lack of moderation, and rendered thoughtless by her female nature. Well, what then did they think about a woman who was condemned as a poisoner? They thought that she must also be unchaste. Why? Because no motive could more easily have brought her to this evil deed than foul desire and immoderate lust; furthermore, they did not think it possible for a woman's body to remain chaste once her mind had been corrupted. And did they observe that the same was true in the case of men? Not at all. Why? Because separate passions drive men to different forms of evil, but in women, one passion alone leads to all evil deeds.

3.12 Cicero *For Caelius* 13.30–16.36. 56 BCE. Cicero defended Marcus Caelius Rufus on a charge of public violence; his rhetorical strategy involved attacks on Clodia, the sister of Cicero's enemy Publius Clodius Pulcher. The year before the trial, Caelius and Clodia had an affair, which ended in bitter recriminations.

There are two charges, one to do with gold and one with poison; one and the same person is involved with both. Gold has supposedly been received from Clodia, and poison procured in order to be administered to Clodia. All the rest are not charges but slanders, belonging more to a loutish quarrel than a criminal investigation. To call a man adulterous, lewd, corrupt – these are insults, not legitimate accusations. For there is no foundation to these charges, no basis for them: they are recriminations flung out by an accuser in a rage, with no authority. I see the person responsible for these two charges; I see their certain source and origin. There was need of gold; he took it from Clodia, without witnesses, and he kept it as long as he wanted. I see a great proof here of an exceedingly intimate relationship. He wanted to kill that same Clodia, he procured poison, he bribed the slaves, he readied the drink, he arranged a place, he brought it with him in secret. Again, I see that an extremely bitter parting has resulted in great hatred. Our whole business in this case, judges, is with Clodia, a woman not only of high rank but notorious. Of her I will not speak except as necessary to repel these charges. But a man of your outstanding experience knows, Gnaeus Domitius,[97] that this matter has to do with her alone. For if she does not say that she loaned Caelius the gold, if she does not declare that he prepared poison for her, then we are acting capriciously in speaking of the mother of a family in a way so different from what is due to the virtue of a Roman matron. But if, without that woman, there is left to his accusers neither a charge nor any other means of attacking him, what are we his advocates to do other than ward off those who pursue him? And indeed, I would do this more vigorously were I not prevented by a quarrel with this woman's husband – brother, I mean – it is a mistake I always make. Now I shall proceed with moderation, and not progress further than duty and the case itself compel me, for I have never thought it necessary to enter into a quarrel with any woman, particularly a woman who is universally thought of as the friend of all rather than anyone's enemy.

Yet I will first seek to inquire from the woman herself, whether she prefers that I deal with her sternly, in a serious manner and according to ancient custom, or that I do so with gentle courtesy and modern refinement. In order to proceed in the old-fashioned manner, I must summon up from the underworld one of those bearded old men, not with one of those neat little beards that she finds delightful, but with the shaggy beard that we see on ancient statues and images. He will rebuke the woman, speaking in my place lest she become angry with me. Therefore, let someone from her own family come forth, that most capable of men, Blind Claudius.[98] He does not have to see her, so he will feel the least grief. And in fact, if he comes forth, he will speak and deal with her thus: 'Woman, what have you to do with Caelius, a very young man? What have you to do with a man who belongs to someone else? Why were you so familiar with him that you loaned him gold, or so hostile toward him that you feared his poison? Had you never seen nor heard that your father, uncle, grandfather, and great-grandfather were all consuls? Did you not, moreover, understand that you were bound in matrimony to Quintus Metellus, a most illustrious and courageous man, and one distinguished for love of his country? A man who excelled nearly all other citizens in virtue, glory and dignity from the moment he set foot outside his door? When you, as a descendant of a very distinguished family yourself, had made such a brilliant match, why then did Caelius become such an intimate of yours? Was he a relative, an in-law, one of your husband's friends? Not at all. What was the reason, then, if not some thoughtless lust? Even if the images of the men of our family had no effect on you, what of my own daughter Claudia Quinta?[99] Did she not admonish you to emulate her glories as a woman and the praise she brought our family? Did you not think of that Claudia, the Vestal Virgin, who embraced her father as he was celebrating his triumph, and saved him from being dragged out of the chariot by a hostile tribune? Why did your brother's vices mean more to you than the virtues of your father, your grandfather, and the other ancestors who have lived since my time – virtues that were apparent not only in the men, but particularly in the women? Was it for this that I broke off the peace-talks with Pyrrhus,[100] so that you could enter every day into pacts of the vilest love? Was it for this I brought water into the city, so that you could use it for your impure amusements? Was it for this I built the Appian Way, so that you could travel accompanied by other women's husbands?'

But why, judges, have I introduced an individual so severe that I fear this same Appius might suddenly turn and begin to reproach Caelius with that solemnity appropriate to a censor? I will attend to this soon, judges, and I trust that I will convince even the strictest arbiters of behaviour that Caelius' habits of life are sound. But you, woman – for now I speak to you myself without an intermediary – if you suppose that we will approve the things you are doing and saying, your accusations, schemes and assertions, you must explain and give a reason why your relationship with Caelius is so very familiar, intimate and close. The accusers speak of lustful desire, love affairs, adultery; of Baiae[101] and beaches and banquets; of revelry, songs, musical entertainments and sailing. They indicate that they speak of all this with your consent. Since you desired these things to be brought to this court and entered into evidence at this trial – in what unruly and rash frame of mind, I do not know – you must yourself either wash away the charges, and show that they are false, or confess that neither your charges nor your statements are credible.

But if you prefer that I deal in a more refined manner with you, I shall do so in the following way. I shall remove that harsh and almost brutish old man, and take up one of these young men; and in preference to others he shall be your youngest brother,[102] whose taste and address are impeccable. He adores you, and on account of some childhood anxiety, I suppose, and a silly fear of something in the night, has always since he was a little fellow slept with his big sister. I imagine him saying to you, 'Why are you in an uproar, sister? What are you raving about? Why do you cause turmoil and make a trivial matter serious? You saw this very young man, your neighbour. His beauty, his height, his face and eyes attracted you. You wished to see him more often. Several times you were present in the gardens when he was there. As a woman of high rank, you wish to hold the affection of this son of a frugal and parsimonious father with your riches, but you cannot. He kicks, he spits you out, he spurns you; he doesn't think your gifts are worth *that* much! Try someone else. You have gardens on the Tiber, carefully situated at the spot where all the young men come to bathe; here you may pick out lovers every day. Why do you harass this one man who scorns you?'

3.13 Catullus *Songs* 57. Ca. 55 BCE. One of the most admired poets of Republican Rome, Catullus produced many examples of invective and made liberal use of sexual insults.

Those nasty perverts get along well,
Mamurra[103] and that faggot Caesar.

No wonder; equally filthy stains,
One a city man and one from Formiae,[104]
They are impossible to wash out.
Twins in their diseased appetites,
These dilettantes in bed together
Have an equal zest for adultery.
Though rivals, they share young girls:
Those nasty perverts get along well.

3.14 Cicero *Philippics* 2.44–5. 44 BCE. Cicero's attacks on Antony were modelled on the speeches Demosthenes made in opposition to Philip of Macedon. In this excerpt Cicero refers to Antony's youthful friendship with Scribonius Curio.

You assumed the dress of a grown man, which you quickly transformed to a woman's toga.[105] At first you were a common whore; you performed disgraceful acts at a fixed price, and it was not cheap. Curio, however, quickly intervened and took you away from the prostitute's way of life. He settled you in a secure and stable marriage, as surely as if he had presented you with a matron's gown. Never was a boy bought for the purpose of sex so completely within the power of his master, as you were within the power of Curio. How often did his father throw you out of the house? How often did he post guards to keep you from crossing the threshold? Meanwhile, assisted by night, encouraged by lust, and compelled by the need for a wage, you had yourself let down through the roof tiles. That house could no longer bear your disgraceful behaviour. Are you aware that I speak of matters on which I am well informed? Remember that time when Curio the father took to his bed in grief; his son threw himself at my feet weeping, and commended you to my care. He begged me to defend you against his own father, if he obtained six million sesterces,[106] for he had promised to stand surety on your behalf for this amount. Indeed, burning with love, he declared that he could not bear a separation, and that he would accompany you into exile.

3.15 Livy *History of Rome* 34.4.1–20, 34.6.16. Ca. 25 BCE. In 195 BCE, the women of Rome demonstrated publicly for the repeal of the Oppian law, which prohibited women from owning more than a half-ounce of gold, wearing brightly coloured garments, or driving carriages in the city except for travel to religious ceremonies. Marcus Porcius Cato spoke against the repeal of the law.

You have often heard me complaining about the extravagance of women, and often too about the extravagance of men, not only private citizens but even public magistrates; also that the state was struggling against avarice and luxury, the two plagues which have toppled every great empire. The better and happier grows the fortune of the republic and our empire day by day – and already we have crossed into Greece and Asia, places filled with tempting pleasures, and we are handling the treasures of kings – the more I tremble with fear that these things may take us captive more than the reverse. Believe me, the statues recently brought from Syracuse to this city are dangerous vanguards. These days I hear far too many people praising and admiring the adornments of Corinth and Athens while they ridicule the clay antefixes on the temples of Roman gods. I prefer that these gods be favourable towards us, and I expect that in future they will, if we allow them to remain in their own dwellings. Our fathers can remember how Pyrrhus tried to corrupt with gifts not only our men, but even our women, through his legate Cineas. This was before the Oppian law kerbing female extravagance had been passed; yet not one woman took his gifts. What do you think was the reason? It was the same reason our ancestors passed no law on this matter: there was no luxury to be restrained. Just as one must know what a sickness is before one can know its cure, so unlawful desires are born prior to the laws that keep them in check. What brought about the Licinian law[107] of 500 *iugera* if not the unbounded desire to join fields together? What was the reason for the Cincian law[108] on gifts and payments, other than the fact that the commoners had already been paying tributes and taxes to the Senate? It is not surprising in the least that neither an Oppian law nor any other law was needed to kerb women's extravagance, when they refused to take gifts of gold and purple cloth freely offered to them. If Cineas were going around today with his gifts, he would find women lining up in the streets to receive them. And for some desires I can find no reason or explanation. For though it may be natural to feel shame or displeasure if something is permitted to another person but not to yourself, what charm does any of you fear that others will miss in you, if all are dressed the same? Indeed, the worst feelings of shame are those associated with stinginess or poverty, but the law separates you from either of these, for that which you are not allowed to possess, you do not possess. 'This is just the kind of equality I cannot bear,' says the rich woman over there. 'Why am I not to stand out from the others in gold and purple? Why is the poverty of other women disguised by this law, so that it seems that, if it were legal, they could own what in fact they cannot afford to possess?' Citizens, do you want to start a competition among your wives, so that the rich ones desire something that no other woman can have, and the poor ones spend beyond their means in order to avoid condemnation of their poverty? Once a woman is allowed to be ashamed of things she should not feel shame about, she will lose her shame in the areas where she ought to feel it. The woman who can afford to buy with her own money will do so; the one who cannot afford it will ask her husband. Pity the poor man who yields, but also the one who refuses, for he will see another man give what he himself does not. Now they publicly solicit other women's husbands, and what is more, they ask for votes to repeal a law and with certain men they succeed. On a matter negatively affecting yourself, your property and your children, you are open to their prayers? Yet once this law ceases to restrain your wife's extravagance, you will never restrain it yourself. Do not imagine, citizens, that in the future things will be as they were before this law was passed. It is safer not to charge a wrongdoer than to acquit him, and extravagance would have been kept to a more tolerable level had we not interfered, than it will be now if we repeal the law; in the same way wild beasts are more dangerous when released from the chains that inflame them. I give my vote against any attempt to repeal this law, and I pray that all the gods may smile on whatever you do.

[Lucius Valerius begins to speak in favour of the repeal, noting that Cato's speech attacked the matrons more than the proposed legislation. He argues that Roman history has seen many instances of the matrons appearing in public for the common good.]

War often repeals laws passed in peacetime, and peace those passed in times of war, just as when one is sailing a ship, some methods are useful in good weather and others in a storm. Since these two types of laws are distinguished by nature, which type is it that we are repealing? Well? Is it an old law from the kings, born at the same time as the city, or – the next best thing – was it written in the Twelve Tables by the Decemviri[109] chosen to codify the laws? Did our ancestors believe that the dignity of the matrons could not be supported without this law? Must we worry that in repealing this law, we may also put an end to the modesty and purity of women? In fact, who is unaware that this is a new law, passed twenty years ago during the consulship of Quintus Fabius and Tiberius Sempronius? Since our matrons lived highly virtuous lives for so many years in the absence of this law, what danger is there that upon its repeal they will be plunged into extravagance? For if the law were an ancient one, or if it had been passed in order to set limits on female desires, there would be cause to worry that its repeal might arouse them. But the date of the law itself explains why it was passed. Hannibal was in Italy, the victor at Cannae;[110] he was successful at Tarentum, then Arpi, then Capua. He seemed ready to march on Rome itself. Our allies had abandoned us; we had no troops in reserve, no naval allies to supervise the fleet, no money in the treasury. We were buying slaves to serve in the ranks, with the understanding that their owners would be paid once the war was over. On these conditions too, the contractors agreed to supply grain and other things needed for the war. We furnished slaves to row the warships in proportion to the census, and ourselves paid for them; following the example set by the senators, we contributed all our gold and silver to the public funds;

widows and orphans put their money in the treasury; we were to take care that nobody had at home more than a certain amount of gold and silver objects, or silver and bronze coins. Were the matrons so given to luxury and ornament that the Oppian law was needed to restrain them, at a time when so many were in mourning that the rites of Ceres had to be suspended, and the Senate ordered that mourning be limited to thirty days? Who does not clearly see that the poverty and affliction of the state wrote this law, because the private property of everyone had to be turned over for public use, and that the law was intended to remain in force only as long as the conditions that caused its enactment?

3.16 Seneca the Elder *Controversiae* 1 Pref. 8–9. Ca. 30 CE. Seneca's work on the art of speechmaking, written when he was an old man, includes his thoughts on the character of the young men of the day.

How sluggish is the natural talent of our lazy young men! They cannot stay awake long enough to accomplish a single honest endeavour. Sleep, dullness and an industrious pursuit of evils more foul than sleep and dullness have assailed their minds. A disgusting enthusiasm for singing and dancing grips these effeminates. It is the distinguishing mark of our youths to braid their hair and thin their voices until they resemble the wheedling tones of women, to compete with women in the softness of their bodies, and to cultivate in themselves elegant refinements that are most unclean. Which of the youths your age, for all his talent and zeal, is actually enough of a man? They are born spineless weaklings, and remain like that for life, assaulting the chastity of others, and careless of their own.

3.17 Martial *Epigrams* 5.61. Second half of first century CE. Martial's twelve books of epigrams were published under the emperors Domitian, Trajan, and Nerva. Many adopt the satirical tone of this example.

What curly-haired man clings so close to your wife?
What curly-haired man, Marianus, is that
Who chatters into the lady's delicate ear,
Draping his arm along her chair,
Whose every finger sports a slender ring,
Whose leg not a single hair profanes?
No answer for me? 'He handles her business', you say.
Yes, a hale and rugged type,
His face proclaims the serious man of business!
Aufidius[111] won't get the better of him!
You deserve a swat upside the head,
Panniculus![112] 'He handles her business'?
That curly-haired man is handling something, all right.

3.18 Juvenal *Satires* 2.82–116, 6.268–341. Early second century CE. The second *Satire* is devoted to ridicule of men who present themselves as rugged, masculine philosophers but in reality practice habits the narrator considers effeminate. They hold a rite for the Bona Dea ('Good Goddess') that reverses the normal order of things: men take the place of women. In the sixth *Satire*, framed as an attempt to dissuade his friend Postumus from a contemplated marriage, Juvenal depicts the secret rites of the Bona Dea as an occasion for outrageous behaviour by women.

2.82–116
Someday you'll progress to pursuits more foul than fashion;
Nobody becomes depraved overnight. Yet gradual
Acquaintance will bring you where they crown their heads
With fillets and load their necks with jeweled collars,
Soothing the Good Goddess with tender pork
And jug after jug of wine, though an evil custom
Strictly bars all females from the door;
The goddess' altars are open to males alone.
'Get out, unholy women!' the cry goes round:
'We'll have no female horn-blowers in this house!'
With secret torch-lit orgies such as these
The Baptae of Athens used to tire Cottyto.[113]
One draws his brows with soot on a needle's edge,
And lifts his fluttering eyelids for the paint;
One folds his luxuriant hair in a golden net,
Clothed in sky-blue checks or green sateen;
The valet swears by Juno, like his master.
Another clutches a mirror like girlish Otho,[114]
Who used that pitiful trophy to admire
Himself in armor, before he gave orders to march.
Let our historians note this innovation:
Each soldier's kit contains a looking-glass!
Only a master general could slaughter Galba[115]
And keep his skin so soft; only a patriot
Could bring the Palace to the battlefield,
Anointing his face with lotion all the while.
Even Semiramis fell short of this
And sorrowing Cleopatra with her fleet.
At this table you'll hear no decent talk;
Instead, Cybele's foul and high-pitched tones.
A white-haired old fanatic acts as priest;

He and his gullet give lessons in gluttony.
But why delay the act that is long overdue,
Lopping superfluous flesh with Phrygian blades?[116]

6.268–341
The conjugal bed is home to strife and bickering
Back and forth; there you will sleep but little.
In bed she is meaner than a tigress stripped of cubs.
Conscious of her guilt, she falsifies complaints;
Grousing about boys or tearfully imagining a mistress.
Plentiful tears are ready in their place, awaiting
Instructions to flow. You think her love is for you,
Poor worm, and kiss her tears away, but what letters
You'd find in the desk of your 'jealous', cheating wife!
If she's caught in the act with a slave or a knight,
'Quick, Quintilian,'[117] says she, 'lend me a story!'
'I can't,' says he, 'Handle it yourself.' 'We agreed
Long since that we both have our freedom,' she tries.
'Shout the sky down, if you wish, but I'm only human.'
No one's more bold than a woman caught in the act;
Censure and blame increase her willful anger.
You ask the source and origin of these monsters?
Humble lives once kept Latin women chaste.
Hard work and little sleep barred sin from the cottage,
Hands roughened by Tuscan fleece, Hannibal
At the gates, and husbands on the Colline tower.[118]
Now we suffer from lengthy peace. Luxury,
More brutal than war, smothers the captive world.
No crime or lustful deed is absent, since the day
Roman poverty perished. Hither to our hills
Flow Sybaris, Rhodes, Miletus, with bold Tarentum,[119]
Soused and wearing a garland. It was filthy money
That first brought foreign ways, and silken wealth
Broke our race with foul self-indulgence.
What cares drunken Venus? She can't distinguish
Groin from head, slurps giant oysters at midnight,
Tops her unmixed wine with perfume, and drinks
From a conch-shaped flask. The room staggers,
The table flies up, and all the lights are double.
Go now and ask why Tullia sniffs with a smirk,
What Maura says to her notorious sibling,
When she passes the ancient altar of Chastity,

How they stop their litters here at night, and piss,
Spraying the goddess' statue with lengthy streams,
Ride each other by turns, and come, as the moon
Looks on, then return home. The next day, you step
In your wife's puddle–before an important meeting.
The 'mysteries' of Good Goddess are hardly a secret,
When flutes stir the groin, and maenads of Priapus
Driven wild by music and wine, swarm about
Howling and flinging their hair. What hot desire
For sex burns in their brains then, and what screams
They utter as the passion pounds within!
What floods of wine drench their thighs! Saufeia
Challenges the call-girls to a competition
In the swiveling of hips, but bows to Medullina,
Queen of the pelvic thrust. The ladies win,
Thanks to skills that match their birth! Nothing
Is faked, it's all for real–enough to stiffen
Even the limp old loins of a Priam or Nestor.
Now her itch can wait no more, and Woman's nature
Prevails, as the cry resounds throughout the den:
'Let in the men! It's time!' If her lover sleeps,
She bids another youth hasten there in his hood;
If he is absent too, she hounds the slaves;
If they are gone, the water-seller is hired;
If a man is not to be found, she loses no time
Arranging her buttocks underneath a donkey.
If only the ancient and sacred rites of our people
Were spared this contamination! But every Moor
And every Indian knows how a 'lady lutist'
Brought a rod longer than Caesar's Anti-Catos[120]
To that rite from which even a mouse must flee,
Ashamed of his tiny balls; and even a picture
Depicting the opposite sex must be hidden away.

3.19 Aulus Gellius *Attic Nights* 6.12. Mid-second century CE. In the *Attic Nights*, Aulus Gellius collected antiquarian, philosophical, and historical notes covering a wide array of topics.

For a man to wear a tunic that covered his arms, his wrists, and reached almost to the fingers was considered improper at Rome and in all Latium. Our countrymen called these tunics 'long sleeves' using a Greek term, and they considered a long and loosely draped garment appropriate for women only, in order to prevent others seeing the arms and legs. But Roman men at first dressed in the toga alone, without a tunic; later they had short, close-fitting tunics ending below the shoulders, which the Greeks call 'sleeveless'. Publius Africanus, the son of Paulus,[121] a man endowed with every useful skill and every virtue, dressed in this older fashion. Among the many objections he had to the effeminate Sulpicius Gallus, he considered it particularly disgraceful that Gallus wore tunics long enough to cover his hands. These were Scipio's words: 'The kind of perfumed man who primps every day in front of a mirror, who shaves his eyebrows, who walks around with plucked beard and thighs, who when he was a youth reclined at parties with a lover, wearing a long-sleeved tunic, who craved not only wine but also men, who would doubt that he has done the same things that perverts do?'

3.20 Curse tablet. *Suppl. Mag.* I.38. Second century CE. The purpose of the magical invocation on this lead tablet from Egypt is to 'bind' a woman and prevent her from having sex with anyone other than the man who purchased the spell.

I bind you, Theodoutis daughter of Eus, to the tail of the snake and the mouth of the crocodile and the horns of the ram and the venom of the asp and the whiskers of the cat and the male member of the god so that you cannot ever have intercourse with another man, so that you can neither be fucked nor buggered nor give oral sex, nor can you do anything for pleasure with another person if not me alone, Ammonion son of Hermitaris. For I alone am *Lampsourē othikalak aiphnōsabaō stēseōn uellaphonta sankistē chphyris.*[122] Fulfill this binding love spell – Isis[123] used this one – so that Theodoutis daughter of Eus may no longer have experience of another man's companionship other than me alone, Ammonion. Let her be enslaved, driven mad, and fly through the air in search of Ammonion son of Hermitaris, and let her bring thigh to thigh and sex to sex for intercourse always for as long as she lives. These are the figures: [crude drawings of a god, a snake, a crocodile, a cat (?), human figures, and magical signs].

3.21 Tertullian *On the Apparel of Women* 1.1.1–3, 2.2.4–6. Early third century CE. Tertullian converted to Christianity as an adult and produced many works, including a group of books setting forth his views on Christian habits and morality.

1.1.1–3
'In pain and worry you bear children, woman; you turn to your husband and he is lord over you.'[124] Do you not know that you are Eve? God's sentence on

this sex of yours lives on in this age; the guilt must live on as well. You are the Devil's door; you are the unveiler of that tree;[125] you are the first to desert divine law; you are the one who persuaded him, whom the Devil was unable to reach; you destroyed the man, God's image, with ease. Because of what you deserved – death – the Son of God had to die, and you think to adorn yourself in something grander than your tunic of animal skin? Come now, if the Milesians had shorn their sheep at the beginning of the world, and the Chinese had spun silk, and the Tyrians dyed cloth, and the Phrygians done embroidery, and the Babylonians tapestry, and pearls had gleamed and precious stones glimmered; if gold had already emerged from the ground along with greed, if the mirror had been allowed to tell such lies as it does now, then I believe that Eve would have coveted these things, even though she was thrust from Paradise and already dead.

2.2.4–6

But why are we dangerous to others? Why do we cause others to feel desire? If God, in amplifying the law, does not distinguish the desire from the deed when punishing fornication, I do not know whether he would spare from punishment the one who caused another's perdition. For as soon as a man desires your beauty and admits thoughts of what he desires into his mind, he perishes; and you have become the sword by which he perishes, so that even if you are blameless, you shall not escape odium. It is just as when a robbery takes place on someone's estate: the owner is not responsible for the crime, yet the area nevertheless gains a bad reputation, and the owner himself is tainted by its infamy. Shall we paint ourselves, if it means that others perish? Then what of 'You shall love your neighbour as yourself'? What of 'Care not for your own welfare, but for your neighbour's'? No pronouncement of the Holy Spirit can be pertinent to the immediate context alone, and each is to be applied and carried out in every circumstance in which it is useful. Therefore, since both we and others are affected by the zealous pursuit of physical charms, know now that you must not only reject the stagecraft of beauty that is artificially and laboriously achieved, you must even blot out your natural good looks by concealment and lack of care, since these are equally grievous to the eyes of those who behold you. For even though physical charm is not to be censured, since it is a bodily happiness, another example of the divine molder's art, and as it were, a good garment of the soul, nevertheless it is to be feared because of the violence and wrongs done by men who pursue it. Even Abraham, the father of the faith, was in great fear because of his own wife's beauty, and earned reproach when he purchased his safety by falsely calling Sarah his sister.[126]

Further Reading

On Pandora, see Loraux 1993, Zeitlin 1995b, and Brown 1997; for a feminist perspective on misogyny in Hesiod, see DuBois 1992. For Hippolytus and Phaedra, see Rabinowitz 1993, pp. 155–88. For Cicero's attack on Clodia, see Skinner 2011; for hostility toward powerful women, see Joshel 1997. For the 'performance' of masculinity and male scrutiny of other males, see Gleason 1995, Corbeill 1996, the essays in Foxhall and Salmon (eds) 1998, and Gunderson 2000; for the accusation of male prostitution against Timarchus, see Lape 2006. For Roman social codes of 'correct' sexual behaviour, see Parker 1997. For sex in Roman satire and other comic writing, see Richlin 1983, Smith 2005a, and Smith 2005b. On erotic magic, see Faraone 1999. For Tertullian's views on women, see Conybeare 2007.

4

Pederasty and Male Homoerotic Relations

Pederasty, or the sexual attraction of adult men for youths, is first attested in Greece in the post-Homeric aristocratic cultures of the emergent city-states, and was institutionalised as an educational practice by which the values of the nobles were transmitted from one generation to the next. The practices of the Dorian Greeks in Crete illustrate the educational function of pederasty in creating relationships between older and younger warrior-citizens; the pederastic relationship was a rite of passage by which a boy reached manhood and began his military service. The historian Ephorus' observations on Cretan customs (4.11) have been partially confirmed by archaeological evidence of the seventh century BCE.[127] Archaic Sparta, another Dorian state, recognised a pederastic relationship as a key element in a boy's education (4.20), although according to Xenophon (4.8) and Cicero (4.13) the sexual element of these friendships was discouraged. Pederastic sex is unambiguously attested for Archaic Thera, a Spartan colony. Explicit graffiti inscribed near the gymnasium (4.1) applaud the good looks of certain boys; dancing and the god Apollo are also mentioned in the graffiti, so the activity may have had a ritual context. During the Classical period, the symposium and the gymnasium were the premier homoerotic environments, but the continuing perception of a relationship between pederasty and homosocial male bonding in the warrior context is illustrated in the legend of the 'Sacred Band' of Thebes, an elite warrior squadron of the fourth century BCE, said to be made up of pederastic couples and renowned for its valor (4.18).

Archaic pederasty typically involved a relationship between two unequal (older and younger) partners.[128] The elegiac verses of the collection attributed to Theognis (4.2) reflect the disgruntled attitude of a mature lover (*erastēs*) toward the boy he loves (*erōmenos*) when the boy appears ungrateful and spends time with rival lovers. A powerful lover had the ability to mentor a boy and enhance his prospects for social and political advancement, while the boy had the ability to give or withhold affection and sexual gratification. In a successful relationship, it was not unusual for ties of affection to persist in later life, even after the lover's passion had faded. Plutarch's description (4.17) of Solon's love for Pisistratus (whether or not historical fact) gives us some sense of the lasting social impact of pederastic relationships in Athens, while the lovers Harmodius and Aristogiton were credited (inaccurately, as Thucydides notes) with bringing down the Pisistratid tyranny (4.5). Anacreon (4.3) and other famous poets sang openly of their love for beautiful boys. So pervasive was boy-love that the Classical Greeks assumed it was the motivation for the strong bond between Achilles and Patroclus in the *Iliad*. In Aeschylus' treatment of the myth, Achilles is portrayed as the *erastēs* and speaks passionately of the dead Patroclus' thighs, a reference to the practice of intercrural (between the thighs) intercourse favoured by Athenians, presumably because it protected the citizen boy from the feminising and corrupting effects of anal penetration.[129]

During the period of democracy in Athens, boy-love began to enjoy a lesser degree of popularity insofar as it was associated with aristocracy and outmoded thinking. Aristophanes' satirical description of the proclivities of Marathon veterans (4.4), penned nearly seventy years after the famous battle, suggests that jokes satirising the old-fashioned brand of pederasty were well received by Athenian audiences, and most references to boy-love in his comedies are negative. Pederasty, however, never lacked enthusiastic advocates within Greek culture until the advent of Christianity. Plato's *Phaedrus* (4.7) described the ideal man-boy relationship as the pathway to the divine: through his initial attraction to physical beauty, a lover aims toward the transcendence of divine beauty. Although emphasising the superiority of celibate but affectionate relationships, Plato condoned those with a sexual element, most likely departing in this respect from the teachings of his teacher Socrates, who while not indifferent to the beauty of youths, seems to have resolutely disapproved of any physical gratification with them.[130] Later in life, Plato apparently turned away from his early idealisation of pederastic love. In the *Laws*, he adopted a more censorious view according to which sexual activity was reserved for procreation alone (4.10, 6.5).

Philosophers debated the sexual ethics of pederasty, including the proper age for relationships to be initiated, and under what circumstances it was acceptable for the boy to physically 'gratify' the lover. In general, boys were expected to be passive 'beloveds' and to receive the attentions of their lovers with warm affection rather than an erotic response (4.9), although the arousal of the *erōmenos* is sometimes depicted in Athenian vase paintings of pederastic couples.[131] They were to avoid greedy demands for gifts, lest they appear to prostitute themselves. Older lovers, meanwhile, were not to take advantage of their superior experience by gaining a boy's affections and then suddenly dropping him in favour of another (4.6). Although the affection of a couple could last a lifetime (4.7), a youth lost his sexual appeal around the time he sprouted a beard. Eventually, each boy was expected to marry and sire legitimate offspring. Thus, the institution of pederasty is not consistent with modern concepts of 'gay' sexual orientation, because there was no assumption that either the lover or the beloved was exclusively interested in same-sex partners.

Erotic relations between men and boys did not enjoy unqualified social approval; as we have noted, pederasty was to a great extent an aristocratic preoccupation, and even among its most ardent supporters there was concern about its potentially feminising effects on citizen boys. This is why strong advocates of pederasty tended to emphasise the educational benefits of the practice and to insist that such relationships must be chaste (Lycurgus in 4.8; Protogenes in 8.19). Skeptics replied that the reality was far different, and derided what they saw as the hypocrisy of men who presented themselves as austere and manly philosophers, but had fleshly pleasures as their true aim. In Plutarch's *Dialogue on Love* (8.19), Anthemion chides Pisias, 'the most morally severe' of Bacchon's lovers, for opposing his marriage in order to continue having the pleasure of seeing him strip naked in the wrestling ring. An anecdote from the *Satyrica* (4.15) tells how the devious Eumolpus gained the confidence of his hosts by pretending to be a stickler for high morals, and then proceeded to seduce their handsome freeborn son. The gritty details of this story, including the boy's greed for gifts and the way he quickly learns to enjoy anal penetration, debunk every element of the pederastic ideal.

Among elite men, having been an *erōmenos* in one's youth created a political liability, for such men could be easily accused of having prostituted themselves. The Attic orators made liberal use of this strategy against their enemies, and it was also employed at Rome. Julius Caesar, whose adult reputation as a womaniser was almost unequalled, nevertheless had to battle politically damaging rumours that he had once been the *erōmenos* of an Eastern king (4.20), while Mark Antony was open to ridicule on the basis of his youthful relationship with Curio (3.14). Cicero, who launched that attack, expressed disapproval of Greek educational institutions such as the gymnasium because they encouraged pederasty (4.14).

In general, the elite Romans of the Republic and early empire disapproved of erotic relations between males of equal civic status, on the grounds that one of them was thereby made effeminate and thus disqualified from the privileges of citizenship. In the Roman context, sexual activity between males possessed little or no educational function and was typically a transaction between master and slave (or freedman), often focusing unambiguously on sexual activity and dispensing with the aesthetic niceties of Greek pederasty, such as the preference for beardless younger males. The scene between Lysidamus and Olympio in Plautus' comedy *Casina* (4.12) is one of many such scenes in Roman comedy illustrating the casual assumption that masters had sexual access to both male and female slaves, and that adult male slaves were not exempt from a master's attentions.

Among educated men, however, even master-slave relationships could be idealised and dignified with the help of prestigious Greek literary models. Vergil's second *Eclogue* (4.13) draws on the conventions of Greek pastoral poetry to tell the love of a shepherd for a beautiful slave boy. His models for this poem, Theocritus' third and eleventh *Idylls*, are stories of heterosexual love and courtship. Statius' poem of consolation to Ursus on the death of a beloved slave, Philetus (4.19) celebrates the erotic and emotional aspects of the relationship between master and slave, but the unequal status of the partners makes this a difficult task. Statius alternates between downplaying the servile status of Philetus in order to emphasise the depth of the emotional relationship between him and Ursus, and inserting reminders that Philetus was in fact a slave, and not Ursus' social equal. One of Martial's epigrams (4.16) presents a more mundane and simple scenario: over the objections of his wife, the narrator insists on his right to have anal sex with a slave boy in a purely physical encounter. Suetonius says in his life of Galba (4.20) that the emperor's 'inclination' was for adult men rather than boys (though he still insisted that they be depilated and thus feminised). His favourite was a freedman, Icelus, and the relationship had begun when Icelus was younger.

Acceptance of pederastic love and master-slave homosexual relations remained ingrained in Greco-Roman culture until the Christian period, when the Judeo-Christian condemnation of same-sex love, drawn in particular from the Hebrew Bible and the writings of Paul (5.10), became part of mainstream culture. In the late fourth century CE, Augustine's *Confessions* drew upon his Classical education for the argument that homosexual acts were contrary to nature (4.22). His ultimate appeal, however, is not to nature but to God the creator and author of nature, who punished the people of Sodom.

4.1 Graffiti from Thera. *IG* XII 3.536, 537, 540, 542, 543, 550. Sixth or seventh century BCE. These graffiti were inscribed in rocks above the gymnasium on the Aegean island of Thera (Santorini), not far from the temple of Apollo.

536 Phidippides had sex. Timagoras and Empheres and I had sex. Empylos too, the faggot. Empedocles wrote this, and by Apollo, he danced.

537a By Apollo Delphinios, Crimon had sex here with Bathycles' son, the brother of [...]

537b Here Crimon had sex with Amotion.

540 (I) Lacydidas is good. (II) Eumelus is the best at dancing. (III) Crimon was the first to delight Simias by dancing the 'dust cloud'.[132]

542 Astydicidas. Samagoras. [...] loves Phanocles.

543 Barbax dances well and gave [...]

550 In front of Dyman, the son of Hermeas, [...] always offered [...]

4.2 Theognis *Elegies* 1259–70. Sixth century BCE. An aristocrat from Megara, Theognis faced political upheavals threatening the dominance of his social class. The collection of elegiac verses by 'Theognis' also contains later material. Many of the verses are addressed to the narrator's beloved, a youth named Cyrnus.

Boy, your form is lovely, but upon your head
Lies a great crown of ignorance.
Your habit of mind resembles the swift-turning kite;
You believe the words of other men.
You, Boy, who repaid my attentions with evil deeds,
Ungrateful for the good you received,
Have never brought me benefit. Although many a time
I served you well, you lack respect.
The minds of a boy and a horse are alike. The horse
Weeps not for his rider in the dust,
But takes his fill of barley, then carries another man.
A boy loves the man beside him.

4.3 Anacreon *PMG* 360, 407. Mid to late sixth century BCE. The Ionian poet's compositions included love lyrics addressed to both males and females.

Fr. 360
Boy with the glance of a girl,
You pay no heed to my pursuit,
Entirely unaware that you
Drive the chariot of my soul.

Fr. 407
Come, dear boy,
Make me a gift of your slender thighs.

4.4 Aristophanes *Clouds* 957–1029. 423 BCE. In this comedy, Socrates stages a debate between Just and Unjust Arguments. Just Argument represents the old-fashioned generation of Persian War veterans who are stern disciplinarians and enthusiastic pederasts.

Chorus [To Just Argument]:
Now, you who crowned our elders with many wholesome habits,
Give utterance to that voice in which you delight,
And tell us of your nature.

Just Argument:
I will now describe how education used to be handled in the old days,
When I, the Just Argument, was in my blooming youth, and moderation was the rule.
First of all, boys were to keep quiet and not be heard uttering even a grunt.
Second, local boys marched down the street in a group to the lyre-master's,
In good order and naked, even if it was snowing as thick as coarse meal.
Then he would teach them to memorise a song, keeping their thighs well apart,
Either 'Awesome Pallas, City-Sacker' or 'The Far-Sounding Lyre's Call',
Raising the pitch high in the way our fathers handed down to us.
If any of them started clowning around or played a fancy flourish,
Like those virtuoso bits they play these days in imitation of Phrynis,[133]
He got a sound and repeated thrashing, for blotting out the Muses.
And in gymnastics the boys had to sit covering themselves with their thighs,
So as not to give onlookers a peek at anything too cruelly delightful;
And then again, they had to sweep the sand when they got up, taking care
Not to leave impressions of their youthful vigour for their lovers.
And at that time, boys did not anoint themselves with oil below the navel,
So their genitals bloomed with glistening down like one sees on a quince.
Nor did any boy greet his lover with a high, effeminate voice,
Fluttering his eyelashes and going about like a prostitute.
Nor were boys allowed when dining to take the heads of the radishes,
Nor to snatch away the dill and parsley from their elders,
Nor to eat delicacies, giggle, or keep their legs crossed.

Unjust Argument:
How antiquated you are, how full of Civic Zeus, cicadas,
Old-fashioned poets and ceremonial ox-killing![134]

Just Argument:
Yet these are the principles on which my educational system reared

The veterans of Marathon, whereas now you teach the boys early
To wrap themselves in their cloaks. It chokes me with anger,
Whenever those who should be dancing at the Panathenaea
Cover their hams with their shields and neglect Lady Tritogenia.[135]
Therefore, boy, boldly choose me, the Better Argument,
And you'll learn to hate the Agora, keep well away from baths,
Feel shame at what is shameful, meet jeers with hot anger,
To rise up from your seat when your elders approach,
And never behave badly to your parents, or do any shameful act,
Because you must mold for yourselves the image of Modesty,
And not to dart after dancing girls, lest while you gape at them,
A little whore hits you with an apple and ruins your good name,
And not to contradict your father in anything, calling him Iapetus,[136]
And reproaching him with old age, who reared you from a chick.

Unjust Argument:
If you listen to this fellow, young man, by Dionysus you'll end up
A confirmed boob, like Hippocrates' dullard sons.[137]

Just Argument:
But you'll work out in the gymnastic clubs, sleek and blooming,
Not babbling rude jokes in the Agora like the boys of today,
Or dragged into court over some contentious quagmire of a lawsuit,
But descending to the Academy, wearing a crown of pale reeds,
You'll run races beneath the olives with a decent lad your own age,
Smelling of greenbriar, the leaf-shedding poplar, and peace of mind,
Rejoicing in the springtime, when the plane tree whispers to the elm.

If you do as I say, and apply yourself,
You'll always have a strong chest, a clear face,
Broad shoulders, a tongue of few words,
A shapely rump, and a dainty prick.
But if you follow the youths of today,
In the first place you will end up with
Jaundiced skin, narrow shoulders,
A hollow chest, a big mouth,
A scrawny rump, a large ham,
And a dangling…decree.
[He points to Unjust Argument]
And that one will set you thinking
How everything shameful is fine,
And everything fine is shameful,

And what's more, it will fill you
With Antimachus'[138] lust for buggery.

Chorus:
O you who cultivate wisdom
Of towering renown,
How sweetly your words
Unfold the blossom of chastity!
Happy indeed were those
Who lived in the days of old!

4.5 Thucydides *History of the Peloponnesian War* 6.54.1–4, 6.56.1–57.4. Ca. 410 BCE. One of the rare digressions from the topic of the Peloponnesian war in Thucydides' history is this discussion of the Athenian 'tyrant slayers' Harmodius and Aristogiton who assassinated Hipparchus, the brother of the tyrant Hippias, in 514. They were killed in turn, but Hippias was soon deposed.

The bold deed of Aristogiton and Harmodius was undertaken because of a love affair, which I will detail at some length in order to demonstrate that the Athenians themselves speak no more accurately about their tyrants than other Greeks, and that their ignorance extends to the incident in question. For when Pisistratus grew old and died, still in possession of the tyranny, it was not Hipparchus who succeeded him, as many believe, but his eldest son Hippias. Harmodius was then in the radiant flower of his youth, and Aristogiton, a citizen of the middle class, became his lover and possessed him. Hipparchus made sexual overtures to Harmodius, but the latter did not return his interest, and told Aristogiton of the matter. Because of his passionate love, Aristogiton was deeply upset and afraid that the powerful Hipparchus might take Harmodius by force. At once he formed a plan to destroy the tyranny, insofar as his circumstances in life permitted. In the meantime Hipparchus again approached Harmodius, but without success. He was unwilling to use violence, but he made arrangements to insult Harmodius by some underhanded means.

[Thucydides digresses in order to describe the character of the Pisistratid tyrants' rule, which, he reports, was generally benevolent, and the circumstances under which Hippias succeeded his father as tyrant.]

When Harmodius rejected his advances, Hipparchus proceeded to insult him as he had planned. He and his friends invited Harmodius' young sister to carry the ritual basket in a procession, and then rejected her, saying that they had never invited her in the first place because she was unworthy. Harmodius was very upset over this, and Aristogiton was provoked to even greater anger for his sake. They had already made their preparations for the deed, but were waiting for the Great Panathenaea,[139] the only day when armed citizens assembling to escort the procession would not be viewed with suspicion. Harmodius and Aristogiton were to begin the attack, and the others were to assist them immediately by closing with the bodyguards. The conspirators were few in number because it was safer that way; they hoped that once those who were not in the plot realised what bold deeds were afoot, they would take up their own weapons to fight for freedom. At last the festival arrived, and Hippias with his bodyguard was arranging the order of the procession, outside the city at the Ceramicus.[140] Harmodius and Aristogiton already had their daggers and were proceeding with the plan, when they saw one of the conspirators talking in a familiar manner with Hippias, who was easy to approach. In a panic they concluded that they had been betrayed and were on the point of being captured. They were anxious to avenge themselves first, if possible, on the man who had done them wrong and on whose account the entire venture had been planned. So they rushed inside the gates with their daggers, and immediately meeting Hipparchus there by the Leocorium,[141] they recklessly made their attack, stabbing and killing him; Aristogiton acted because he was an outraged lover, and Harmodius because he had been insulted. Aristogiton at first eluded the bodyguards, escaping through the crowd, but was later captured and dealt with harshly; Harmodius was killed on the spot.

4.6 Plato *Symposium* 181c–184c. Ca. 385 BCE. Plato's account of a party at which each guest gave a speech in praise of Eros includes this extract from a speech by Pausanias. Little is known about Pausanias except that he was the lover of the dramatic poet Agathon, the host of the party. For more of his speech, see 2.10.

But the Eros of Heavenly Aphrodite, first of all, does not partake of the female, but only the male – this is the love of boys – and secondly, she is older, and free of violent lust. Therefore those who are inspired by this Eros turn toward the male, welcoming that which is more robust in its nature and has more understanding. And in the custom of boy-love itself, one can recognise those who are impelled by this type of Eros, for they only love boys when they begin to possess some understanding, about the time they first get hair on their chins. Those who begin to love at this point, I believe, are prepared to stay together and to share everything as long as they live. They don't act deceptively and take advantage of a boy's youthful inexperience, mocking him and running off to someone else. But the law ought to forbid the love of younger boys, because it is wasteful to expend so much effort on something uncertain. For one does not know whether a young boy will end up being virtuous or vicious in body and soul. Good men make this law for themselves, and we ought to force those 'common' lovers to follow it too, just as we compel them, as much as possible, to exclude freeborn women from their attentions. These are the men who have brought the love of boys into disrepute, so that some even go so far as to say that it is shameful to gratify a lover, because they observe that these men approach boys who are too young, and with bad intentions. But surely whatever is done in a decent and lawful manner cannot justly bring censure.

Furthermore, whereas the rules with regard to Eros in other cities are well defined and easy to understand, here and in Sparta they are complicated. In Elis and Boeotia, and wherever they are not skillful with language, they have made a simplistic rule that it is a good thing to gratify lovers. Nobody, either young or old, would say that it is a shameful thing, and I suppose this is because they don't want the trouble of trying to persuade the young, seeing that they are poor speakers. But in Ionia and other places where they live under the rule of the barbarians,[142] it is considered shameful. For the barbarians, because of their despotic form of government, suppose that not only this, but even philosophy and training in gymnastics are shameful. It does not profit their princes, I believe, to have high ideals planted in the minds of their subjects, nor to permit any strong friendships or associations, which these activities, and especially Eros, tend to produce. The tyrants here certainly learned this by experience, for the love of Aristogiton[143] and the affection of Harmodius[143] were strong enough to destroy their power. Thus, in places where they consider it shameful to gratify a lover, this is due to the poor character of those who set the standards, both the arrogance of the princes and the cowardice of their subjects. And wherever they have a simplistic rule that it is a good thing, this is due to the lazy minds of those who set the standards.

Here we have laid down far better rules, but as I said, they are not easy to understand. Consider our belief that it is better to love openly than in secret, and also that it is better to love a boy of excellent family and character, even if he is less than good-looking. Think also of the remarkable encouragement a lover receives from us all; he is not regarded as doing anything wrong. We believe that lovers who get what they seek are deserving of honour, while those who fail should be ashamed. And in pursuit of his success, we permit the lover great latitude to win praise by astonishing acts, which, if performed with any other end in view, would earn him only the greatest reproach. For example, if a man in pursuit of someone's money, or political office, or any other type of power were to behave the way lovers do with their boyfriends, begging and pleading in a needy fashion, swearing oaths in proof of their love, sleeping in doorways, and willingly submitting themselves to the sort of slavery that not even a slave would put up with, both friends and enemies would try to restrain him from acting this way. His enemies would censure him for his fawning, servile behaviour, while his friends would admonish him and feel ashamed on his behalf. But we look favourably on a lover who does all these things, and under our rules he may do them without censure, for the goal he pursues is completely honourable. The strangest thing of all is that most people believe the gods look leniently on lovers who break their oaths – and only lovers, for they say that an oath sworn in the heat of passion is no oath.

Thus both gods and men have given great freedom to the lover, as is the rule at Athens. And so it might be supposed that here in our city both being a lover and showing affection to a lover are considered wholly honourable. But in fact fathers give their sons escorts when they become objects of desire, and do not permit them to talk to lovers, and the escorts have strict instructions on this. And if a boy is observed talking to a lover by his age-mates and friends, they reproach him, but their elders do not prevent this or reprove them for speaking wrongly; seeing all this someone might well draw the conclusion that here such behaviour is considered an utter disgrace. But the truth, I think, is more complex. As I said in the beginning, loving is neither a good nor a bad thing in and of itself: it is good if done well, and bad if done poorly. Gratifying a vile lover in a vile manner is a bad thing, and gratifying a virtuous lover in a virtuous manner is a good thing. By 'vile' I mean that 'common' lover who feels desire for the body rather than the soul; he will not endure, for he does not love that which endures. As soon as the body he loves begins to lose its bloom, he 'flutters away and is gone', dishonouring all his fine words and promises, whereas a lover of virtuous character remains for a lifetime, because he has joined himself to something enduring.

Our rules put these lovers to the test well and truly, and distinguish those who deserve gratification from those who ought to be shunned. That is why we encourage lovers to pursue, and boys to flee, for this is the way we judge the competition and test whether each lover and each beloved is vile or virtuous. This explains first why we consider it disgraceful if the boy yields too quickly, for there ought to be a period of delay, and time is an excellent test. And secondly, it is disgraceful if a boy yields for the sake of material or political gain, whether his circumstances are poor and he reacts with cowardice rather than steadfastness, or whether he fails to show the proper scorn at the prospect of benefiting financially or politically. For in these benefits there is nothing enduring or certain, except the fact that a noble friendship cannot be based on them. Indeed, our rules leave only one acceptable circumstance in which a boy can gratify his lover, for just as it is not considered fawning or blameworthy if a lover becomes a willing slave, so also there is another type of willing slavery that is not blameworthy, and that is the pursuit of excellence. We believe that if a boy wishes to serve a man in the belief that this man will make him better, whether in wisdom or in one of the other elements of excellence, this willing slavery is neither fawning nor shameful.

4.7 Plato *Phaedrus* 255a–256d. Ca. 370 BCE. In this famous speech from a dialogue comparing love and literature as divinely inspired phenomena, the speaker is Socrates. He describes the impact of lover and beloved on one another's souls, which are metaphorically described as pairs of mismatched (good and bad) horses driven by a charioteer.

The beloved receives every attention from the lover, as though he were a god. The lover is not pretending, but truly feels love, and the boy is by nature friendly toward the one who serves him, even though in earlier days he may have been misled by his schoolmates or others who said that it was a shameful thing to have sexual relations with a lover, and because of this he may have driven away the lover. As a result of all these things, the boy's time of life and a feeling of destiny eventually lead him to accept the lover into his circle of friends. For it is the decree of fate that bad can never be a friend to bad, while good must always be a friend to good. And once the lover is permitted to enter the conversation and share the company of the beloved, his goodwill, now experienced on a more intimate footing, amazes the object of his love, and he perceives that all the affection of his friends and family cannot compare to this divinely inspired friendship. And as they spend more time together and the lover draws closer and has physical contact with him in the gymnasium, and on other occasions, then indeed that flowing stream which Zeus called 'Longing' when he was in love with Ganymede[144] rushes over the lover, some of it pouring into him, and some rolling off him when he is full. And just as a breeze or an echo bounces back from a hard, smooth surface and returns to its source, so the stream of beauty flows back into the beautiful boy through his eyes, the natural path to the soul, and moistening the pathways for the feathers, it stimulates their growth, causing the boy's soul to be filled with love and to take wing. He is in love, but does not know with whom; he does not understand what he is experiencing, and has no words to describe it. He is like one who has caught a disease of the eyes from someone else, but is at a loss to explain how. He does not realise that in the lover he sees himself, as though in a mirror. And whenever the lover is present, like him the boy feels relief from pain, and when the lover is absent, the boy feels a yearning, just as the lover yearns for him. In his mind is the image of mutual love, but he speaks of it and thinks of it as friendship, not love. Like the lover, but to a lesser degree, he desires to see his friend, to touch him, kiss him, lie down with him, and as you might expect, he soon does these things. Now, while they are lying together, the lover's undisciplined horse has something to say to his charioteer, and insists that he deserves to have a little enjoyment in return for his troubles. Meanwhile the boy's undisciplined horse has nothing to say, and full of confusion and overwhelming desire, it kisses and hugs the lover, embracing him as a true friend. Whenever they lie together, the bad horse for its part would not deny the lover any favour he might ask, but the other horse and the charioteer resist all this with modesty and reason. If the better intentions prevail in both partners, leading to a life lived in the pursuit of order and wisdom, their existence here below is blessed and harmonious. They practice moderation and self-control, holding in subjection the part that creates troubles in the soul, and giving free rein to the part that produces excellence. When they die, they become ethereal and winged, for they have been victorious in the first match of the three true Olympic games.[145] Neither human wisdom nor divine madness can bring a greater good than this. But if they live a coarse way of life without love of wisdom, and in pursuit of self-glorification, then when they have been drinking, or at some other moment of carelessness, the two undisciplined horses will take their souls by surprise, and lead them to perform the act which most people consider the happiest choice of all. And once they have done it, they continue the practice afterwards, but not often, for only a part of their minds approves. So these two remain friends both at the time of their love and afterwards, though in a lesser sense than the others who abstained, and they believe that they have exchanged such firm pledges of their faith that it would be unthinkable for them ever to break them and become enemies. When death comes, their souls exit the body without wings, but they have begun to sprout feathers, so the madness of love brings them no small prize. For it is the law that once souls have begun their journey toward heaven, they never again pass into darkness and the paths under the earth, but they lead a happy existence in the light, journeying together, and their love for one another ensures that when their wings grow, they will have matching plumage.

4.8 Xenophon *Constitution of the Lacedaemonians* 2.12–14. First half of fourth century BCE. The soldier and historian Xenophon was a follower and contemporary of Socrates.

I think I should say something about boy-love, since this is a topic that has to do with education. Among the other Greeks, such as the Boeotians, a man and a boy form a very intimate couple, while among the Eleans they gain enjoyment of a boy's youthful bloom through favours. Some, on the other hand, completely exclude lovers from talking with boys. Lycurgus[146] formed opinions in opposition to all of these customs. If someone was himself of good character and, in admiration of a boy's soul tried to make him a friend without reproach and be close to him, he approved and considered this the finest sort of education. But if someone was clearly interested in the boy's body, he condemned this as most disgraceful, and he brought it about that in Sparta, lovers abstained from their favourites no less than parents abstain from sexual relations with their children, or brothers and sisters with each other. I am not surprised that some people don't believe this, for in many cities the laws are not opposed to the desire for boys.

4.9 Xenophon *Symposium* 8.16–22. Ca. 365 BCE. Socrates discusses the ideal pederastic relationship, which is based on love of the soul, in contrast to relationships in which the lover focuses on the body of his beloved. While the lover (*erastēs*) feels passion for the boy, the boy himself 'returns the affection' (*antiphilein*) of the lover but does not himself experience *erōs*.

Now, no argument is necessary to establish that a soul blooming with freedom's beauty and with a modest and noble disposition, a soul is that kindly and a leader among his fellows, will feel admiration and affection for the object of his love. But it is likely that such lovers will also have their affection returned by the boys they love, and this I shall demonstrate. First, who could hate someone if he knew that person regarded him as fine and noble? And then, if he also saw that his lover was more interested in his welfare than in the lover's own pleasure? And in addition to this, if he felt assured that his lover's affection would never fail, even if he suffered some misfortune or lost his good looks through illness? Where there is mutual affection, people inevitably enjoy gazing at one another; they have pleasant conversation; each one trusts and is trusted by the other. They look out for one another, and feel glad when things are going well, and they grieve when there is a setback. They lead their lives cheerfully when both are healthy, but when one of the two falls sick, they spend even more time together, and each is more preoccupied with the other when he is absent than when he is present. Aren't these all the charms of Aphrodite? It is for the sake of these things that those with a mutual love of friendship continue to enjoy it right through to old age. But why should a boy return the affection of one whose attention is all for the body? Because that man allots to himself all that he desires, and gives the boy only what will cause him great shame? Or because he takes pains to conceal his real intentions from the boy's relatives? As for the notion that he does not force the boy, but persuades him, this is all the more despicable. The man who rapes a boy proves that he himself is a villain, but the one who uses persuasion corrupts the boy's soul. And what about the boy who sells his youth for money? Why will he feel any more affection for the buyer than someone who sells and deals in goods in the marketplace? Because he is young and the other is the opposite of young, or because he is handsome while the other is no longer handsome, or because he associates with someone whose passion he does not return? Certainly he will not feel affection because of these things. For unlike a woman, a boy does not share with a man in the joys of sex, but soberly watches as the man is intoxicated by Aphrodite. Therefore it is not surprising if he feels disdain for his lover.

4.10 Plato *Laws* 636b-d. Ca. 350. In this late work of Plato describing a utopian state, the 'Athenian Stranger' debates a Cretan and a Spartan on the value of their respective customs and institutions.

Although these gymnasiums and dining halls provide many benefits to the cities, they are problematic when it comes to civil strife, as the youths of Miletus, Boeotia, and Thurii[147] show us. And what is more, these practices seem to have utterly destroyed a law that is both ancient and in accord with nature, the law governing the pleasures of sex in human beings as well as in beasts. And for these problems one could hold your cities responsible, as well as the others that particularly favour the use of gymnasiums. Whether one considers this question jokingly or in earnest, it must be noted that when the female and male natures come into union for the purpose of procreation, the pleasure that results is in accord with nature, whereas male joining with male or female with female deviates from nature, and that the first people to dare this deviation did so out of an inability to control their appetite for pleasure. We all accuse the Cretans of inventing the story about Zeus and Ganymede. Since they believed that their laws came from Zeus, they attributed this tale to Zeus, in order to follow a god in the pursuit of this pleasure. But let us have done with the subject of myth.

4.11 Ephorus of Cyme *FrGrHist* 70 F 149. Mid-fourth century BCE (quoted in Strabo *Geography* 10.4.20–1. Early first century CE). The historian Ephorus' description of pederastic customs among the Cretans reveals traditional connections between pederasty and the training of youths as warriors. The groups of adolescent boys undergoing training were known as 'Herds'.

The most important of the Cretan institutions are as follows, according to Ephorus. Among the Cretans, all the boys selected from a Herd at one time are compelled to marry simultaneously. They do not bring home the girls they have married immediately, but only when the girls have gained sufficient knowledge of how to manage a household. A girl's dowry, if she has brothers, is half of a brother's share. Boys are expected to learn not only letters, but also the songs specified by their laws and certain forms of music. Those who are even younger are brought into the dining hall, known as the 'men's hall', and they sit together as they eat, dressed in threadbare clothes winter and summer alike; they wait on the men and also serve one another the food. And those who eat together join combat with one another, and with the boys from other dining halls. A supervisor of boys presides over each men's hall. The bigger boys are brought to the Herds; these are organised by the most notable and influential boys, each one gathering as many members as he can. The leader of each Herd is usually the father of the boy who assembled it, and he has the authority to lead them out in hunts and races, and to punish anyone who is disobedient. The Herds are fed at public expense, and on certain days one Herd is pitted against another, marching to battle to the rhythm of the pipes and lyre, just as they do in real wars, and the boys show the marks of battle, some dealt by fists, and others by iron weapons.

They have a distinctive custom with regard to love affairs, for they win the boys they love not by persuasion, but by abduction. The lover tells the boy's friends three or more days in advance that he is going to carry out the abduction. For them to hide the boy away or not allow him to go by the appointed road is considered quite a disgraceful thing, an admission that the boy is not worthy of such a lover. When they meet, if the abductor is the boy's equal or superior in social standing and in other respects, the friends pursue and oppose him only for a time, in order to satisfy the custom, and then they turn the boy over to him gladly. But if the abductor is unworthy, they take the boy away from him. The pursuit ends when the boy is brought to the men's hall of the abductor. They believe that the most desirable boys are not the best-looking ones, but those who stand out because of their manliness and good behaviour. The abductor gives the boy presents, and then takes him to a country retreat of his choice, and those who attended the abduction accompany them. After feasting and hunting for two months (it is not permitted to detain a boy longer than that), they return to the city. The boy is released after receiving as gifts military dress, an ox, and a drinking cup; these are the gifts required by law. And other gifts are given, so many and costly that a collection is taken up among the lover's friends to cover the expense. The boy sacrifices the ox to Zeus, and holds a feast for those who came to the country with him, and then he makes a statement about the relations with his lover, whether they were pleasing to him or not. The law allows this, so that if the boy experienced any force at the time of his abduction, he has a chance now to get revenge and rid himself of the lover. It is shameful if a boy with a handsome appearance and illustrious ancestors fails to obtain a lover, because they assume that this is the result of the boy's poor character. The boys 'who stand beside them' (for this is how they refer to those who have been abducted) receive honours, taking the most prestigious places in the dances and at the races, and they are allowed to dress differently from the rest, in the military outfits given them by their lovers. And not only then, but even after they are grown men, they wear a distinctive dress by which they can be recognised as 'famous'. For they call the chosen boys 'famous', and the lovers they call 'those whose hearts bear affection'. These are their customs in regard to love affairs.

4.12 Plautus *Casina* 449–70. Early second century BCE. Plautus' comedy centres around the efforts of the Athenian Lysidamus to obtain sexual access to the lovely slave girl Casina. In this scene, Lysidamus discusses these plans with his slave steward Olympio, as the two are secretly observed by Chalinus, a slave belonging to Lysidamus' wife.

Olympio:
I have been able to meet your needs very well!
I've given you the way to your heart's desire.
Today you'll possess your love, without your wife's knowledge.

Lysidamus:
Hush.
By the gods' love, I can hardly keep from kissing you,
My darling, because of that business.

Chalinus:
[aside] What! You want to kiss him? What 'business'? 'Your 'darling'?
By Hercules, he wants to drill the steward's bladder!

Olympio:
Do you really love me, now?

Lysidamus:
Gods, yes, more than I love myself!
May I put my arms around you?

Chalinus:
[aside] What do you mean, 'put my arms around you'?

Olympio:
Yes, you may.

Lysidamus:
Touching you is like licking honey to me!

Olympio:
Enough, lover-man. Take yourself off my back.

Chalinus:
[aside] So that's why he made this guy his steward.

Once the same thing happened, when I went with him:
He tried to make me his 'doorman' behind the door!

Olympio:
How obedient and charming I have been today!

Lysidamus:
May I love you more than myself as long as I live.

Chalinus:
[aside] By Hercules, I think they are up to more than footsie.
The old man really goes for the bearded ones.

Lysidamus:
Today I get to kiss Casina! And do fun things
Of all sorts, without my wife knowing!

Chalinus:
[aside] Aha! I'm finally back on the right track now.
The master's the one who is dying to have Casina.
I've got them!

4.13 Vergil *Eclogues* 2.1–27. Ca. 40 BCE. Vergil's shepherd Corydon laments his
unrequited love for the beautiful slave boy Alexis.

Corydon the shepherd burned for shapely Alexis,
The darling of his master, and had no hope at all;
Yet among the thick beeches and shaded crags
He ranged, and poured forth with useless zeal
These lonely uncouth verses to the woods and hills:
'Cruel Alexis, have you no interest in my songs,
Nor pity for me? In the end, you'll be my death.
Now even the cattle gain the cooling shade,
Now the thornbush shields the green lizard,
And Thestylis pounds thyme with fragrant herbs
To soothe the reapers tired from the fiery heat.
But the sun blazes and hoarse cicadas sound
As I track your footsteps through the orchards.
Wouldn't I have fared better braving the angry
Amaryllis with her proud ways, or Menalcas,
Though he is a dark lad, and your skin is fair?

O beautiful boy, don't pride yourself on looks!
White privet is cut, and the dark berry picked.
Alexis, you scorn me and don't ask who I am,
How rich in flocks or well supplied with milk.
My thousand lambs roam the Sicilian hills;
Fresh milk is mine in seasons of cold and heat.
I sing as Dirce's Amphion[148] did of old,
Calling his cattle on the peaks of Aracynthus.
Nor am I ugly; once I caught sight of myself
In the calm and wind-stilled sea. If that image
Was true, I'd dare to stand beside Daphnis[149]
Even with you as judge.'

4.14 Cicero *On the Republic* 4.3–4. Ca. 51 BCE. In this fragmentary section from a treatise on government, Cicero discusses the education of youths at Rome and compares the Roman system to that of the Greeks.

On the matter of educating a nation's youth, a goal toward which the Greeks have laboured long and fruitlessly, this is the one area in which Polybius,[150] as a guest in our land, finds our institutions negligent. For the Romans have not made it their policy to fix or determine by legislation the nature of instruction, nor to set forth a uniform system of public education. [...] that young men be naked. Such rules as some basis for modesty can be traced back to ancient times. But how absurd is the Greeks' practice of sending their youths to gymnasiums! How frivolous a method of training young men for military service, and how free and unrestrained are their fondlings and love-affairs! I refer to the Eleans and Thebans, among whom the pleasure of loving freeborn youths is given unrestrained licence. And the Spartans themselves, while they grant every freedom in the love of youths except actual fornication, create only a very tenuous obstacle to the act they disallow, for they permit lovers to sleep together and embrace with only the bed linens between them.

4.15 Petronius *Satyrica* 85–7. Ca. 60 CE. In this vignette from Petronius' picaresque satire written during the reign of Nero, the poet Eumolpus describes his seduction of a respectable freeborn boy, the son of his host.

When I went to Asia to do my military service on the staff of the quaestor,[151] I was given lodging in Pergamum. I stayed there willingly, not only because my rooms were elegant, but also because the host had a son who was extremely good-looking. So I thought up a plan whereby the father would not become suspicious that I was pursuing his son. Whenever the dinner conversation involved any mention of the enjoyment of handsome boys, I became extremely red-faced and refused in a pained and severe tone of voice to have my ears sullied with such obscene talk. So vehement was I that the mother came to look on me as quite the philosopher. And now I began to escort the young man to the gymnasium, and to organise his lessons. I instructed him and cautioned him not to allow any sexual predator into the house...

It happened that once on a holiday we were reclining in the dining room, when the games had drawn to a close, and the lengthy celebrations had made us too lethargic to retire to bed. Right around midnight, I noticed that the boy was awake, so in the softest of voices I spoke a prayer: 'Lady Venus, if I kiss this boy and he doesn't notice it, tomorrow I will give him a pair of doves.' When he heard the price of my pleasure, the boy began to snore, so I went over to him as he pretended to sleep, and stole some little kisses. Satisfied with this beginning, I rose early the next morning and fulfilled my vow by presenting the expectant youth with a choice pair of doves.

On the next night, when the same opportunity arose, I changed the prayer and said, 'If I fondle this boy with my wicked hands, and he doesn't feel a thing, I will give him two ferocious gamecocks for his trouble.' At this promise, the young man moved over toward me of his own volition; I think he began to fear that I had fallen asleep! I eased his worries about that, and became utterly absorbed in exploring his entire body, stopping just short of the summit of pleasure. Then in the morning, much to the boy's delight, I brought him the gift I had promised.

When the third night gave me my chance, I whispered...in his ear as he pretended to sleep, 'Immortal gods! If I am able to enjoy the full satisfaction of sex with this sleeping boy, in return for this happiness I will give him an excellent Macedonian thoroughbred horse tomorrow, though only on the condition that he does not feel a thing.' Never did a young man sleep more soundly! So first I filled my hands with his milky white breasts, then I clung to him in a long kiss, and finally all my desires were joined into one. In the morning, he sat down in his room to wait for my usual visit. Now, you know how much easier it is to buy some doves or cocks than a thoroughbred; and besides, I was afraid that such an expensive gift would make my friendly attentions seem suspicious. So I took a walk for a couple of hours, and when I returned to the lodgings, I merely gave the boy a kiss. And looking about as he embraced me, he said, 'Please, sir, where is the thoroughbred?'

When, on account of the broken promise, the access I had previously enjoyed was closed to me, I resorted to my former bold devices. In a few days, when circumstances allowed a similar opportunity and I heard the father snoring, I began to beg the youth to be friends again, and said that I would make it up to him, and all the other things that a man's swollen lust suggests he should say. But he was clearly angry and only replied, 'Go to sleep, or I'll tell my father.' Now, there is no obstacle that a wicked will cannot overcome with force. While he was saying, 'I'll wake my father', I crept up to him and forcibly took my delight while he weakly resisted. My villainous act did not displease him, and after he had complained for a while that I had deceived him and caused him to be laughed at by his fellow students, to whom he had bragged of my wealth, he said 'I won't be like you. If you want, do it again.' I was back in his good graces, and all my sins forgotten, so I took advantage of his generous offer and then dropped off to sleep. But he was at that ripe age when young men are keen to submit, and he wasn't satisfied with a second time. So he woke me from a sound sleep, saying, 'Don't you want something?' And it was certainly no burdensome task. So I panted and sweated, grinding away, and when he had finally got what he wanted, I collapsed into sleep again, worn out by pleasure. Less than an hour had gone by before he started to jab me with his hand, saying, 'Why aren't we doing it?' Then, incensed at being woken up so many times, I gave him a taste of his own medicine: 'Go back to sleep, or I'll tell your father!'

4.16 Martial *Epigrams* 11.43. Late first century CE. A Latin poet from Spain, Martial wrote twelve books of epigrams on a wide variety of subjects.

Wife, you catch me in the act with a boy,
And pointedly state that you too have an ass.
Juno said as much to her horny Thunderer,[152]
Yet still he sleeps with big Ganymede.
Instead of his bow, the man who came from Tiryns
Used to bend Hylas[153] over; do you suppose
That Megara, Hercules' wife, was bereft of buttocks?
Runaway Daphne put Phoebus on the rack,
But his tortures were banished by the Spartan lad.[154]
Briseïs often lay with her back to Achilles,
Yet his beardless friend was closer still.[155]
So wife, don't flatter your bits with masculine names,
And don't convince yourself you have two cunts.

4.17 Plutarch *Life of Solon* 1.2–3. Late first century CE. Solon was a statesman and lawgiver credited with laying the foundations for the Athenian democracy; he lived during the late seventh and early sixth centuries BCE. Although composed centuries later, Plutarch's biography is one of the principal sources for his life.

Heracleides of Pontus relates that Solon's mother was a cousin of Pisistratus'[156] mother. And the friendship between these two men was due in great part to their kinship, but also in great part to Pisistratus' youthful good looks, for some say that Solon had a strong sexual attraction to Pisistratus. And this may be why later on, when they fell into disagreement over politics, their feud did not carry with it harsh or wild emotion, but a sense of fair play remained in their souls, and preserved the pleasing memory of their love, 'a still-smouldering flame of Zeus' fire'.[157] And one gathers from his poems that Solon was not immune to good looks, and not so bold as to fight Eros 'confronting him fist to fist, like a boxer'.[158] He also wrote a law stating plainly that slaves were not permitted to anoint themselves with oil in the wrestling schools, nor to become the lovers of boys, thus distinguishing this practice as one that was honoured and dignified, and in a way summoning the worthy to participate in that from which he barred the unworthy.

4.18 Plutarch *Life of Pelopidas* 18. Late first century CE. In his biography of the Theban statesman Pelopidas (died 364 BCE), Plutarch tells how Pelopidas was victorious against the Spartans with the help of an elite force of Theban warriors known as the Sacred Band.

Gorgidas, they say, first formed the Sacred Band from three hundred chosen men, whose training and upkeep was supplied by the city, and who had their camp on the Cadmeian citadel.[159] They were also called the City Band, for an acropolis in those days was properly referred to as 'the City'. Some say that the company was composed of lovers and beloveds, and they mention the witty comment of Pammenes[160] on this subject. He said that Homer's Nestor was no tactician when he commanded the Greeks to organise themselves by tribes and clans,

That clan might support clan, and one tribesman another,[161]

since what he ought to have done was station lovers beside their beloveds. For when in danger, clansmen do not give much thought for clansmen, nor men of a tribe for one another, whereas a company of men bound together by the affection of lovers cannot be destroyed or broken. They will remain beside each another in times of danger, one group out of fondness for the beloved, and the other out of a proper wish not to appear cowardly before a lover. Nor is this surprising, since they value more the opinion of a loved one who is absent than that of other men who are present, as was the case with the downed man whose enemy was about to kill him. He begged the enemy to pierce his chest with the sword, in order, he said, 'that my beloved may not see my corpse with a wound in the back and feel ashamed of me.' It is also said that Iolaus[162] was the beloved of Heracles and shared his Labours, fighting beside him. And according to Aristotle, even down to his day the tomb of Iolaus was the place where lovers and beloveds pledged their faith to one another. It was fitting, therefore, that the band was called Sacred, for Plato also says that the affection of a lover is divinely inspired. It is said that the Band remained undefeated until the Battle of Chaeronea.[163] And after that battle, when Philip was viewing the dead, he stopped at the place where the three hundred lay after facing his long spears, all in their armor and mingled together. He was filled with admiration, and when he learned that they had been lovers and beloveds, he wept and said, 'May he die a miserable death, whoever believes that these men either did anything shameful or allowed anything shameful to be done to them.'

4.19 Statius *Silvae* 2.6.35–58. Ca. 93 CE. Statius, a Latin poet who lived in the time of the emperor Domitian, composed the *Silvae*, a book of poems written for special occasions. In this poem of consolation to a master on the death of his favourite slave Philetus, the narrator addresses the dead beloved.

How lovely you were! You excelled boys and men
In beauty, surpassed by your master alone. Only he
Outshone you, as the bright moon leads lesser lights,
Or the Evening Star subdues all others in the sky.
No soft charms or woman's looks adorned your face,
Like the dubious features of boys, transformed
By the criminal knife; you were pleasingly virile.
Your glance was not brash, but sweet and serious,
The image of Parthenopaeus[164] without his helmet.
You wore your hair simple, tousled and unstyled,
Your cheeks glowed, still free of their first flower.
Eurotas rears such youths beside the pool of Leda.[165]
With Jove at Elis[166] such perfect boys sojourn
To offer up their years. How could my song recall
His modest cast of mind, and even-tempered ways,
His spirit so much greater than his tender years?
With zealous work and lofty counsel, the slave
Advised his willing master; your joys and sorrows
He shared; his face always mirrored your thoughts,
Worthy to surpass in fame the Haemonian friend
And the Athenian pledge.[167] But let his praises be
Only those fortune allows: not even sad Eumaeus[168]
Awaited more loyally the tardy return of Ulysses.

4.20 Suetonius *The Twelve Caesars* 1.49 (Caesar); 7.22 (Galba). 121 CE. Suetonius was a historian working under the emperor Hadrian. In the first selection, he tells how the young Julius Caesar was sent to Bithynia to bring back a fleet and there met King Nicomedes. This episode gave rise to a persistent rumour that Nicomedes had become Caesar's lover. The second selection is an anecdote about Galba, who reigned during the 'year of four emperors' in 69 CE.

2.49

Besides his attendance on Nicomedes, nothing else damaged his reputation for chastity; that, however, created a serious and long-lasting scandal, and exposed him to universal reproach. I leave out discussion of Licinius Calvus'[169] famous verses:

> He possessed all Bithynia
> And screwed Caesar too.

I pass over the orations of Dolabella and the elder Curio,[170] in which Dolabella called him 'the mistress who rivaled the queen, the mattress in the royal litter' and Curio called him 'Nicomedes' bordello and Bithynia's brothel'. I omit the edicts of Bibulus,[171] in which he proclaimed that his colleague was the queen of Bithynia: 'Once he desired a king, now a kingdom.' As Marcus Brutus[172] says, that was the occasion when a certain Octavius, who was very talkative because of a mental disorder, called Pompey 'king' in front of a great crowd, and followed this by saluting Caesar as 'queen'. And Gaius Memmius[173] even throws out the taunt that he acted as cupbearer to Nicomedes, with other debauched youths, at a banquet attended by several Roman merchants, whose names he cites. Cicero was not content to write in certain of his letters that Caesar, led by attendants into the king's chamber, lay down on a golden bed dressed in a purple robe, and that 'the youthful flower of one sprung from Venus was defiled in Bithynia.' Once when Caesar was speaking in the Senate in support of Nicomedes' daughter Nysa, and noting the king's generosity to himself, Cicero even said, 'Enough of that, I beg you! Everyone knows what he gave you – and what you gave him.'

7.22

[Galba's] sexual tastes inclined toward males, and he preferred them strong and full-grown. When Icelus, one of his old lovers, brought him news in Spain of Nero's death, not only did he single him out with ardent kisses, but he also begged Icelus to have his body hair removed without delay, and took him aside into a private room.

4.21 Aelian *Various History* 3.10. Ca. 230 CE. Aelian, a contemporary of the emperor Septimius Severus, wrote a collection of historical anecdotes in Greek. This extract describes the attitude of the Spartan ephors (civic leaders) toward pederastic lovers.

Concerning the ephors of the Lacedaemonians,[174] I have many other excellent things to say, which I plan to do later, but for now I will tell the following. If one of the beautiful among them preferred a rich lover to a poor but deserving one, they assessed him a fine, punishing his love of money with a loss of money. If some other man of good birth refused to be the lover of any of the boys who were well brought up, they fined him too, because even though he was worthy, he did not love. Clearly he could have made that boy, and even others, worthy like himself, for the goodwill of lovers produces excellence in their favourites, whenever they themselves are worthy of high respect. It was also the law among the Spartans that whenever a young boy did wrong, they excused him on account of his lack of age and experience, but they punished his lover, for they expected him to examine and oversee the actions of his beloved.

4.22 Augustine *Confessions* 3.8. 397–8 CE. Written in his early 40s, Augustine's autobiography describes his wild youth and conversion to Christianity.

Can it ever or in any place be unjust to love God with all one's heart, soul, and mind, or to love one's neighbour as oneself? Therefore disgraceful acts that are contrary to nature, like those that occurred among the people of Sodom, are always and everywhere to be hated and punished. Even if every nation did them, they would all be judged guilty of a crime according to the same divine law, which did not create human beings to use another in this way. For the fellowship that ought to exist between God and us is violated, when that nature of which he is the author is polluted by perverted lusts.

Further Reading

Dynes and Donaldson (eds) 1992 is a collection of classic papers on the subject of homosexual behaviour in the ancient world; Hubbard ed. 2003 provides an extensive selection of primary sources. Dover 1989 (first published in 1978) is a foundational work on Greek pederasty; for more recent views and controversies, see the essays in Hubbard ed. 2000. For visual sources, see Devries 1997, and Lear and Cantarella 2008; for myth, see Sergent 1986. On pederasty in Sparta and Athens respectively, see Cartledge 1992 and Konstan 2002. On perceptions of Achilles and Patroclus as lovers, see Clarke 1992; for the Sacred Band at Thebes, see Leitao 2002. For pederasty and male homoerotic relations at Rome, the authoritative work is Williams 2010; for homosexual behaviour and Christianity, see Boswell 1980; Brooten 1996.

5

Female Homosocial and Homoerotic Relations

Because of the paucity of female voices in our sources, little is known about intimate female friendships or same-sex erotic relationships from the perspective of women. The role of homoerotic relationships in female socialisation during the Archaic and Classical Greek period continues to be debated, but it appears that in certain traditional contexts, intimate relations between females were perceived as part of the preparation for marriage, just as pederasty had a role in the education of boys and their transition to adulthood. As part of their education, aristocratic girls were trained to dance and sing in religious festivals. The female singers in Alcman's compositions (5.1) express their admiration and desire for the girls who lead the chorus (Hagesichora and Agido in Fr. 1 and Astymeloisa in Fr. 3). Although a man composed these songs, they are thought to be representative of the prevailing culture among girls undergoing choral training as part of their transition to adulthood in Archaic Sparta. Interestingly, Alcman attests relations among girls of the same age, rather than relations between an adult mentor and a younger girl. Much later, however, Plutarch refers to noblewomen of early Sparta taking girls as lovers in a custom parallel to the male practice of pederasty (5.12).

A focus on a private world of female beauty, ornament, fantasy, and sensuous experience, often tied to ritual celebrations as in Alcman's songs, is also found in the poetry of Sappho, the only female poet from Archaic Greece whose work has survived (2.4; 5.2). Sappho is frank about her desire for women, and rejects overtly masculine cultural values (such as a preference for the beauty of warriors) in favour of her own aesthetic, which features the sensuous natural settings and luxurious objects of female adornment associated with Aphrodite. Sappho's mastery of poetic technique caused her to be widely admired, but her homoeroticism could be misinterpreted. By the Classical period, comic plays and fanciful 'biographies' cast her as a short, ugly woman who turned to other females because of her unattractiveness, as the rejected lover of the fictional, Adonis-like youth Phaon, or as a prostitute (since female homoerotic acts were associated with prostitution in the minds of many men).[175] Even in Plato's fable (2.10) about the origins of the human desire for sexual union, which attributes the same origins to same-sex and opposite-sex desire, the speaker Aristophanes has no word by which to name a woman desiring other women except *hetairistria*, which connotes prostitution.

Aristophanes' speech makes homosexual desire a part of the natural order, arising from the fact that there were three primordial sexes: the fully male, the fully female, and the male-female. Although the *Symposium* idealises male pederasty, the fable throws a mantle of legitimacy over same-sex female desire as well – perhaps because Plato knew of the existence of female 'pederasty' in Archaic Sparta, the city-state that was to inspire his greatest work, the *Republic*. Another fanciful tale about the origins of same-sex desire, preserved in Phaedrus' collection of fables (5.9), attributes same-sex desire to a drunken error by humanity's creator Prometheus, who attached male genitals to some female bodies and vice versa. This version, lacking both Plato's aristocratic bias toward pederasty and the spark of his poetic imagination, expresses the more mainstream, 'common man's' view that attraction must necessarily be based on the meeting of opposite genders and that every sexual relationship and act requires the partners to play the physical and social roles of 'man' and 'woman'.

In the virtually encyclopedic repertoire of sexual jokes used by Aristophanes, the fact that sex between two women goes unmentioned suggests that it was too sensitive a topic for the public scurrility of the comic stage. Aristophanes uses the verb *lesbiazein* to refer to fellatio, for the inhabitants of Lesbos were stereotypically associated with this act.[176] Hence, it is unclear whether a poem of Anacreon (5.3) about the narrator's rejection by a girl from Lesbos refers to a preference for other females, or to her desire to engage in fellatio with men younger and more vigorous than the narrator. By Lucian's day in the second century CE, however, Lesbos had clearly come to be associated with women who desired women (5.16), and not merely because Sappho was known to be a native of the island. Perhaps as a result of Sappho's fame, 'Lesbian' relationships were condoned there. Also in the second century CE, this time in Egypt, we learn of the existence of a woman named Heraïs (5.14) who tried to attract the woman she desired by means of magic. Such 'binding spells', written on papyrus or lead and deposited in tombs, used conventional formulas that did not vary with the gender of the persons involved, so little can be known about Heraïs' specific situation except that she was willing to use the same methods as other desperate lovers who turned to coercive magic (3.20).

Sappho inspired not only male poets, but also a few women such as Nossis, whose extant poems (5.4) declare her allegiance to a Sapphic aesthetic, address themselves to a notional audience of women, and express admiration for female beauty. The Hellenistic interest in female emotion and interior life, anticipated in the tragedies of Euripides, gave rise to new subjects for poetry, including salacious portraits of intimate female conversations and interests as imagined by males. Herodas' *Mimes* include scenes of Alexandrian middle-class ladies discussing with one another their enjoyment of dildos (5.5), a theme that was already sounded in Aristophanes' *Lysistrata* (8.7) and in Athenian vase painting. While female sexual desire was readily acknowledged in antiquity, the possibility that female desire could be satisfied without a penis, or a penis-substitute, was virtually unheard of in Classical Greece. But by the Roman period, female same-sex lovers were often referred to using the noun *tribas*, a loan word related to the Greek verb *tribō*, 'I rub'. Martial's Philaenis (5.11) is primarily attracted to other women and indulges in cunnilingus, a practice considered particularly distasteful among elite men, although she is also said to 'screw' young people of both sexes (the verb used in the case of her male partners is *pedicāre*, which refers to anal penetration). Martial's ridicule of Philaenis and other *tribadēs* focuses primarily on their presumptuous attempts to act like men, or to exclude men from their circles.

In Hellenistic and Roman texts authored by men, female same-sex desire generally meets with disapproval because it is perceived as a deviation from normal gender roles. In most cases, however, it does not provoke feelings of outrage, the response expected when one man seduces another's wife, but a vaguer sense that such activities are 'not right', as in the epigram by Asclepiades (5.6), or shameful and strange, yet fascinating, as in Lucian's titillating sketch (5.16) of a young prostitute seduced by a female couple. When a married woman at Rome engages in a same-sex affair, there is hesitancy about whether this fits the definition of adultery, since the wife's partner lacks the ability to penetrate (5.8), yet the activity is clearly considered off-limits and unacceptable. A less censorious view of same-sex desire is presented by the urbane Ovid, whose tale of Iphis' love for Ianthe (5.7) dwells extensively on the 'unnatural' pairing of same-sex partners as an obstacle to true union, but is sympathetic toward Iphis and the love she believes is hopeless. It is notable that Iphis does not attempt to usurp the male role, but has it thrust on her by circumstances and the will of the goddess Isis, who ultimately transforms Iphis into a man so that her story can end happily.

The concept of female same-sex desire as 'unnatural' is also illustrated in the dream-interpretation handbook of Artemidorus (5.13). His chapter 80, on 'unnatural sexual intercourse', classes sex between women with the entries for oral masturbation and intercourse with gods, the dead, or animals, thus defining this type of sexual activity as extreme and bizarre. Like other male authors, Artemidorus conceptualises every sex act between a couple as having a dominant and a submissive partner: one 'is gratified' and the other 'gratifies'. To dream of such activity, however, indicates nothing about the dreamer's sexual preferences, but is simply a prediction of future events. Interestingly, female same-sex love presages the 'sharing of secrets', which could be a positive or negative event depending on the context.

Not surprisingly, female same-sex desire was strongly condemned by early Christian authors, who reinforced its traditional association with prostitution. That Sappho must be a prostitute because of her sexual interest in other women was taken for granted by the Christian ascetic Tatian (5.15), who belittled her as a 'sex-mad little whore' and contrasted her sexual freedoms with the opportunities afforded celibate women to play more active roles in the life of the church. Tatian traced his complete rejection of sex to the apostle Paul, who encouraged total celibacy and specifically condemned homosexual acts, whether male or female (5.10). Tertullian, an ascetic who paid special attention to the sexual connotations of clothing, complained of matrons on the streets of Carthage who appeared at first glance to be either prostitutes or *frictrīcēs* (literally 'women who rub', the Latin equivalent of *tribadēs*). In another work (5.18), Tertullian expresses disgust at the idea of drinking from a cup used by a *frictrix*, a castrated priest of Cybele (whom he assumes to be a participant in homosexual acts), a gladiator, or an executioner. Thus the most impure persons Tertullian could imagine were homosexual lovers and people whose occupation was the shedding of human blood. Such negative Christian attitudes toward same-sex desire were to remain influential in Western culture to the present day.

5.1 Alcman *PMG* Frs. 1.36–101, 3.61–85. Seventh century BCE. Alcman is famed as the first known choral poet. In Fr. 1, a 'maiden song' composed for performance by young women, the girls first sing the heroic story of the Spartan kings Hippocoon and Tyndareus (omitted here). They continue with descriptions of one another's beauty, focusing on the two chorus leaders Agido and Hagesichora. The occasion of the poem seems to be the festival of a goddess Orthria, perhaps a goddess of the dawn. In Fr. 3, another choral song, the singers express their admiration of Astymeloisa, whose name (as the poem suggests) means 'she for whom the town cares'. The opening of the song (omitted here) is an invocation to the Muses of Olympus and evokes a picture of the girls' chorus, dancing on tender feet and shaking their blonde hair.

Fr. 1.36–101
The vengeance of the gods is real.
Fortunate is he who weaves
His day to the end in gladness,
Without tears. I sing
The light of Agido. I see her
Like the sun, which Agido
Calls to shine as our witness.
But the renowned leader of our chorus
Allows me neither to praise nor find fault with her
In any way. For she herself
Seems to stand out, just as if someone
Set a horse among the herds,
Well-built to carry off prizes with thundering hoof,
A dream-horse from beneath the rocks.

Don't you see? She is a Venetic racehorse.[177]
But the mane of my cousin
Hagesichora blooms
Like pure gold.
And her silvery face –
Why do I need to say anything?
This is Hagesichora.
And the second in beauty after Agido
Will run like one of Colaxes' horses
Racing an Ibenian opponent;[178]
For the Pleiades[179] battle us,
Rising like the star Sirius
Through the ambrosial night
As we carry a robe to Orthria.

Abundant robes of purple
Are not sufficient for protection,
Nor a snake all of gold,
Intricately worked, nor a headband
From Lydia, the delight
Of violet-eyed girls,

Nor Nanno's hair,
Nor even Areta like a goddess,
Thylakis, or Cleësithera.
Nor will you go to Aenesimbrota's house
And say, 'If only Astaphis were mine,
I wish Philylla would look at me,
And Damareta, and lovely Ianthemis.'
No, it is Hagesichora who guards me.[180]

For isn't Hagesichora here,
She with her lovely ankles?
Doesn't she stay close beside Agido
And with her applaud our festival?
You gods, accept their prayers;
To fulfill and bring to pass
Belongs to the gods. Chorus-leader,
If I may speak, I am only a girl,
An owl screeching from the rafter
In vain. Yet I long to please
Aotis[181] most of all, for she
Was the healer of our pains.
And because of Hagesichora,
The girls traversed the path
Of lovely peace.

For like the lead-horse of a team,
[line missing]
One must heed the helmsman
Especially. She is not richer in song
Than the Sirens, for they are goddesses,
But we ten sing as well
As a chorus of eleven.
We sing like a swan on the streams
Of the Xanthos river,[182] and she
With her lovely yellow hair
[four missing lines]

Fr. 3.61–85
[missing lines]
With longing that loosens the limbs, more melting
Than sleep and death is her glance.
That sweetness is not without power.

But Astymeloisa gives me no reply.
Instead, holding her garland,
She flies through the heaven
Like a radiant star,
A sapling of gold, or a light down feather.
[one line missing]
...she strode away on her long legs
...the moist charm of Cinyras[183]
Sits on the tresses of the maidens,
But as for Astymeloisa, through the crowd
...the darling of the people
[4 fragmentary lines]
...to see if she might love me
If she came closer and took my tender hand,
Soon I would be begging at her feet.
But now...the girl...deep thoughts...
[missing lines]

5.2 Sappho Fr. 1, 16 Lobel-Page. Late seventh to early sixth century BCE. The
renowned lyric poet lived on the Aegean island of Lesbos. Most of her poetry
has been lost, and much of the surviving material is fragmentary.

Fr. 1
Jewel-throned, Immortal Aphrodite,
Wile-weaving child of Zeus, I beg you
Do not conquer my heart with anguish
And hurt, O Queen.

But come, if ever before you listened,
Hearing my far-off voice, and departing
The golden abode of your father
You came to me here,

Your chariot yoked with lovely sparrows,
Swift birds, whose ever-whirring wings
Brought you from heaven over dark earth
Through the middle air,

And soon arrived. You, blessed one,
Asked with your immortal smile
What was wrong this time, and why
This time I called you,

And what my mad heart most wished
For myself. 'Who is she this time,
The one I am to persuade to your love?
Who wrongs you, Sappho?

For if she flees, she shall soon pursue,
If she rejects gifts, soon she shall give.
If she loves you not, she shall love, even
Against her will.'

Come to me now again and deliver me
From harsh care; fulfill all the things
My heart longs to fulfill, and yourself
Fight beside me.

Fr. 16
Some say a host of horsemen, some
Of soldiers, others of ships is the finest
Thing on the black earth, but to me it is
Whatever one loves.

It is perfectly easy to make this clear
To everyone, for Helen, far surpassing
All others in beauty, left behind
Her noble husband,

And sailing to Troy she went without
A thought for her child or dear parents
But … led her on…
[one line missing]

[two lines missing]
She reminds me now of Anactoria
Who is not here.

I would rather see her lovely walk
And the bright sparkle of her face
Than the chariots and armored men
Of the Lydians.[184]
[at least twelve missing lines]

5.3 Anacreon *PMG* 358. Mid to late sixth century BCE. In the works of the lyric poet Anacreon, male same-sex relations are mentioned often, but female desire for other females very rarely.

Golden-haired Eros once again
Strikes me with his purple ball,
Summoning me to frolic with a girl
Who wears fancy sandals.
But she hails from the lovely land
Of Lesbos. Because my hair is white,
She scorns it, and gapes eagerly
At someone else – a girl.[185]

5.4 Nossis *Greek Anthology* 5.170, 6.275, 9.604. Ca. 280 BCE. Seven of Nossis' surviving eleven epigrams were written about women. In several of the poems, the narrator's voice guides the group through a temple of Aphrodite, describing lifelike portraits of beautiful women.

5.170
Nothing is sweeter than love. All else is second;
Even honey I spit from my mouth.
Nossis says: She whom Cypris does not cherish
Cannot recognise the rose.

6.275
Let us visit the temple and view the statue
Of Aphrodite, worked in gold,
A gift of Polyarchis, who enjoys the wealth
Gained from her body's splendor.

9.604
How well this panel shows shapely Thaumareta,
Her lively bloom and gentle eyes.
Your puppy, set to guard the house, would wag
Her tail, thinking it was you.

5.5 Herodas *Mimes* 6. First half of third century BCE. In this dialogue, Metro visits her friend Coritto, who is attended by slave girls. The two discuss a leather dildo that has been passed around among their friends, and the shoemaker Cerdon who manufactures these prized objects.

Coritto:
Sit down, Metro. You, get a chair for the lady!
Must I tell you everything? Wretched girl!
Won't you do one thing on your own? A lump,
Not a slave, lives here. But when you are fed,
You count every crumb. And if one bit is lost,
All the livelong day you mumble and fume,
Fit to bring the house down. And you choose now
To wipe and shine the chair, when we need it?
Thief! Be grateful she is here, for otherwise,
You'd soon have a taste of the back of my hand.

Metro:
Dear Coritto, we chafe under the same yoke.
Night and day I too gnash my teeth, and bark
Like a hound at these unspeakable slave girls.
But the reason I came…

Coritto:
Leave us now, and be off with you, schemers,
Made of nothing but ears, tongues and laziness!

Metro:
I beg you, dear Coritto, tell me the truth now;
Who was it stitched you the scarlet dildo?[186]

Coritto:
But Metro, where have you seen it?

Metro:
Erinna's daughter Nossis[187] had it a few days ago.
My goodness, what a lovely present that was!

Coritto:
Nossis? From whom did she get it?

Metro:
Will you get me in trouble if I tell?

Coritto:
By these sweet eyes, dear Metro, nobody will hear
One word you say from the mouth of Coritto.

Metro:
Eubule the wife of Bitas gave it to her, and said
That no one must know.

Coritto:
Women! This one will be the death of me someday.
She begged me incessantly, so taking pity on her,
I gave it before I had a chance to use it myself.
Then she snatches up the treat, and passes it on
To the wrong people. My dear, it's goodbye to her,
Such as she is, and let her find another friend.
Not if I had a thousand would I give up even one
To Nossis, Medoces' daughter – may Adrastea[188]
Overlook a woman's grumbling – no, not even
An old rotten one!

Metro:
Now, Coritto, don't let it get up your nose
The minute you hear a piece of bad news:
'An honest woman's duty is to endure all.'
But I am to blame for speaking of this; in fact,
I ought to have cut out my own tongue first!
Yet on that particular point I mentioned,
If you love me at all, tell me who stitched it.
Why do you give me that smile, and look as if
You don't know me? Why so coy about this?
I pray you Coritto, tell me no more lies, but
Give me his name.

Coritto:
My, what's all this fuss? Cerdon stitched it.

Metro:
But which Cerdon? For there are two of them.
One's that grey-eyed neighbour of Myrtiline,
Cylaethis' wife. But he couldn't stitch a plectrum![189]
The other lives near Hermodorus' lodgings,
On Broad Street. He was really something,
Till he got old. Dear departed Pylaethis
Had an affair with him, bless her memory.

Coritto:
As you say, Metro, it is neither of them. He
Hails from Chios or Erythrae, I don't know which.
He's bald and short – you'd say he was Prexinus,
For they look as much alike as two figs. And yet
You'll know it's not Prexinus when he speaks.
He works at home and sells his wares in secret,
For today every door shudders at the taxman.
But as for his work! You'd think Athena's hands
Had done it, not Cerdon's. He brought two, Metro,
And the minute I saw them my eyes popped.
Just between us two, no man's part is that firm,
And not only that, but silky smooth as a dream,
And the straps are more like wool than leather.
Search though you might, you'd never find
A more considerate shoemaker for a woman.

Metro:
But why then did you leave the other one?

Coritto:
I did all I could to persuade him, Metro –
I kissed him, patted his bald head, poured him
Sweet drinks, and called him by pet names.
The only thing I didn't give was my body.

Metro:
Even if he asked that, you should have agreed.

Coritto:
Yes, I should have, but it wouldn't do to be rude.
Bitas' wife Eubule was here grinding grain,
For day and night she wears out our millstone
To save a few obols on buying her own.

Metro:
And how did this fellow find his way here,
Dear Coritto? Tell me no lies.

Coritto:
Artemis, the wife of Candas the tanner
Pointed out our house and sent him here.

Metro:
Oh, Artemis is always up to something.
She puts the procuress Thallo to shame.
But since you couldn't purchase the pair,
I hope you asked who ordered the other one?

Coritto:
I begged him, but he swore he wouldn't tell.
It seems he had quite a crush on her, Metro.

Metro:
Then I must be off. Soon I shall visit Artemis,
And learn all about this Cerdon. Farewell,
Coritto, it's time I go feed my hungry husband.

Coritto:
Shut the door, you there, girl! Count the hens,
To see if they're safe, and toss them some food.
A bird-thief may rob a chick right from your lap.[190]

5.6 Asclepiades *Greek Anthology* 5.207. Mid-third century BCE. Asclepiades, a poet from Samos, is known as one of the early masters of Hellenistic erotic epigram and lyric.

Bitto and Nannion from Samos are not willing
To obey the goddess' rules when they visit Aphrodite;
They go astray and do what isn't right. Lady
Cypris, be hateful toward those who flee your bed.

5.7 Ovid *Metamorphoses* 9.702–97. 8 CE. In this episode from Ovid's mythological epic, a husband has commanded his pregnant wife Telethusa to have their child killed if it turns out to be a girl. Comforted by a vision of the goddess Isis, the mother saves the baby girl by passing her off as a son named Iphis.

Rising from bed, the woman joyfully prayed,
Stretching pure hands to the sky, that her vision be true.
When the pains brought her burden into the world,
And a girl was born without the father's knowledge,
The mother succeeded in passing her off as a boy,
And none knew the secret except the child's nurse.
The father repaid his vows and named the child

For Iphis, its grandfather, and the mother rejoiced,
That a name of common gender required no lies.
The tender falsehood was skillfully concealed;
The child's dress was male, and the child's face
Lovely, whether it belonged to boy or girl.
And so when thirteen years had passed, Iphis,
You were pledged by your father to blonde Ianthe,
Telestes' daughter, a maiden whose dowry of beauty
Was highly esteemed by all the women of Crete.
Equal in age and looks, the pair received
Childhood's lessons from the selfsame teachers.
In this way, young love touched both their hearts
And wounded both, yet how different their hopes!
Ianthe awaits the wedding torch and the pledge
Of union, believing her affianced spouse is a man.
Iphis loves where she has no hope of fulfillment,
But this only spurs her desire; girl burns for girl!
Near tears, she asks 'Where will it end for me,
Gripped by a strange new love, unknown to any?
If the gods wished me no ill, they should have spared me.
But if they desired my end, at least they ought
To have bestowed a natural and normal ruin.
Neither cow nor mare craves her own kind;
Ewes love rams, and each doe loves her stag.
So the birds mate, and in all the animal kingdom,
No female ever aches with desire for the feminine.
I wish I had never been born! Yet Crete knows many
Marvels, for the daughter of the Sun[191] loved a bull,
Manifestly a male. If we confess the truth,
My love is less sane, for she had hope of fulfillment.
The seductress won her bull in a heifer's guise!
Were every genius in the world to gather here,
If Daedalus[192] should return on his wings of wax,
Could he reverse my sex by his clever arts?
Or transform you, Ianthe? No, Iphis, be strong.
Compose yourself and shake off these useless fits
Of mindless, foolish passion. That you were born
A female is clear-- unless you delude yourself.
Do what is right, and love as a woman should!
It is hope that begets, hope that nurtures love,
And you have none. No watchful guardian,

No jealous husband or troublesome father obstructs
Her dear embrace, nor does the girl herself
Reject your love. Yet you cannot possess her,
Nor, though gods and men do all in their power,
Can you be happy. My prayers were not in vain;
The gods have willingly given me all they could.
Ianthe and both of our fathers have agreed.
But nature, stronger than they, withholds consent;
Nature alone impedes me. Now the day
Of our wedding is here, the day so long desired;
I shall have Ianthe, yet not possess her.
In the midst of a flooded stream, I shall be thirsty.
Why, oh Bridesmaid Juno, and Hymenaeus,[193]
Attend a rite with no bridegroom, but two brides?'
So she spoke. Ianthe is no less ardent,
And begs you, Hymenaeus, to speed your way,
While fearful Telethusa puts off the wedding,
First pretending illness, then pleading omens
And visions. But every excuse had now been used,
As the time for the wedding torch drew near.
Only one day remained. Drawing the chaplets
From her own and Iphis' head, she prayed
With loosened hair as she embraced the altar:
'Isis of Paraetonia, Mareota and Pharos,[194]
You who guard the seven-horned Nile,
I beg you, bring us help and heal our fears!
Once, goddess, I saw you and your signs;
I knew the sistrum[195] and the following throng,
And I was careful to mind all your commands.
Thus Iphis lives and I bear no punishment:
Behold, this is your counsel and your gift.
Have pity and aid us both!' Then she wept.
The goddess seemed to move, the altar shifted,
The doors of the temple shook; her crescent horns
Flashed like the moon and the sistrum loudly rattled.
Still uneasy, but gladdened at the omen,
She leaves the temple, and beside her Iphis walks
With strides longer than usual, and her skin
Darkens; her muscles expand, while her face
Grows less round, and her hair is plain and short.
The former woman's body is filled with strength;

Female no more, you have become a man!
Now free from fear, rejoice and offer gifts!
They offer gifts at the temple, and a tablet
On which they inscribe a single verse:
IPHIS THE MAN REPAYS VOWS MADE AS A WOMAN.
The next day dawns and brings a brighter world.
Venus, Juno and Hymenaeus arrive,
Torches gleam; and Iphis wins his Ianthe.

5.8 Seneca the Elder *Controversiae* 1.2.23. Ca. 30 CE. The participants in Seneca's conversation on rhetoric discuss the best way to deal with cases in which someone has been accused of sexual misconduct: orators should make their case forcefully but without recourse to vulgar or obscene remarks.

Scaurus[196] used to say that this fault [vulgarity] could be traced to the Greek declaimers, who stopped at nothing and won their cases. He said that once Hybreas[197] was delivering a declamation on a husband who caught two women having sex,[198] one of them his wife, and killed them both. He began by repeating the reaction of the husband (who should not have been forced to make such a shameful examination), saying: 'but I looked at the man first, to see whether he was natural or sewed on.'

5.9 Phaedrus *Fables* 4.16. Ca. 45 CE. In the earliest surviving collection of Aesop's fables, Phaedrus tells how Prometheus made a mistake when he was creating human beings.

Someone asked how women who love women[199]
And girlish males came to be. The old man
Explained: That very same Prometheus
Made them, who molded people from clay,
And was punished when he offended Zeus.
Once he spent all day shaping the parts
Which modesty hides, separately, so that
He might fit each set to the right bodies.
Then Liber[200] called him suddenly to dine,
Where his veins were flooded with nectar,
And home he went with tottering steps.
Then with drowsy mind, unsure from drink,
He pasted the maiden's part on the men,
And the man's part he placed on women.
Thus lust now enjoys improper pleasures.

5.10 Paul *Letter to the Romans* 1.22–32. Ca. 56 CE. Paul's letter to the Romans includes a vehement denunciation of those who refuse to recognise God's revealed truth and choose an earthly life over a spiritual one. For Paul, participation in homosexual acts is an expected outcome of such refusal.

Declaring that they were wise, they became fools, and exchanged the glory of the incorruptible God for what only resembled it, the image of a corruptible human being, and for creatures that fly, walk on four feet, and crawl. That is why, since their hearts were full of lustful desires, God handed them over to the unclean state of dishonouring their own bodies and those of others – they who exchanged the truth of God for a lie, and worshiped the created things rather than the creator, who is blessed for eternity, amen. That is why God handed them over to dishonourable passions, for the females exchanged the natural use of their bodies for one that was unnatural, and likewise the males, forsaking the natural use of the female, became inflamed with appetite for one another, male for male, cultivating obscene conduct and bringing upon themselves the due recompense for going astray. And when they did not see fit to live in the knowledge of God, he handed them over to a disreputable cast of mind, to improper behaviour, glutted with every form of wrongdoing, wickedness, arrogance, vice, and full of envy, murder, strife, evil habits; they became whisperers, slanderers, hated by God, insolent, arrogant, boastful, contrivers of evil things, disobedient to their parents, witless, faithless, heartless and pitiless. They know God's ordinances, and that whoever does these things is worthy of death, yet they not only practice them, but approve of others who do so.

5.11 Martial *Epigrams* 1.90 (ca. 86 CE), 7.67 (ca. 91 CE). Martial wrote a series of epigrams satirising the sexual and personal habits of others. Among his targets were women who had sex with other women.

1.90
I never saw you together with men, Bassa,
And not one rumour assigned you a lover.
Always women clustered about you,
Filling every need, with no man in sight.
Indeed, I considered you like Lucretia[201]
But in truth you were just a fucker.
You dare to join twin cunts together –
Your monstrous clit thinks it's a cock.
You pose a riddle worthy of the Sphinx:[202]
Adultery is here, but here is no man.

7.67

Philainis the dyke screws boys,
And bruises eleven girls a day,
More cruel than a horny husband.
She girds herself up to play handball,
Gets yellow with sand, and easily
Hefts weights too great for athletes.
Muddy from the wrestling ring
She's pummeled by an oiled trainer.
She neither reclines nor eats dinner
Till she's puked seven cups of wine,
And thinks it's good to drink more,
After disposing of ten thick steaks.
When this is done and she wants sex,
Sucking men isn't manly enough,
But she gladly gobbles up girl-parts.
Philaenis, may the gods keep you,
Who think it's manly to lick a cunt.

5.12 Plutarch *Life of Lycurgus* 18.4. Late first century CE. In his discussion of male pederasty in early Sparta, Plutarch mentions that a similar custom was practiced among the women.

The boys' lovers shared their reputations, for good or ill, and it is said that once when a boy uttered an ignoble cry during a fight, the archons penalised his lover. This type of love was so valued among them that even the nobly-born women took girls as lovers, yet there was no jealousy about it, but those who loved the same boys made this the foundation of their friendship, and worked together diligently with the goal of making the beloved boy into an excellent man.

5.13 Artemidorus of Daldis *Interpretation of Dreams* 1.80. Second century CE. Artemidorus' book provides a catalogue of dream events and what they portend for the dreamer.

If a woman dreams that she gratifies another woman, she will share her secrets with the woman she has gratified. But if she does not know the woman she has gratified, she will work at vain pursuits. If a woman dreams that she is gratified by another woman, she will be separated from her husband or widowed, and what is more, she will learn the secrets of the woman with whom she has had sex.

5.14 Magical Papyrus with binding spell. *PGM* 32. Second century CE. In this papyrus found in a cemetery in the Fayum region of Egypt, a woman Heraïs asks the spirit of the dead man Evangelos and the underworld gods to assist her by 'binding' the woman she desires.

I magically summon you, Evangelos, by Anubis and Hermes[203] and all the rest of the gods down below: bring and bind Sarapias whom Helen bore[204] to this Heraïs whom Thermoutharin bore, now, now, quickly, quickly. Bring Sarapias herself in her soul and heart, whom Helen bore in her own womb, *maei ote elbōsatok alaoubētō oeio* [...] *aēn*. Bring and bind the soul [and heart of Sarapias] whom [Helen] bore, to this Heraïs, whom Thermoutharin [bore] in her [womb], [now, now, quickly, quickly].

5.15 Tatian *Address to the Greeks* 33. Second century CE. A Christian from Syria, Tatian opened a school at Rome modelled on the philosophical schools. In his *Address to the Greeks*, he tries to demonstrate that Christian culture and moral habits are superior to those of pagans. An ascetic who rejected sexual activity of any kind, he was particularly hostile to Sappho.

Therefore I have been eager to prove, from the things that you consider deserving of honour, that our customs are sound and sober, whereas yours are close to utter madness. You, who say that we spread nonsense to the women and boys, to the girls and old women, and make a joke of us because we are not with you: hear how ridiculous the Greeks are. For the models you value are laughable, and you disgrace yourselves in matters to do with women. Lysippus cast a statue of Praxilla, who said nothing useful in her poems, and Menestratus one of Learchis, and Selanion one of Sappho the courtesan[205]...

[Tatian continues with the catalogue of women poets and the sculptors who portrayed them, listing fourteen women in all.]

My wish in bringing up these women is that you may not consider our ways strange, and that with these examples before your eyes for comparison, you may not make a joke of the women who pursue philosophy among us. This Sappho is a sex-mad little whore, and she sings about her own lewd acts. But all the women among us are chaste, and the maidens at their spinning sing songs about God in a manner more worthy than that girl of yours. Therefore you ought to be ashamed, you who make yourselves students of women, yet scoff at the women among us who have a role in governance, and their assemblies.

5.16 Lucian *Dialogues of the Courtesans* 5. Late second century CE. Lucian composed many witty and satiric dialogues, with interlocutors including the dead, the gods, and courtesans. This is one of the rare instances where the courtesans discuss sexual acts, and is one of the few places in Greek literature where sex between women is described.

Clonarion:
We hear some odd things about you, Leaena – that Megilla, the rich woman from Lesbos, loves you just like a man, and that you sleep together and do I don't know what with each other! What's this? Are you blushing? But tell me if it's true.

Leaena:
It's true, Clonarion. But I'm ashamed, because it's strange.

Clonarion:
By the nurturing goddess, what's going on? What does the woman want? And what do you do when you are together? See, you don't care for me or you would not hide such things.

Leaena:
I care for you as much as I do any other woman. But this woman is amazingly like a man.

Clonarion:
I don't understand what you mean, unless perhaps she is a woman-lover.[206] They say that there are women like that in Lesbos, who look like men, and they won't do it with men, but they have sex with women as though they themselves were men.

Leaena:
It's like that.

Clonarion:
Well, Leaena, tell me all about it – how she first came on to you, how you ended up agreeing to it, and what happened after that.

Leaena:
She was organising a drinking party with Demonassa, a Corinthian woman who is also rich and practices the same arts as Megilla. They brought me along to play the lyre. But when I had finished playing, and it was late and time to go to bed, and they were drunk, Megilla said 'Come on Leaena, it's high time we were in bed. Now sleep here between the two of us.'

Clonarion:
And did you sleep there? What happened after that?

Leaena:
At first they kissed me like men, not just putting their lips together with mine, but opening their mouths. And they embraced me and squeezed my breasts. Demonassa even bit me while she was kissing me, and I wasn't sure what to think of it. After a while Megilla got hot and took off her wig, which looked real and was a tight fit, and you could see that her head was shaved, just like the manliest of athletes. When I saw this, I was troubled, but she said, 'Leaena, have you ever seen such a good-looking young man?' 'But I don't see a young man, Megilla,' I said. 'Don't make me into a woman,' she said. 'I call myself Megillus and I married Demonassa here a long time ago. She's my wife.' I laughed at that, Clonarion, and said, 'So you are in fact a man and we didn't realise it, just like Achilles hidden among the maidens in his purple robes? And do you have what a man has?' 'I don't have that, Leaena, but I don't need it at all. I have my own way of getting together, a much better one, as you will see.' 'But you are not a hermaphrodite, are you,' I said, 'one of the people they say have both man's and woman's parts?' For I still didn't understand, Clonarion. And she answered, 'No, but I'm all man.' I said, 'I've heard the Boeotian flute-girl Ismenodora telling the fireside tales they have about how someone in Thebes was changed from woman to man, and he was also a very great prophet, I believe, by the name of Tiresias.[207] Nothing like that happened to you, did it?' 'No, Leaena,' she said, 'I was born female like the rest of you, but my thoughts and desires and everything else are those of a man.' 'And is desire all you need?' I asked. 'If you don't believe me, give me a chance,' she said, 'and you will learn that I'm as good as any man. I have a substitute for what a man has. Just give me a chance, and you'll see.'

Well, I gave her a chance, Clonarion, because she begged so much and gave me a very costly necklace and dresses of the finest linen. Then I threw my arms around her just as though she were a man, and she kissed me and then got busy, breathing hard, and seemed to enjoy it beyond anything.

Clonarion:
What did she do, and how, Leaena? You must tell me!

Leaena:
Don't ask for the details. It's a shameful thing, so by heaven I won't tell!

5.17 Tertullian *On the Pallium* 4.9. Early third century CE. Discussing his own decision to abandon the Roman toga in favour of the *pallium*, or philosopher's gown, Tertullian argues that changes to traditional dress are acceptable unless they offend nature or modesty.

Let us turn to women. You have only to look at what Caecina Severus[208] sternly impressed upon the Senate: the problem of matrons appearing in public without their formal robes.[209] In fact, according to the degree enacted under the augur Lentulus, the penalty for any women who had put themselves beyond the pale in this way was the same as for fornication. This was because certain women had zealously sought to bring an end to the wearing of these garments, the outward signs and guardians of respectability, because they were obstacles to their making prostitutes of themselves. But now they do in fact make a show of themselves as prostitutes, in order that men may identify and approach them more readily, by swearing off robes, scarves, shoes and hats, and even the litters and sedan chairs by which they used to be conveyed in privacy and discretion through public places. But one man closes his eyes, while another will not open his. Look at the harlots, those traffickers in public lust, and also at the women who have sex with each other.[210] Even though it is better to avert your eyes from the sight of chastity murdered in public by shameless women, nevertheless look higher, and now you will see matrons.

5.18 Tertullian *On the Resurrection of the Flesh* 16.6. Early third century CE. Tertullian argues that God's judgement is on both the soul and the flesh, and that both will be resurrected. As part of his argument, he uses the metaphor of a cup to describe the ways in which the flesh can be tainted by an individual's actions.

A cup is not condemned because someone has mixed poison in it; nor is a sword given over to the beasts because someone used it to commit a robbery. Therefore the flesh is innocent in so far as evil deeds are not attributed to it, and nothing prevents its salvation on the ground of innocence. Although the flesh is not responsible for good deeds (nor yet evil ones), still it better fits the beneficent divine to absolve the innocent. Doers of good deeds he must absolve, but it is characteristic of the greatest goodness to grant even more than is necessary. And yet, a cup – I do not mean a poisoned one into which some doomed person has spewed, but one contaminated with the breath of a woman who has sex with other women,[211] or a chief Gallus,[212] or a gladiator or an executioner – I wonder whether you could condemn it any less than kisses from these people.

Further Reading

For homoerotic themes in Alcman and Sappho, see the essays in Greene ed. 1996, Calame 1997 pp. 244–57, and Snyder 1997. For Nossis, see Skinner 2002. On the figure of the *tribas* at Rome, see the classic article by Hallett, most recently reprinted as Hallett 1997. On female same-sex love in Ovid, see Pintabone 2002 and Greene 2005. For Lucian's *Dialogues of the Courtesans*, see Haley 2002 and Gilhuly 2006. For the use of the dildo in Greek homoerotic contexts, see Rabinowitz 2002; and for the salacious portraits of women in Herodas' mimes, Finnegan 1992. For overviews of the evidence for female same-sex love in antiquity, see Brooten 1996 (focusing on the Christian period), and Rabinowitz and Auanger (eds) 2002. For Tatian's hostility toward Sappho, see Gaca 2003, pp. 235–8.

6

Philosophical and Medical Models of the Body and Sexuality

Greco-Roman thinkers and physicians derived their models in part from traditional beliefs, which lent support to existing assumptions about gender and power. As early as the eighth century, a folk tradition cited by Hesiod held that men were more susceptible than women to the drying influences of the summer heat, which affected their sexual vigour via the head and knees (6.1). Later, the Hippocratics (6.2) and Galen (6.14) taught that the production of semen, drawing on reserves of vital fluid from the entire body, has the potential to drain and enervate a man. Men had to be careful not to overindulge in sexual activity, for by doing so they ran the risk of depleting their *pneuma*, or vital spirit, an invisible substance contained in bodily fluids and equated with the life force (6.6, 6.14). Thus the ideology of masculine self-control, which justified male social and political dominance (6.10), dovetailed neatly with ancient medical theories.

Similarly, the doctors of the Hippocratic school perceived women's bodies as radically different from those of men, cold and moist where men were hot and dry. For Aristotle too, reproductive and other differences between men and women resulted from the colder nature of the female, for her coolness rendered her incapable of 'cooking' blood into semen as males do (6.6). Whereas the male provided the seed from which the new life would grow, the female provided the matter (blood/menstrual fluid) of which it would be composed. Aristotle considered the female body an inferior version of the male, yet like the Hippocratics allowed for the possibility of essential differences between female and male sexual response, physiology, and anatomical structures. Galen agreed that women's bodies were inferior because of their colder temperature, but took the idea in a different direction, developing a 'one sex' model according to which the female reproductive parts were an inverted and inferior version of the male (6.13).

On the controversial question of contributions to the reproductive process, Aristotle denied emphatically that women produce seed (6.6). Soranus, whose book *On Semen* is lost, says in his *Gynecology* that females produce a kind of seed, but that it does not contribute directly to the reproductive process, as it is excreted externally.[213] Instead, the male seed alone is 'taken up' by the uterus and develops into the fetus (6.12). Galen stood at the other end of the spectrum from Aristotle and agreed with the earlier Hippocratic doctors who taught that both sexes contributed seed to the offspring.[214]

Opinions about the role of pleasure in reproduction varied. The Hippocratic author of *On Generation* believed that female pleasure in intercourse was less intense than that of the male (6.2), though in both the male and female, pleasure was associated with the release of fluids. Galen and Soranus (6.12) taught that a woman could not conceive unless she took pleasure in the act of intercourse or at least possessed the bodily urge for it, whereas Aristotle was aware that female pleasure was a more complex matter and independent of conception (6.6).

While recommending that men use moderation in the enjoyment of sex, most ancient medical authorities agreed that sexual intercourse was necessary for female health. According to the Hippocratics, regular intercourse kept the womb in good working order and ensured the proper flow of menstrual fluid. When retained, this fluid could putrefy and lead to madness and suicidal tendencies (6.3), particularly in young women who had not yet married. Soranus was an iconoclast in this respect, insisting that abstention led to better outcomes for a woman's health and basing his argument on observations of spayed sows, and priestesses who were required to abstain from sex for ritual reasons (7.14). While the Classical Greeks subscribed to the idea that the uterus was a mobile organ and that its independent movements caused a host of physical problems in women (6.4), by Alexandrian times the practice of dissection had shown that the uterus was held in place by ligaments and could not move, for example, into the chest.

Philosophers of the Classical and early Hellenistic periods adopt a positive attitude toward pederasty, which they associate with education and friendship rather than sexual gratification. Plato is the best-known exponent of this position, and he advocates celibate friendships as the ideal (4.7). Notwithstanding their views on the need to control the passions, the early Stoics taught that the wise man experiences *erōs*; he will devote himself to a friendship with a young person who possesses personal beauty (6.15 on Zeno; compare Aristotle in 2.12). The Stoic founder Zeno, in particular, was said to be an enthusiastic pederast.[215] The Stoics also interpreted the ancient concept of the sacred marriage allegorically in their cosmological theory. Chrysippus (6.16), another early Stoic, described a painting of Hera performing fellatio on Zeus as the reception of the seeds of order by the unformed matter of the universe, while Dio Chrysostom (6.11) evoked an awe-inspiring vision of the Mind of the cosmos (Zeus) penetrating matter (Hera) in the form of a thunderbolt. The Epicureans, on the other hand, tended to reject *erōs* as a harmful passion (6.8, 6.15 on Epicurus). More accepting of sexual pleasure than his philosophical master Epicurus, the Roman Lucretius notably depicts heterosexual intercourse as an activity characterised by mutual desire and pleasure (6.9). Emphasising the dangers inherent in amorous passion, however, he advises his male audience to avoid falling in love if possible. While sexual feelings were normal for both men and women, overindulgence led to physical, emotional, and financial ruin.

Some philosophers discouraged sex for purposes other than procreation, arguing that sex for pleasure was 'unnatural' and emphasising the traditional virtues of moderation (*sōphrosynē*) and self-control (*enkrateia*). In Plato's late work, the *Laws*, the Athenian speaker adopts this view (6.5), proposing that in an ideal state, both peer pressure and the legal system should be used to discourage any sexual activity not leading to orderly procreation within heterosexual marriage. He envisions a society in which homosexual acts, prostitution and even masturbation are condemned in the same way as incest. The Stoic Musonius Rufus focused less on societal change and more on the moral responsibility of the individual to keep his or her activity in conformity with (unwritten) natural and (written) human law (6.10). Musonius Rufus critiques prevailing cultural assumptions about the sexual status of slaves, insisting that men who use their slave women for sex are acting in an unlawful fashion and that they lack the all-important virtue of self-control. The Jewish philosopher Philo of Alexandria similarly emphasised the need to kerb sexual pleasures. In his explanation of the Jewish custom of circumcision for a pagan audience, he avoided the scriptural explanation that circumcision was the outward sign of God's covenant with the Jewish people in favour of alternative explanations that were more compatible with Greek cultural values. He provides the first known explanation of circumcision as a hygienic procedure, and sees circumcision as a symbol of philosophical virtues such as indifference to bodily suffering and the ability to control physical appetites.

The argument from 'nature', invoked by Plato and Musonius Rufus to justify societal strictures on sexual behaviour, could also be used to justify a variety of sexual urges as normal and acceptable when indulged in moderation, a view that Aristotle seems to have adopted (6.7). Moreover, it could be pushed much further in order to weaken cultural limits on sexual behaviour and to support the position that natural urges should be satisfied without shame or punishment. The Cynic philosopher Diogenes advocated the free exchange of sexual partners according to personal preference, and taught that there was no shame in satisfying bodily urges, even in public (6.15 on Diogenes).

6.1 Hesiod *Works and Days* 582–8. Eighth century BCE. In folk wisdom, the summer heat caused women's sexual desires to increase, while men's vigour as lovers was decreased. This lassitude was caused by the drying-up of the fluids in the head and knees, thought to be areas important for the production of semen.

But when the thistle flowers and the trilling cicada
Perches in a tree pouring down a high-pitched song
From under his wings, all day in the wearisome heat,
Then goats are at their fattest and wine is best,
And women are most lustful, but men are weak,
For Sirius[216] dries them up in head and knees.

6.2 Hippocrates *On Generation* 1.1–3, 4 Joly. Late fifth century BCE. Followers and students compiled the large collection of works attributed to Hippocrates. None has been proven to the work of Hippocrates himself, though most date from the fifth and fourth centuries BCE.

1.1–3
Law governs everything. A man's semen comes from all the fluid in the body, and it is the strongest part that is separated out. The evidence that the strongest part is separated is that when we have sexual relations, even though we release only a small amount of semen, we become tired. Here is the way things are: veins and sinews extend from every part of the body to the penis; when these are rubbed, and heated, and filled, a kind of tickling feeling results, which brings about pleasure and warmth in the whole body. As the penis is rubbed through the movement of the man's body, the moisture in the body is heated, diffused, and churned by the motion and it becomes foamy, just as all other fluids become foamy when they are churned. Just in this way, in a person the strongest and fattiest part is separated from the foaming fluid, and passes into the marrow of the spine. For passages extend to the spine from all parts of the body, and there is diffusion from the brain to the groin and over all the body, and the spinal marrow, and there are passages extending from the spine so that fluid can enter and exit. When the semen arrives at the spinal marrow, it passes to the kidneys, for here there is a passage through the veins, and if there is ulceration in the kidneys, it sometimes happens that blood flows along with the semen. From the kidneys, it passes through the middle of the testicles to the penis, not where the urine passes, but by another channel which is there. And

those who have wet dreams do so for the following reasons: when the fluid in the body becomes very diffused and heated either through fatigue or for some other reason, it becomes foamy, and when it is being separated out, there comes to one's mind a vision of sexual activity; the fluid acts the same as during actual sex. But I am not concerned with dreams, nor yet with this disorder in general, nor its effects, nor why it takes the place of an orgasm...

4.1–3

I assert that when a woman's vagina is rubbed and her womb is agitated, a kind of tickling feeling results and provides feelings of pleasure and warmth to these and other parts of the body. The woman also releases fluid from the body, sometimes into the womb, so that the womb becomes moist, and sometimes outside the body, when the entrance of the womb gapes open too far. She feels pleasure during intercourse from the beginning, and the entire time until the man releases her. But if she has an orgasm during intercourse, she releases fluid before the man does and no longer feels the same pleasure. If she does not have an orgasm, she ceases to feel pleasure at the same time the man does. It is as though one pours cold water into boiling water: the water ceases to boil. In the same way, when the semen falls from the man into the womb, it extinguishes both the heat and the pleasure of the woman. The pleasure and the heat both flare up when the semen falls into the womb, and then they subside. Just as when someone pours wine onto a flame, and the flame initially flares up and is increased for a short time by the pouring of the wine, and then subsides, so in a woman the heat flares up in response to the man's semen, and then subsides. In intercourse, a woman's pleasure is far less than a man's, but lasts longer. The man experiences more pleasure because the separation from the fluid occurs more suddenly for him and by means of a stronger disturbance than in the woman. The following is also the case for women: if they have intercourse with men, they are healthier, and if they do not, they are less healthy. For the womb becomes moist with intercourse and not dry; when the womb is too dry, it contracts violently, and this powerful contraction causes pain. At the same time, by heating the blood and making it more fluid, intercourse facilitates the passage of the menstrual flow. Now, when the menstrual flow does not pass, the bodies of women become ill. Why they become ill, I will discuss in *Diseases in Women*. That is all I have to say on this subject.

6.3 Hippocrates *On Diseases of Virgins* 8.468 Littré. Late fifth century BCE. The author describes the symptoms that ensue when the flow of menstrual blood is blocked and backs up into the heart and diaphragm.

When these things happen, girls are maddened by the pain of the inflammation, they become murderous as a result of the putrefaction, they are terrified and made fearful by the darkness, and as a result of the pressure on their hearts, they hang themselves. Because of the foulness of the blood, the mind is pained and sorely distressed, and draws evils to itself. Even terrible ideas it calls by another name, and these ideas command the girl to wander, and to throw herself into a well or hang herself, as though such actions were preferable and advantageous in every way. Even when the visions abate, the girl experiences a certain pleasure, which causes her to desire death, as though it were a good thing. When this person regains her senses, the women dedicate to Artemis the most expensive of women's garments and other things also on the advice of the seers, but they are deceived. For relief from this condition comes when the menstrual blood is not impeded from flowing out. When young girls suffer with this problem, I instruct them to cohabit with husbands as soon as possible. For if they become pregnant, they are healthy. If not, either when puberty arrives or soon after they will fall prey to this illness, if not some other one. And among wives who have sex regularly, the barren ones are susceptible to this illness.

6.4 Plato *Timaeus* 91b-d. Ca. 360 BCE. This famous passage describes the 'wandering womb', a traditional concept that was to have a long afterlife in Western medical thought.

Therefore in men, the nature of the genital organ is disobedient and willful, like an animal that is not amenable to reason, and spurred on by its desires, it tries to dominate everything. And again in a woman, for the same reasons, the matrix or what is called the womb is a creature within her that desires the procreation of children. Whenever it remains unfruitful long past the right time, it does not bear this well and becomes irritated. Wandering in all directions through the body and stopping up the airways, it interferes with breathing, causing extreme distress and all sorts of other illnesses until desire and love unite the two sexes.

6.5 Plato *Laws* 838a–841a. Ca. 340 BCE. In this excerpt from Plato's late work, the character called the Athenian advocates social limitations on sexual behaviour.

Athenian:
We know that at present most men, even if they are lawbreakers, are prevented in a very effective way from having sex with certain beautiful people, and that this is not against their will, but very much according to their wishes.

Megillus:
When do you mean?

Athenian:
Whenever a man has a beautiful brother or sister. And for sons and daughters too, the same unwritten law is quite sufficient to prevent men from sleeping with them either openly or in secret, or otherwise to embrace and fondle them. Indeed, desire for this sort of sex never comes at all to most men.

Megillus:
That is true.

Athenian:
Isn't it the case, then, that a brief message extinguishes all such desires?

Megillus:
What sort of message do you mean?

Athenian:
The message that these acts are in no way permitted by divine law, but hateful to the gods, and the most shameful of shameful acts. And isn't the reason for this that nobody speaks of them otherwise, but that from the day of our birth, each of us hears this being said always and everywhere, not only in comedies but also often in serious tragedy, whenever some Thyestes or Oedipus comes onstage, or Macareus secretly having sex with his sister,[217] and these characters are clearly ready to kill themselves, as the just punishment for their wrongdoing?

Megillus:
You are quite right to say this much: that public opinion is surprisingly powerful, since no one tries in any way whatsoever to breathe a word against this law.

Athenian:
Then isn't what I said just now true, that when a lawgiver wishes to subjugate one of those desires that especially enslave people, it is easy at least to determine in what way he should go about it? That is, he should cause this opinion to be hallowed in the eyes of all alike, slave and free, children and women, and the entire state. In this way he will establish the law most securely.

Megillus:
Certainly. But how will he ever be able to bring it about that everyone is willing to say such a thing?

Athenian:
You ask a good question. This is the reason for what I said before: that with regard to this law, I have a method for engaging in reproductive sex in a way that is

consistent with nature – on the one hand, abstaining from sex with males, and not deliberately killing the human stock, or sowing seed on rocks and stones, where it can never become firmly rooted and have fruitful growth, and on the other hand, by abstaining from every female field in which you would not want the seed to grow. Once this law has been recognised continuously for a long time, if it prevails in other areas, just as it has now with respect to intercourse with one's parents, it brings about innumerable benefits. First of all, it is in agreement with nature, so it prevents sexual rage and madness and all sorts of adultery, and all overindulgence in food and drink, and it causes husbands to be properly affectionate toward their own wives. Many other benefits would result, if this law could prevail. Perhaps, though, some high-spirited youth who is standing by, full of sexual vigour,[218] on hearing of the promulgation of this law would revile us for passing legislation that is foolish and impossible, and would fill the air with shouting. With this possibility in view, I said that I possessed a method, which is at the same time both the easiest and the most difficult of all methods, to ensure the permanence of this law once it is passed. For while it is easy to perceive how this is possible and by what means – since we assert that once this rule is sufficiently hallowed, it will subjugate every soul and because of their dread, people will obey absolutely once the law is enacted – yet it has now come about that people think this would not happen. In just the same way, they disbelieve that the whole state can flourish while permanently instituting common meals, and they say this in spite of the fact that such meals exist in your countries, although even among you it is considered unnatural for women to participate. Because of the strength of this disbelief, I said before that it is extremely difficult to have such laws enacted permanently.

Megillus:
What you said was correct.

Athenian:
In order to show that it is not beyond the ability of people to achieve this, but that it is possible, would you like me to attempt a plausible argument?

Clinias:
Certainly.

Athenian:
Then, is someone more likely to abstain from sexual pleasures and to duly comply with this ordinance, if he keeps himself in good physical condition, not neglecting exercise, or if he is in poor shape?

Clinias:
He will comply much more readily if he is not in poor shape.

Athenian:
Haven't we heard about Iccus of Tarentum[219] and his contests at Olympia and elsewhere, how because of his love of winning, his skill, and the combination of courage and wisdom in his soul, they say that he never touched either a woman or a boy during the whole period of his training? And they say the same thing about Crison and Astylus and Diopompus and very many others. And yet, Clinias, not only were these men less well educated with respect to their souls than your citizens and mine, but also their bodies possessed a greater sexual appetite.

Clinias:
Yes, the ancient authors confidently state that this is what happened with these athletes.

Athenian:
Well, then, if they could bear to abstain from an activity that most men consider a source of great happiness, and all for the sake of victory in wrestling, running and the like, won't our boys be able to endure this in pursuit of a much more noble victory? The noblest of all victories, as we will beguile them into believing, by telling them tales and proverbs and singing them songs starting in early childhood.

Clinias:
What victory is that?

Athenian:
The victory over pleasures. If they exercise control over these, their lives will be happy, but if they yield to them, very much the opposite. And furthermore, will not the dread of doing that which is utterly in contradiction to divine law give them the ability to master what lesser men have mastered?

Clinias:
That is likely.

Athenian:
Now that we have come to this point regarding the rule, but have run into difficulties because of the cowardice of the many, I assert that our rule must simply proceed on the strength of the argument that our citizens ought not to be inferior to the birds and many other wild animals that are born in large broods, but live pure and untouched without sexual union, until they arrive at the age for breeding, and then they pair off, male with female and female with male, as they are attracted to one another. From that point on, they live

in a way that is holy and just, remaining faithful to their first commitment of affection. Our citizens must at least be better than these animals. But if they are corrupted by most of the other Greeks and the barbarians, seeing and hearing that among them, the so-called 'lawless Aphrodite' has great power, and thus they are unable to overcome that power, then our Guardians of the Laws must become Lawgivers, and devise for them a second law.

Clinias:
What law do you advise them to enact, if the one now in place slips away from them?

Athenian:
Clearly, Clinias, it should be the law that comes second to this one.

Clinias:
What do you mean?

Athenian:
That we should weaken the force of pleasure through disuse, by directing its influx and nourishment to other parts of the body through physical labour. This could happen, if shame were attached to sexual pleasure. For if people engaged in it only rarely, because they felt ashamed, they would find it a less powerful mistress as a result of this rarity. So let discretion in these acts be considered a good thing, a usage upheld by both custom and unwritten law, and let lack of discretion be shameful, but not total abstention. Thus we will have a second law regarding what is shameful and honourable, which comes second in its degree of righteousness. And individuals of corrupt character, whom we describe as 'inferior to themselves',[220] and who all belong to the same type, will be forced by three different means not to break the law.

Clinias:
By what means?

Athenian:
By respect for the gods, love of honour, and desire for beautiful souls rather than beautiful bodies. What I am describing now may seem like an unattainable dream, but if only it could come true, it would certainly be the best thing for every state. And soon, if God grants it, we might compel people to comply with one of two rules regarding sexual matters: either that no man should dare to touch anyone who is of good birth and freeborn except his own wedded wife, nor sow any unworthy or bastard seed in mistresses, nor again any unfruitful

seed by unnatural association with males. Or the law could say that we do away entirely with sexual relations between males, and as for women, if a man has sex with any woman who comes to his house except with the sanction of the gods and holy matrimony, whether she is a slave or has been acquired by some other means, if that act is detected by anyone, man or woman, we would likely consider it right for the lawgivers to decree that such a man be excluded from civic commendations, as one who is in fact an alien. So whether we call this one law or two, let it be enacted regarding sexual pleasures.

6.6 Aristotle *Generation of Animals* 727b–728a (selections), 737a. Mid to late fourth century BCE. In Aristotle's biological works, he considers human bodies side by side with animal bodies.

727b–728a (selections)
Here is an indication that the female does not release semen in the way that the male does, and that there is not, as some say, a mixture of semen from both: often the female becomes pregnant even though she has had no pleasure from the act of intercourse. And conversely it is no less true that when male and female derive pleasure equally, she does not bear offspring unless a suitable amount of so-called menstrual fluid is present...

There are those who think that the female contributes semen during intercourse because females sometimes take nearly as great a delight in it as males, and because this occurs together with a fluid secretion. This fluid does not contain seed, and depends on the specific body part in each woman; a discharge from the uterus happens in some women but not in others. Generally speaking, it happens in fair-skinned, feminine women and does not happen in dark, masculine-looking women. In those who have it, this emission is sometimes different from a male's semen in that there is far more of it. Furthermore, differences in diet also greatly affect whether there is less or more of it; for example, some pungent foods cause a noticeable increase in the amount. The pleasure that comes with intercourse is due not only to the release of semen, but also to the release of vital spirit, the collection of which results in ejaculation. This is evident in boys who cannot yet emit semen, although they are near the age, and in men who are infertile, for they all take pleasure in sexual stimulation...

A boy's shape resembles a woman's, and a woman is like an infertile male; in fact, a creature is female as a result of a disability: not being able to cook the nourishment in its final state (either blood, or its counterpart in bloodless animals) into semen, because of the coldness of its nature...

A sign that the female does not release semen is the fact that during the contact of intercourse, pleasure is produced in the same place as for males, and yet the liquid is not emitted from there.[221]

737a

Because semen is a residue and possesses the same property of movement by means of which the body grows and partakes of the ultimate nourishment, whenever it arrives in the womb, it 'sets' the female residue and imparts the same property of movement that it possesses. For the female contribution is a residue, and potentially contains all the parts of the body, but in actuality none. Potentially, it includes those parts of the body by which the female is distinguished from the male. Just as deformed parents sometimes produce deformed offspring and sometimes not, a female sometimes produces a female, and sometimes a male. This is because the female is like a deformed male, and menstrual discharge is semen, but in an impure state. There is only one thing that it lacks, the principle of Soul. And this is why, in those animals that produce wind-eggs,[222] the egg is constituted with parts of both sexes, but it lacks this principle, and thus it does not become a living thing. This is the contribution of the male's semen. And whenever the female residue partakes of this principle, conception occurs.

6.7 Aristotle *Nicomachean Ethics* 1118a 8–9. Mid to late fourth century BCE. Aristotle discusses the sense of touch, which includes eating and sexual activity, and classifies types of desire.

Moderation and lack of self-discipline thus have to do with the pleasures that are held in common with other animals, and that is why these pleasures seem slavish and bestial, namely, the pleasures of taste and touch. But even taste seems to play little or no role, since it has to do with the discrimination of flavours, as when people taste wine or prepare seasoned dishes. They do not delight in these precisely, or at least undisciplined people do not, but in the contact itself, which is all to do with the sense of touch, in eating and drinking alike, and also in what are called the pleasures of Aphrodite. This is why a certain gourmand prayed that his gullet would become longer than a crane's, because it was the contact that he enjoyed. Thus lack of self-discipline has to do with the sense that is most universal, that of touch, and it seems appropriate that this sense is considered highly suspect, since we partake of it not as human beings but as animals. Therefore it is brutish to delight in and welcome the pleasures of touch in excess. The noblest versions of this pleasure, such as rubdowns and warm baths in the gymnasium, are exempted, for the tactile pleasure of the undisciplined person has to do not with the whole body, but with certain parts.

There are two kinds of desires, those common to all, and those that are specific and acquired. For instance, the desire for nourishment is natural, since everyone in need of solid food or drink desires one of these, and sometimes both. And a young man in his prime has a desire for sex, as Homer says.[223] But not everyone desires this or that type of nourishment, nor does everyone like the same food. Therefore this desire seems to be specific to us as individuals. But this is also something natural, for different things taste good to different people, and some delicacies are tastier to everyone than everyday foods.

6.8 Epicurus *Sententiae Vaticanae* 51 Muehll. Late fourth or early third century BCE. Epicurus' advice to a follower on the subject of sex.

I hear from you that excitement of the flesh has resulted in a strong disposition toward the pleasures of sexual intercourse. As long as you do not contravene laws, or disturb well-established customs, or bring grief to people around you, or ruin your health, or squander your property, you may indulge your inclination as you wish. But in fact there is no way to avoid every one of these pitfalls. For sexual pleasure never did anyone good, and it is a lucky thing if it does no harm.

6.9 Lucretius *On the Nature of Things* 4.1037–1208. Ca. 60 BCE. A follower of Epicurus, Lucretius adopts in this didactic poem a rationalist view of sexuality and love, describing the physical processes that lead to desire and their psychological and social consequences.

As I said before, the seed is stirred in us
When first as adults our bodies grow strong.
For different causes provoke varied results;
One force calls forth the human seed in man.
As soon as it is cast forth from its place,
It departs the limbs and the body entire,
Gathering in a certain part of the groin
And rouses directly the genitals themselves;
Inflamed, they swell with seed and exert
The will, in straining toward awful desire.
What has wounded the mind, the body seeks,
For each is subject to its wound, as blood
Spurts toward the stroke that caused the cut,
And reddens the enemy who is close at hand.
Thus he who is hit by the shafts of Venus,
Whether cast by boys with lovely limbs,
Or women whose entire bodies dart love,
Strains and exults to join what has hit him,
And eject the fluid drawn from his frame.
For that speechless craving foretells pleasure.
This we call Venus; here Love gets its name.

This sweet droplet of Love distilled
In the heart is soon replaced by chill care,
For even absent, the beloved form is seen
And the sweet name is heard in the ear.
It is right to dispel such images, drive
Away Love's food, turn the mind elsewhere,
And expel the gathered fluid among many,
Rather than hoard it for one love alone,
Ensuring cares and sorrows for yourself;
For the sore grows deeper by daily feeding,
And the madman finds his labours heavier,
Unless he counters the fresh wound with new
Strokes, and follows Venus as she wanders,
Or can direct his passion to other ends.
Nor does he who shuns Love lack Venus'
Benefits; rather he avoids their penalty.
Sexual pleasure is greater for the hale
Than for the sick at heart. At the moment
Of union, lovers' passion is indecisive;
They don't know what to see and touch first.
They seek and grasp some part, causing pain,
Or clamp teeth on lips too often as they plant
Kisses, because the pleasure is not unmixed,
And they feel an urge to harm the very thing
Which gives rise to their frenzied desire.
But Venus' gentle touch redeems the price,
And pleasure soothes the sting during Love.
For their hope is that the body they desire
Will quench the very flames it ignited.
But in Nature they find utter opposition:
The more we satisfy this one desire,
The more it burns dreadfully within us.
For our bodies take in food and drink,
Which since they abide in certain parts,
Easily fill the need for water and bread.
But from the human face and lovely form
Our bodies enjoy nothing but an image,
A poor empty thing dispersed by the wind.
As a man in dreams strives to quench thirst,
But receives no water to cool his limbs,
And vainly pursues the mirage of moisture,
Thirsting even as he swallows amid a flood,

So Venus deceives lovers with empty shadows.
They cannot sate desire by gazing face to face
Nor rub matter from the beloved's tender limbs,
As their hands wander fitfully over the body.
At last with limbs entwined they enjoy the bloom
Of youth, now as their bodies foretell delights
And Venus is here to sow the womanly fields,
They lock themselves together and eagerly
Mingle saliva and breath, pressing lips on teeth.
To no purpose, for nothing can rub off,
Nor penetrate body wholly within body,
For this is what they seem to struggle to do.
So locked by desire in Venus' embrace
Their limbs melt with powerful pleasure.
When at last the desire gathered in the groin
Is spent, the raging flame briefly abates.
But the fury returns and that frenzy comes
Again, when they crave and long for the touch,
And lack any device to conquer their illness.
Perplexed, they waste away from hidden wounds.
To this add wasted strength and deathly toils,
And a youth spent at the service of another;
Duties languish, while their good name staggers.
Meanwhile estates dissolve in costly Babylonian
Scent, and pretty shoes from Sicyon sparkle
On her feet; while, no doubt, great green emeralds
Glow in gold, and sea-blue gowns are frayed
With overuse, and drink the sweat of busy
Venus. Ancestral lands are no more, changed for
Bands, scarves and cloaks from the isle of Cea.
Dinners with finest food and linen, games,
Glassware, perfume, and wreaths are supplied,
In vain, since amid this fountain of pleasures,
Despite the flowers, grows a drop of bitterness
Or the guilty mind gnaws harshly at itself,
Regretting years lost to slothful indulgence.
Her verbal darts may give rise to a doubt,
Fixed and burning in his longing heart;
Or she gazes far too much at other men
And he sees a trace of laughter in her face.
These ills are found in lasting and prosperous love;
But when love grows hateful and needy,

You can see endless troubles with eyes closed.
So best to be watchful before it happens,
And guard against temptation by the method
I've shown. Far easier to avoid the snares
Of Love than to escape the net once caught
And burst from the tight knots of Venus.
Yet with feet entangled, escape can be had
From harm, unless it's you who block the way,
Overlooking every fault of mind and body
In the woman you seek out and prefer.
For people blinded by desire often do thus,
Assigning virtues their loves do not possess.
Thus we see the ugly and misshapen
Thriving as their lovers' honoured darlings.
They chuckle at others and counsel indulgence
Since their friends are afflicted by foul Loves;
Ignoring all the while their own disasters.
The dark skinned girl's 'like honey', the filthy
One is 'au naturel', the cat-eyed is 'Athena',
The nervous and flighty is 'gazelle-like'.
The short girl is 'one of the Graces', the dwarf
Is 'zestful', the big and clumsy is 'impressive',
The stutterer 'lisps' and the mute's 'modest'.
The annoying chatterbox is 'bright and witty',
The scrawny scarecrow is a 'slender gamine'
The one half-dead from coughing is 'delicate'
And the top-heavy is 'Ceres suckling Iacchus'.[224]
A pug-nosed girl is 'a female Silenus',[225]
And the fat-lipped one is 'utterly kissable'.
It would be too long a task to tell them all.
But even though her face be lovely as you like,
And the charm of Venus rise from her limbs,
Pretty girls abound, and you survived before
You met her. Yes, and we know she does the same
As the ugly girl, anointing her wretched self
With vile perfume, while her maids stand away
And secretly titter, and the tearful lover, shut out,
Covers the threshold with garlands of flowers,
Paints the proud doorposts with marjoram oil,
And wretchedly kisses the doors. If he got in,
And was hit by one whiff, he'd make his excuses
To flee, dropping his long-planned speeches.

Then he would curse his stupid self, and see
That he placed her higher than mortals should sit.
Our Venuses know this, and therefore they try
With every art to hide the life behind the scenes
From those they wish to hold in bonds of Love.
In vain, since by reason you can drag it all to light
And uncover the secrets that cause those smiles.
And if she is charming and kind, in return
Let it pass and yield to the human condition.
Neither does woman always feign love's sighs,
When she joins her body to man's embrace,
Wetting their kisses with lips pressed tight,
For often she acts from the heart, and seeking joys
In common, urges him on to run Love's course.
This is why the birds, the cattle, wild beasts,
Flocks of ewes and mares submit to the male,
For their nature is lustful and their plentiful heat
Gladly takes on the partners as they mount.
Do you see how even those who share pleasure
Are tortured and bound in a strong embrace,
How dogs in the crossroads attempt to separate
And eagerly strain with all their might to part,
When Venus has joined them with powerful bonds?
Not so, if they had never felt the mutual joys
Which caught and held them tight in chains.
Therefore I say again, the pleasure is shared.

[Lucretius continues (1209–77) with a discussion of infertility. This is caused by incompatibility between the man's semen, which may be too thick or thin, and the woman's seed and womb. He describes vaginal intercourse from the rear as the position most advantageous for conception.]

6.10 Philo of Alexandria *The Special Laws* 1.1–2. Early to mid-first century CE. The Jewish philosopher and biblical exegete Philo attempted to harmonise the Jewish scriptures (known to him primarily through the Greek Septuagint) with Stoic philosophy.

I will begin with a topic that many people find laughable, for they ridicule the circumcision of the genitals. Many other nations zealously observe this practice, and in particular the Egyptians, who are considered the most populous, ancient, and wisdom-loving of nations. Therefore, it would befit the critics to cease their childish mockery, and pursue a more thoughtful and serious inquiry into the reasons for the prevalence of this custom, instead of prematurely adopting a prejudice against the great nations who are in fact displaying fortitude. The critics ought to reason that since thousands in every generation undergo the operation, themselves suffering this painful and difficult severing of a body part and having it performed on their family members, that many reasons support the continued performance of that which was introduced by the ancients. The four principal reasons are as follows. One is that it delivers men from that painful disease of the foreskin, difficult to heal, which they call 'hot coals', I believe, from that smouldering inflammation it causes, and to which men who keep their foreskins are more susceptible. Second, it improves the cleanliness of the entire body, which is appropriate for men consecrated to priesthoods, and that is why the Egyptians carry this idea even further, shaving the bodies of their priests. For certain substances that need to be cleaned away collect gradually and inconspicuously in both the hair and the foreskin. Third, it makes the circumcised member more like the heart. For both are made for the purpose of generation, since the vital spirit in the heart generates thoughts, and the reproductive organ generates living creatures. That is why the earliest men determined that the visible and apparent member, through which things perceived by the senses come into being, should be made similar to the unseen and superior faculty through which thoughts are organised. The fourth and most compelling reason is that it increases fertility, for it is said that it keeps the semen on the right path, without scattering or dripping into the folds of the foreskin. That is apparently why the nations who practice circumcision are the most prolific and populous.

These are the reasons that have been handed down to us, through the efforts of inspired men who studied the ancient lore and made profound inquiries into the writings of Moses. To these I add that I consider circumcision to be symbolic of two most cogent principles. One is the cutting away of pleasures that bewitch the mind. Among the spells that draw us toward pleasure, sexual intercourse between a man and a woman surpasses all others. That is why the lawgivers decided to dock the organ that ministers to such intercourse, expressing figuratively that by circumcision we must circumscribe pleasure that is excessive and out of bounds, and not this one alone, but all the others too that are represented by this most overpowering of pleasures. The other reason is that a man ought to know himself, and to thrust from his soul the grievous disease of self-conceit. For some have congratulated themselves on their ability to produce, like talented sculptors, a human being, that most beautiful of living things. Swollen with boastfulness, they have deified themselves, ignoring the fact that God is the true cause of all that exists, even though they could correct their delusion by looking at their neighbours. For among them are many men who cannot beget children, and many infertile women, whose acts of intercourse are fruitless, and who grow old without offspring. This evil idea, then, needs to be cut out from the mind, along with any other ideas that are deficient in the love of God.

6.11 Musonius Rufus 12 (*Concerning Sexual Pleasures*) Lutz. Mid-first century CE. Known as the 'Roman Socrates', Musonius Rufus was a Stoic philosopher who focused on ethics and practical advice for daily life.

Sexual pleasure forms no small part of the luxurious life. Those who live in luxury feel a need for a variety of lovers, lawful as well as unlawful, female as well as male. They hunt now for one object of love, now for the next, and unsatisfied with those who are available, they aim for those who are difficult of access, and seek out obscene forms of embrace; all of these things are serious reproaches to humanity. Those who do not pursue a life of luxury and evil ought to consider sexual pleasure justified only in the context of marriage, when it is undertaken in order to beget children, since this is lawful, but unjust and unlawful when it is pursued purely for the sake of pleasure, even in marriage. Of other types of embraces, those involving adultery are the most unlawful, and those involving two males are no more tolerable, because they are bold trans-gressions against nature. Even aside from adultery, intercourse with women that is contrary to law is in every case shameful and is practiced because of a lack of self-discipline. Therefore no man of moderation could abide relations with a courtesan, or with a free woman outside of marriage, no, not even with his own maidservant. Because these sexual relationships are not lawful or proper, they are a great shame and reproach to men who seek them. No one is comfortable doing such things openly, even if he scarcely has the ability to blush, and those who are not completely lost to decency dare to do such things only secretly and behind closed doors. And yet, attempting to conceal an act is itself an acknowledgement of wrongdoing. 'Yes indeed,' someone may say, 'but unlike an adulterer who wrongs the husband when he corrupts the wife, someone who has sex with a courtesan or indeed, an unmarried woman does no wrong, because he destroys no one's hope of children.' I continue to hold that everyone who errs outright and does wrong, even if he harms no one near him, nevertheless reveals himself as a worse and less honourable person. For whoever does wrong is a worse and less honourable person to that extent. Even setting aside the injustice, a lack of self-discipline necessarily attaches to anyone who yields to shameful pleasures and delights in filth, just like swine. This most certainly includes the man who has sex with his own slave woman, a thing that some people think is perfectly blameless, since they suppose that every master has full authority to use his own slave as he wishes. In reply to this, I have just one thing to say. For if it seems neither shameful nor strange for a man to have sex with his own slave, especially if she happens to be without a husband, let him consider what his reaction would be if the mistress of the house had sex with a male slave. Would it not seem intolerable, not only if a married woman admitted a slave to her bed, but even if a woman without a husband did so? Yet surely no one considers men inferior to women, or less able to school their own desires, since this would make those stronger in judgement inferior to the weaker, and the rulers inferior to the ruled. For men ought to be far better than women, if they expect to exercise power over them, and surely if they clearly have less self-control, they will in fact be worse. Why is it even necessary to state that for a master to have sex with a slave woman demonstrates a lack of self-control? Everyone knows this.

6.12 Dio Chrysostom *Orations* 36.55–6. Late first or early second century CE. The philosopher Dio presents a Stoic version of the sacred marriage. Here 'Mind' (Greek *nous*), the active principle that organises the universe, is identified with the god Zeus.

For when the Mind alone had been left, and had filled infinite space with itself, pouring itself evenly in all directions, nothing dense remained within it, but a looseness of texture prevailed throughout. At this point it was very beautiful, having taken on the purest nature of undiluted light, but immediately it yearned for the existence it had in the beginning. And conceiving a love for that guidance and rule and oneness of mind which it had maintained over the three natures of the sun and moon and other stars, and over every single animal and plant, it set out to procreate and distribute each thing and to fashion the universe then existing into one far better and more splendid because it was newer. And it sent out a perfect bolt of lightning, not a disordered or foul one such as storms often create when the clouds are driven violently, but a pure bolt, unmixed with any darkness. And quick as thought, it easily brought about a transformation. Mindful of Aphrodite and procreation, it calmed and relaxed itself, and extinguished much of its light, turning into a fiery mist of gentle heat. Then having intercourse with Hera and sharing in perfect sexual relations, it released anew at the end of this process the full complement of the seed of all that exists. The sons of the wise sing of this blessed marriage of Hera and Zeus in secret mysteries.

6.13 Soranus *Gynecology* 1.8 (33), 1.10 (37). Late first or early second century CE. Soranus was a physician who practiced in both Alexandria and Rome. Although he was a prolific author, only his work on gynecology and obstetrics has survived. In these passages he discusses the right age for a girl's first sexual experience, and the role of sexual appetite in conception.

1.8 (33) Since the male merely emits semen, there is no danger to him from the first intercourse. But the female both receives the semen and conceives the substance of the living being. Because she accordingly runs a risk if she is deflowered earlier or later than appropriate, it is reasonable for us to inquire into this problem. Some people suppose that it is a good thing for the female to continue in a state of virginity as long as there is not yet an urge for intercourse, for nature itself produces certain stings and stimulates urges in both the animals without speech and in humans, with regard to the appointed time for intercourse. And by this point, the body has produced an urge for the pleasures of sex. But these people do not realise that animals without speech, operating according to nature alone and pure circumstance, make no contribution of their own to their desire. Therefore in most animals the time when the urge for intercourse appears is fixed in advance, but in humans it is not fixed; often under the influence of reason, the timing of the urge varies because some new pleasure or fancy is introduced. Accordingly, since virgins who have not been wisely brought up and lack education manifest premature desires, these urges are not to be trusted. It is good to maintain them in a virginal state, until such time as menstruation begins by itself, for this will be the signal that the uterus is already able to fulfill its proper functions, which include conception, as we said before. It is dangerous when the emitted semen brings about conception in a uterus that is still of small size. The embryo in this case is chafed as it grows larger, and can either be utterly destroyed, or suffer the destruction of individual features. Or at any rate, at the time of birth it will cause danger to the pregnant woman by making its way through the narrow and undeveloped area around the mouth of the uterus. Under these conditions it also happens that some embryos atrophy because the uterus is not yet interwoven with large blood vessels, but fine ones, which do not carry sufficient blood to nourish the womb and its occupant. But in fact the first menstruation in most cases takes place around the fourteenth year. This age, then, is the natural one and indicates the time for defloration. On the other hand, defloration is not safe after the passage of many years, for the neck of the uterus remains folded, like the members of males who abstain from sexual pleasure. In such cases the semen takes shape and develops into a living being within the spacious cavity of the uterus, but at the time of birth it causes great disturbance and danger because of its inability to pass easily through the narrow neck. Therefore the time mentioned above, when the generative areas of the body have developed and are able to support conception, is the appropriate time for defloration.

1.10 (37). Just as the male cannot discharge semen in the absence of appetite, so it cannot be taken up by the female in the absence of appetite. And just as food swallowed in the absence of appetite and with distaste does not settle well and fails to be properly digested, so the semen cannot be taken up, and once it is grasped, a pregnancy cannot be carried through, unless urge and appetite for intercourse are present. For although some women have conceived after being raped, one may nevertheless say that a state of appetite existed in them too, but was obscured by their mental resolve. In the same manner, the appetite for food often exists in women who are mourning, but is obscured by their grief over their misfortune. Indeed, overwhelming hunger eventually compels them to nourish themselves.

6.14 Galen *On the Usefulness of the Parts of the Body* 14.2, 14.6 (selections), 15.3. Late second to early third century CE. Galen was a court physician to the emperors Marcus Aurelius and Commodus. His medical writings are voluminous and include these passages on the function and structure of the human reproductive organs.

14.2 Nature has given instruments of conception to all animals, and has added to these instruments a remarkable capacity for pleasure in reproduction. And to the soul that is to use them, Nature has given a wondrous and indescribable desire for their use, so that it feels the sting of arousal, even if it is dull-witted, young, and altogether without reason, and it provides for the continuance of the race just like a creature fully endowed with wisdom. For knowing, I suppose, that the substance from which it fashioned them is not compatible with perfect wisdom, Nature gave to animals instead the only incitement they could receive for the purpose of securing and protecting the race, by making the use of these body parts extremely pleasurable…

14.6 The female is less perfect than the male first and foremost because she is colder. For if among animals the warm one is more active, then the colder animal is less perfect than the warmer one. The second reason becomes apparent during dissection. This is the little matter that I hinted just now would be difficult for me to explain. But since this is the right moment, I must attempt it, and you who are following these writings must not question the whole truth of it before you have seen what I describe with your own eyes, for I know well that viewing the parts will make up for what my argument lacks. All the parts that men possess also belong to women, with one difference, which must be kept in mind throughout the argument, and that is that a woman's parts are internal, whereas a man's are external, in the region known as the perineum. Considering first whichever of the two you wish, turn the woman's parts outward, or turn the man's parts inward and fold them double: you will find them the same. Now, consider first the man's parts turned inward and together located between the rectum and the bladder. If this were the case, the scrotum would necessarily take the place of the uterus, with the testicles lying outside of it on each side. The penis of the male would make the neck of the cavity thus formed, and the skin at the end of the penis, which we call the foreskin, would become the female external genitals…

Now just as a human being is of all animals the most perfect, so within the human race the man is more perfect than the woman. The cause of this perfected state is his superabundance of heat, for heat is Nature's most important instrument. In those animals with less of it, Nature's work is necessarily less perfect, and so it is no wonder that the female is less perfect than the male to the same degree as she is colder. In fact, just as the mole possesses imperfect eyes, though not so imperfect as in those animals that wholly lack any trace of an eye, the woman is likewise less perfect than the man with respect to the genital parts. For the parts were formed within her when she was still a fetus, but could not emerge and project downwards to the outside because of her deficiency of heat. Although this made the animal that was being formed less perfect in every respect, it provided no small benefit to the race, for there must be a female. Do not suppose that our creator would make half of the entire human race imperfect and, as it were, mutilated, unless this mutilation were to be greatly useful.

15.3 As to the outgrowths of skin at the ends of the genitals of both sexes, in women they are present for the sake of ornament, and were placed there as a covering to prevent the uterus from becoming chilled. In men, in addition to being ornamental, it was not possible for them to be wholly lacking, if we recall the previous discussions in which I showed how male and female animals are formed. The part known as the clitoris provides a covering for the uterus and prevents it from becoming chilled in the same way the uvula covers the pharynx, for it is situated on the female external genitals over the opening of the neck of the uterus.

6.15 Galen *On Semen* 1.16 (selections). Late second to early third century CE. Galen warns that overindulgence in sex can compromise a man's health.

If a man engages in sex immoderately, the testicles draw the semen more continuously from the convolution of the vessels and completely empty them. And if you dissect an animal in this condition, you will not find seminal fluid in it, just as if you dissect an animal that has been kept from sexual activity, you will find quite thick and abundant seminal fluid...

In animals that have been kept from sexual intercourse with the female, all the parts are full of semen, first the varicose assistant, then the entire sperm duct, then the epididymis,[226] then the entire testicle, and then the convolution of the vessels. But if all the semen is drained out by continuous indulgence in sex, that animal has semen neither in the convolution nor any other part. In such a case, the testicles draw whatever seminal fluid is available from the veins lying above them, but this is a small amount, and mixed with the blood like dew. But it was shown that the veins too require this type of fluid. So when they are forcibly deprived of it by the testicles, which are much more powerful, the veins draw from the veins that lie above them, and those in turn draw from the next, and those from the veins next to them, and this process does not stop until the transfer reaches all parts of the body, so that in the entire animal, all the body parts are emptied of their proper nutrients. For a part that is completely emptied always draws from a part that is full, as though snatching it away by force. Since this is always happening and they are all transmitting fluid to one another as if in a dance, all the vessels and parts of the animal are necessarily drained until the strongest is filled up. And at such a time, the animal's body parts all lose not only the seminal fluid, but also the vital spirit, for this is drained from the arteries along with the semen-bearing moisture. So it is no wonder that those who indulge immoderately in sex turn out to be weaker, since the entire body loses the purest part of both substances, and besides this there is a rush of pleasure, which all by itself is enough to destroy the vital tone. Indeed, in the past some have died from overstimulation. Let these things be said as a side matter, though they are not digressions, for they pose this question as often as any other, why sexual intercourse is especially tiring. And they have many false things to say about it, because they are ignorant of the first principles, from which this result necessarily follows.

6.16 Diogenes Laertius *Lives of Eminent Philosophers* 6.2.46, 72; 7.1.129–31; 10.1.118. Third century CE. In spite of his late date, Diogenes Laertius is one of the principal sources for the lives and opinions of the Greek philosophers.

[On Diogenes of Sinope, one of the founders of the Cynic school of philosophy]
6.2.46
When he was short of money, he told his friends that he was not asking them for money but demanding repayment. Once when he was masturbating in the marketplace, he said that he wished it were as easy to relieve hunger by rubbing his stomach. Seeing a youth going off to dine with satraps,[227] he tore him away, brought him to his friends and asked them to watch him carefully. When an elaborately adorned youth asked him a question, he refused to answer unless the youth pulled up his robe and showed whether he was a man or a woman. 6.2.72. He made light of noble birth, the opinions of other people, and all such things, calling them the ornaments of moral failure. The only right form of government was the commonwealth of the universe. He said that wives should be held in common, and valued marriage not at all, arguing instead that sex should happen between any persuasive man and consenting woman. And for the same reasons, he thought that sons also should be held in common.

[On Zeno of Citium, one of the founders of Stoicism, and other Stoics]
7.1.129–31 Furthermore, they say that the wise man will be a lover of youths

who by their personal beauty show that they have a natural disposition toward excellence. Zeno says this in his *Republic*, Chrysippus in the first book of his work *On Ways of Living*, and Apollodorus in his *Ethics*. They say that *erōs* is an application of the mind toward establishing an affectionate relationship with another because of that person's manifest beauty, and that it is not to do with sexual relations, but with affection. At least, they point to the fact that Thrasonides,[228] even though he had the woman he loved in his power, kept away from her because she hated him. Therefore they say that *erōs* is affection (just as Chrysippus says in his book *On Erōs*), that it is not sent by the gods, and that youthful beauty is the blossoming of excellence.

Of the three ways of living, the contemplative, the practical, and the rational, they say that we ought to choose the third, because a rational creature has been designed by nature for both contemplation and achievement. They say that when a wise man has good reason to do so, he will put an end to his own life, for the sake of his country or his friends, or if he suffers unbearable pain, mutilation, or incurable sickness. They also expressed the view that among wise men wives should be held in common with a free interchange of partners, as Zeno says in his *Republic* and Chrysippus in his work *On the Republic*. Under these conditions we will feel an equal paternal affection for all the children, and adultery caused by jealousy will be eliminated.

[On Epicurus, founder of the Epicurean school of philosophy, and his followers] 10.1.118 Even under torture the wise man is happy. Only the wise man will feel gratitude towards friends, present and absent alike, and show it by word and deed. To be sure, however, if he is under torture, he will moan and cry out. The wise man will have a sexual relationship with no woman who is forbidden to him by law, as Diogenes says in his summary of Epicurus' ethical doctrines. He will not punish his servants, but will have compassion towards them and will at times make allowances for those who take their work seriously. The Epicureans do not think a wise man should fall in love, nor should he pay any attention to burial rites. They say that *erōs* is not sent by the gods, as Diogenes[229] states in his twelfth book. A wise man will not be a fine speaker. And they say that sexual activity is never of benefit, and that we should be content if it does no harm.

6.17 Origen *Against Celsus* 4.48. 248 CE. In this attack on paganism, Origen mentions a teaching of the early Stoic philosopher Chrysippus (mid-third century BCE). No other such depictions of Zeus and Hera are attested, and we do not know whether the picture Chrysippus discussed was what he purported it to be.

But why should I recount the strange stories told by the Greeks about their gods, which are in themselves shameful, even when interpreted allegorically?

Take for example the passage where Chrysippus of Soli, who is deemed to have ornamented the Stoic school with many wise writings, interprets a painting in Samos[230] showing Hera performing an unmentionable act on Zeus. This venerable philosopher says in his writings that Matter receives the spermatic principles of God, and holds them within herself for the purpose of creating order in the universe. For in the Samian painting, Hera is Matter and Zeus is God. It is because of these and countless other similar myths, that we are unwilling, even in name only, to call the God of all things Zeus, or the sun Apollo, or the moon Artemis.

Further Reading

For the influence of traditional culture on medical thought, see Carson 1990. For the Hippocratics' views on female bodies, see Dean-Jones 1994, and Flemming and Hanson (eds) 1998. On the wandering womb, see Faraone 2011. For the disagreements between Aristotle and Galen, see Connell 2000; for Soranus, see Hanson and Green 1994. For Galen and the 'one sex' model, see Laqueur 1990. For Musonius Rufus and Stoic sexual ethics, see Nussbaum 2002 and Gaca 2003, pp. 59–116. On Lucretius' view of erotic love, see Brown 1987 and Nussbaum 1994, pp. 140–91. For the impact of medical thought about sexuality and the body in late antiquity, see Rousselle 1993. For Philo of Alexandria, see Gaca 2003, pp. 190–217.

7

Virginity, Chastity, and Modesty

In the language of myth, female virginity indicates purity, but also autonomy and freedom from subjection to a husband. This freedom is essential, in different ways, to the personalities of Athena and Artemis (7.2), while Hestia's virginity relates to the integrity of the home and the purity of fire. Perpetual virginity or celibacy for male deities was unheard of, with the possible exception of the self-castrated Attis (1.10, 1.13, 1.15). In spite of the symbolic value of virginity for certain goddesses, permanent virginity was rarely considered desirable for either men or women in Greco-Roman culture. Even the famous Vestal Virgins of Rome (7.13) were not required to maintain lifelong virginity; once their period of service was concluded, they were free to marry. The requirement of celibacy during their service, however, was absolute and the punishment for transgressions was death.

To a greater degree than the Greeks, the Romans associated the virtue of chastity (deified as the goddess Pudicitia) with the safety and security of the state. Thus, Romans spoke in reverent tones of the Vestals or praised the chastity of the emperor's wife (7.12). In Roman legends, sexual abuse of free women was the inevitable result when excessive power was concentrated in the hands of one man, and this abuse was portrayed as the catalyst for political change, as in the stories of Lucretia (7.12, 9.12) and Verginia (7.12). Although a woman's chastity could be threatened or lost through no fault of her own, its loss was considered such an irreparable stain on the family that stories of honour killings (for example, Verginius' and Aufidius' executions of their daughters) were admired as examples of moral excellence.

Sexual abstinence was associated primarily with distinctive religious obser-vances. In ancient thought, sexual intercourse brought about a temporary miasma or pollution that had to be washed away before a man or woman approached the sanctuaries or altars of the gods; childbirth carried a similar taint. The ritual law from the Greek colony of Cyrene in North Africa (7.7) provides instructions on maintaining ritual purity for women about to be married, new brides, and those who have given birth. At these times in a woman's life, she was expected to pay honours to the virgin goddess Artemis. The law also specifies a penalty for women who have premarital sex with their affianced husbands, and for pregnant women who fail to abstain from sex during the goddess' festival. The Roman elegiac poet Propertius, meanwhile, amusingly reproaches the goddess Isis for a similar requirement that his lover Cynthia abstain from sex during a festival period (7.10).

A standard of virginity before marriage and chastity afterward was used to control female sexuality; both men and women in the community participated in the enforcement of cultural norms. From Homer's *Odyssey* we learn that in the early Archaic period, female modesty required that a girl avoid being seen in conversation with a male stranger (7.1). On the other hand, Nausicaa considers it more important to avoid the censure of others (particularly males) who might ruin her reputation than actually to avoid conversation with a potential marriage partner as attractive as Odysseus. Virginity was highly valued in brides; in Catullus' wedding song (7.8), the bride's reluctance to consummate the marriage is interpreted as a confirmation of her virginal state. The impact of prolonged virginity on women's health was much debated in medical circles. The physician Soranus went against the traditional medical consensus in his insistence that virginity was healthful for women (7.14); he cited the example of priestesses who were required to abstain from sex, and even argued that intercourse was by its very nature harmful to both men and women.

Citizen males, meanwhile, were expected to be sexually active, but were raised to observe ideals of self-control in furtherance of their gender roles. A lack of self-control in sexual matters meant that a free man did not deserve the privileges he enjoyed for the sake of his gender and social status. For many ancients, Socrates embodied the virtues of *enkrateia* (self-control) and *sōphrosynē* (moderation), because he resisted sexual temptations and demonstrated mastery of his body in other ways (7.5), such as an ability to endure extremes of cold and heat. For men, chastity and modesty were related to the idea that the male body must maintain its integrity, which meant that it must not be penetrated. Therefore during most of Roman antiquity, a man who was a passive partner in anal sex or used his mouth to sexually gratify a partner was thought to have lost his chastity, while a man who engaged in normative sexual intercourse with his wife or with sexual partners sanctioned by society (including prostitutes and slaves) was considered chaste so long as he indulged only moderately and took an active role. The requirement of chastity was predicated on a man's freedom and social status, since slaves and freedmen were subject to varying degrees of sexual servitude (7.11).

Both Greeks and Romans were shocked by sexual attitudes and practices that differed from their own. In a breathless (and no doubt exaggerated) account of sexual habits among the Etruscans (7.6), the Greek historian Theopompus sounds alternately outraged and envious. The passage reveals that many Greeks of his day valued privacy for sexual activities, even to the point of requiring darkness, and that they carefully censored references to sex in their speech. Cornelius Nepos, a more sophisticated commentator (7.9), uses Roman shock at the Greeks' acceptance of marriage with a half-sibling, and the fact that respectable Spartan women of the time appeared on the stage, to make his point that attitudes vary by culture. In his *Histories*, Herodotus had already adopted a humane and relativist perspective, privileging Greek customs yet insisting that his readers acknowledge cultural difference. The story of Candaules and Gyges (7.3) addresses differences in cultural attitudes about revealing the body. Herodotus uses the anecdote about nakedness to show his readers that the Lydians had more conservative views than the Greeks on this matter. Yet the two cultures agreed on the basic indecency of displaying a married woman's nakedness.

Complete celibacy was not unknown among the early Greeks, but was associated with sectarian and esoteric religious groups such as the Pythagoreans and Orphics. In Euripides' *Hippolytus*, the title character has Orphic leanings and wishes to remain a virgin like the goddess Artemis. Yet the 'meadow' of Hippolytus' song (7.4) is a sexual symbol, and his rapturous devotion to Artemis suggests not a neutralised sexuality but the sublimation of sexual energies in religious asceticism. The Stoics and especially the Epicureans had ambivalent attitudes toward sex, but not until the advent of Christianity was celibacy preached as a universal virtue. The apostle Paul (8.14) urged both the men and women in his flock to remain celibate if they could. This teaching arose from the Christian belief in the imminent return of Jesus to inaugurate the Kingdom of God, making procreation unnecessary. Celibacy and permanent virginity were particularly popular with women, as shown in the apocryphal *Acts of Paul and Thecla*, where Thecla's ecstatic acceptance of Paul's teachings regarding chastity (7.15) recalls the joy of the celibate Hippolytus.

By the third century CE, pagan culture and Christian culture had begun to converge in the high value both placed on virginity and sexual abstinence for men as well as women. In Heliodorus' novel *Aethiopica*, both hero and heroine maintain their virginity until marriage and resist the strong temptation to have sex even when they are left alone together (7.16). The ordeal by fire used to test their virginity, meanwhile, resembles the miracles associated with Christian martyrs, and the crowd is surprised and impressed that the handsome Theagenes has remained a virgin. Celibacy in men was highly prized by pagans of the late Imperial period as an indicator of wisdom and moral superiority. The emperor Julian studied philosophy, and according to his biographer Ammianus Marcellinus, remained celibate after the death of his wife (7.17); his behaviour was much admired, although not considered a realistic goal for most people.

7.1 Homer *Odyssey* 6.251–88. Late eighth century BCE. When shipwrecked Odysseus washes up on the shore of the Phaeacian people, the princess Nausicaa agrees to help him.

But white-armed Nausicaa had another idea.
She placed the folded clothes in the pretty wagon,
Yoked the strong-hoofed mules, and took her seat.
She roused Odysseus, and addressed him saying:
'Now take heart, stranger, and travel toward the city,
To the house of my prudent father, where I believe
You will come to know all the noble Phaeacians.
You seem a man of good sense, so do as I say:
Follow my maids behind the mules and wagon
Until we reach the fields of men at work,
And I will lead. But once we near the city,
High-walled, with a lovely harbour on each side,
The way grows narrow, lined with curving ships,
And in the dockyard each man claims his space.
There lies a lovely square by Poseidon's shrine,
Paved with quarried stones set into the earth.
Here they turn their minds to the black ships' rigging,
The cables and sails, and the sharpening of the oars.
The Phaeacians have no interest in arrows and quivers,
But instead love masts, and oars, and steady ships,
In which they delight to glide over seas of grey.
Their bitter talk I wish to avoid, lest someone
Reproach me later, for haughty men fill this town;
Some lowborn man might say when passing us,
'What stranger follows Nausicaa, handsome and tall?
Where did she find him? A husband for her, no doubt.
Perhaps she leads from his ship some vagabond,
A man from a far-off land, for few live here.
Or perhaps in answer to many fervent prayers,
A god came down from heaven to hold her forever.
A better thing, if she found a husband abroad,

Since she has no respect for men of Phaeacia,
Though many nobles are suitors for her hand'.
These words, if spoken, would be a reproach to me.
I too would blame a girl, if she did such things,
Crossing her parents' will while they still live,
And meeting with men before she is openly wed.'

7.2 Homeric *Hymn to Aphrodite* 1–44. Seventh century BCE. The first section of the hymn contrasts the virgin goddesses Athena, Artemis, and Hestia with the goddess of sexual desire.

Muse, tell me the deeds of golden Aphrodite,
Cypris, who rouses sweet longing in the gods,
And masters the tribes of humans doomed to die.
The hovering birds above and wild beasts
As many as land and sea together nurture,
All heed the works of flower-crowned Cytherea.
Three minds only she fails to persuade or trick:
Grey-eyed Athena, the aegis-bearer's daughter
Rejects the deeds of golden Aphrodite;
She is pleased by war and the works of Ares,
Contests, battles and pursuit of glorious feats.
She first taught the craftsmen on the earth
To fashion chariots and horses' tack from bronze.
She teaches soft-skinned maidens in the home,
Filling their minds with thoughts of splendid works.
Aphrodite who loves laughter never tames
Raucous Artemis, she of the golden arrows;
The bow pleases her, the slaughter of beasts in the hills,
Dances, and lyres, and the women's piercing cry,
Shady groves, and the cities of righteous men.
Nor does Aphrodite please shy Hestia,
The firstborn child of crooked-counseling Cronus,
Yet youngest, because of aegis-bearing Zeus;[231]
A queen, wooed by Poseidon and Apollo,
But she rejected both and spoke out firmly,
And swore a great oath (which has been fulfilled):
Touching the head of her aegis-bearing father,
The goddess vowed to remain a virgin forever.
Zeus gave her a privilege in place of marriage:
Seated within the house she receives rich food,
Accepts a share of honour in every shrine,

And precedes the other gods in mortal affairs.
The minds of these three she fails to persuade or trick,
But of the rest, not one has escaped Aphrodite,
Either from blessed gods or mortal humans.
Zeus who delights in thunder she leads astray,
The greatest god with the greatest share of honour.
Even his crafty mind she beguiles when she wishes,
And easily brings him to bed with mortal women
All unknown to Hera, his sister and spouse,
Whose beauty surpasses that of other goddesses,
The glorious daughter of crooked-counseling Cronus
And Mother Rhea. But in his imperishable wisdom,
Zeus made Hera his modest and capable wife.

7.3 Herodotus *Histories* 1.8–12. Ca. 440. Herodotus produced one of the first accounts of the rise of the Persian empire and its war with the Greeks. Here he describes events in Lydia when it was still an independent kingdom. Candaules is thought to have ruled from 735–718 BCE.

This Candaules fell in love with his own wife, and in his passion he believed that she was by far the most beautiful woman in the world. As a result, he endlessly praised her beauty when speaking to his favourite bodyguard, Gyges son of Dascylus,[232] for he confided all his most important business to Gyges. After some time went by, the ill-fated Candaules said to Gyges, 'Gyges, I do not think you believed me when I spoke of my wife's beauty. Since people more readily believe their eyes than their ears, you must contrive to see her naked.' Crying out in protest, Gyges said, 'Master, what a sick idea, ordering me to see the Mistress naked! A woman removes her modesty with her clothes. Long ago people discovered the right rules of behaviour, and we must learn from these; one is that a person ought to mind his own business. I believe that she is the most beautiful of all women, and I beg you not to ask me to do what is lawless.'

Gyges said these things in opposition to the idea, because he dreaded that something bad would be the result for him. But Candaules replied, 'Courage, Gyges! Do not fear that I am testing you when I say this, or that you will come to any harm from my wife. I will arrange it so she will never know that you have seen her. I will place you in the bedchamber where we sleep, behind the open door. After I enter the room, my wife too will come to bed. Near the entrance of the room, there is a chair. Upon this she will lay each article of clothing as she takes it off. This will allow you plenty of time to see her. Then, when she moves from the chair to the bed and has her back to you, be careful she does not see you as you go out the door.'

Since Gyges could not escape, he agreed. When Candaules judged it was time for bed, he brought Gyges to the bedchamber, and soon afterward, his wife came in. And once she had entered and was laying down her clothing, Gyges saw her. When the wife turned her back on him to get into bed, he slipped out of the room, but she observed his departure, and understood what her husband had done. Although she felt shame, she did not cry out or let on that she knew, because she intended to avenge herself on Candaules. For among the Lydians and most other foreign peoples, it is a great humiliation even for a man to be seen naked.

For the present, then, she revealed nothing and kept quiet. But as soon as day came, she prepared the servants whom she knew were loyal to her, and summoned Gyges. Believing that she knew nothing of what had been done, he answered the summons, for he was accustomed to come when the queen called. When Gyges arrived, the wife said, 'Now, Gyges, two paths lie before you. I give you a choice; decide which one you wish to follow. You must either kill Candaules and take both me and the Lydian kingdom, or die immediately yourself, so that in future you do not follow all Candaules' orders and see what you should not. For either Candaules must die, who planned these things, or you who saw me naked, and did that which is unlawful.' For a while Gyges stood silent in astonishment at her words, and then he begged her not to force him to make such a choice. But when he failed to persuade her, and he saw that indeed it was necessary for him either to kill his master or to be killed himself, he chose to survive. And he questioned her, saying, 'Since you are forcing me against my will to kill my master, I would like to know by what means we are to lay hands on him.' And she answered, 'The attack will proceed from the same spot where he made a show of me naked: you will attack him while he is asleep.'

When they had completed their planning, and evening arrived, Gyges followed the wife into the bedroom, for he had not been released, and either he or Candaules must perish. She placed a dagger in his hand, and hid him behind the same door. Gyges slipped out and killed Candaules as he was sleeping, and possessed both the wife and the kingdom.

7.4 Euripides *Hippolytus* 73–87. 428 BCE. Hippolytus' speech in praise of Artemis emphasises that his chastity makes him worthy to be her companion.

Hippolytus:
From an untouched meadow I bear this crown
I have braided for you, O Lady,
A place no shepherd would graze his flocks,
Where no scythe of iron has ever come,
The spring bee roams this untouched meadow
And Reverence tends the plants with river dew,

For those whose chastity, untaught, inheres
By nature always, and in all they achieve.
These have the right to pick the blooms,
But for the base, it is unlawful.
But, dear Lady, receive from my reverent hand
This diadem for your golden hair.
To me alone of mortals is given this prize:
I consort with you and we converse,
I hear your voice but never see your face.
May the end of my life match the beginning!

7.5 Xenophon *Memorabilia* 1.2.1–2. Ca. 360 BCE. Xenophon's collection of Socratic dialogues describes the famed philosopher's self-discipline in matters pertaining to the body.

It amazes me that some believed the charge that Socrates corrupted the youth. First, in addition to what I have already said, of all men he had the most self-control when it came to the pleasures of sex or of the stomach. Moreover, he was most patient in enduring extremes of cold, heat or physical exertion. And he was so well accustomed to moderation that although he had very few possessions, he was quite content. Since this was his character, how could he have made others impious, lawbreakers, gluttonous, over-indulgent in sexual pleasures, or lazy in their work? Instead, it was thanks to him that many dropped these vices, because he made them aspire to excellence, and gave them hope that if they looked after themselves, they would become men of the best kind.

7.6 Theopompus of Chios *FGrHist* 115 F 204. Mid-fourth century BCE (quoted in Athenaeus *The Philosophers at Dinner* 12.517d–18a. Early third century CE). Theopompus' historical works focused on the events of the fourth century BCE, in Greece and around the Mediterranean. Athenaeus quotes Theompompus in the context of a discussion of luxurious living as practiced by Greeks and other peoples.

In the forty-third book of his *Histories*, Theopompus says that it was the custom among the Etruscans to have their wives in common. The women are much concerned with their bodies and often take exercise, even with men, and sometimes with one another. To appear in the nude causes them no shame. What is more, they dine not with their own husbands, but with any men who happen to be present, and they drink toasts with anyone they wish. They consume shocking amounts of wine and are very good-looking. The Etruscans rear all the babies that are born, without knowing who the father is in each case. And these, in turn, live the same sort of life as those who nurtured them, throwing many drinking parties and having sex with all the women. The Etruscans feel no shame if they are seen having sex in the open, and they do not even feel ashamed to be the passive partner, for this too is the custom in their country. And they are so far from thinking of it as shameful that whenever the master of the house is indulging in this type of sex, and someone comes to see him, they say, 'he is having such and such a sex act done to him', openly calling the act by its disgraceful name. When they congregate for fellowship or family gatherings, this is what they do. First, when they have stopped drinking and are ready to retire, the servants bring in courtesans to them while the lamps are still lighted, and sometimes beautiful boys, and sometimes also their wives. When they have enjoyed these, the servants bring young men in the prime of life, who take the active role in sex with them. They indulge in sex and practice this activity sometimes in full sight of each other, but usually with screens set up around their couches; the screens are made of wicker with robes thrown over them. Now, they gladly have sex with women, certainly, but they delight much more in relations with boys and youths. Among the Etruscans, these are extremely good-looking, because they live luxuriously and keep their bodies smooth.

7.7 Ritual law from Cyrene, *LSCG Supp.* 115.A11–15, B 1–23. End of fourth century BCE. This section of the law (from the Greek colony of Cyrene in North Africa) describes the requirements for ritual purity in relation to the cult of Artemis.

A 11–15
A man who has spent the night with a woman may sacrifice [whenever] he wishes. If he has slept with her by day, after washing he may [...] go wherever he wishes, except [2 lines missing].

B 1–23
[most of 1 line missing] [must pay a penalty] to Artemis, and she herself may not be under the same roof as her husband nor become polluted, until she comes to Artemis. If any woman voluntarily becomes polluted without doing this, she shall purify the temple of Artemis and in addition she shall sacrifice as a penalty a full-grown animal, and then go to the sleeping-room. But if she becomes polluted involuntarily, she shall purify the shrine.

A bride must go down to Artemis in the bride-room, whenever she wishes during the festival of Artemis, but the sooner the better. If any bride does not go down, she shall offer [what is customary] at the festival of Artemis, and because she did not go down, she shall purify the shrine and in addition she shall sacrifice as penalty a full-grown animal.

[Before giving birth, a pregnant woman] shall go down to Artemis in the bride-room [...] she shall give to the Bear-priestess[233] the feet and head and skin. If she does not go down before giving birth, she shall go with a full-grown animal. A woman who goes down shall remain pure on the seventh, eighth and ninth, and a woman who has not gone down shall remain pure on these days. But if she becomes polluted, she shall purify herself, purify the shrine, and in addition she shall sacrifice as penalty a full-grown animal.

7.8 Catullus *Songs* 61.46–118. Ca. 55 BCE. In this extract from a wedding song in the form of a hymn to the wedding god Hymenaeus, the poet praises the beauty and modesty of the bride Aurunculeia.

What other god should anxious
Lovers seek? What other god
In heaven is more honoured?
O Hymen, Hymenaeus.

To you the quaking parent
Prays, virgins loosen belts
For you; the nervous groom
Awaits your song eagerly.

Into the wild youth's hands
You give the blossoming girl
From her mother's bosom,
O Hymen, Hymenaeus.

Without you Venus takes
No action in good repute;
With you, she thrives. Who
Would rival such a god?

Without you the house and
Father lack issue; with you,
Offspring abound. Who
Would rival such a god?

Without your rites the land
Lacks defense; with you,
The borders are secure.
Who would rival such a god?

Open the bolted gates;
The virgin arrives. See how
The bright torches flicker?
[1 missing line]

Hearing this, the modest
Bride walks with slower
Step, and sheds a tear
For now she must go.

Don't cry! No woman
More lovely than you,
Aurunculeia, will see
Day shining from the east.

Such is the hyacinth bloom
In the wealthy man's dappled
Garden. The light fades;
You delay; come forth, bride!

Come forth, bride, if now
All is well, and hear my word.
See how the bright torches
Flicker? Come forth, bride!

No man of yours will stray
In fickle pursuit of foul
Betrayal, sleeping apart
From your tender breasts.

But as the pliant vine clings
Closely to the trees, your arms
Shall enfold him. But the
Light fades; come forth, bride!

O marriage bed, which all
[2 missing lines]
The couch with white feet.

What joys for your husband,
What delights in the brief night

And in the midday! But the
Light fades: come forth, bride!

Raise the torches, boys:
She comes in crimson veil.
Come, sing all together:
O Hymen, Hymenaeus.

7.9 Cornelius Nepos *Lives of Eminent Commanders* Preface 1–8. Mid-first
century BCE. In the preface to his biographical work on famous generals,
Nepos alludes to the differing cultural norms held by Greeks and Romans in
regard to female chastity.

I have no doubt, Atticus, that many will consider this type of writing trivial, and
not worthy of the most eminent men, when they find recorded here the name
of Epaminondas'[234] music teacher, or that fact that his talents included graceful
dancing and playing the flute skillfully. But these will be just the people who,
lacking an acquaintance with Greek literature, think nothing is right unless it
conforms to their own customs. If these readers will grasp that the same things
are not honourable or scandalous for all peoples, but that every custom is
judged by what a people's forefathers have established, they will not wonder
that in describing the virtues of Greek men I have paid attention to their habits
of life. For Cimon,[235] a great man among the Greeks, did not find it scandalous
to marry his half-sister, since his fellow-citizens accepted this practice, but
among us, the same action is considered unlawful. In Crete, they consider it
praiseworthy for a young man to have as many male lovers as possible. No
widow in Lacedaemonia is so highborn that she will not accept payment to
appear on the stage. Throughout all Greece it was considered a great honour
to be proclaimed a victor in the Olympic games, and indeed, nobody of this
nation thought that it was a scandal to go on the stage and become a public
spectacle. Yet among us all these practices are considered both disreputable and
characteristic of the lower classes, far from the behaviour of respectable people.
On the other hand, many things that seem appropriate to us are considered
scandals among them. What Roman man is ashamed to bring his wife to a
dinner party? What Roman wife does not occupy the best room in the house,
and take her part when people are gathered there? In Greece it is far different.
For a wife does not attend a dinner party except among relatives, nor does she
occupy rooms other than those in the interior of the house, which is called the
'women's quarters', and nobody goes there unless he is a close relation of hers.

7.10 Propertius *Elegies* 2.33a. Ca. 24 BCE. Propertius laments a ritual
requirement of the rites of Isis. In Greco-Roman culture, Isis was identified

with the Greek heroine Io, priestess of Hera/Juno who was transformed to a
cow and traveled to Egypt.

Now the solemn date returns, to my sorrow:
Cynthia is elsewhere for ten nights.
May they perish, the rites Inachus' daughter[236]
Sent from the Nile to Italy's women!
Whoever she is, how harsh a goddess, to keep
Eager lovers apart so very long.
From your secret trysts with Jove, no doubt,
You learned what it is to wander, Io,
When Juno decreed that you, a girl, should grow horns
And made your voice the moan of a cow.
How often you dined in your stall and bruised your lips
Chewing the leaves of oak and arbutus!
Now because Jove has restored your human face,
Have you become so proud a goddess?
Aren't the dark daughters of Egypt enough for you?
Why seek such a long journey to Rome,
And what use is it to you that girls sleep alone?
Believe me, your horns will return, and then
We'll hound you from our city, O cruel one!
Tiber and Nile were never good friends.
And as for you, who enjoy my plight overmuch:
We'll love three times when next we meet.

7.11 Seneca the Elder *Controversiae* 4 Preface 10. Ca. 30 CE. In this section of
his work on rhetoric, Seneca is speaking about a much-repeated remark of
the orator Haterius, who had died only a few years before.

While he desired to say nothing that was not elegant and brilliant, he often
ended up saying that which could not escape ridicule. I remember how once
when he was defending a freedman against a charge of sexually serving his
former master, he said, 'lack of chastity is a crime in the free, a necessity for the
slave, and a duty for the freedman'. This became the basis for jokes, such as
'you aren't doing your duty by me', and 'he is very dutiful toward him'. As a
result, for some time afterward, whatever was unchaste or obscene was termed
'dutiful'.

7.12 Valerius Maximus *Memorable Deeds and Sayings* 6.1.1–4. First half of
first century CE. Valerius wrote a book of historical anecdotes that demonstrate his rhetorical training.

Chastity, the chief support of men and women alike, from what place shall I summon you? You inhabit the hearth consecrated by ancient religion to Vesta; you lie upon the couch of Capitoline Juno;[237] you are in regular attendance on the revered domestic gods of the Palatine's peak[238] and the most holy marriage bed of Julia;[239] with your help the emblems of childhood are protected; out of respect for your divinity, the flower of youth remains intact; through you the matron is judged worthy of her robe. Come, therefore, and learn of things that you yourself willed.

Lucretia, who led the way in Roman chastity, and whose manly spirit Fortune by an unkind error had allotted to a woman's body, was forcibly subjected to rape by Sextus Tarquinius, the son of the king Superbus. In a family council, she complained of the injury done her in the most solemn terms, and then killed herself with a sword she had brought hidden in her clothing. By such a courageous death, she gave the Roman people cause to exchange kingly authority for that of the consuls.

Lucretia could not bear the injury done to her; Verginius, a man of plebeian family but a patrician in spirit, sacrificed a child of his own blood in order to keep his house free of infamy. For when the Decemvir Appius Claudius,[240] relying on the power of his office, repeatedly attempted to violate his daughter, he brought the girl to the Forum and killed her, preferring to end the life of a chaste daughter rather than be father to a defiled one.

Nor was the mind of the Roman knight Pontius Aufidius any less resolute. When he learned that his daughter's virginity had been given up to Fannius Saturninus by her tutor, he was not content with applying the penalty of death to the wicked slave, but he also killed the girl herself. In this way, rather than celebrate a repugnant marriage, he gave her a premature funeral.

Again, what a stern guardian of chastity was P. Maenius! When he learned that a freedman, a great favourite of his, had kissed his daughter, who was of the age for marriage, he punished the freedman with death, even though the act could have been the result of error rather than lust. But Maenius judged it important to implant the discipline of chastity in the girl's still tender feelings through the harshness of the punishment, and by this very sad lesson he taught her that she must bring to her husband not only intact virginity, but unsullied kisses.

7.13 Plutarch *Life of Numa* 9.5–10.7. Late first century CE. This biography of the Roman king Numa is an important source for the rules surrounding the priestesses of the hearth goddess Vesta, known as the Vestal Virgins.

He was also the overseer of the sacred virgins called Vestals, for they credit Numa with both the consecration of the Vestal Virgins and the ritual honours surrounding the immortal fire which they guard; and they are virgins either because the pure and incorrupt nature of fire is to be entrusted to persons who are untouched and undefiled, or because the sterility and unfruitfulness of fire is associated with virginity. Wherever a perpetual fire is kept in Greece, as at Pytho[241] and Athens, it is not virgins but widows no longer married who tend it, and if by any chance it goes out, as at Athens the sacred lamp is said to have been extinguished during the tyranny of Aristion, and at Delphi the temple was torn down by the Medes,[242] and during the Mithridatic wars and the Roman civil war the altar together with the fire was obliterated, they say that it must not be lighted from another fire, but that it is necessary to make a new one, igniting it from a pure and undefiled ray of the sun. They usually do this with concave mirrors, whose hollow area corresponds to the sides of an isosceles right triangle, converging from the rim to a single point in the centre. When one of these is positioned to face the sun, so that the rays striking from all sides are gathered and intertwined at the centre, the air itself becomes rarefied, and very light and dry objects placed there quickly ignite because of the resistance, as the rays gain the substance and force of fire. Now, some maintain that the sacred virgins keep watch over nothing but this perpetual fire, while others say that certain other hidden objects exist, which must not be seen by anyone else. I have written as much as can lawfully be spoken and learned concerning these things in my *Life of Camillus*. They say that Numa first consecrated Gegania and Verenia, and then Canuleia and Tarpeia; and that when Servius[243] later added two others, the group was maintained at this size to the present day. The king ordained thirty years of purity for the sacred virgins, of which the first decade is spent learning their duties, the second performing them, and the third teaching the others. When this time has passed, she who desires it is permitted to partake of marriage and lead a different life, once she has been released from her sacred duties. But they say that not many accepted this freedom, and that those who did so found it gave little satisfaction, but spent the rest of their lives in regret and sorrow and cast the others into a superstitious fear, so that they steadfastly continued in their virginal state until old age and death.

But Numa gave them great honours, including the right to make a will while their fathers were still living, and to manage their own affairs without a guardian, like women who have given birth to three children. When they go out, bearers of the *fascēs*[244] precede them, and if they happen to meet with someone being led to execution, he is reprieved, but the virgin must swear that the meeting was involuntary and the result of chance, not a prearranged plan. Anyone who passes under the litter on which they are carried is put to death. For minor misbehaviour, the virgins are punished with a whipping, and the Pontifex Maximus[245] sometimes carries out this punishment on the naked offender, in a dark place with a linen cloth hung between them. But if one of them dishonours her vow, she is buried alive near the Colline gate. Here a ridge of earth runs for a distance along the interior of the city wall; it is called 'the mound' in Latin speech. Here a small underground room is built, with steps leading down from above. In this room they place a couch with bedding, a lighted lamp, and small offerings of life's necessities, such as bread, water in a jug, milk, and olive oil, in order to absolve themselves of the guilt of starving to death a body that had been consecrated to the highest state of holiness. Then the culprit herself is placed on a litter, which is tightly covered and lashed down with cords, so that no cry can be heard from inside. This is carried through the Forum, and all the people stand out of the way in silence, and escort the litter without speaking, in terrible sorrow. No other spectacle is more horrifying, nor is any other day in the city gloomier than this. When the litter reaches its destination, the attendants loosen its bindings and the chief priest stretches his hands to the heavens and speaks some secret prayers before what must occur takes place. Then he removes the heavily veiled offender from the litter, places her on the steps leading down to the chamber, and turns his face away, along with the other priests. When she has descended, the steps are removed and large quantities of earth are used to hide the chamber, so that it is level with the rest of the mound. In this way they punish those who give up their sacred virginity.

7.14 Soranus *Gynecology* 1.7 (30–32). Late first to early second century CE. In this chapter, the physician examines the arguments for and against the proposition that permanent virginity is injurious to health.

Regarding permanent virginity, some have said that it is healthy, and others that it is unhealthy. The first group says that desire causes illness in the body, and indeed we see the bodies of lovers are pale, weak and thin, whereas virginity bypasses desire because it lacks experience of sex. Moreover, all excretion of seed is harmful, for males just as for females. Virginity, then, is healthful, because it is a hindrance to the excretion of seed. The animals without speech also bear witness to what has been said, because mares that have not been bred are far better runners, and sows that have had the uterus removed are larger, better nourished, stronger, and firm-fleshed like males. This is clearly also the case in humans, for males who remain pure are stronger than the rest and larger, and spend their lives in greater health. Correspondingly, it follows that virginity is generally healthy for females, for conception and birth are exhausting to the female body and take a heavy toll, whereas virginity should necessarily be considered healthful because it removes the female from these sources of harm. However, those of the opposite opinion say that virgins as well as wives have a desire for sexual pleasures, and that some virgins at any rate suffer more from passion than wives, for the one antidote to the craving is the practice of intercourse, not abstinence from it. Maintaining virginity, then, does not abolish desire. And some say that the discharge of seed is not harmful in itself either for males or females, but only in excess, for the body is harmed by continuous discharge of seed, but it is aided by secretion at regular intervals, so that difficulty in movement and discomfort is relieved. Indeed, after intercourse many people feel more agile and adopt a more noble bearing. Others say that the emission of seed causes muscular weakness, and because of this it actually harms people, yet when it happens only occasionally and at the proper time, it is rather helpful in another way, namely, the unobstructed discharge of the menstrual flow. For, as movement of the whole body typically causes perspiration, and lack of movement hinders and prevents it, and just as vigorous use of the voice leads to an increased excretion of saliva, which accompanies the passage of the breath, so during sex the movement taking place around the female genital area relaxes the whole body. And for this reason it also relaxes the uterus, and protects against any hindrance to menstruation. Indeed, many women whose menses came painfully and with difficulty because they lived as widows for a long time, have experienced an unobstructed flow again after remarrying. And sows that have had the uterus removed become more robust because they wholly lack the organ that supports menstrual excretion. Now, just as someone without feet cannot have foot disease, and someone whose eyes have been struck out cannot have a squint, given that he does not possess the body part that contracts the illness, so in the same way a woman with no uterus cannot be afflicted with a malady arising from the uterus. But virgins possess a uterus, so if they abstain from sexual embraces, there is a danger that the normal functioning of the uterus may be lost. And in response to the argument that women who have no intercourse are saved from the ills of childbirth, they say that lack of intercourse harms women in much worse ways, because the menstrual cleansing is obstructed. Certainly they become fat and excessively full of compounds that accumulate over time rather than being eliminated through the cleansing process. Absolute virginity, therefore, is harmful. These are the arguments they make on either side. But we say that permanent virginity is healthy, because the very activity of intercourse is harmful, as has been shown at greater length in the book *On Health*. We see that even among the animals without speech, the more robust females are those that have been kept from engaging in intercourse. And among women, those who avoid sexual relations because of the custom in worship of the gods and those who are kept virgins as ordained by law are more resistant to illnesses. If there is difficulty in menstruation, fat, and abnormal bodily proportion, this is the result of laziness and failure to exercise the body, for many women who are kept in a state of virginity spend their time as observers and guardians without partaking of the necessary exercise, even passive exercise, or realising its benefits. For this reason, they are susceptible to the problems we have discussed. Therefore, permanent virginity is healthy for females just as for males, but sexual relations would seem to be consistent with the general law of nature, by which the two sexes support the continuity of life. And we must discuss these matters in more detail later.

7.15 *Acts of Paul and Thecla* 7–12. Second century CE. This influential text, part of the New Testament apocrypha, was translated from its original Greek into Latin, Syrian, Armenian, and Coptic. It recounts the life of the (likely fictional) Thecla, a woman of Iconium in central Asia Minor, who travelled as a missionary with the apostle Paul.

And as Paul was saying these things in the midst of the assembly in Onesiphorus' house, a certain maiden Thecla who was the daughter of Theoclea, and betrothed to a man named Thamyris, was sitting in the window nearby and listening night and day to the arguments concerning purity that Paul was making. And she did not turn away from the window, but was led by faith to rejoice greatly. And what is more, as she saw many wives and maidens going in to Paul, she herself yearned to be considered worthy to stand before Paul and to hear the word of Christ. For she had not yet seen what Paul looked like, but only listened to his words.

So she did not stand up from the window, and her mother sent for Thamyris. He came joyfully, as if he were about to marry her, and he said to Theoclea, 'Where is my Thecla?' And Theoclea said to him, 'I have news for you, Thamyris. For three days and three nights, Thecla has not stirred from the window either to eat or to drink, but stares intently as though at a glad sight. She is devoted to this strange man teaching deceitful and intricate arguments–so much so, that her sense of modesty has been overturned in a way that surprises me.

Thamyris, this man is shaking up the city of the Iconians, and your Thecla too, for all the women and youths go in to him and are taught by him. He says that they must fear one god alone and live in purity. And what is more, my daughter, bound like a spider at the window by his words, is mastered by a new desire and a terrible passion, for the girl hangs on his words and falls prey to them. But go and speak to her, for she is betrothed to you.'

Thamyris went to her, feeling both tender affection and fear at her mental disturbance, and said, 'Thecla my betrothed, why do you sit this way? What passion makes you so disturbed? Turn back to your Thamyris. You should be ashamed of yourself!' Her mother too said the same thing: 'My child, why do you sit there looking down, and make no answer, but remain stricken?' And they lamented terribly, Thamyris because he had lost his wife, Theoclea her child, and the maidservants their mistress; the house was filled with a great confusion of grief. While this was going on, Thecla did not turn around, but remained fixated on the words of Paul.

But Thamyris leapt up and went out into the street, and closely observed those going in to Paul and coming out. He saw two men fighting bitterly, and he said to them, 'Men, tell me who you are, and who is inside with you, this man who misleads and deceives the souls of young men and maidens, so that there may be no weddings, and so that they remain as they are. I promise to give you a great deal of money if you tell me about him, for I am a leading man in the city.'

And Demas and Hermogenes said to him, 'We do not know who this man is, but he robs the young men of wives and the maidens of husbands, saying "There is no resurrection for you unless you remain pure and do not defile the flesh, but guard your purity."'

7.16 Heliodorus *Aethiopica* 5.4.4–5, 10.7.6–10.9.4. Third century CE. In this novel Chariclea, the daughter of the Ethiopian queen, is separated from her mother at birth and ends up a priestess at Delphi. She falls in love with the handsome Theagenes and runs away with him, though she makes him swear to preserve her virginity. They ultimately arrive in Ethiopia, where Chariclea is reunited with her family and marries Theagenes.

5.4.4–5
Left alone in the cave, Theagenes and Chariclea made the best of their terrible situation. For the first time, they found themselves on their own with nothing to disturb them. They took their fill of embraces and kisses without holding back, forgetting everything else as though they had grown together into one. Still, they satisfied themselves with a chaste and virginal love, mingling their warm hot tears and exchanging pure kisses. For whenever Chariclea noticed that Theagenes' manly urges were becoming too strong, she restrained him with a reminder of his oath. He had no difficulty in practicing moderation and easily held himself back, for while love had overpowered him, he was the master of his pleasures.

10.7.6–10.9.4
[Hydaspes and Persina, king and queen of the Ethiopians, and the true parents of Chariclea, are presiding over the crowd as prisoners are led forth for sacrifice. Seeing the beautiful Chariclea, Persina pities her and suggests taking Chariclea into her household as a servant. Hydaspes responds.]

You know that our law requires us to offer and sacrifice a man to the Sun and a woman to the Moon. This woman was the first to be captured and was brought to me as the intended victim for the sacrifice today; the people would disapprove if we spared her. Only one thing could preserve her: if she undergoes the trial by fire, and is found to lack purity in her associations with men. For the law commands that the woman who is given to the goddess must be untainted, and likewise the man who is given to the Sun, and for the sacrifice to Dionysus, it makes no difference. But consider whether a girl who the fire shows has consorted with men would be suitable to receive into your household. Persina answered, 'Let the fire show this, if only she is saved! Captivity, war and banishment so far from her own land render her blameless if that is what has happened, especially in the case of this girl, whose beauty is great enough to incite violence.'

While she said these things and wept, trying to hide her tears from those who were present, Hydaspes ordered that the brazier be brought forward. Then the attendants, taking young children from the crowd (for only they could handle the fire and not be harmed), brought it from the temple, and placing it in their midst, commanded each of the prisoners to walk on it. All those who walked on it burned their feet, and some could not bear to touch it even for a short time, for the golden spits in the fire were endowed with the power to burn anyone who was not pure or had broken an oath, but the pure could walk on them without hurting their feet. So these prisoners were allotted to Dionysus, except for two or three girls whom the fire had recognised as virgins.

When Theagenes stepped into the fire and it was clear that he was a virgin, everyone was amazed at his height and good looks, and wondered how a young man in his prime could be unacquainted with the pleasures of Aphrodite. So he was made ready for the sacrifice to the Sun. Then he spoke softly to Chariclea: 'They have a fine reward in Ethiopia for those who live a pure life! Are sacrifice and slaughter to be the prizes for chastity? Dearest, why do you not reveal your identity? What are you waiting for, the moment when they cut our throats? Speak, I beg you, and declare yourself. Perhaps you will save me, if you are recognised and you plead on my behalf. And if not, surely at least you will escape the danger. It is enough for me to die knowing that you are saved.' 'The contest is at hand,' she said, 'and our fate lies in the balance.' Without waiting for a command from those in charge, she put on the sacred tunic from Delphi, interwoven with gold and glittering ornaments. This she drew from the small bag she carried with her. Then, letting her hair down, she ran and leaped onto the brazier like a woman possessed, and stood there for a long time without harm. From the high place where she stood, her beauty was apparent to all and shone out brighter than ever. Because of her dress, she seemed to the crowd more like the image of a goddess than a mortal woman. Amazement seized them all, and a single, indistinct murmur resounded throughout the crowd, demonstrating their wonder. Above all they marveled that she had remained untouched although she was lovelier than any mortal woman and in the bloom of her youth; her chastity was a greater ornament than her physical beauty.

7.17 Ammianus Marcellinus *History* 25.4.2–3. Ca. 380. One of the last great Roman historians, Marcellinus recorded the deeds of the Roman emperors in the fourth century. He was an admirer of Julian (331–63), the emperor who rejected Christianity in favour of a return to paganism informed by Greek philosophy.

Most especially he was distinguished for his inviolate chastity, so that after he lost his wife, he was steadfast in avoiding sexual relations, citing what can be read in Plato, that when the tragic author Sophocles, having grown very old, was asked whether he still slept with women, he said no, adding that he rejoiced at having escaped from the love for such things, as from some fierce and cruel master. Likewise, in order to further strengthen this principle, he often repeated the saying of a lyric poet he loved to read, Bacchylides, who declared that just as a skilled painter makes a face beautiful, so chastity is a lofty adornment to a life of aspiration. He so carefully avoided this failing in the mature vigour of his prime, that there was never the slightest suspicion of lechery, nor did the attendants closest to him accuse him of it, as often happens.

Further Reading

On virginity in antiquity, see Sissa 1990, and MacLachlan and Fletcher (eds) 2007. For virgin goddesses, see Irwin 2007. For the social context of the Greek term *aidōs*, see Cairns 1993; for Gyges and Candaules, see Cairns 1996. On attitudes toward veiling, sexual modesty, and privacy, see Llewellyn-Jones 2003 and 2007. On the Vestal Virgins, see Beard 1995 and Parker 2004. On *pudicitia*, see Langlands 2006; on modesty and shame among the Romans, see Barton 1999. On the chastity of Hippolytus, see Zeitlin 1985 and Cairns 1997. On Christian celibacy and virginity, see Brown 1990, E. A. Clark 1995 and G. Clark 1998; for Thecla, see Bremmer 1996. For virginity and chastity in the Greek novel, see Konstan 1994 and Chew 2003.

8

Marital Sexuality

In the Greco-Roman world, marriage was less closely linked to love and romance than it is today. The families of prospective spouses arranged most marriages with a view to increasing their wealth or benefiting their social status. While personal emotional fulfillment for the spouses was recognised as one possible outcome of marriage, its main purpose was perceived as the procreation of legitimate heirs and the building of economic and social capital to the benefit of both partners. Besides bearing children, the wife's primary duty was overseeing the management of the household (8.10). Adult lifespans were shorter than they are today and divorce was common, with the result that many people were married more than once. Still, both the Greeks and Romans considered ideal those marriages in which the partners were devoted to one another, and the erotic aspects of marriage were not ignored, especially in the rituals surrounding weddings (1.18, 7.8). Among philosophers, the Stoics were the most accepting of marriage, and Musonius Rufus argued (8.13) that because marriage was not required for procreation, its most important aspects were 'companionship' (*symbiōsis*) and the partners' mutual care. Interestingly, however, he did not view sexual pleasure as an essential part of the ideal marital relationship, but stated instead (6.11) that spouses ought to have sex only in order to beget children.

In Homer's epic poem, Odysseus meets the virginal princess Nausicaa (8.1) and expresses to her his hope that she will find happiness in a marital relationship with a husband 'of like mind' (*homophrōn*). While Nausicaa sees Odysseus as husband material, he himself is thinking of his wife Penelope, who is a match for him in intelligence and resourcefulness. When he returns home after a twenty-year absence, she proves this by testing the stranger who claims to be her husband (8.2). Her test demonstrates to her husband not only her like-mindedness, but also the great lengths to which she has gone to maintain loyalty to Odysseus and fidelity to the marriage. Odysseus' account of how he built the couple's nuptial chamber, in turn, is not merely the final proof of his identity, but also reveals to Penelope that the emotional significance he invests in their marriage has not wavered over a twenty-year separation.

In Classical Greek culture, marriage was a rite of passage by which a young woman shed her previous identity and realigned her interests from those of her natal family toward those of her husband. This transformation, which accompanied her first sexual experience, could be metaphorically viewed as a kind of death, while premature death itself is sometimes presented as a marriage to Hades (8.3; compare 1.4 on Hades' rape of Persephone). In Sophocles' tragedy *Antigone*, the title character laments that she must accept 'Acheron' (the name of an underworld river used by metonymy for Hades) as her husband in place of a living spouse, and questions the cultural expectation that a woman's loyalty belongs solely to her husband.

Greek culture enshrined a double standard whereby men's extramarital affairs with socially sanctioned partners were condoned, whereas wives were expected to remain chaste in order to ensure the legitimacy of the couple's children. Women were not immune to sexual jealousy. Euripides' Medea insists (8.4) that nothing incenses a woman as much as the threat that her husband may be tempted away from her bed. Plutarch's advice to a young couple on the occasion of their wedding (8.15) represents the conventional sentiment of upper-class, well-educated men regarding infidelity: a man should not insult his wife's dignity by subjecting her to drunken carousing or rough sex; if he felt compelled to engage in such activities, he should indulge in them with women of lower social classes. Instead of feeling resentment in such cases, the wife ought to be grateful. Only among the philosophers did the concept of male marital fidelity circulate; the Pythagoreans and later the practical philosopher Musonius Rufus (6.11) advocated that both spouses be sexually faithful. The apostle Paul also expressed this idea, but in a new context, the Christian ideal of celibacy (8.14). He advised total abstinence from sex for his followers in Corinth, but if they were not capable of this, he recommended marriage and mutual fidelity.

The ideal wife was faithful, industrious and chaste, although both Greek tragedy and comedy show wives taking a keen interest in marital sex. The wives in Aristophanes' *Lysistrata* initially balk at the idea of withholding sex from their husbands, because they enjoy it too much to forego its pleasures (8.7). Their zestful enjoyment of sex is exaggerated for comic effect, and reflects a cultural belief in the lascivious character of women (3.4, 3.18, 5.5, 6.1). For dramatic reasons, Aristophanes ignores the fact that his male characters could easily satisfy their physical needs with partners other than their wives. Even setting aside a husband's potential pederastic interests, the passage from the oration *Against Neaera* on the complementary roles of prostitutes, courtesans, and wives suggests a bleak outlook for Athenian

wives who wished to be the sole objects of their husband's sexual attentions (8.11). Attitudes such as this may have prevented wives from taking
the sexual initiative, for fear that their husbands would find their behaviour
too similar to that of prostitutes (8.15). In Xenophon's *Symposium*, marital
sexuality between Dionysus and his bride Ariadne is presented in a positive
light (8.9), but Ariadne, while a willing partner, conducts herself 'like a modest
woman'. The Athenian gentleman Ischomachus, whose methods of 'training'
his young wife for her role are described in Xenophon's *Economics*, reflects
the attitudes of many well-educated men in both Greece and Rome, particularly in his rejection of cosmetics for married women (8.10). He alludes to the
fact that he has sexual access to the female servants in the house, and that
his wife can compete with them most successfully by emphasising the differences: she is a willing partner, cleaner, and more expensively dressed.

In spite of the sexual double standard, many married couples were loving,
affectionate, and even passionately attached to one another. The speech
by Isaeus (8.8) describes a suitor who pursued his bride without regard to
considerations of financial gain. In Euripides' play *Helen*, an ecstatic and
faithful Helen is reunited with Menelaus after many years of separation and
mutual longing (8.6). The Euripidean heroine Evadne (8.5) demonstrates what
may have seemed to contemporaries an unseemly degree of passion in her
determination to burn herself on her dead husband's pyre. Her speech draws
upon the common metaphor of the flame for erotic desire, and she describes
her suicide in sexual terms as a form of union with her husband.

The younger Pliny wrote to his wife (8.21) expressing a type of marital
affection that must have often resulted even from arranged marriages.
When his wife is absent, Pliny clearly misses their emotional as well as their
sexual intimacy. Much as they do today, gravestones in antiquity provided
a public medium for spouses to express affection for each other; typically a
husband's praise for his deceased wife emphasised her chastity and sexual
fidelity. While the sentiments displayed on gravestones were often dictated
by convention, they sometimes go beyond the standard formulas in order
to express the lasting devotion of one spouse the other (8.12) The opposite
point of view is represented in Aulus Gellius' report of a speech delivered
during the Republican period, in which Roman men are portrayed as reluctant
husbands who must be convinced to suffer the daily irritations of marriage in
order to fulfill their patriotic duty to populate the state (8.22).

Josephus' portrait of the marital relations between Herod and Mariame
(8.20) demonstrates not only the potential for erotic attachment in marriages
arranged for political purposes (typical among the elites in the Greek and
Roman worlds), but also the drawbacks of a match between partners of
disparate social class. In Josephus' interpretation, Mariame's sense of her
dignity and entitlements as Hasmonean royalty led her to reject the authority

that the lowborn Herod held over her, both as sovereign and as husband. In spite of Herod's passion for her, his distrust and her contempt combined to seal her fate.

It is no coincidence that several selections from Plutarch appear in this chapter, because among ancient authors he is one of the strongest advocates of marriage, and the most assiduous in recording ancient marital practices. In his *Dialogue on Love*, Daphnaeus and Plutarch extol the benefits of marriage even in the unusual case of Ismenodora, a wealthy widow who wished to marry a teenaged boy (8.19). Although Bacchon and his mother seem to have doubts about the unequal match, Ismenodora's champions hold that Bacchon can only benefit from her superior status and wealth. The main area of contention in the dialogue, however, is the relative value of pederastic and heterosexual attachments, and their relationship to *erōs*. While their opponent Protogenes, an advocate of pederasty, argues that genuine love (*erōs*) is found only in chaste pederastic friendships, Daphnaeus and Plutarch maintain that a sexual relationship provides the foundation for loving and affectionate relations in marriage.

Plutarch's interest in marriage, including its sexual component, is equally apparent in his biographical works. In the *Life of Solon*, he approves of Solon's legislation stipulating that the husbands of heiresses must have regular intercourse with them (8.17). While this provision may have been intended to facilitate the conception of male heirs, Plutarch interprets it as a method of strengthening the personal relationship between individuals forced by circumstances to marry. In the *Life of Lycurgus*, he similarly praises the Archaic Spartan custom of bride-capture because it forces newly-wed couples to practice moderation and thereby increases their mutual desire (8.16). The relationship between marriage and the needs of the state is illustrated in the 'wife-swapping' custom of the Archaic Spartans, whereby the claim of a man to both wife and children, like personal property, was thought to be contingent and limited; the state's need to produce healthy children for the Spartan war machine was the most important consideration and outweighed the desires of the individual. Traces of a similar eugenic and duty-based attitude can be discerned in the behaviour of the younger Cato, who agreed to give up his wife so that another man could make use of her in order to father children (8.18). Cato's decision may reflect the views of Greek philosophers who advocated a community of wives (6.16).

8.1 Homer *Odyssey* 6.175–85. Late eighth century BCE. Shipwrecked Odysseus asks for assistance from the Phaeacian princess Nausicaa.

Have pity, queen, for first to you I came,
After many sufferings, unacquainted

With the others, who hold this land and city.
Show me the town, and give me a covering,
If you have some extra cloth on hand.
And may the gods bestow all you desire:
A home and husband, and that noble gift
Like-mindedness. For nothing is stronger or better
Than when a man and woman think alike,
Dwelling together, a grief to their enemies,
But a joy to their friends, and especially to each other.

8.2 Homer *Odyssey* 23.164–232. Late eighth century BCE. After Odysseus kills the suitors who have invaded his home, he feels frustration because Penelope still refuses to recognise him.

Then once more he sat in the chair opposite
His wife, and spoke a word to her, and said:
'Strange woman! The gods who hold Olympus
Made your heart all too hard for a female.
No other wife could bear to remain aloof,
When her man had suffered such ill fortune
And after twenty years come home at last.
Come, nurse, spread a couch for me alone,
Since this woman's heart is made of iron.'
Then wise Penelope said to him in reply,
'Strange man, neither do I proudly scorn you,
Nor am I surprised, for I had your measure
When you departed Ithaca in long-oared ships.
Eurycleia, spread the stout bed, outside
The inner chamber that he built himself.
Bring the stout bed for him, and blanket it well,
With fleeces and woolen mantles and shining rugs.'
She spoke, and tested her spouse. Odysseus
Replied to his prudent wife in a burst of anger,
'Woman, this word of yours sickens my heart.
Who set my bed elsewhere? That would be difficult,
Even for a man of skill, unless by chance
A god should come and move it effortlessly.
But no man alive, even though young and strong,
Could pry it loose with ease, for I and no other
Built a great token into the well-carved bed.
A long-leafed olive tree once grew in the courtyard,

Thriving, strong, and wide as a pillar. Round this
I constructed the chamber with dry-stone blocks,
And carefully fitted the roof and jointed doors.
Then I cut the long-leafed olive branches,
Trimming the trunk from the root, and smoothing it
With bronze and skill, keeping the line in true;
The bedpost once complete, I pierced with an auger.
And this was the starting point of the bed I built,
Inlaid with plaques of ivory, silver and gold.
On the frame I stretched bands of crimson oxhide.
This token, woman, I confide to you, not knowing
Whether my bedpost still stands firm, or by now
Some man has cut and moved it from its root.'
So he spoke, unbinding her knees and heart,
For she knew the sturdy bedpost he described.
Then in a burst of tears she ran to Odysseus,
And taking him in her arms, kissed him and said,
'Do not be angry, you who were always wise.
The gods have given us grief as a companion,
For they begrudged that we should stay together,
Enjoying youth and reaching the brink of old age.
Lay aside anger and blame me not, if at first
I failed to give you welcome, for always my heart
Feared to fall prey to some man's deceptive words,
And many are those who scheme for evil profits.
Even Argive Helen, who was born from Zeus,
Would not have gone to bed with a foreign man,
Had she foreseen that the warlike Achaeans' sons
Would lead her home again to her native land.
Some god aroused her to that wrongful deed:
Before, she never had thoughts of the ruinous madness
That was destined to carry sorrow to us as well.
But now, since you have clearly named the sign
Of our marriage bed, which no man else has seen,
But only you and I and one serving maid,
Actor's daughter, my father's wedding gift,
She who watched the doors of our bridal chamber,
I am convinced, though my heart was cruel before.'
She spoke, and the urge to cry welled up within him;
He wept, embracing the mate of his heart, his wife.

8.3 Sophocles *Antigone* 806–16, 890–925. 438 BCE. Antigone addresses the chorus after learning that Creon, the ruler of Thebes, has condemned her to be buried alive for providing funeral rites to her brother Polynices.

806–16
Antigone:
Watch, citizens of my native land, as I make my last
Journey, beholding the sun's light for one last time,
And then never again. But Hades, who lays all to rest,
Is leading me, still living, to the strand of Acheron,[246]
Though I have had no share in marriage, and no one yet
Has sung my wedding song. Instead I shall become
Acheron's bride.

[Creon gives the final command for Antigone's execution.]

890–925
Antigone:
My tomb, my bridal chamber, my everlasting
Abode deep in the earth, where I travel to find
So many of my kin, now ruined corpses all,
Those Persephone has welcomed to her realm.
Last of all and prey to the greatest misery
I shall descend before my allotted time.
Yet I nourish great hopes that my arrival
Will be welcome to my father, and to you,
Mother, and to you, my dearest brother,
For my own hands washed you when you died;
I bathed and dressed you, and at the burial place
Poured drink. But now, Polynices, I win
This reward for laying out your corpse.
Indeed, the wise admit I knew your worth.
For had I been mother to children, or seen a husband
Die and decay, never would I resolve
To take on this task against the citizens' will.
What law, you may ask, do I observe in this?
Should my husband die, I could find another,
And bear his child if one of mine were lost,
But with Father and Mother both below in Hades,
No brother will ever again be born for me.
Under this law I honoured you most of all,

My brother, but to Creon's mind I did wrong,
And dared to commit a terrible deed.
And now I lie within his powerful grasp,
A virgin still unwed and deprived of my share
In marriage and the nurturing of children.
Bereft of friends and doomed to an evil fate,
Alive I descend to the dead deep in the earth.
What decrees of the gods have I transgressed?
Why in my misery do I still look to them?
To whom could I cry out, since reverent acts
Now convict me of irreverence?
If these events are pleasing to the gods,
Pain may cause me to confess my error.
But if these men have erred, I pray that they
Suffer no more than the wrong they do to me.

8.4 Euripides *Medea* 214–66. 431 BCE. Euripides' tragedy tells how the hero Jason planned to leave his foreign wife, Medea for a Corinthian princess, and how Medea took revenge by murdering the children she had with Jason. In this scene, Medea laments the woman's lot in marriage.

Medea:
Women of Corinth, I have come from the house
To forestall your blame. Many people, I know,
Are proud whether indoors or in the public eye.
Others seem uncaring to their neighbours,
Living quietly. Justice fails, when mortals
Hate a man on sight, who never wronged them,
Before they gain clear knowledge of his heart.
A foreigner must keep the ways of the city;
I disapprove those whose willful ignorance
Brings sharp pain to their fellow citizens.
But this unexpected blow casts utter ruin
Upon my soul. No joy in life remains;
I wish only to die, my friends. My husband,
He who was my all – how well I know it! –
Has shown himself to be the worst of men.

Of living things endowed with breath and thought
We women were born to the greatest misery.
First, we must purchase at excessive cost

A spouse, to be lord and master of our bodies.
And our whole life's fortune depends on this:
Whether he is bad or good. For divorce is ruin
To a woman's name, nor can she refuse to wed.
She enters a strange house, amid new customs
She never learned at home, and is expected
To read the omens of her husband's mood.
If a wife completes these difficult labours,
And her husband accepts the yoke of marriage,
She is to be envied; if not, she is better off dead.
When a man is weary of domestic company
He soothes his heart's annoyance outside the home.
But we must direct our gaze to one face alone.
They say we live a carefree life at home,
Safe from danger while they fight with the spear.
How wrongly! Sooner would I take my stand
Three times with a shield, than give birth once.

But our stories diverge: you have a home
And city; you enjoy friends' company,
While I, deserted and without a country, suffer
My husband's abuse. I was his foreign plunder;
No mother or brother lives here to shelter me
From this disaster. So I shall ask this favour:
If I discover some means by which to avenge
My husband's ill treatment of me, keep silence.
In many matters, a woman is filled with fear
And shrinks from feats of strength and steel,
But if she suffers an insult touching her bed,
No mind is more intent on bloody slaughter.

8.5 Euripides *Suppliants* 990–1030 Diggle. 423 BCE. When Evadne's husband Capaneus, one of the Seven Against Thebes, is killed by Zeus' thunderbolt, she decides to throw herself onto his funeral pyre. This portion of the play has serious textual problems and some elements of the translation are conjectural.

Evadne:
With what radiant beams
The sun's chariot shone
And the moon in the heavens

As swift-moving nymphs
Rode through the dark sky
On the day the city of Argos
Raised high the cheerful song
For my wedding and groom,
Alas! Capaneus clad in bronze.
I run to you straight from home,
Frantic to tread the bright flame
And share the same tomb,
To dissolve my tedious life
And weary burdens in Hades.
Yes, for the sweetest death
Is to die with dying loved ones
If fate will accomplish it.

Chorus leader:
You see the pyre and stand
Above it, Zeus' treasure house.
There lies your husband,
Brought low by the fiery bolt.

Evadne:
I see my goal from where I stand;
May good luck lead my feet.
For glory's sake I will rush
Headlong into the flames
From these rocks, to unite
My body in the fiery blaze
With that of my spouse.
Pressing his dear flesh to mine
I will reach Persephone's realm;
Never will my soul betray you,
As you lie dead in the earth!
Away with light and weddings,
Let righteous marriage beds
And songs shine forth in Argos
For my children, as a pious
Steady husband is fused
With the guileless breeze
Of a wife born to nobility.

8.6 Euripides *Helen* 625–59. 412 BCE. In the Euripidean version of Helen's story, she does not travel to Troy with Paris, but is whisked away to Egypt by Hermes, while Paris is joined by a phantom Helen. When her husband Menelaus finds her, the pair are rapturously reunited.

Helen:
Menelaus, dearest of men,
The time was long, but delight is now at hand.
Friends, I receive my husband in gladness,
Embracing one who is dear to me
After many a light-bearing dawn.

Menelaus:
And I embrace you. Amidst so many thoughts,
I hardly know how to begin to express them.

Helen:
The hair on my head stands on end, and tears
Drip from me, so joyous am I.
I throw my arms about your neck, husband,
To feel this pleasure all the more.

Menelaus:
You are the dearest thing I see. I place no blame.
I possess the daughter of Zeus and Leda.
Beneath the wedding torches, your brothers gave blessings,
Blessings, those twin youths on white horses.
That was before. But the god who deprived me of you,
Leading you from home, now drives us
Toward a fortune better than this.
After long years, a happy evil led you to your husband.
May I enjoy the good fortune that is mine.

Chorus:
May you enjoy it! I join my prayer with yours,
For when there are two, one does not suffer a pain alone.

Helen:
My dear, dear friends, for that which is past
I heave no sighs, nor do I feel pain.
I have my husband, whose arrival from Troy
I longed for these many years.

Menelaus:
You have me, and I have you. The innumerable days
Of separation were difficult, yet I understand now
The ways of the goddess. My joy is tearful,
Yet I feel more delight than sorrow.

Helen:
What words can express this? What more could a mortal wish?
I hold you to my heart, against every expectation.

Menelaus:
And I hold you, whom I thought lost to Ida's city
And the careworn towers of Troy.

8.7 Aristophanes *Lysistrata* 99–166. 411 BCE. In this famous comedy, the
women of Athens and Sparta plot a sex strike during the Peloponnesian war
in order to force the warring cities to make peace.

Lysistrata:
Don't you yearn for your children's fathers
Who are away at the war? I've a good idea
Not a single one of you has your man at home.

Calonice:
That wretched man of mine's been in Thrace
For five months, keeping an eye on Eucrates.[247]

Myrrhine:
And mine's spent a full seven months in Pylos.

Lampito:
As soon as mine gets clear of one battle line,
He straps on his shield and flies off to another.

Lysistrata:
Even our lovers are gone without a trace.
And ever since the Milesians switched sides,
There is a dire shortage of leather dildos,
Those ten-inchers that help a girl in need.
If I can devise a plan, do you all agree
To help me put an end to the fighting?

Myrrhine:
Yes, by the Two Goddesses![248] I'd even pawn
This blouse, and drink the proceeds down!

Calonice:
And I'll help even if I'm split like a sole,
And half of me goes to the anti-war fund.

Lampito:
I'd climb to the peak of Mount Taygetus,[249]
Just to catch a glimpse of peace at last.

Lysistrata:
Then I'll tell you; no need for secrets.
Ladies, if we really and truly intend
To force our husbands to make peace
We must refrain –

Myrrhine:
From what? Tell us.

Lysistrata:
Will you really do it, then?

Calonice:
We'll do it, even if it kills us.

Lysistrata:
Then – we must forego the pleasures of the penis.
Why are you turning away? Where are you going?
Why do you grimace and shake your head?
Why the pale, drawn faces and the flow of tears?
Will you help me or not? What will you do?

Calonice:
No, by Zeus, I won't do it. Let the war continue!

Myrrhine:
Me neither, I won't do it. Let the war continue!

Lysistrata:
Is that so, Mrs. Sole? Just now you told us all
You'd gladly be cut in two for the sake of peace!

Calonice:
Is there no other way? I'll walk through fire,
If you say we must. But not give up the penis.
Oh, Lysistrata, there's nothing else like it!

Lysistrata:
And you?

Another Wife:
I'd rather walk through fire, too.

Lysistrata:
Our female sex can think of nothing but sex!
It's no wonder the tragic poets feast on us.
We keep replaying Poseidon and the boat.[250]
But, dear Spartan, if you agree to help me,
The plan might still work. Support my cause!

Lampito:
By the Two Goddesses, it's a great hardship
To sleep alone, without the comfort of a cock.
But so be it, for the sake of making peace.

Lysistrata:
Darling! Only you deserve the name of woman.

Calonice:
But if, God forbid, we do the thing you suggest,
Would peace come any sooner because of this?

Lysistrata:
By the Two Goddesses, much sooner.
If we sit inside, with our faces made up,
And our crotches plucked neat and smooth,
In those see-through silks from Amorgos,
Our husbands will grow hard and hot for sex.
When we refuse them and keep well away,
They'll make peace soon enough, believe me.

Lampito:
So Menelaus threw down his sword, they say,
When he got a look at Helen naked!

Calonice:
But what if our husbands simply leave?

Lysistrata:
Then as a wise man said, you go it alone.

Calonice:
Bah, no imitation pricks for me. But what if
They drag us into the bedroom by force?

Lysistrata:
Then grab on to the doorposts.

Calonice:
And if they beat us?

Lysistrata:
Then give in, but be sullen and reluctant.
For they have no pleasure when it's forced.
Then find other ways to make them suffer.
They'll give in soon enough. When his wife
Won't put out, a husband can never be happy.

Calonice:
Well, all of us will do as you think best.

8.8 Isaeus 10.18–20. First half of fourth century BCE. In this speech composed by Isaeus for his client in a lawsuit, the client describes his father as an eager lover who would not give up his intended bride for considerations of money.

Perhaps some of you, gentlemen, will wonder at the delay, asking how we could allow such a long time to pass, and why, although we had been defrauded, we took no action in the matter but only now press our claim. I believe that it is an injustice if someone receives less than what is due to him because he was unable to ask for it, or neglected to do so. For what requires examination is not failure to ask, but whether the claim is itself just or unjust. Yet we can furnish an explanation, gentlemen, even for this delay. When my father became engaged to my mother and married her, he received a dowry. But whereas these men were reaping the benefits of the estate, he had no recourse, for they threatened that they would gain legal control over her, and that one of them would marry her, if he were not satisfied to keep her with no more than the dowry. But in order to avoid being deprived of my mother, my father would have allowed them to enjoy an estate of even double the value. That is the reason why my father never proceeded with a lawsuit.

8.9 Xenophon *Symposium* 9.1–7. Ca. 365 BCE. At the end of a drinking party attended by Socrates and his friends, hired actors present an entertainment portraying the god Dionysus with his bride Ariadne.

Here the conversation ended. Since this was the hour when Autolycus usually took a walk, he rose to leave. As his father Lycon was departing to accompany him, he turned and said, 'By Hera, Socrates, you are a man of true nobility.'

After this, an armchair was placed in the room first of all, and then the man from Syracuse came in and said, 'Gentlemen, Ariadne will now enter the bedchamber she shares with Dionysus. After that, Dionysus will come to join her, slightly intoxicated from drinking with the gods, and they will frolic together.'

After this, Ariadne came in dressed as a bride and sat in the armchair. Although Dionysus had not yet appeared, the flutist played a Bacchic song. Then the audience felt admiration for the choreographer, because as soon as Ariadne heard the music, she reacted in such a way that everyone perceived her joy in it. Although she neither went to greet him nor even stood up from the chair, it was clear that she could barely restrain herself. And when Dionysus caught sight of her, he came dancing toward her and lovingly sat down in her lap, wrapping his arms about her and kissing her. She conducted herself like a modest woman, yet returned his embrace with affection. When the guests saw this, they clapped all together and shouted, 'Again!' After Dionysus got to his feet and gave his hand to Ariadne to rise, the spectators looked on as they clung together and kissed each other. They saw a truly handsome Dionysus and a truly lovely Ariadne, not playing for laughs but exchanging real kisses with their lips, and as they viewed this scene, they became aroused. For they heard Dionysus asking her if she loved him, and she vowed that she did, in such a way that not only Dionysus, but all those present would have sworn that this boy and girl truly cared for one another. To all appearances, they were not actors taught to play a scene, but two people now free to satisfy desires they had felt for a long time. Finally, the guests saw the couple leave for bed with their arms entwined about one another. At this, those who were unmarried swore that they would take brides, while the married men leapt onto their horses and hurried home to bed their wives.

Socrates and the others who were left went out with Callias to join Lycon and his son on their walk. And that is how the party that night broke up.

8.10 Xenophon *Economics* 10.2–13. Ca. 360 BCE. Xenophon's dialogue recreates a conversation between Socrates and Ischomachus in which they discuss the training of Ischomachus' young wife for her household duties. The dialogue also touches on more intimate aspects of the relationship between husband and wife.

At that Ischomachus said, 'Well, Socrates, one day I saw that she had rubbed a great deal of white lead onto her face, in order to look even more light-skinned than she was, and that she was applying rouge in order to make her cheeks more rosy than was truly the case, and wearing shoes with thick soles in order to appear taller. So I said to her, "Tell me, my wife, would you judge me more worthy of your affection as a co-owner of our mutual assets if I showed you each thing just as it is, without exaggerating or concealing the extent of our possessions, or if I deceitfully tried to convince you that we have more than we do, showing off counterfeit silver coins, gilded necklaces that are wood underneath, and cloth made purple with cheap dyes that fade?"

"Don't say that," she interrupted right away. "And you must not become that sort of man, because if you did, I could not be glad about our marriage."

"Then, my wife," I answered, "is the sharing of our bodies with each other not also a part of our union?"

"That's what people say, at any rate," she replied.

"Then would I seem more worthy of your affection as a co-owner in this partnership of the body if I take careful measures so that the body I present to you is healthy and vigorous, and so that the colour in my cheeks is real, or on the other hand if I display myself to you with red lead daubed on my cheeks and flesh-coloured makeup under my eyes, and when we are in bed together, I deceive you so that you see and touch red lead instead of my own skin?"

She replied, "I would much prefer to touch you than red lead, to see your skin instead of makeup, and your eyes healthy instead of smeared with ointments."

"Then you must realise that I too prefer your own skin to white lead and rouge, and that just as the gods made horses to find other horses most pleasing, and cattle to prefer other cattle, and sheep other sheep, so also one human being is pleased with the pure and unadorned body of another. Perhaps these tricks may deceive outsiders, who have no way of determining the truth, but people who live together are bound to be caught, if they try to deceive each other. For the ruse is detected when they get out of bed in the morning to dress; they are betrayed if they sweat, convicted if they shed a tear, and their true appearance is exposed when they take a bath."'

'Good heavens,' I said, 'what was her answer to that?'

'Nothing, except that from that day on she never occupied herself with such things, and always tried to present herself to me in her pure and unadorned state, as is right. She did ask me, however, whether I could advise her on how to be truly beautiful, rather than only seeming so. And this was my advice, Socrates. I told her to avoid always sitting around like a slave, and instead to try, with the help of the gods, to behave like the mistress of the household. She should stand at the loom and teach whatever she knows better than others, while learning whatever she doesn't know. She should keep an eye on the slave who makes the bread, stand beside the housekeeper while she is measuring out supplies, and go all around the house looking to see that each thing is in its proper place. I thought that this would give her something to do, as well as a walk. I said that it is also good exercise to mix flour and knead dough, and to shake out and fold cloaks and blankets. If she exercises in this way, she will have a better appetite, be healthier, and the colour in her cheeks will be real. And whenever her looks are compared with those of a female servant, she will be cleaner and better dressed, and altogether more stimulating, especially since she is willing to gratify me, whereas a female servant is compelled to do so. But wives who always sit about like grand ladies cause others to think they are overdressed frauds. And now, Socrates, you can rest assured that my wife's dress and habits of life are those I have taught her, just as I have described.'

8.11 Pseudo-Demosthenes *Against Neaera* 59.122. Ca. 340 BCE. Erroneously attributed to the orator Demosthenes, this speech from an Athenian trial was actually authored by Apollodorus, who prosecuted the case. In this section, he discusses the sexual roles of different groups of women.

For this is what it means to be married: a man fathers children and presents his sons to the members of the clan and the township, and he gives his daughters in marriage to their husbands with the understanding that they are his offspring. We have courtesans for the sake of pleasure, and mistresses for the daily care of our bodies, but the role of the wife is to produce legitimate children and be a trustworthy guardian of the household. Therefore, if Stephanus previously married a citizen woman, and these children belong to her and not Neaera, he could have demonstrated this most convincingly by handing over these maidservants for torture.

8.12 Roman gravestone. *CIL* I² 1221. First half of first century BCE. This gravestone was set up by Aurelius Hermia for his wife. On each side of a sculpted relief showing the couple, one of the spouses 'speaks'.

Aurelius Hermia, the freedman of Lucius, a butcher on the Viminal Hill. This woman, who preceded me in death, chaste of body and with a loving heart, was my only wife. She spent her life faithful to her faithful husband with equal devotion, since greed never caused her to fail in her duty. Aurelia, the freedwoman of Lucius.

Aurelia Philematio, the freedwoman of Lucius. When alive I was named Aurelia Philematium. I was chaste, modest, and knowing nothing of the rabble, I was faithful to my husband. I am without my husband, alas, who was freedman to the same Lucius. In fact and truly, he was far more than a parent to me. He took me to his bosom when I was seven years old. At the age of forty years, I am stronger than death. Through my tireless care he flourished in the eyes of all.

8.13 Musonius Rufus 13a (*On the Goal of Marriage*). Mid-first century CE. The Stoic philosopher was an advocate of marriage, and taught that the emotional relationship between the spouses was of the greatest importance.

The husband and the wife must come together, he said, in order to live with one another, to beget children together, and to consider all their goods held in common, and nothing individually owned, not even their own bodies. The birth of a human being that results from this union is a great thing indeed, but it is not sufficient to define a married person, for procreation could take place as a result of other types of embraces, entirely apart from marriage, in the same way that animals mate. But in marriage, above all, there must be companionship, and the husband and wife must look after one another in health, in sickness and in every circumstance, since this in addition to the begetting of children is what each of the two aimed for when embarking upon marriage. When the caretaking role is perfected, and when the partners achieve full reciprocity, each striving to excel the other, this is a model marriage and it is a thing to envy, for such sharing is beautiful. But when each partner cares only for his or her own concerns and neglects the other, or indeed, when one partner is acting this way and lives in the same house, but fixes his or her mind elsewhere and is unwilling either to strive for common goals or to yield to the other, then their partnership will necessarily suffer destruction. Although they live together, their affairs will go badly, and in the end they either separate from one another or suffer a continuing connection that is worse than loneliness.

8.14 Paul *First Letter to the Corinthians* 7.1–9. Ca. 55 CE. This letter, part of the canonical New Testament, was written by Paul after he founded a Christian church in Corinth and moved to Ephesus to continue his missionary work.

Now, concerning what you wrote to me, it is good for a man not to touch a woman. But because of the danger of fornication, let each man have his own wife, and let each wife have her own husband. Each husband should give his wife what is due to her, and likewise each wife her husband. The wife does not exercise authority over her own body, but the husband. Likewise, the husband does not exercise authority over his own body, but the wife. Do not deprive one another, unless you both agree to do so for a time, in order to be free to devote yourself to prayer, and then come together again, so that Satan does not tempt you because of your lack of self-control. I say this as a concession, not as a command. I want everyone to be like me, but each person has his own gift from God, and each is different. And to the unmarried and the widows, I say that it is a good thing if they remain as I am. But if they lack willpower, they should marry, for it is better to marry than to burn.

8.15 Plutarch *Advice on Marriage* 16–18 (= *Moralia* 140b–146a). Late first century CE. Happily married himself, Plutarch wrote this essay as a wedding gift for a young couple.

The lawful wives of the Persian kings sit beside them at dinner, and feast with them. But when they desire amorous play and drunkenness, they send their wives away and call in their music-girls and mistresses. They are right to do this, because they do not cause their wives to share in their debauchery or drunken misbehaviour. Therefore if a man in private life, who is ill-bred and lacks self-control with respect to his pleasures, goes astray with a courtesan or maidservant, his wedded wife should not feel irritation or violent anger over this, but should reason that he shows her respect by sharing his violent, unrestrained and drunken misbehaviour with another woman.

Kings who love music and the arts make many musicians, those who love literature make poets, and those who love sports make athletes. In the same way, a husband who loves his own body makes a wife who cares only for adornment; one who is overly fond of pleasure makes an undisciplined wife who acts like a courtesan, and a husband who loves what is good and beautiful makes a wife who is chaste and well-behaved.

A young Spartan girl, when asked by someone whether she had approached her husband for sex, said, 'No. He approached me.' This, I think, is the way the mistress of the household ought to act, neither shying away and being reluctant to endure her husband's sexual overtures, nor initiating them herself. The latter behaviour is overly bold and too much like a courtesan, whereas the former is haughty and lacks natural affection.

8.16 Plutarch *Life of Lycurgus* 15.3–9. Late first century CE. The rules governing the marital conduct of the Spartans were attributed to the lawgiver Lycurgus. If Lycurgus was a historical figure, he would have been active during the first half of the seventh century BCE.

The women were wedded through abduction, not when they were small and too young, but when they were in full bloom and ripe for marriage. When a bride was carried off, a woman known as the 'bridesmaid' took charge of her. She cut the bride's hair close to the scalp, fitted her out in a man's cloak and sandals, and laid her on a straw mat, alone in the dark. Then the bridegroom, not drunkenly or weakened by excessive carousing, but soberly, having dined as usual in the men's mess hall, came to her side. He then untied her virgin's belt and carried her in his arms to the bed. After spending a short time with his bride, he went away calmly to his previous quarters, where he slept alongside the other young men. And from then on, this was his practice, spending his days with his fellow youths and taking his rest with them, but visiting his bride secretly and cautiously, full of bashful trepidation lest any of the household might notice his visits. The bride, too, would plot and arrange with him opportunities for them to meet privately. And they did this not for a brief time, but long enough that some of the husbands became fathers before they ever saw their own wives in daylight. Not only were such meetings good practice in self-control and moderation, they also brought together the spouses in sexual union when their bodies were ready for procreation and their affection for one another was new and fresh, rather than sated and dulled by unrestricted relations. In this way, when they parted they always felt some remnant of delight and a mutual spark of desire for one another. After making such provisions for marriages to be conducted with modesty and good order, Lycurgus also removed from them the empty and womanish passion of jealousy, by making it honourable for deserving men to share in common the begetting of children, yet keeping the institution of marriage wholly separate from any violent lust or unworthiness. For Lycurgus scorned those who would protect their spousal rights as exclusive and inalienable by resorting to murder and wars. For example, if the older husband of a young wife approved of and held in high regard some noble youth, it was permitted for him to introduce this youth to his wife, and to adopt as his own the children produced as a result of her impregnation with noble seed. Likewise, if a worthy man admired some fertile and chaste woman who was married to someone else, it was permitted for him to sleep with her, provided the husband gave his consent, and to plant in this soil, so productive of beautiful progeny, noble children who would share the same blood as a noble family.

For in the first place, Lycurgus believed that children were not the private property of their fathers, but belonged in common to the state, and therefore, he wanted the citizens to be born not from random parents, but from the best. And secondly, he observed much foolishness and ignorance in the laws on these matters enacted by other people, who seek out the best sires they can obtain by fee or favour when it comes to breeding their horses and dogs, but keep their wives under lock and key, so that the children are fathered by them alone. They think this is justified even if they are foolish, elderly, or diseased, as though children who arise from worthless stock do not demonstrate their worthlessness first to those who possess and rear them, and conversely, children who arise from good stock demonstrate their goodness. The way things were done at that time for the physical and political health of the state is so far removed from the looseness later attributed to Spartan women, that for them adultery was unthinkable.

8.17 Plutarch *Life of Solon* 20.2–3. Late first century CE. Plutarch's biography of Solon includes detailed discussion of the laws he promulgated for Athens ca. 590 BCE. Solon's legislation extended to matters of marital sexuality.

The law allowing an heiress to be married to the next of kin, in case the man who legally has power over her is unable to have intercourse with her, seems absurd and wrong. There are some who say that this was justifiable protection against men who would take an heiress for the sake of property, though they are unable to have sex, and so use the law to violate nature. For when they see the heiress sleeping with whomever she wishes, they will either put an end to the marriage, or stay the course under these shameful circumstances, thus receiving the punishment for their arrogance and love of riches. And he is right to legislate that an heiress may not choose just anyone, but only one of the kinsmen of her husband, so that the children who are born may be of his family and lineage. Consistent with this is the law that the bride must eat a quince and be shut in a chamber with the bridegroom, and that the man who takes an heiress as his wife must come to her three times a month without fail. For even if there are no children, a husband still ought to honour a chaste wife in this way. His kindness removes many of the disagreements that arise in such situations, and prevents the pair from becoming estranged as a result of their differences.

8.18 Plutarch *Life of Cato the Younger* 25.2–5. Late first century CE. Cato was a statesman of the Roman Republic and a practitioner of Stoic philosophy, noted for his personal integrity. The incident Plutarch describes probably took place sometime around 56 BCE.

Of the many people who were lovers and admirers of Cato, some showed their feelings more openly and conspicuously than others. One of these was Quintus Hortensius,[251] a man of brilliant reputation and excellent character. In his desire to be not merely an associate or even a companion of Cato, but to bring his entire household and family line into a shared kinship with him, he tried to persuade Cato, whose daughter Porcia was married to Bibulus and had produced two children, to give her in turn to him as noble soil in which to plant offspring. Although most people found such an act strange, he said, it was a good thing, in accord with nature and beneficial to the state, that a woman in the prime of her life should neither allow her productive power to be quenched in idleness, nor trouble her husband and reduce him to poverty by bearing more children than were required. Furthermore, having a community of heirs among worthy men would ensure an abundance of virtue and spread it widely in their families, and the state would be strengthened by the intermingling of their kinship lines. If Bibulus was very devoted to his wife, Hortensius would return her as soon as she had given birth, and in this way he would be intimately related to both Bibulus and Cato because of the children they had in common. Cato responded that he had great affection for Hortensius and approved of the idea of shared kinship with him, but thought it was strange for him to suggest marriage with a daughter who was already given to someone else. Then Hortensius quickly changed tactics and did not scruple to reveal his true intent, asking Cato for his own wife, since she was still young enough to bear children and Cato had plenty of heirs. And it cannot be said that Hortensius did this in the belief that Cato was not attached to Marcia, for we are told that she was pregnant at the time. And when he saw that Hortensius was serious and had his heart set on this, Cato would not refuse, but said that Marcia's father Philippus must also give his approval. Therefore Philippus was consulted and expressed his agreement, but stipulated that he would not promise Marcia in marriage unless Cato himself was present and joined in the pledge.

8.19 Plutarch *Dialogue on Love* 749d–750a, 750b–e, 751b–52a. Late first century CE. One of the speakers in this dialogue is Plutarch's son, who recounts his father's participation in a long-ago conversation at Thespiae, where a festival of the god Eros took place. A substantial portion of the dialogue focuses on the relative merits of marriage and pederasty and their relationship to love (*erōs*).

There lived at Thespiae a woman well known for her wealth and ancestry, who without a doubt also led a well-ordered life in other respects. She had been a widow for some time without encountering criticism, even though she was young and quite good-looking. Now Bacchon was the son of a close friend of hers, and while she was arranging a match between him and a girl of her own family, Ismenodora herself had many meetings and conversations with the young man and began to feel something for him. Then, in the course of hearing and speaking many kind words about him, and observing that he had attracted many male lovers of good family, she fell in love with him herself. She resolved to do nothing that was unworthy of her birth; her intention was to celebrate their marriage publicly and spend the rest of her life with him. Yet the situation was highly unusual and the youth's mother worried that the grandeur and pomp of Ismenodora's house made the match with her son too unequal. Meanwhile Bacchon's hunting companions scared him by dwelling on the difference in age between him and Ismenodora, and by their ridicule did more to discourage the match than those who opposed their marriage for serious reasons. On the verge of adulthood, the young man felt shy about marrying a widow, but dispensing with the rest of his advisors, he left it up to

Pisias and Anthemion to make the decision. The elder of these two, Anthemion, was his cousin, and Pisias was the most morally severe of his lovers. Therefore Pisias opposed the marriage and attacked Anthemion for handing over the youth to Ismenodora, while Anthemion for his part told Pisias that although a worthy man in other respects, he did wrong to imitate those petty lovers who would deprive his friend of an estate, an alliance, and great resources, all in order to enjoy the frequent sight of him naked in the wrestling ring, youthful and untouched by a woman. And so in order to avoid provoking one another and falling little by little into an angry dispute, they chose my father and his companions as judges and arbiters of the matter.

[Anthemion finds among the arbiters an advocate for his views, Daphnaeus, while Pisias finds a fellow supporter of pederasty in Protogenes.]

'So you think that I am at war against Love,' said Protogenes, 'and not fighting on his behalf against intemperance and insolence when they try to force the most shameful acts and passions into the company of those things that we name most beautiful and honourable?' Daphnaeus replied, 'Are you referring to marriage, the union of a man and woman, as "most shameful"? Never, either now or in the past, has there existed a joining more sacred than this.'

'Since marriage is necessary for procreation,' said Protogenes, 'there is nothing wrong with legislators treating it reverentially and singing its praises to the masses. But authentic love has nothing whatever to do with the women's part of the house, and I assert that whenever you have doted on women and girls, what you felt was not love any more than flies love milk or bees love honeycombs, or any more than cooks and butchers feel tender affection for the calves and birds they are fattening in the dark. Just as nature gives us a moderate and sufficient appetite for bread and tasty foods, and an excess of this produces the vices called gluttony and gourmandising, so it is natural that men and women have a need for the pleasure they derive from one another, but when the impulse to this pleasure becomes powerful and overwhelmingly difficult to restrain, it is a mistake to call it love.

Love is that which attaches itself to a young soul with the proper aptitude, and through friendship brings it to a state of excellence. But the desire for a woman, however well it may turn out, excels in no area other than the harvest of pleasure, and the enjoyment of a ripe body. Aristippus testified to this when he made his reply to someone who charged that Laïs felt no affection for him. He answered that he didn't think his wine or his fish felt affection for him either, but he gladly enjoyed them both. So you see that the object of desire is pleasure and enjoyment. Love, on the other hand, does not wish to stand by once the possibility of friendship has been lost, and cultivate to ripeness that which can only be a source of grief, even at the peak of its beauty, when there is no chance of recompense in the fruit of a disposition suited to friendship and excellence.'

[Protogenes continues to argue that heterosexual desire is characterised by pleasure, which makes men soft and unmanly, while boy-love focuses on the pursuit of virtue. He cites Solon, the Athenian lawgiver, in support of his views.]

Though Protogenes was eager to say even more, Daphnaeus cut him off, saying 'By Zeus, you were right to bring up Solon, and we must make him the standard of the man in love. Solon wrote:

> Until he cares for a boy in the lovely flower of his youth,
> Longing for thighs and sweet lips.[252]

Add to Solon this passage from Aeschylus, who says:

> You lacked reverence for the wonder of your thighs,
> Ungrateful for my many kisses.[253]

Others, of course, jeer at those who urge lovers to inspect thighs and loins, as though they were about to wield the knife at a sacrifice and read the omens. But I consider this a strong argument in favour of women. For if intercourse against nature between males does not destroy or harm a lover's feelings of goodwill, it is reasonable to suppose that the love of women, which is entirely natural, is more likely to lead to friendship through the charm of gratification. For the ancients referred to it as charm, Protogenes, when the female yielded to the male. This is why Pindar said that Hephaestus was born to Hera "in the absence of charms"[254] and Sappho addresses a girl who is not yet ready for marriage saying,

> You seemed to me a little girl without charm.[255]

And someone once asked Heracles,

> Did you persuade the girl or gain her charm by force?

But what takes place when males come together, whether unwillingly by force and plunder, or willingly with weakness and effeminacy, allowing themselves in Plato's words "to be mounted like a beast and go through the motions of reproduction"[256] against nature – this is entirely lacking in charm, unseemly, and contrary to the will of Aphrodite. That is why I think that Solon wrote those lines when he was still young and "full of semen", as Plato says,[257] but when he got older, this is what he wrote:

Now I delight in the Cyprus-born and Dionysus
And the Muses, who bring merriment to men.[258]

He says this as though he has redirected his life from the tempestuous storms
of boy-love to the calm sea of marriage and philosophy. If we contemplate the
truth, Protogenes, we see that strong emotions for boys and women amount to
the same thing: both are forms of Love. But if in your fondness for argument
you should choose to distinguish them, you would note that this boy-love goes
out of bounds, and like a late-born child, a bastard born in obscurity and out
of season, it attempts to drive out the Love that is legitimate and older.[259] For
it was only yesterday and recently, my friend, after youths began to strip and
show themselves naked, that boy-love began to creep into the gymnasium. At
first he only made gradual and quiet inroads, but then little by little he grew
wings in the wrestling-ring and can no longer be restrained. Instead he reviles
and tramples on the institution of marriage, the means of immortality for
mortals, which kindles again through the generations our fragile and extin-
guishable light.'

[The debate continues and a messenger brings word that Ismenodora has
kidnapped Bacchon and proceeded with a wedding. Anthemion and Pisias leave
hurriedly order to investigate matters, while Plutarch entertains the others with
a discourse on love and marriage. The dialogue closes with the news that Pisias
has been reconciled to the marriage of Bacchon and Ismenodora.]

8.20 Flavius Josephus *Antiquities of the Jews* 15.7.2–6 (selections). Ca. 94
CE. Josephus' voluminous history of the Jewish people starts with Adam and
Eve and continues through the events of his own time. He wrote a detailed
account of the relations between Herod the Great, whom the Romans
installed as King of Judea in place of the previous Hasmonean dynasty,
and his beautiful and imperious wife Mariame, one of the last heirs of the
Hasmoneans. Mariame died in 29 BCE and Herod in 4 BCE.

[When departing his kingdom in order to report to his patrons Mark Antony
and (later) Octavian, Herod left orders that if he should not return, his
wife Mariame and his mother-in-law Alexandra were to be killed in order
to preserve the succession rights of his blood relations. On both occasions,
Mariame learned of Herod's plans.]

And now Herod sailed home delighted at his great and unexpected good fortune,
and announced these things first to his wife, as was proper. He honoured her
by greeting her alone of all the rest of the court, because of the love he felt for
her and the intimacy between them. When he told her of his success, however,

far from rejoicing, she almost seemed disappointed, and she was not able to conceal her resentment. Conscious of her superior birth, and feeling contempt for him, she responded to his embrace with a groan, and showed that she felt more dejection than delight at his tale. Her antipathy toward him, not merely suspected but openly revealed, troubled Herod. Perceiving his wife's unconcealed and unexpected hatred, he felt both anguished and aggrieved over the matter, yet unable to withstand his love for her, he could neither remain angry nor reconcile himself to her. And so he vacillated first in one direction and then the other, completely at a loss. Caught thus between hatred and affection, he was often on the verge of repaying her arrogance, but because his soul was overwhelmed, he did not have the strength to rid himself of this woman. In short, although he would gladly have punished her, he feared that in exacting vengeance by putting her to death, he would bring a much greater punishment on himself.

When Herod's sister and mother realised the state of his feelings toward Mariame, they thought that the time was ripe to act on their hatred. They excited Herod's anger through long harangues filled with false accusations that were serious enough to provoke both hatred and jealousy. Although he was not unwilling to listen to what they had to say, neither did he seem to credit their words enough to take any action against his wife. Still, he thought all the worse of her, and the feelings of both were inflamed, for she did not hide her disposition toward him, and the love he felt for her was constantly being transformed to wrath. Just as he was about to do something irreversible, he heard the news that Caesar had prevailed in the war, and had taken possession of Egypt, for Antony and Cleopatra were dead. In his hurry to get to Caesar, Herod left everything in his household as it was.

[Herod is successful in his meeting with Caesar and expands his power.]

As a result of these successes, Herod's magnificence increased, and he escorted Caesar as far as Antioch. But on his return home, he found his prosperity in expanding his external dominions matched by the unhappiness of his domestic affairs, particularly in regard to his marriage, which previously had seemed a stroke of good fortune. For the love he felt toward Mariame was by no means inferior to those loves that are justly celebrated in books of history. She possessed the virtue of moderation in other respects, and she was faithful to him, but there was something both feminine and irksome in her nature. She took considerable delight in the fact that he was enslaved to his desire for her, and because of her untimely failure to take into account that he was the king, and that she was subject to his rule, she often behaved insolently toward him; yet he usually passed these moments off humourously, and bore them with self-discipline and patience. She also scoffed openly at his mother and sister because of their lowly birth, and spoke ill of them, so that the irreparable enmity already established among the women of the household gave rise to even worse accusations. The atmosphere of suspicion grew and lasted for a full year after Herod returned from his visit to Caesar. Finally, however, that trouble which had previously been kept within bounds burst forth in the following manner. As the king was lying down to take his rest at midday, he called for Mariame to join him because of the affectionate love he always had for her. She came in, but refused to lie down with him, and although he was eager in his attentions, she not only poured contempt on him, but reproached him as well, saying that he had killed her father and brother. He was angered at this insult,[260] and was on the point of doing something rash. Perceiving that his agitation was greater than usual, the king's sister Salome sent in his cupbearer, who had long since been prepared for his role in this plot, directing him to say that Mariame had bribed him to help her administer a love potion to the king.

[Herod has Mariame's eunuch tortured, and acting on an erroneous suspicion of Mariame's infidelity, he tries and executes both her and her mother. Mariame goes to her death with dignity, while Herod is nearly driven mad as a result of her loss.]

So died a woman who was truly noble both in respect to her self-mastery and the greatness of her soul, but she was not a reasonable person, and by nature too fond of quarrels. Yet both her physical beauty and the impact of her presence were more compelling than words can convey.

8.21 Pliny the Younger *Letters* 7.5. Ca. 100 CE. Calpurnia was Pliny's third wife. In this letter, he expresses his passion for his young bride by alluding to a theme common in poetry, the lover who is turned away from the door of his beloved.

Gaius Plinius to his wife Calpurnia.
Such great longing for you possesses me that it is hardly to be believed. The main reason for this is my love for you, and also the fact that we have not grown accustomed to being apart. That is why I lie awake for a great part of the night thinking of you; and during the day, at the times when I used to see you, my feet lead me to your room 'of their own accord', as people so truly say. When I find you are not there, I return disappointed and heartsick, like a lover who has been shut out. The only reprieve from these torments comes when I wear myself out making speeches or conducting lawsuits for my friends. Think what kind of life I have, when my only rest lies in work, and my only consolation in misery and worries. Farewell.

8.22 Aulus Gellius *Attic Nights* 1.6.1–6. Mid-second century CE. Aulus Gellius' collection of historical anecdotes mistakenly attributes a famous speech on marriage to the Roman censor Metellus Numidicus. The speech was in fact made by a different Metellus, consul in 143 BCE.

Several learned men were listening as the speech of Metellus Numidicus was read; he was a serious and eloquent man, who spoke to the people in his role as censor on the subject of taking wives, and urged them to enter purposefully into the responsibilities of matrimony. In that speech he wrote as follows: 'If we could manage without a wife, citizens, we would all forego that irritation, but since nature has decreed that we can neither live with them comfortably, nor live at all without them, we must give consideration to our lasting welfare rather than to temporary pleasures.' Some of the listeners thought that since Quintus Metellus was urging the people in his role as censor to take wives, he should not have alluded to the irritation and lasting inconvenience of having a wife, and that his words acted more to dissuade and deter than to encourage. They said that the speech should have instead taken the opposite tack, affirming that for the most part there was nothing irritating in the married state, and if after all annoying problems sometimes occurred, they were minor, insignificant, quite bearable, and completely forgotten in the greater advantages and pleasures of marriage. And furthermore, not everyone faced these problems, nor were they inherent in the state of matrimony, but they were instead the result of the wrongdoing and bad behaviour of certain couples. But Titus Castricius thought that Metellus had spoken rightly and in a way appropriate to his office. 'A censor,' he said, 'ought to speak in one way, and an orator in another. We allow orators to make statements that are untrue, daring, sly, deceptive and fallacious, as long as they resemble the truth and can by some clever trick insinuate themselves into people's minds and influence them. Furthermore, it is a disgrace for an orator, even if defending a bad case, to abandon it or make halfhearted arguments. But it would ill become Metellus, a pious man who enjoyed a reputation for dignity and integrity, addressing the Roman people after such a distinguished career, to speak anything other than what he and others believe to be the truth, especially on a matter of everyday knowledge that was part of the common and shared experience of life. Therefore, once he had admitted the irritations of which everyone is well aware, and established that he deserved his reputation for earnestness and honesty, it was no difficult matter to convince them of a principle that is more sound and true than any other: without numerous marriages, the state cannot be healthy'.

Further Reading

On marriage in the *Odyssey* and the 'like-mindedness' of Penelope and Odysseus, see Zeitlin 1995a, Bolmarcich 2001 and Emlyn-Jones 2009. On marriage in Greek tragedy, see Foley 2001 and Kaimio 2002; for the connection between marriage and death in Greek thought, see Rehm 1994 and Redfield 2003, pp. 346–85. For Xenophon's *Economics* and Ischomachus, see Scaife 1994–5. On the religious lives of matrons at Rome, see Stehle 1989 and Staples 1998. For Catullus' wedding poetry, see Thomsen 2002 and Ancona 2005; on the relationship between *amor* and marriage in the *Aeneid*, see Gutting 2006. On Herod and Mariame, see Richardson 1996, pp. 216–20. For the younger Cato's marriage in its social context, see Cantarella 2002. For Plutarch's views on marriage and sexual matters, see Walcot 1998; for Ismenodora and Bacchon, see Goldhill 1995, pp. 144–61 and Rist 2001.

9

Transgression and Deviance

Adultery is the form of sexual transgression most often mentioned in Greek and Roman sources. For a woman, adultery meant sexual relations with a man other than her husband. For a man, it meant sexual relations with another man's wife. In an ancient marriage, one of the primary duties of the wife was to produce legitimate offspring who could inherit the family goods. Therefore the fidelity of wives fell under special scrutiny, and this scrutiny took culturally specific forms. In early Rome, for example, women were forbidden to drink wine because its consumption was associated with adultery. Later this prohibition was lifted and Roman men, following the customs of the Etruscans, dined in mixed company with their wives (7.6, 7.9). In the Classical Greek world, on the other hand, married women whose social and financial status exempted them from working outside the home did not dine with men or participate in social interactions with men who were not part of the family circle.

Two archetypal stories of adultery are featured in the Homeric epics. In the *Iliad*, the war is ascribed to the Trojan prince Paris' seduction of Helen, the wife of his Greek host Menelaus (9.1). The wayward and irresponsible Paris, more skilled in bedroom matters than in warfare, is contrasted with his dutiful brother Hector, a loving family man and accomplished warrior. Demodocus' song in the *Odyssey* (9.2) shows that on Olympus, the gods interact according to the social mores governing human marriage. A man's marital infidelities can be condoned only if they do not encroach on the rights of another man. When his wife Aphrodite is caught in bed with Ares, Hephaestus is entitled to compensation for the harm he has suffered through the actions of Ares. In both Classical Greece and Rome, outraged husbands actually had the right to kill their wives' seducers under certain circumstances

(9.8). Guilty wives bore less legal responsibility than male seducers, though their husbands were expected to divorce them, and they could be punished with severe penalties such as banishment, especially under the harsh laws first instituted by the emperor Augustus (9.18).

One of Augustus' motivations was to clean up what he viewed as the lax moral habits of the late Republican period; this was a time when upper-class women enjoyed a great deal of sexual freedom. Clodia, a married woman who indulged in affairs with the poet Catullus and a number of other lovers, was attacked by Cicero for her behaviour (3.13), but his real target was a political enemy, her brother Clodius, and his professed moral outrage is unconvincing. Julius Caesar's reputation as an habitual adulterer, meanwhile, harmed him far less than the story that as a young man he was a sexual favourite of the Bithynian king (4.20).

Like adultery, the seduction of a virgin daughter was far beyond the pale, though in some cases the offense might be repaired if the girl's family considered the seducer suitable as a husband. In Archilochus' epode (9.3), we witness an encounter between a young girl and a very persuasive seducer, who nevertheless stops short of claiming her virginity. Taken as a whole, Archilochus' poems convey the persona of a hard-drinking maverick who rejects the social conventions of his time, and the biographical tradition links him romantically with Neoboule, the elder sister of girl depicted in the epode. This poem, presumably intended for a male audience, seems to demonstrate that the conquest of virgin girls, frowned upon by society, was a matter for boasting – if the seducer was not caught. It is just this consideration that caused Horace and others to argue that a man is always better off with a prostitute, who brings with her no dangerous entanglements (10.8).

Rape plays an important role in the myths of the gods, where it often seems to be exempted from human moral standards; the principal male members of the Greek pantheon attempt rape at one time or another, with varying degrees of success. Zeus himself has recourse to both rape and seduction in his relations with females, but these affairs (1.1), which result in the birth of heroes and gods, only confirm his virility. Ancient definitions of rape and standards of consent differed from our own. With respect to females, a criminal violation was not legally defined by the rape victim's lack of consent, but by the lack of consent of her father, husband, or guardian. Thus in the Homeric *Hymn to Demeter*, Persephone's abduction by Hades (1.4) is not perceived as a rape by Zeus and Hades, who have agreed on an arranged marriage. From the perspective of Persephone's mother Demeter, who is not consulted in the matter, and that of Persephone, who is forcibly abducted, the experience is what we would consider a rape. In the treatment of sex crimes, Greco-Roman cultures employed a double standard based on the social status of the victim. For example, slaves had no ability to give consent or withhold it. While sexual and other physical abuse of slaves was recognised as a punishable offense (9.9, 9.18), it was not necessarily criminal unless it happened without the consent of the slave's owner. Under certain circumstances, as when cities were captured in wartime, the rape of free women was considered unremarkable; yet commanders who prevented captive citizen women from being raped were praised for respecting societal norms even in the context of war (9.17).

Livy's history of early Rome includes two contrasting stories of rape (9.12), one condoned and the other depicted as a heinous crime. The young Romans under Romulus engineered their abduction and rape of the Sabine virgins with the goal of obtaining wives and fathering legitimate children in order to build the Roman state. By contrast, Sextus Tarquinius, the son of an arrogant king, raped Lucretia, whose virtuous chastity was symbolic of the security and welfare of the state itself. These didactic stories can be contrasted with the view of 'date rape' expounded by Ovid in the *Art of Love* (9.13), which he presents as a book of advice for the common man on how to conduct love affairs. Ovid suggests that if a woman is willing to kiss a man, he is foolish to walk away without having satisfied his desires fully, whether or not she cooperates. Daringly, Ovid includes married women at Rome among those who are open to seduction. It is not surprising that this poet ran afoul of the moralistic emperor Augustus, and ended his life in exile.

Greek myths reveal a fascination with many types of sexual deviance, including rape, incest, and, in the case of Minos' wife Pasiphaë, sexual relations with a bull (9.5). Whereas more mundane forms of transgression such as adultery were viewed as occasions for moral outrage, the Greeks attributed extreme and uncanny forms of deviance in mythic contexts to divine intervention and fate. This is the defense used by Pasiphaë against the recriminations of her husband, who is depicted in Euripides' play as a reckless and harsh tyrant, bent on punishing Pasiphaë for circumstances over which she had no control. In Sophocles' *Oedipus The King*, incest between mother and son is a cause for horror, and the poet dwells on the paradox of Jocasta's womb as host to a 'begetter' and a 'begotten' who are one and the same (9.6). Yet the chorus and the audience feel compassion for the pair, whose inadvertent transgression was unavoidable because fated by the gods. Euripides, on the other hand, makes King Pentheus in the *Bacchae* share the responsibility for his deviance (9.7). Pentheus' horrific death at the hands of his crazed female relatives is a punishment for his refusal to acknowledge the divinity of Dionysus, but the play suggests that his voyeuristic desire to see female family members engaging in illicit sex is merely brought to the surface through the god's action in bringing about a loss of inhibitions.

Beyond the nearly universal human prohibition on sex between parent and child, definitions of incest are culturally determined. The Greeks accepted certain marital matches (uncle-niece or half-sibling) that the Romans considered incestuous (7.9), but the practices of both Greeks and Romans were considered unacceptably lax by Jews (9.10), a factor that contributed to political unrest in the East under Seleucid and Roman rule. Accusations of incest were common (and therefore presumably effective) weapons in Roman invective, as we can see from Cicero's attack on Clodia (3.13), and Catullus' poems ridiculing a rival lover (9.11). By long tradition, the most horrific sex crimes were attributed to tyrants, monarchs, or emperors, whose unlimited power over their subjects allowed them to indulge their sexual proclivities. An example from Archaic Greece is the necrophilia of the Corinthian tyrant Periander (9.4), who supposedly had sex with his wife after murdering her. The historian Suetonius was a diligent cataloguer of gossip concerning the Roman emperors' sexual transgressions. He attributes a wide variety of deviant behaviours to Nero (9.15), who uses his unlimited power to break virtually every taboo. To Roman sensibilities, the story of Nero's attempt to cast himself as the bride in his 'marriage' to Doryphorus (called Pythagoras in other sources) was especially shocking. By adopting the female role, Nero stripped himself of the masculine authority considered integral to the function of a ruler; his bizarre antics undoubtedly contributed to the rebellion that ended in his death.

Gender deviance is treated in more detail in Chapter 3, but merits additional discussion here in relation to Petronius' *Satyrica*, a product of the age of Nero. Although fragmentary, this works yields a phantasmagoric portrait of Italian street life with its plentiful brothels, violent gangs, and thieves (9.14). It is one of very few works written from the narrative point of view of a member of the lower classes. Its protagonist Encolpius makes no attempt to adopt the hypermasculine stance of the elite Roman male, who must abide by a strict set of rules or be labeled effeminate by his colleagues. The *Satyrica* illustrates that 'deviance' was a relative concept. Because of their low social status, Encolpius and the other characters are free to express feelings and conduct themselves in ways that would be labeled as deviant in more privileged members of Roman society. Even in the *Satyrica*, however, the figure of the *cinaedus* remains repugnant and ridiculous. The *cinaedus* is a man who rejects his gender identity by dressing effeminately and willingly engaging in acts that were off limits to 'masculine' men, such as being penetrated orally or anally. Providing oral sexual gratification to another person was unthinkable for upper-class members of Roman society, who typically believed that such activity fouled or polluted the mouth of anyone who engaged in it (9.16).

Religious rituals, particularly those led by women or from which men were excluded, often gave rise to suspicions that the women were taking advantage of freedom from supervision to plot adultery or other crimes. Among both the Greeks and Romans, the rites of Dionysus/Bacchus fueled fears of this type

(1.11, 9.7), and stories of scandalous Bacchic rites during the second century BCE led to stern suppression of the cult in Italy. Petronius (9.14) draws on this background for his description of comical and pornographic 'mysteries of Priapus' involving sexual abuses masterminded by a priestess of the phallic god. The mysteries culminate in a travesty of the sacred marriage performed by the youth Giton and the female child Pannychis.

9.1 Homer *Iliad* 3.38–75. Eighth century BCE. Hector reproaches his brother Paris for bringing trouble on the Trojans through his deviant behaviour in running away with Helen, another man's wife, and for his failure to take responsibility for his actions.

Seeing him, Hector spoke words of rebuke and blame:
'Evil Paris, you handsome, girl-mad cheat,
I wish you had never been born, or had died unwed.
This I would prefer, and it would have been better
Than to live in disgrace this way, despised by others.
I suppose the long-haired Achaeans will laugh aloud,
When they tell of a prince who is foremost among us
For looks, but lacking in strength of mind and valor.
Were you like this when you and your trusty comrades
Sailed in seafaring ships, mingling with strangers,
And brought from a distant land a shapely woman,
A daughter of spearmen, a grievous harm to your father
And city, a joy to our foes, and a sorrow for you?
Will you not meet Ares' favourite, Menelaus?
Then you would learn of the man whose wife you possess.
The lyre will be no help, nor the goddess' gifts,
Nor hair and handsome looks, when you sprawl in the dust.
The Trojans are timid, for otherwise long ago
A cloak of stone would have repaid your deeds.'
Godlike Alexander spoke in his turn and said:
'Hector, your harsh rebuke is not unearned –
For always your heart is like a tireless axe,
Sent through a beam by the skillful man who shapes
The planks of the ship, and it strengthens his blow –
Just like the axe, the heart in your breast is fearless.
But blame me not for the goddess' lovely gifts.
The glorious gifts of the gods are not to be spurned,
What they give freely, no man could take for his own.
But now if you wish me to practice war and combat,
Direct the Trojans and Achaeans to take their seats.

Send me the favourite of Ares, Menelaus
Among them to battle for Helen and all that she owns.
Whichever one wins and proves the stronger man,
Let him go home with all the wealth, and the woman.
May the rest of you, after swearing friendly oaths,
Inhabit fertile Troy, while the Achaeans return
To Argos where horses and beautiful women thrive.'

9.2 Homer *Odyssey* 8.266–370. Late eighth century BCE. Demodocus, the
bard of Alcinous, king of the Phaeacians, sings the tale of the adulterous love
of Ares and Aphrodite, and its consequences.

With lyre and voice he began the beautiful song
Of love between Ares and fair-crowned Aphrodite,
How first in the Hephaestus' house they came together
In secret, and Ares' many gifts brought shame
To Lord Hephaestus' bed. But soon came Helius
As messenger, who saw them making love.
When Hephaestus heard the painful news,
He went to his forge pondering evil thoughts,
And setting the anvil on the block, he struck
Unbreakable bonds to hold the lovers fast.
And when the snare was complete, still angry at Ares,
He went his way to the chamber where stood his bed,
And all round the posts he spread the bonds,
And many, too, hung down from the beams of the roof.
Like slender spider-webs, undetectable even
To blessed gods, for they were artful works.
And when he had laid the trap about the bedposts,
He pretended to leave for the well-built town of Lemnos,
Most dear to him of all the places on earth.
Now Ares of the golden reins kept careful watch,
And when he saw the famous craftsman depart,
He went his way to the home of renowned Hephaestus
Craving the love of fair-crowned Cytherea.
She had just come from her mighty father Zeus,
And was taking her seat when Ares entered the house.
He clasped her hand, and spoke a word to her, saying:
'Come, dear, let us delight in the bed together,
For Hephaestus is not at home, but away, I think,
In Lemnos, with the rough-voiced Sintians.'[261]
He spoke, and she was glad to lie down with him.

These two went to sleep in the bed, and about them fell
The artful bonds, inventions of clever Hephaestus,
So they could neither move nor raise their limbs;
And then they knew that there was no escape.
The famous god with two lame feet approached,
Having turned back before he came to Lemnos,
For Helius watched on high and told him the news.
So he returned to his house, with aching heart,
And stood in the doorway, full of wild anger.
With an awful cry, he shouted to all the gods:
'Father Zeus and blessed immortal gods,
Come and see a horrible, laughable sight,
How Zeus' daughter Aphrodite rejects
Her crippled spouse, and loves destructive Ares.
He enjoys good looks and health, while I
Was born a weakling. Yet I am not to blame,
But my mother and father who wrongly begot me.
You will see where these two slept in my bed
Together in love, a sight that is grievous to me.
They will not wish to lie there a moment longer,
I think, however loving they might be.
Neither will wish to sleep, yet my trap will bind them,
Until her father returns all the bridal gifts,
Those I gave for the sake of this shameless girl,
For his daughter is lovely, but cannot restrain herself.'
He spoke, and the gods arrived at the brass-floored house,
Poseidon the earth-embracer, and Lucky Hermes,
And Lord Apollo, the Far-Shooter. But the goddesses
Modestly stayed, each one, at home. The gods,
Who give to each his own, stood in the doorway;
Laughter rose unquenched among the Blessed,
As they surveyed the arts of clever Hephaestus.
And thus one looking on would say to his neighbour:
'Bad deeds fail, and the slow one catches the swift,
Just as slow Hephaestus has now caught Ares,
Swiftest of all Olympians. Though he is lame,
He used his arts, and the other must pay the price.'
So they declared, as they spoke one to another.
And Zeus' son, Lord Apollo, said to Hermes,
'Zeus' son, Guide who gives each his own,
Though closed inside a trap, would you be willing
To lie down in bed with Golden Aphrodite?'

And the Guide, the Slayer of Argus, responded,
'Let me be held by three times the number of bonds,
Even though you and all the goddesses watch,
So long as I lie with Golden Aphrodite.'
He spoke and laughter shook the immortal gods.
But Poseidon did not laugh, and kept entreating
Hephaestus, famed for crafts, to release Ares.
Addressing him, he spoke with winged words:
'Free him, and I promise, as you demand,
All that is due he shall pay, before the gods.'
The renowned god with two lame feet replied,
'Poseidon, embracer of earth, do not ask for this,
Or make a sorry pledge for a sorry fellow.
How could I bind you before the immortal gods,
If Ares both defaulted and slipped his bonds?'
And Poseidon the shaker of earth responded,
'If Ares should flee and default on his debt,
I myself shall pay to you all he owes.'
The renowned god with two lame feet replied,
'Your word I neither can nor should refuse.'
So mighty Hephaestus spoke, and loosed the bonds.
The pair leaped up, freed from the strong restraints,
And Ares quickly went his way toward Thrace
While the laughter-loving goddess went to Cyprus,
To Paphos, home of her shrine and fragrant altar.
The Graces bathed and rubbed her body with oil,
Ambrosial oil such as gods have for their use,
And wrapped her in a wondrous, lovely robe.
So sang the glorious bard, and Odysseus
Rejoiced at heart as he heard the song, as did
The Phaeacian men, famous for long-oared ships.

9.3 Archilochus Fr. 196a West Vol. 1. Ca. 650 BCE. Archilochus, one of the earliest lyric poets whose work has survived, was a soldier and colonist who helped to settle the island of Thasos. In this fragmentary poem, the narrator describes the seduction of a young, virginal girl.

[missing lines]
'If your heart is set on this and you feel so strongly,
Even now in our house
There is a lovely, tender girl
Longing for you. I think you will find nothing

To complain of in her looks.
Make her your own girl.'
That is what she said. And to her I said in answer,
'Daughter of Amphimedo,
That good and wise woman
Whom now the dank earth covers completely,
For young men the goddess
Provides many delights
Besides the divine thing. One of these will be enough.
In the quiet time of evening,
Once it gets dark outside,
You and I and the gods will consider this matter.
I will do just as you ask,
Much […]
I'll come over the wall as far as the gates. Surely
You won't grudge me this, dear.
I'll stop at the grassy garden.
Now this you must know: As to Neoboule,
Let some other man have her.
Ai! She is overripe
And worse. Her maidenly flower has faded away
Along with her former charms.
She could never get enough.
Even in her prime, the woman was crazy.
To hell with her!
This doesn't […]
May I never become a joke among my neighbours
By taking such a wife.
I much prefer you.
You are not a faithless, two-faced cheat,
But she's a sharp one
With dozens of lovers.
If I let myself go with her, I'd be afraid
Of getting blind puppies
Like the "hasty bitch."'[262]
That's what I said. I took hold of her and leaned back
On a lush bed of flowers,
Sheltered by my soft cloak.
I cradled her neck in the crook of my arm
As she kept completely still,
In her fear, like a fawn.
I gently stroked her breasts with my hands

By the feel of her skin,
She was nearly a woman.
Caressing the length of her beautiful body
I let go my white force,
Lightly touching her blonde hair.

9.4 Herodotus *Histories* 5.92G.1–4. Ca. 440 BCE. This story of the Corinthian tyrant Periander is part of a digression detailing the excesses and injustices of tyrants. Periander succeeded his father Cypselus in 627 BCE.

Whatever slaughter or persecution Cypselus had left undone, Periander brought to completion. In the space of one day, he stripped all the Corinthian women naked, for the sake of his own wife Melissa. He had sent messengers to the Oracle of the Dead on the river Acheron in Thesprotia[263] to inquire the whereabouts of a hoard of money left by a friend, but in an apparition, Melissa said that she would not give a sign nor tell where the hoard was deposited, for she was cold and naked. The cloaks buried with her had not been burned and thus were of no use to her. Then, as evidence for her husband that she spoke the truth, she said that Periander had put his loaves into a cold oven. When this was reported later to Periander, he believed the message, because he had had intercourse with Melissa's corpse. Immediately after the message, he made a proclamation that all the women of Corinth should come out to the sanctuary of Hera. They came as if for a festival, wearing their most beautiful garments. And posting guards there, he had them all stripped naked, ladies and servants alike, and heaped the garments into a pit, where he burned them as he prayed to Melissa. When he had done this and sent a second message, the ghost of Melissa told him where the friend's hoard was located.

9.5 Euripides *Cretans TrGF* 5.1 F 472e lines 4–52. Ca. 435 BCE. This fragmentary play tells the story of the Cretan queen Pasiphaë, who mated with a bull and gave birth to the monstrous Minotaur. When the bestial liaison is discovered, her husband Minos puts her on trial.

Pasiphaë:
No denial from me could change your mind,
For the facts in the matter are well known.
If I had given over my body to a man,
And secretly sold the delights of Cypris,
Justly would I be condemned in your eyes.
But in fact I suffer a madness sent by a god.
I grieve for this evil I did against my will.
Does it not seem unlikely, that a sick passion

Would gnaw my heart as I gazed at a bull?
Was he handsome to look at in his robe?
Did his red hair attract me, his flashing eye,
The wine-dark beard, so glossy on his cheek?
His body was hardly that of a bridegroom!
For this love I dressed in the skin of a cow,
And walked about on my hands and feet.
I had no wish to make this spouse a father.
Why, then, did I fall ill with this madness?
This man's fate heaped its evils onto me;
Minos is truly the one who bears the guilt.
When the bull appeared, the sea god's omen,
He vowed its sacrifice, but broke that vow.
Thus you incurred the vengeance of Poseidon,
But the punishment of sickness fell on me!
Now you rage and call the gods to witness,
When it was you who brought about my shame.
I gave birth, yes, but the fault was not mine;
I kept the secret of this god-sent calamity.
But you proclaim your wife's plight to all,
As though you played no role. You haughty,
Evil man! What fine news to tell the world!
You are my destruction. The fault was yours,
The illness came from you. For this, you wish
To drown me in the sea? Then drown me.
You are skilled at bloodshed and murder.
Or is it your desire to devour my flesh raw?
By all means, have your feast! I shall die
Guiltless and free, for the wrong you did.

Chorus:
Clearly this misfortune is from the gods,
My lord. You must restrain your anger.

Minos:
Have you stopped her howls with a muzzle?
Come, keep your spearpoints leveled at her.
Seize this depraved woman and let her perish;
Her accomplice too. Bring them to the palace
And let both women be shut in the dungeons,
Where the sunlight will never see them again.

Chorus:
My lord, delay your decision, for this matter
Is worthy of thought. Wise men are not hasty.

Minos:
My judgement is final and allows no delay.

9.6 Sophocles *Oedipus the King* 1205–21. 429 BCE. When Oedipus, king of Thebes, discovers the secret of his true parentage, the chorus reacts first by lamenting the changeable fate of humankind. Then they reflect on the horror of Oedipus' unwittingly incestuous marriage.

Now what man's story is more wretched?
What man's life is more transformed,
Stamped with ruin and pain so savage?
Alas for Oedipus, known to all.
The same harbour sheltered father and child,
Bridegrooms both.
How, O man of misery, was it possible
That the furrow your father ploughed
Bore you in silence for so long?

All-seeing Time has found you out,
Against your will, and judges
This marriage that is no marriage;
This begetter who is the begotten.
Ah, child of Laius
I wish I had never seen you.
I grieve like one from whose lips
Pours the funeral dirge.
Truth to tell, it was you who renewed my light,
But now darkness covers my eyes.

9.7 Euripides *Bacchae* 912–62. 405 BCE. Euripides' drama deals with resistance to the new god Dionysus in his hometown of Thebes, and the god's punishment of his opponents. As his wits fall under the sway of Dionysus, the hostile king Pentheus decides to dress like a Bacchant, or female worshiper of the god, so that he can spy on his wayward female relatives. For more of the *Bacchae*, see 3.6.

Dionysus:
You, Pentheus, avid to see what you should not,

And eager to pursue what should be left alone,
Come forth from the palace and let me see you
Dressed in the garb of a Bacchic madwoman,
Ready to spy on your mother and her band.
[Pentheus emerges]
You shine forth like one of Cadmus' daughters.[264]

Pentheus:
Now two suns appear to my eyes, and twin
Towns of Thebes, the city of seven gates.
You seem to be a bull leading me forth,
And on your head grow horns. But what
Were you before, who now appear as a bull?

Dionysus:
Formerly hostile, the god now walks with us
Under a truce. Now you see what you should.

Pentheus:
How do I look? Don't I hold my body
Just like Ino or my mother Agave do?

Dionysus:
In appearance you are exactly like them.
But this strand of hair has fallen loose
From where I tucked it beneath your hairnet.

Pentheus:
It slipped its mooring as I shook my head
To and fro, practicing my Bacchic moves.

Dionysus:
But I, who have the role of your attendant,
Shall restore it. Now hold up your head.

Pentheus:
Yes, arrange it. I rely on you completely now.

Dionysus:
Your belt is far too loose, and the folds of your gown
Do not hang well in pleats about your ankles.

Pentheus:
I'm inclined to think the problem is my right leg;
On the left the gown flatters my figure well.

Dionysus:
Surely you'll count me the best among your friends,
When you learn the Bacchae are in fact chaste.

Pentheus:
Shall I grasp the thyrsus on the right or left?
Which way makes me more like a Bacchant?

Dionysus:
Hold it in your right hand, and raise it in time
With your foot. I applaud your change of heart.

Pentheus:
Could my shoulders carry the weight of all
Mount Cithaeron's glens, and the Bacchic women?

Dionysus:
They could if you wished. Your mind was ill
Before, but now you think as you should.

Pentheus:
Shall we bring levers, or shall I tear them up
By hand, wedging my shoulder beneath the peaks?

Dionysus:
Take care not to destroy the shrines of the nymphs
And Pan's dwellings, where he plays the pipes.

Pentheus:
You're right. The women must not be subdued
By force. I shall lose myself among the pine trees.

Dionysus:
You shall lose yourself as you should be lost,
Coming as a crafty spy among the maenads.

Pentheus:
I can see them already, like birds in a thicket,
Caught in the sweetest nets of lovemaking.

Dionysus:
You are dispatched to guard against this event.
You may catch them unless they catch you first.

Pentheus:
Escort me throughout all the lands of Thebes.
I alone have courage to do this deed.

9.8 Lysias *On the Murder of Eratosthenes* 1.30–33. Ca 400 BCE. In this extract from the speech on the murder of an alleged adulterer, the Athenian orator Lysias argues in defense of the killer Euphiletus.

Read out the law inscribed on the pillar on the Hill of Ares.
You hear, gentlemen, how the Court on the Hill of Ares itself, which both in our fathers' time and in our own has had jurisdiction over cases of murder, specifically stated that whoever catches an adulterer in the act with his wife and imposes this punishment shall not be convicted of murder. And the lawgiver was so utterly convinced of the justice of this provision in the case of married women, that he imposed the same penalty in the case of mistresses, who are a less worthy group. Therefore it is clear that if he had known of a greater punishment for the case of married women, he would have used it. But since he was not able to discover a stronger punishment for their case, he deemed the same fit for the case of mistresses also. Read out this law also. You hear, gentlemen, how he ordains that if someone commits a shameful act against a free adult or child using force, he shall be liable to double damages. And if he commits a shameful act against a woman in one of the situations where it is permissible to kill him, the same damages apply. So he believed that rapists deserved a lesser penalty than seducers, for he condemned seducers to death, but exacted double damages from rapists, reasoning that rapists are hated by the people they forcibly ruin, but seducers function by corrupting the souls of their victims, so that they make other men's wives more loyal to themselves than to their husbands. They bring the whole household over to their cause, and make it uncertain who has fathered the children, the husband or the adulterer. For these reasons, he who made the law decreed that their penalty was death.

9.9 Aeschines *Against Timarchus* 1.14–16. 347 BCE. The orator Aeschines discusses Athenian laws and penalties for transgression involving physical violation of another person (*hubris*).

And what other law has been established to guard your children? The law against pandering, which calls for very great penalties against anyone who procures a freeborn child or woman for prostitution. And what other law? The law against physical violation, which includes all such acts under one heading, and wherein it is explicitly written that if someone violates a child (and surely he who does the hiring commits the violation), or a man or woman, whether free or slave, or if someone commits any illegal act against one of these, there is to be prosecution for violation and a penalty, and it states the punishment or fine to be exacted. Read the law.

Law: If any Athenian commits physical violation against a freeborn child, the guardian of the child shall bring an accusation to the Thesmothetae,[265] specifying a penalty. If the court condemns the accused, let him be handed over for execution the same day. If he is sentenced to pay a fine, let him pay within eleven days of the trial, and if he is not able pay immediately, let him remain confined until payment is made. Those who abuse the persons of household slaves shall be held responsible under the same conditions.

9.10 *Leviticus* 18 (Septuagint). Second century BCE. Leviticus, one of the five books of the Hebrew Torah, deals with religious laws for the priests and people. While the Hebrew text reached its present form between the sixth and fourth centuries BCE, the book became accessible to Hellenised, Greek-speaking Jews throughout the Mediterranean world in the second century BCE, when it was translated into Greek.

And the Lord said to Moses, 'Speak to the sons of Israel and say to them: I am the Lord your God. You shall not conduct yourselves according to the customs of the land of Egypt, where you used to live. And you shall not conduct yourselves according to the customs of the land of Canaan, where I am leading you. You shall not follow their laws. You shall keep my judgements and guard my ordinances. I am the Lord your God. Guard all my ordinances and all my judgements, and practice them; the person who practices them will live in them. I am the Lord your God.

A person shall not approach a close relative in order to uncover that person's shame.[266] I am the Lord.

The shame of your father and the shame of your mother you shall not uncover. She is your mother and you shall not uncover her shame. You shall not uncover the shame of your father's wife. That is a shameful thing for your father. You shall not uncover the shame of your sister, either your father's daughter or your mother's, whether she was born in your house or outside. You shall not uncover the shame of your son's daughter or your daughter's daughter. That is a shameful thing for you.

You shall not uncover the shame of the daughter of your father's wife, a sister born to the same father as you. You shall not uncover the shame of your father's sister. She is a close relative of your father. You shall not uncover the shame of your mother's sister. She is a close relative of your mother. You shall not uncover the shame of your father's brother, and you shall not approach his wife, for she is your kin.

You shall not uncover the shame of your daughter in law. She is your son's wife; you shall not uncover her shame. You shall not uncover the shame of your brother's wife. That is a shameful thing for your brother.

You shall not uncover the shame of both a woman and her daughter. You shall not take hold of her son's daughter or her daughter's daughter in order to uncover their shame. They are your relatives, and this is an unholy act. You shall not take hold of your wife's sister as a rival wife, in order to uncover her shame while your wife is living. You shall not approach a woman during her seclusion for impurity in order to uncover her shame. And you shall not sire offspring in the bed of your neighbour's wife and defile yourself with her. You shall not sire offspring to hand over to the worship of an idol, and you shall not profane the name of the holy. I am the Lord. And you shall not lie with a male as one does with a woman. That is disgusting. You shall not expend your seed in relations with a four-footed creature and defile yourself with it. A woman shall not be placed with any four-footed creature to have relations with it. That is loathsome.

Do not defile yourselves in any of these ways, for in all these ways the nations defiled themselves, those that I shall drive out before you. Even the land was defiled, and I punished them because of this wrong, and the land was angry with its inhabitants. Guard all my laws and all my ordinances. The native born person and the stranger among you shall not do any of these disgusting things. For all these things were done by the people who were before you in the land, and the land was defiled. You shall not do these things, lest the land become angry with you for defiling it, as it was angry with the nations who were before you.

As for anyone who does any of these disgusting things, these souls shall be obliterated from their people. You shall guard my ordinances so that you will not practice the disgusting customs that were before you. And you shall not defile yourselves with them. I am the Lord your God.'

9.11 Catullus *Songs* 89–91. Ca. 54 BCE. In this trio of poems, the narrator attacks one Gellius for his alleged incestuous relations with a variety of relatives. In the third poem we learn the motive for the attacks: Gellius has also had a liaison with the girl the narrator loves.

89

Gellius is thin; why not? With such a good mother,
So healthy and hale, such a charming sister,

Such a good uncle, and so very many girl cousins,
How can he avoid becoming so lean?
Even if he touches nothing but what is forbidden,
You'll see he has reason to be so lean.

90

Let a magus[267] be born from Gellius' heinous coupling
With his mother; let him learn Persian omens,
For a magus ought to be born from a mother and son,
If the wicked Persian religion is true:
A son who pleases the gods, so that after the chant
He may pour on the flame the melting fat.

91

I didn't expect you to do right, Gellius,
When it came to my miserable, desperate love
Because I knew you or thought you capable
Of restraining yourself from a filthy deed;
No, it's because the girl whose love devours me
Is neither your mother nor sister. And while
I've had dealings with you many a time,
I didn't know that would be reason enough.
For you, it was. That's how much you enjoy
A guilty deed, as long as it's evil.

9.12 Livy *History of Rome* 1.9, 1.58. Ca. 25 BCE. In the first book of his history, Livy recounted the legendary events associated with the city's origins, including the rape of the Sabine women by the men of Rome. The episode with the Sabine women would have taken place in the mid-eighth century BCE. The rape of Lucretia by the son of the Roman king Tarquin led to the expulsion of the kings and the founding of the Roman Republic. If she was a historical figure, Lucretia must have died ca. 508 BCE.

1.9

Rome was now strong enough to engage in war on equal terms with any of the neighbouring states. But due to the lack of women, the city's greatness was likely to last only one generation, for the Romans had neither the hope of offspring at home, nor the right to intermarry with women from adjoining states. Therefore, on the advice of the Senate, Romulus sent envoys around to the neighboring peoples, seeking for his new nation an alliance and the right to intermarry. Cities come from the humblest origins, the envoys argued, like all other things. But with time, those who are aided by the gods and their own virtues create for themselves great prosperity and renown. They expressed their confidence both that the gods had been favourable to the birth of Rome, and that its citizens would not be deficient in virtue; therefore, it would be no burden to their neighbours to mingle their blood and lineage with that of the Romans, who were their fellow men. This embassy was nowhere favourably received. Even as the neighbours grew to fear the great edifice growing in their midst, they spurned it, both for themselves and their descendants. As they sent away the envoys, several of them asked whether the Romans had also opened a refuge for female outcasts, since only in this way would they make suitable matches.

The Roman youths could scarcely bear this treatment, and it seemed inevitable that the matter would end in violence. In order to give them an opportune time and place for this, Romulus concealed the sorrow in his heart and spared no effort to prepare ceremonial games in honour of Horseman Neptune; he called this festival the Consualia.[268] Then he ordered that this spectacle be announced to the neighbouring peoples, and the Romans directed all their knowledge and ability toward the goal of preparing for the festival, in order to ensure that it was much discussed and eagerly awaited. Many people gathered for the festival out of a desire to see the new city, and most especially those living closest: the people of Caenina, Crustumia, and Antemnae. A great crowd of the Sabines came too, with their children and wives. They were hospitably received in every home, and when they saw how the city was situated, its walls, and its many buildings, they were amazed at the speed with which the Roman state had grown. When the time came for the show, and people's minds and eyes were thus preoccupied, the pre-arranged show of force was carried out. When the signal was given, the Roman youths ran in all directions, carrying off the virgins. Most of them were snatched up at random, but certain girls notable for their looks were carried off by plebeians charged with this task, and delivered to the homes of the leading senators. One girl in particular, who stood out from all the rest for her face and figure, was carried off by a group under the command of a certain Talassius. The men shouted over and over, in answer to the many questioners, that she was destined 'for Talassius' and that nobody should lay a hand on her. This is the origin of the cry 'Talassio' at weddings.

The panic brought the games to a halt, and the grieving parents of the virgins fled, crying that the laws of hospitality had been wickedly violated, and calling upon the god whose games they had attended, only to be victims of treacherous deceit. The girls were equally downcast and indignant. But Romulus himself went about visiting them, explaining that their fathers' pride was the cause of this deed, for they had refused their neighbours the right to intermarry. In spite of this, the girls would be wedded, and would share the property and civic rights of their husbands; furthermore they would be the mothers of freeborn children, and nothing was dearer to the human heart than this. They should lay aside their anger, he said; fortune had given their bodies to these men, and they should give the men their hearts. Feelings of hurt often gave rise to affection, and because of this experience their husbands would be more kind to them, for each would exert himself to the utmost and make it his occupation to console his wife for the parents and homeland she had lost. The husbands then caressed their wives with sweet words, excusing their deed on the grounds that they were overcome with desire and love; such pleas are the most appealing to a woman's nature.

1.58

After a few days, Sextus Tarquinius went to Collatia without Collatinus'[269] knowledge, taking with him only one attendant. He was warmly received, for no one suspected his plan, and after dinner he was conducted to a guest room. Burning with passion, he waited until everyone seemed to be asleep and it was safe to move about. Then, drawing his sword, he came to Lucretia as she slept, and holding her down with his left hand on her chest, he said, 'Be silent, Lucretia. I am Sextus Tarquinius, and I am armed. You will die if you make a sound.' The woman started from her sleep, terrified, but saw no hope of aid, only the likelihood of immediate death. Tarquinius then began to speak of his love, to beg her to yield, mixing his pleas with threats, and tried every trick he could to subvert her woman's heart. When he saw that she was resolute and that not even the fear of death swayed her, he added disgrace to fear, saying that once she was dead he would kill his slave and place the naked body upon hers; then people would say that he had killed her in the act of a filthy adulterous liaison. At this terrifying prospect, his savage lust prevailed as though by force over her resolute chastity. Tarquinius the brave departed, having taken by storm a woman's honour, while the grief-stricken Lucretia sent the same message to her father at Rome and her husband at Ardea, that each should come and bring a trusted friend, and that they must do so quickly, for something horrific had happened. Spurius Lucretius came with Publius Valerius, the son of Volesus, while Collatinus brought Lucius Junius Brutus,[270] with whom he happened to be returning to Rome when he met the messenger from his wife. They found the grieving Lucretia sitting in her chamber. Her friends' arrival brought tears to her eyes, and when her husband asked whether all was well with her, she replied, 'Not at all. For how can a woman be well when she has lost her chastity? Collatinus, a stranger has left his imprint in your bed. Only my body has been violated; my mind remains guiltless. My death will be the evidence of this. But swear to me that the criminal shall not go unpunished. He is Sextus Tarquinius, who last night repaid our hospitality by making himself our enemy. Armed and by force, he brought ruin upon me, and upon himself – if you show yourselves to be men – when he stole his noxious pleasure.' Each man pledges himself in turn; they soothe the heartsick woman by assigning the offence to the doer of the deed rather than the victim. It is the mind that sins, they say, not the body, and where there is no intent, there can be no guilt. 'It is for you to determine what is owed to him,' she said. 'As for me, although I consider myself guiltless, I do not exempt myself from the penalty. No unchaste woman shall use Lucretia as her excuse.' And taking a butcher's knife, which she had concealed beneath her dress, she plunged it into her heart and collapsed forward onto the wound, dying as she fell. Her husband and father cried out in lament.

9.13 Ovid *The Art of Love* 1.659–78. Ca. 1 BCE. This early work by Ovid offers advice to men on how to seduce and keep a woman. Ovid later added a third book addressed to women, with advice on how to be attractive to men.

Weep: with tears you'll move a heart of steel.
If you can, let her see your wet cheeks.
If the tears won't come (it's not easy to cry on cue)
Then rub your eyes until they water.
The wise man mixes his kisses with sweet words.
If she refuses, take kisses anyway.
She may fight at first and cry, 'you wicked man!'
Yet in fact she wants to be overcome.
But don't be too rough or bruise her tender lips;
Be sure she has no cause to complain.
A man who gains a kiss and fails to take the rest
Doesn't deserve what he has won.
Such a short path from kisses to your heart's desire –
Blunders, not scruples, hold you back!
You shrink from force? But girls like to be forced;
They long to yield against their will.
She who is taken in a moment's violent passion
Delights, and the deed is like a gift.
But she who comes untouched from the struggle,
Though she smiles, is secretly sad.
Phoebe was raped, and her sister taken by force;
Both victims found their rapists pleasing.[271]

9.14 Petronius *Satyrica* 16–26. Ca. 60 CE. Petronius' fragmentary novel, written and set during the reign of Nero, tells the adventures of Encolpius and his lover, the slave boy Giton, in the criminal underworld of Rome. In this selection, the priestess Quartilla confronts Encolpius, Giton, and their companion Ascyltus after the three have accidentally viewed secret rites devoted to the phallic god Priapus. She then subjects them to sexual abuse in the guise of initiation into the cult of the god.

Thanks to Giton's good work, we were just stuffing ourselves with dinner when there came a loud pounding on the door. We were frightened and asked who was there. 'Open up,' came the reply, 'and you'll find out.' As we were about to answer, the bar fell of its own accord from the door, which swung open to admit the visitor. It was a woman with her head veiled, who said, 'Did you think you could scorn me? I am the maidservant of Quartilla, whose rites you disturbed in front of the grotto. She herself is coming to this house and she wants to speak with you. Don't worry yourselves. She isn't accusing you of wrongdoing, and she's not going to punish you. In fact, she is wondering what god sent such elegant young men her way.'

We were silent up to this point, showing no sign of acquiescence, when Quartilla herself came in, attended by a virginal girl, and seating herself on my bed, burst into a lengthy bout of weeping. Even then, we couldn't bring ourselves to say anything, but waited in astonishment for the display of contrived tears to end. When the ostentatious storm had passed, she removed the mantle from her proud head, and stretched her hands out in front of her until the knuckles cracked, saying 'What boldness is this? And where did you learn this thievery that outstrips the storybooks? By the gods, I pity you, for whoever gazes upon that which is forbidden does not go unpunished. To be sure, this part of town is so full of supernatural powers that you're more likely to stumble upon a god than a human being. But don't think I've come here to get revenge. I place more importance on your youth than on the injury to myself. You have, quite unintentionally, I think, committed a crime for which there is no atonement. Indeed, that night I was shaken with such dangerous fits of the chills, that I thought I'd contracted a tertian fever.[272] I sought a cure in my dreams, and I was commanded to seek you out and to soothe the onset of my illness by the exact methods revealed to me. But my main concern is not a cure for myself; much greater is the sadness I feel in my heart – which may yet be the death of me – that you will reveal to the general public the counsels of the gods, and profane the mysteries of Priapus, which you witnessed in the chapel as a result of your youthful recklessness. Therefore, I am at your knees, stretching forth my hands to beg and pray that you not subject our nocturnal rites to derision and scorn, or betray the secrets kept for so many years, which scarcely a thousand people have known.'

After this plea, she again dissolved into tears, and shaken by great sobs, pressed herself face down on my bed. At this, I was filled with pity and fear, and told her to cheer up and that she need not worry on either count: nobody would profane the sacred rites, and what is more, if the god had revealed to her some cure for the tertian fever, we would assist divine providence, even at risk to ourselves. Once this promise was made, the woman became quite cheerful, kissing me soundly, and her tears turned to giggles as she stroked the hair over my ears with a lingering hand. 'I will call a truce with you and drop the charges I filed,' she said. 'If you had not agreed to this medicine I seek, a gang of men would have come tomorrow to avenge the wrong you did and restore my honour.'

Disrespect is truly vile,
Making the rules is more my style.
Here's what puts me at my ease:
I go exactly where I please!
For even a person who's hale and wise
If spurned, will give you a nasty surprise.
When ladies refrain from killing their men,
They become winners, again and again.

Then clapping her hands, she gave a bark of laughter so loud and sudden that we were frightened. She was joined at once by the maid who had arrived first, and the little virgin who had come in with her.

Their farcical laughter echoed from every wall. Meanwhile we had no idea what had given rise to this sudden change of mood, and gazed in astonishment first at one another, and then at the women... 'I have forbidden that any mortal enter this inn today, in order that I may receive my cure from you without interruptions.' When Quartilla said this, Ascyltus stood stunned and gaping, while I was deprived of speech by a chill that felt colder than a northern winter. But the fact that my companions were there kept me from feeling too dejected. For even if they tried anything, they were only three weaklings, mere women, whereas we were if nothing else, at least of the male sex, and our clothing didn't hinder us as theirs did. Indeed, I had it all worked out that if there was going to be a fight, I would take on Quartilla myself, while Ascyltus would face the maidservant, and Giton the virgin...

Then all our resolution dissolved in amazement, and certain death rose up before our wretched eyes...

'Please, my lady,' I said, 'if you have anything worse in store for us, get it over with quickly. Our offense was not so great that we deserve to die under torture.' The maidservant, whose name was Psyche, carefully spread a blanket on the floor...

She got to work on my groin, which was now as cold as though I were a corpse a thousand times over...

Ascyltus covered his head; presumably he had learned how dangerous it was to meddle in other's people's secrets...

The maidservant drew two scarves from her bosom and tied our feet with one, our hands with the other...

Now that the conversation had flagged, Ascyltus said, 'What about me?

Don't I get to have a drink too?' In response to my laughter, the maidservant clapped her hands and said, 'I put it right there. Young man, did you drink up all the medicine yourself?' 'What's that?' put in Quartilla, 'Did Encolpius drink all the satyrion[273] that was left?' And her sides shook with a laugh that was not unattractive...

Finally Giton couldn't help laughing, especially when the little virgin threw herself on his neck and showered the unresisting boy with countless kisses...

We wanted desperately to scream, but there was nobody near to help us, and besides, Psyche had a sharp hairpin, and whenever I seemed about to call out to my fellow citizens for aid, she jabbed it in my cheek, while from the other side the girl descended on Ascyltus with a paintbrush soaked in satyrion...

Finally there appeared a pervert[274] fitted out in a rough, myrtle-coloured tunic, which he had hitched up to his waist...

First he would fall upon us, wrenching our buttocks apart, and then befoul us with stinking kisses, until Quartilla, with her skirt girded up and grasping a whalebone rod, declared that it was time to give the poor unfortunates a respite...

Both of us swore in the most solemnly religious terms that such a terrible secret would go with us to our graves...

Several masseurs came in and restored us, making use of the right type of oil. Once we had shaken off our fatigue, we dressed in dinner clothes again and were led to the next room, where three couches stood ready amid the preparations for a splendid banquet. We were told to lie down, and after an excellent first course we got started on a flood of Falernian wine. Once we had eaten several courses, we began to feel sleepy, but Quartilla said, 'What is this? You intend to sleep, when you know that we must devote the whole night to the spirit of Priapus?'...

When Ascyltus fell asleep, exhausted by so many trials, the maidservant whom he had roughly pushed away rubbed soot over his entire face, and then, when he did not awake, she painted his shoulders and sides with pictures of big penises.

[Encolpius and the others fall into a drunken sleep, only to be awakened when two Syrian thieves sneak into the house to rob the silver, causing a commotion as they fight over the loot. The servants rise, rubbing their eyes, and a cymbal-player begins to play festive music, while the party starts up again.]

The pervert came in, a most absurd individual and clearly well suited to that house. He began to snap his fingers and wail out a song something like this:

Naughty perverts hasten here,
Come every one and gather near.

Nimble buttocks, grasping hands,
Come, old fags and eunuch bands!

When these verses were done, he planted on me an incredibly foul and
slobbering kiss. Then he got up on my couch and forcefully ripped the covers
off me, even though I resisted. He laboured over my groin for a long time, but
in vain. Gummy rivulets of sweat poured from his face, and there was so much
white makeup caked in the wrinkles on his cheeks, it made me think of an old
plastered wall in a rainstorm.

I was very close to tears, but at last, in the depths of my sorrow, I said,
'Please, my lady, I was sure your orders were that I was to be given a drinking
horn?' Quartilla gently clapped her hands and said, 'Oh, you clever man, what
a fountain of native wit you are! What? You didn't understand that "Drinking
horn"[275] is our name for a pervert?' Then, since misery loves company, I said,
'For heavens' sake, is Ascyltus the only one in this room enjoying a holiday?'
'You're right,' Quartilla replied, 'let Ascyltus receive the drinking horn!'

At this the pervert changed his mount, and moving over to my companion,
he ground away at Ascyltus with his buttocks and lips. All this time Giton was
standing there, laughing himself to pieces. Observing this, Quartilla asked with
deliberate care whom he belonged to. When I said that he was my boyfriend,
she replied, 'Well, why isn't he kissing me, then?' and leaned up against him,
her mouth seeking his. Her hand soon found its way to his lap, and getting hold
of his inexperienced member, she cried, 'This will serve as a lovely appetiser
tomorrow; after the sea-bass I'm not inclined to sample a sardine!'

As she said this, Psyche broke into a huge grin and came over to say
something to Quartilla. 'Yes, yes,' she cried, 'what a good suggestion! Since
this is a perfect opportunity, why not have our girl Pannychis deflowered?'
Immediately a girl who appeared to be no more than seven years old was led
forward, the same one who had come into our room with Quartilla. I gaped
as everyone applauded the idea and called for the nuptials, and then I asserted
that Giton, who was after all a very shy boy, was not capable of such freakish
behaviour, nor was the girl old enough to play a grown woman's role. But
Quartilla said, 'Is she any younger than I was when I had my first man? May my
Juno frown on me if I can even remember when I was a virgin! Even as an infant
I liked a bit of fun with my playmates, and later on I used to occupy myself with
older boys, until I came of age. I suppose that's where that proverb got started,
the one that says if you can carry a calf, you can carry a bull!' Anxious that
something even worse could happen to my boyfriend if I was not there, I rose
to attend the marriage rites.

Psyche had already draped the girl in a flame-coloured wedding veil, and
now 'Drinking horn' led the procession carrying a torch, as the applauding,

drunken women formed a long line; they had already decked the bridal chamber with obscene pictures. Aroused by these hijinks, Quartilla herself got to her feet, and grabbing hold of Giton, dragged him into the chamber. Giton was by no means unwilling, nor indeed did the poor girl tremble at the idea of her 'wedding night'. While they lay together behind the closed door, we sat at the threshold. Quartilla was the first to put her attentive eye up to a suspiciously convenient crack in the wall, watching their childish play with lewd concentration. She gently drew me over to view the scene, and because our faces were side by side, whenever she grew weary of watching, she would move her lips my way, harassing me with stolen kisses…

Throwing ourselves down on the bed, we spent the rest of the night without fear.

9.15 Suetonius *The Twelve Caesars* 6.28–9 (Nero). 121 CE. In his life of Nero, the historian Suetonius catalogues stories of the emperor's debaucheries and sex crimes.

Besides using freeborn boys for sex and sleeping with other men's brides, he forced himself on the Vestal Virgin Rubria. He came very close to making the freedwoman Acte his lawful wife when he suborned some men of consular rank to commit perjury by swearing that she came of royal blood. After castrating the boy Sporus and attempting to transform him into a woman, he married him with all the usual ceremonies, including the dowry and the marriage veil, and had him escorted to his house by a great crowd. A clever witticism on this remark is still repeated: 'It would have been a benefit to the human race if Nero's father Domitius had had such a wife.' This Sporus, dressed in all the ornaments of an empress and riding in a litter, he took to the legal assemblies and markets of Greece (fondly kissing him all the way), and later in Rome to the Sigillaria, the market for figurines. That Nero had a strong desire to sleep with his mother, and that he was only prevented from doing so by her detractors, who feared that this vicious and headstrong woman would gain the upper hand by granting these favours, nobody doubted, especially after he added to the number of his concubines a prostitute who reportedly had a close resemblance to Agrippina. Yet even before that, they say, whenever he rode in a litter with his mother, his incestuous pleasure was betrayed by the stains on his clothing.

He exposed his own chastity to so much dishonour that, after polluting virtually every part of his body, he at last devised a completely new sort of game. Covered in the skin of a wild animal, he was released from a cage and attacked the genitals of men and women who were tied to stakes. When he had practiced this savagery to the point of weariness, he was brought to a sexual climax by his freedman Doryphorus. Just as he had made Sporus his wife, he himself had become the wife of Doryphorus, even imitating the cries and laments of a virgin being forcefully deflowered. Quite a few people have told me that he was utterly convinced that no person is truly chaste or pure in any part of the body, but that most hide their vices and shrewdly keep them secret, and that therefore he would overlook other crimes if people confessed to him their sexual vices.

9.16 Artemidorus of Daldis *Interpretation of Dreams* 1.79. Second century CE. Artemidorus explains the significance of dreams about oral sex. He includes oral sex in the category of sex acts that are 'contrary to law'.

A man who dreams that he has had the unmentionable act performed on him by a friend or relative, or a child who is no longer an infant, will grow to hate the one who performed the unmentionable act, but he who has had the unmentionable act performed by an infant will bury the child. For it is no longer possible for him to kiss the child. He who has the unmentionable act performed on him by an unknown person will pay a fine of some sort, because of the useless emission of semen. But if a man dreams that he himself performs the unmentionable act on someone he knows, either a man or a woman, he will grow to hate that person because it is no longer possible for their mouths to be joined together. If he does not know the person, the dream foretells harm for all except those who earn their living by their mouths, such as flute-players, trumpeters, public speakers, sophists, and any other such persons.

9.17 Pausanias *Description of Greece* 4.16.9–10. Late second century CE. Pausanias relates an episode involving the Messenian hero Aristomenes, who was celebrated in his homeland for his ability to outwit the Spartan enemy. Unless Aristomenes is purely a figure of legend, he lived during the late eighth and early seventh centuries BCE.

He set a daytime ambush for the girls who performed the dances for Artemis at Caryae,[276] and capturing those who were wealthiest and whose fathers were most respected, he brought them to a village in Messenia, and turned over the guardianship of the maidens to his men while he rested for the night. There the young men tried to rape the girls, perhaps having lost their reason as a result of drunkenness. When Aristomenes opposed these actions as things no Greek would do, they ignored him, so that he was forced to kill the most violently drunken ones among them. And when he had recovered the captives, he ransomed them for a good price and returned them in a state of virginity, just as he had taken them.

9.18 Julius Paulus Prudentissimus *Opinions* 2.26.1–17. Second to third century CE. Paulus was an influential Roman jurist. Here he summarises provisions of the Julian law concerning adultery, which was first established under the emperor Augustus (17 BCE), and related laws.

Concerning Adultery

1. In the second chapter of the Julian law on adultery, either an adoptive or a natural father is permitted to kill with his own hand an adulterer of any social status whom he has caught in the act with his daughter in his own house, or that of his son in law. 2. If a father who is himself under paternal control should catch his daughter in the act of adultery, it is inferred from the wording of the law that he cannot kill her, yet it ought to be permitted for him to do so. 3. The fifth chapter of the Julian law sets forth that it is permitted to detain an adulterer caught in the act for twenty hours, calling neighbours to witness. 4. A husband may not kill anyone taken in adultery other than disreputable people, and those who make a profit from their bodies, and also slaves. But it is forbidden for him to kill his wife. 5. It has been decided that a husband who catches his wife with an adulterer and kills her should be punished more leniently, because he committed the act in the impatience of righteous suffering. 6. When a husband kills an adulterer, he must immediately send away his wife and publicly state within the next three days with what adulterer and in what place he caught the wife. 7. A husband who surprises his wife in adultery can only kill the adulterer if he catches him in his own house. 8. It has been decided that a husband who does not immediately send away a wife whom he has caught in adultery is subject to prosecution for pandering. 9. Slaves of the husband as well as the wife are subject to torture in cases of adultery, and freeing the slaves will not give them immunity from torture. 10. It should be noted that two adulterers can be accused at the same time with the wife, but more than two cannot be accused at the same time. 11. It has been decided that adultery is not applicable if the woman in question has charge of a public business or tavern. 12. Anyone who commits a sexual offense with a free male without his consent shall be punished with death. 13. He who of his own free will submits to impure and disgraceful sexual acts will be punished with the loss of half his property, and will not normally be permitted to make a will. 14. It has been decided that a woman convicted of adultery will be punished with the loss of half her dowry and a third of her property and she will be banished to an island. An adulterous man will likewise forfeit half his property and be banished to an island, provided that the two are banished to different islands. 15. It has been decided that the punishment for incest, which is deportation to an island for a man, will not be applied to a woman, provided she has not been convicted under the Julian law on adultery. 16. Committing a sexual offense

with female slaves is not considered to rise to the level of an injury unless their value deteriorates as a result, or an attempt is made against their mistress through them. 17. Postponements cannot be granted in adultery cases.

Further Reading

For sexual transgression in Greek law, see Cohen 1991a, Carey 1995, and Odgen 1997. For the Julian law on adultery, see Cohen 1991b, and more generally on using the Roman sources, Richlin 1981. On the concept of *stuprum*, see Fantham 1991; on sexual transgression in Hellenistic Jewish and early Christian thought, see Gaca 2003, pp. 119–217. For rape in mythology and in the *Metamorphoses* of Ovid, see Curran 1984 and Lefkowitz 1993. For rape in Greek and Roman comedy, see Peirce 1997. On the rape of Lucretia and Verginia and their relationship to Roman self-definition, see Joshel 1992, Moses 1993, and Arieti 1997. For tyrants and sexual transgression, see Parker 1998. On incest, see Moreau 2002 (in French), Watson 2006; and for Oedipus, Edmunds 1981.

10

Prostitutes and Courtesans

The Greeks and Romans did not consider prostitution a scandal, though the social position of most prostitutes was degraded; male and female sex workers were typically slaves and prostitution was regulated by the state. While it was a serious crime to act as a pimp to one's own free family members or other free persons (9.9), entrepreneurs openly purchased slave children to rear as sex workers. Often these brothel-keepers were themselves veterans of the profession. Prostitutes varied in price and status from the lowly, cheap, and unattractive to the sought-after, exclusive, and beautiful. Greek *hetairai* ('companions') were in some cases educated and independent, able to buy their freedom and to attract the devotion of powerful men such as Pericles (10.14). Among the Greeks, the exceptional social status of these women occasionally won them political influence and substantial wealth; Athenaeus collects (10.21) many of the anecdotes about them, and he quotes from numerous books written on the subject of courtesans. Such women, however, seem to have garnered less respect and power in the Roman system, though they were celebrated by the poets.

At all periods, officials took an interest in making legal distinctions between 'respectable' women of the citizen class who were sexually off limits, and those who did not fall into this category; thus the dress of the prostitute or convicted adulteress (e.g. a toga in Rome) might be legally prescribed by the state. At Rome, prostitutes were required to register with the authorities for tax and identification purposes. But clear distinctions between commercial sex and other sexual arrangements were not always easy to identify, and did not always correspond to modern ideas of what constitutes prostitution. Citizen women could be punished for blurring the line between prostitution, which was not a crime, and adultery, which was. We know of at least one

Roman wife who sought to gain greater sexual freedom by registering as a prostitute, but when her husband failed to punish her, the Senate did so (10.18). Husbands who condoned their wives' adulterous activities could be charged with pandering.

The attitude toward prostitution of the 'man on the street' in Classical Athens is illustrated in a fragment from a comedy by Philemon (10.5). It reveals the absence of guilt or shame about purchasing the services of a prostitute, and relief at the prospect of easily available sex with no entanglements. One of Horace's *Satires* echoes these sentiments, contrasting the straightforwardness of a sexual transaction for money with the dangers and frustrations of pursuing married women (10.8). The more beautiful and sought-after a prostitute was, however, the more she was able to exercise selectivity in the choice of her male companions, and the more such relationships involved passionate desires rather than the simple satisfaction of physical needs. The theme of the courtesan or prostitute who loses her beauty was popular in poetry because it explored universal human fears about ageing and mortality: even the most beautiful of women must grow old and die. At the same time, the misogynistic thread in Greco-Roman culture ensured that some men relished the tradition of invective against ugly prostitutes, particularly those who once spurned would-be lovers. Treatments of this theme ranged from the sympathetic (10.6, 10.7) to the brutal (10.9).

The topic of 'sacred prostitution' has been much debated by scholars. Traditionally, historians described this institution as an import to Greece from Near Eastern cities such as Babylon, where Herodotus says there was a ritual requirement that all women sell their bodies once during their lifetimes (10.2). Whether Herodotus' story has a factual basis is unknown, and it may be based on misunderstanding and a desire to contrast barbarian behaviour (condemned by the historian as 'most shameful') with Greek practices. There is evidence, on the other hand, that some Greek sanctuaries of Aphrodite owned prostitutes whose earnings generated income. For example, the choral poet Pindar wrote a song (10.1) for Xenophon of Corinth, who vowed to dedicate one hundred courtesans to Aphrodite if he was victorious at the Olympic games; the song was a musical accompaniment to the banquet. One of the principal ports of Greece, Corinth was famous as a centre of prostitution, and its patron goddess was Aphrodite. Writing much later, Strabo (10.10) also says that the sanctuary of Corinthian Aphrodite once possessed consecrated slaves. While Aphrodite was the goddess of prostitutes, and many of them certainly felt a special relationship with her, it is unlikely that sex with such a prostitute had a sacral meaning. At Rome, prostitution and sexual revelry were tied to certain religious cults and festivals, including those for the goddess Flora (10.12).

Most prostitutes were female, and their feelings about their work are inaccessible to us, except insofar as male authors have described them.

One example is the conversation between Theodote and Socrates recounted by Xenophon (10.3). Socrates aims to convince Theodote that by practicing her profession within certain ethical boundaries, she will benefit not only her lovers but also herself; Theodote appears receptive to his advice, or at least his potential patronage. Beautiful courtesans such as Theodote became celebrities, and anecdotes about them were long remembered. Among the most famous of these were Phryne and Laïs, both of whom lived during the fourth century BCE. Laïs was a native of Corinth; in Athens she established a reputation as the most beautiful woman of her time. The collection of verse known as the *Greek Anthology* contains several epigrams about her by later poets (10.6, 10.7). Phryne too was celebrated (10.21) for her beauty and noted for the wealth she amassed; she was immortalised as the model for the sculptor Praxiteles' famous nude statue of Aphrodite. The former courtesan Neaera, who also belongs to the fourth century BCE, gained involuntary notoriety as the focus of a lawsuit intended to discredit her husband Stephanus by showing that their marriage was illegal and that Stephanus had broken the Athenian law against marriage to a non-citizen. The oration against Neaera (10.4), handed down as part of the works of Demosthenes, was actually composed by Apollodorus, the greatest enemy of the politically active Stephanus. Again, we know nothing of what Neaera herself thought about the case, because as a woman she was not allowed to testify at the trial.

Most courtesans never became famous, yet derived a substantial living from their ability to attract generous lovers. This form of prostitution, a step up from the sordid brothels, continued to be popular during the Roman imperial period. The satirical writer Lucian penned a whole series of dramatic dialogues with prostitutes as characters. In one of these (10.19), a mother (likely a retired courtesan herself) has introduced her daughter to a life of prostitution and relies on the daughter's beauty to provide a comfortable living for them both. In this case, the prostituted daughter Philinna struggles to reconcile her personal reactions to her lover's behaviour with the need to ensure his continued financial support.

Prostitutes varied in price, from the streetwalkers whom Martial describes using tombs as improvised shelters (10.15), to the denizens of the brothels that were fixtures of every city, to courtesans. They included musicians, dancers, and actresses whose sexual services were assumed to be part of the price when they were hired to entertain at dinner parties. The Romans in particular equated a woman's appearance on a public stage with prostitution (7.9). Written sources provide some information about the conditions in ancient brothels to complement the data from archaeological sites such as Pompeii. Graffiti from the brothels of Pompeii show that both men and women worked as prostitutes (10.13). From the Elder Seneca (10.11) and

Juvenal (10.16) we learn that brothel workers stood in front of small cubicles with their nicknames and prices scribbled on a placard above them; when customers approached them, they retired to the cramped confines of the cubicle, which was blackened by soot from lamps. As described by Horace (10.8) and in other sources, prostitutes on duty were either naked or dressed in garments that revealed the 'merchandise' to prospective customers.

Seneca's hypothetical legal case (10.11) of a virtuous woman kidnapped by pirates and sold to a brothel is not completely fanciful, for slavery was the main method by which brothels were supplied with workers, and pirates were common in the Roman world. The attitude adopted by the jurists contemplating her case gives us some idea of the stigma attached to prostitution in the eyes of elite Roman men and women; prostitutes were considered tainted or unclean, and they had the ability to spread this pollution to those with whom they associated. Juvenal's vicious attack on Messalina (10.16), the third wife of the emperor Claudius, also illustrates this concept. Messalina had a reputation for both promiscuity and political intrigue (she was executed by Claudius for plotting against him with her lover Silius). Accusations of sexual depravity were effective weapons against powerful women.

In spite of the mainstream acceptance of prostitution as a legal and morally legitimate cultural institution, there were voices of dissent. The Stoic philosopher and orator Dio Chrysostom (10.17) was an impassioned opponent of the practice, arguing that it was by its very nature morally corrupt and dangerous to society, and that sex workers were victims of brutal exploitation. The early Christian condemnation of prostitution focused on sexual activity outside of marriage as inherently sinful, and made connections between prostitution and other elements of pagan culture and religion. In particular, the widespread practice of infant abandonment was criticised as a stimulus to prostitution, for such children were often collected and reared by brothel-keepers. In contrast to Chrystostom's compassion for enslaved prostitutes, however, Justin's moral condemnation (10.20) encompasses the prostitutes themselves, as well as those who profit from them.

10.1 Pindar Fr. 122 Snell-Maehler. Ca. 460. According to Athenaeus (*The Philosophers at Dinner* 13.33.573e), Pindar composed this song for Olympic victor Xenophon of Corinth, who dedicated one hundred prostitutes to Aphrodite in fulfillment of his vow. The song is fragmentary.

Young women, hospitable to many, handmaidens
Of Persuasion in rich Corinth,
You who burn the golden tears of pale incense;
Often you fly in your thoughts
To Heavenly Aphrodite, the mother of Loves.

She gave to you, girls, without blame,
To pick the fruit of soft youth
On beds of desire.
With necessity, all is good...[277]

[missing lines]

But I wonder, what will they say,
The lords of the Isthmus, of the beginning
I found for this song of honeyed thoughts,
A consort for women who are shared?
With a pure touchstone we learn the worth of gold.

[missing lines]

Lady of Cyprus, here to your grove,
Rejoicing in his prayers fulfilled,
Xenophon brought a hundred-limbed herd
Of grazing girls.

10.2 Herodotus *Histories* 1.199.1–5. Ca. 440 BCE. The topic of Herodotus' book is the wars between Greece and Persia. He provides background material on many cultures of the Near East, including the Babylonians.

This is the most shameful of the Babylonian customs: every woman of the land must take a seat in the sanctuary of Aphrodite[278] once during her life in order to have sex with a stranger. Many who are arrogant because of their wealth, and consider themselves too important to mingle with the rest, drive to the temple in covered carriages and stand there with a great crowd of attendants. But here is what most do: they sit in the sanctuary of Aphrodite with wreaths of cord on their heads, and great numbers of women come and go. Passages marked by lengths of rope run in every direction through the crowd, and the strangers pass through these making their selections. Once a woman sits down there, she is not released to return home until one of the strangers has tossed money at her knees and had sex with her outside of the temple. When he tosses the money, he must say, 'I invite you in the name of the goddess Mylitta.' For Mylitta is what the Assyrians call Aphrodite. The amount of money does not matter. The woman will not refuse it, for that would not be right; this act makes the money sacred. She follows the first man who tosses money, and rejects no one as unworthy. After she has sex, she has fulfilled her obligation to the goddess and is released to return home, and after that, you will buy her with no amount of money, however great. Now, the women who are tall and good-looking quickly depart, but those who are ugly remain for a long time, unable to fulfill the law. Some remain for three or four years. There is a custom similar to this in some parts of Cyprus.

10.3 Xenophon *Memorabilia* 3.11.1–15. Ca. 360 BCE. The Athenian historian and soldier Xenophon was also a student of Socrates. He wrote a collection of dialogues in which Socrates is a character.

Once there was a beautiful woman in the city by the name of Theodote, who used to sleep with men who won her consent. One of the bystanders mentioned her, declaring that the beauty of this woman was inexpressible, that artists visited her in order to paint her portrait, and that she showed as much of her body as was allowable. 'We must see her,' said Socrates, 'for one cannot learn by hearsay that which is inexpressible.' 'Then follow me right now,' said the man who had described her. So they went to the house of Theodote, and upon arriving they found her posing for a painter, and stood by to watch. When the painter had finished, Socrates said, 'Gentlemen, should we thank Theodote for showing us her beauty, or should she rather thank us for observing it? If she profits more by showing it, should she be grateful to us? Or, if we gain a greater benefit from the sight, should we be grateful to her?' When someone said that this was a fair question, he answered, 'Well, she already benefits from our praise, and when we spread the word, she will profit even more, whereas at this moment we long to touch what we have seen, and we will go away smitten with her, and miss her once we leave. As a result, it seems likely that we will become her servants, and she will enjoy our devotion.' And Theodote said, 'Good heavens, if that is the case, I ought to be grateful to you for looking at me.' Here Socrates observed that she was dressed expensively, and that her mother, sitting beside her, was dressed and cared for in no ordinary manner, and that there were many good-looking servants, who were far from neglected, and that the house was liberally furnished.

'Tell me, Theodote,' he said, 'do you own a farm?'

'Not I,' she answered.

'Then do you own a house, that brings you rental income?'

'No house,' she said.

'Some slave artisans?'

'Nor any slave artisans.'

'Then where do you get the necessities of life?'

'When someone is friendly toward me and wishes to treat me well, I make my livelihood from this,' she said.

'By Hera,' he said, 'that is a fine property indeed, and better by far than having your own herd of sheep and goats and cattle. But do you trust in luck, waiting for these friends to light upon you like flies, or do you rely on some trick of your own?'

'How could I come up with a trick for that?'

'Indeed, you could do so in a more convenient way than the spiders, for you know how they hunt for a living. They weave a fine web, I believe, and whatever falls into it serves as their nourishment.'

'Then is your advice to me to weave a net of some sort?' she said.

'Oh no. Do not suppose that you will hunt for friends, the worthiest of prey, so unsystematically. Did you know that even in the hunt for the least valuable prey, the hare, people use many cunning tricks? Since hares feed at night, they hunt them with special hounds trained for this purpose; and since hares run away and hide in the daytime, they acquire other hounds who track them by their scent from the feeding-grounds to their warrens, and so catch them; and since hares are very fast and likely to escape once they reach open ground, still other swift hounds are procured, who can outrun them. And because some of the hares still escape, they set up nets in their path of escape, so that running against these, they become utterly entangled.'

'Then could I hunt for friends,' she said, 'with tricks like these?'

'Oh, certainly,' he said, 'if instead of a hound you acquire an agent to track down rich men who are lovers of the beautiful, and devise a way of throwing them into your nets.'

'And what kind of nets do I have?'

'You have one that entangles a man very well, I believe – your body! And within that body, your soul lets you perceive both how to favour a man with a glance, and gladden him with a word. It tells you to cheerfully welcome the serious man, but close the door on the frivolous one; to be thoughtful enough to visit a friend when he is sick, and gladly rejoice with him when things are going well;

and if a friend cares greatly for you, to exert yourself to please him with all your heart. As for lovemaking, I am certain that you know how to do that, not only tenderly, but with kindness, and to show your friends that they are pleasing to you not only through your words, but by your actions.'

'Good heavens,' said Theodote, 'I don't give thought to accomplishing any of those things.'

'And yet it makes all the difference whether you behave yourself with a man in a way that is both natural and genuine. For certainly you cannot catch and hold onto a friend by force, but kindness and pleasure capture this creature and keep him close by your side.'

'That is true,' she said.

'First, you must ask those who care for you to do only those favours that will cause them the least trouble; and likewise you must be sure to grant them a return for their favours. In this way, their friendship will become long lasting and greatly to your benefit. And you will gratify them most if you wait until they ask for your company. For you see that the tastiest of foods, if served before they are desired, seem unpleasant, and even cause nausea in those who are satiated; but even poor food is delicious when served to a man who has been kept hungry.'

'But how can I keep them hungry for my fare?'

'Indeed, you must first avoid serving it to those who are satiated, or reminding them of it until they are not quite so full, and are again asking for more. Then you must put them in mind of it by being a model companion, while appearing reluctant to provide favours and seeming to withdraw, until their need is very great; for at that point the same gifts have far more value than if they are offered before they are wanted.'

And Theodote said, 'Socrates, why don't you become my partner in the quest for friends?'

'By all means I shall,' he answered, 'if you persuade me.'

'But how can I persuade you?'

'You will investigate this yourself and come up with a method, if indeed you desire my help.'

'Then come and see me often,' she replied.

10.4 Pseudo-Demosthenes *Against Neaera* 59.17–25. Ca. 340 BCE. In these passages from a speech preserved with the works of Demosthenes, Apollodorus attacks his political rival Stephanus by impugning the status of his wife Neaera and their children. He emphasises the fact that Neaera was raised as a slave and a prostitute.

Gentlemen of the jury, you have just heard the law that prohibits an alien woman from marrying a male citizen, or a citizen woman from marrying an alien man and procreating through any legal device or loophole whatsoever. And if anyone breaks this law, it provides for an indictment against them, the alien man or the alien woman, before the Thesmothetae.[279] And if they are convicted, it directs that they be sold as slaves. I wish, therefore, to demonstrate for you, conclusively and from the beginning, that this woman Neaera is an alien.

Nicarete, the freedwoman of Charisius the Elean and wife of his cook Hippias, purchased these seven little girls while they were still young children. She was skilled at recognising good looks in young children, and she knew how to rear them and train them from long experience, for she set herself up in this trade and from these girls she derived her livelihood. She called them her daughters in order to charge the highest possible prices to those who wished to have sex with them under the impression that they were free. When she had drained all the profit from their youth, she sold off all seven of them: Antea, Stratola, Aristoclea, Metanira, Phila, Isthmias and this Neaera. Who purchased each of them, and how they were set free by those who bought them from Nicarete, I will explain in the course of my speech, if time allows and you are willing to hear. I wish to return to the point that this woman Neaera belonged to Nicarete, and that her line of work was hiring out her body to those who wished to have sex with her.

Now Lysias the sophist was in love with Metanira, and he wished to have her initiated in addition to the other sums he spent on her, for he thought that all the other expenditures were going to the woman who owned her, but that whatever he spent for the festival and the initiation would win favour with the girl herself. So he pleaded with Nicarete to come to the Mysteries[280] bringing Metanira so that she could be initiated, and he promised that he himself would see to her initiation.

When they arrived, Lysias did not bring them to his own house out of respect for his wife, who was his niece, the daughter of his brother Brachyllus, and for his mother, who was elderly and living in the same house. He thus established them, Nicarete and Metanira, at the house of Philostratus, a friend from Colonus who was still a bachelor. They were accompanied by this Neaera, who had already begun to work as a prostitute although she was younger and had not reached adolescence.

As a witness to the truth of what I am saying, that she belonged to Nicarete, accompanied her, and sold herself to anyone who could pay, I call Philostratus himself.

Testimony: Philostratus son of Dionysius, from Colonus, testifies to his knowledge that both Neaera and Metanira belonged to Nicarete, and that they stayed at his house when they came to town for the Mysteries, being residents of Corinth; and that Lysias son of Cephalus established them at his house, since he was a friend and the arrangement was convenient.

And again, Athenians, after these events Simus the Thessalian arrived here with this woman Neaera for the Great Panathenaea. Nicarete accompanied her, and they stayed with Ctesippus son of Glauconides of Cydantidae, and Neaera drank and dined in front of them all, just like a courtesan. As a witness to the truth of what I am saying, I call these witnesses. Please call Euphiletus, son of Simon, from Aexone, and Aristomachus, son of Critodemus, from Alopece.

Testimony: Euphiletus, son of Simon, from Aexone, and Aristomachus, son of Critodemus, from Alopece testify to their knowledge that Simus the Thessalian came to Athens for the Great Panathenaea, and that with him were Nicarete and Neaera, the present defendant; and that they stayed with Ctesippus son of Glauconides, and that Neaera drank with them just like a courtesan, while many others were present and drinking in the house of Ctesippus.

10.5 Philemon *The Brothers* PCG 7, Fr. 3. End of fourth century BCE. This fragment of the Athenian playwright Philemon's comedy *The Brothers* (*Adelphoi*) describes how the statesman Solon set up brothels as an outlet for the energies of the city's young men. Considering the comic source, the story should be taken with a grain of salt.

But you discovered a law for all men's use;
For they say that you, Solon, were first to see
The need for this popular lifesaver, O Zeus!
(It is right and fitting, Solon, that I speak.)
Seeing the city packed full of young men,
Who had certain needs of an urgent kind,
Which led them astray to the wrong places,
You bought women to place round the town,
Equipped to serve the needs of one and all,
And naked, without deceit. Take a look!
Maybe you're not yourself, feeling down?
Well? The door's wide open, for just an obol![281]

Come on in! No coy nonsense or resistance,
Just what you want, and the way you want it.
All done? Away with her, she's nothing to you!

10.6 Plato (?) *Greek Anthology* 6.1. Date unknown; possibly Hellenistic.
Although this epigram is attributed to the philosopher Plato, it is unlikely that
he authored it.

To the Paphian[282] I, Laïs, give my mirror
Who once laughed in triumph over Greece,
Who once held a throng of lovers at my door.
I will not look at myself as I am,
And cannot look at myself as I was.

10.7 Antipater of Sidon *Greek Anthology* 7.218. Late second century BCE. A
native of the Hellenised Phoenician city of Sidon in what is now Lebanon,
Antipater wrote poetry including epitaphs (poems commemorating the dead,
originally inscribed on tombstones).

Her who reveled in gold and purple with Eros,
More delicate than tender Cypris,
I hold: Laïs, the citizen of sea-belted Corinth.
Brighter than the clear spring water of Pirene,[283]
That mortal Aphrodite, whose noble suitors
Outnumbered those of Tyndareus' daughter,[284]
All plucking the fruits of the love she sold.
Even now her tomb smells sweetly of saffron,
Her bones are moistened with fragrant oils,
Her shining hair exudes a breath of incense.
For her Aphrodite's lovely cheeks were torn,
While Eros in his grief moaned and wailed.
Had she not enslaved her bed to all in common
In pursuit of gain, for Laïs' sake all Greece,
As for Helen, would have dared any task.

10.8 Horace *Satires* 1.2.82–105. Ca. 35 BCE. A contemporary of the emperor
Augustus, the poet Horace used a conversational style in his *Satires* to
explore the application of Greek philosophy to everyday life in Rome.

Often the girl in the toga[285] has the advantage.
She presents her wares without deceit, and quite openly
Displays what she has to sell, and if she's a pretty girl,

She doesn't boast and preen while trying to hide her flaws.
When a tycoon buys a horse, he examines it covered up,
In case a lovely shape, supported by a too-tender hoof
Persuades him to buy, as he gazes raptly on the pretty
Hindquarters, the delicate head, the long graceful neck.
This is the right way. So don't linger with Lynceus' eye[286]
On the finer points, and be more blind than Hypsaea[287]
When viewing flaws. 'What a leg, what arms!' you cry,
But miss the flat behind, long nose, short waist, big feet.
You can see nothing of a married woman but her face;
Unless she's like Catia,[288] her long robes hide all the rest.
But if you crave the forbidden and it's the fortified wall
That excites you, many obstacles will stand in your way:
Slaves to guard her, sedan chairs, hairdressers, hangers-on.
Her dress will cover her ankles, while a voluminous cloak
And other garments will grudge you the sight you seek.
With the other, none of that. In Coan silk, she's nearly
Nude, and can't hide a malformed leg or gnarly foot.
You may measure her body with your eye. Or do you prefer
To be swindled and separated from your money, before
You even see the goods?

10.9 Horace *Odes* 1.25. Ca. 20 BCE. Horace drew on Greek models to develop a uniquely Roman lyric style for his four books of *Odes*. In this example, the narrator spitefully describes how the courtesan Lydia will be despised once her beauty has faded.

Eager youths shake your shutters
Less now, with hurled pebbles;
You sleep soundly, and your door
Stays firmly shut,

Though before the hinges swung
Freely. You hear now less and less:
'Lydia, can you sleep all night while
I die of love?'

An old hag in the street, despised by
Scornful lovers, in turn you'll weep
While the North wind rages under
The moonless sky.

Then that burning love and lust,
The itch that maddens mares in heat
Will rage about your cankered heart
With a lament

That happy youth takes its delight
In the green ivy and dark myrtle
But tosses withered boughs to Hebrus,[289]
Friend of winter.

10.10 Strabo *Geography* 8.6.20. Ca. 24 CE. Strabo was a Greek geographer who travelled widely and visited the port city of Corinth. He speaks of Aphrodite's temple slaves using the past tense, perhaps indicating that they did not exist in his time.

The temple of Aphrodite was so wealthy that it owned more than one thousand temple slaves, courtesans who had been dedicated by both men and women. And because of these women the city grew crowded and rich, for the sea captains readily spent all their money; for this reason they repeat the saying, 'Not for every man is the journey to Corinth.' And what is more, they say that when someone reproached a certain courtesan for her lack of interest in working with or even touching wool, she replied, 'Yet such as I am, in this short time I have already lowered three uprights of the loom.'[290]

10.11 Seneca the Elder *Controversiae* 1.2.5–7. Ca. 30 CE. This school exercise in declamation deals with the hypothetical situation of a girl who is kidnapped and sold to a brothel. She manages to escape with her virginity intact but kills a man in the process. Now she wishes to become a priestess. The debate among the speakers includes a sketch of conditions in a Roman *lupānar* or brothel.

Arellius Fuscus the elder: Never fear, young woman, you are chaste. But that praise recommends you to a husband, not a temple. You were called a prostitute, you stood in a public place, a sign was hung above your cubicle, and you welcomed whoever came. As for the rest, if I should find myself 'in a public place', I would keep quiet about it.

Pompeius Silo: The prostitutes greeted her with kisses and taught her how to flatter and move her body seductively. You other women seeking the priesthood, cover your ears while I tell the rest. I shall tell you nothing that is in doubt; you will hear nothing other than what the whole neighbourhood saw.

You, a priestess? What if you had been only a captive, only a prostitute, only a killer, only a defendant?

Romanius Hispo: Will you deny that you struggled with the man and that while you were rolling about, he must at first have been on top of you? According to the pimp, this soldier deserved to be killed, because he dared to do more than is permitted with a prostitute. You won over the people; did you also win over the pimp, and the pirate, whom you could not kill?

Argentarius: She says, 'I killed an armed man', but what about the ones who were unarmed? She boasts of the murder of a man, but she may have killed him too late.

The formal statement of Cestius Pius: She was guarded at home, yet she was kidnapped. She was dear to her family, yet they did not ransom her. The pirates spared her after she was kidnapped, yet they sold her to a pimp. The pimp bought her in order to sell her. She was at the mercy of her visitors, yet she had need of a sword. When her name was tossed into the urn, it did not come out, but was ejected. Now was the time to draw lots, but the urn had been cleaned out.[291] Young woman, you offered yourself in a brothel. Even if nobody violated you, you are tainted by the place itself. You offered yourself along with the prostitutes, and beautified yourself in order to please the masses, in a dress supplied by the pimp. Your name hung at the door, you accepted pay for fornication, and the hand that you hoped would offer sacrifice to the gods instead held unsavoury profits. When you begged off the embraces of the clients, you obtained everything else you asked for, but had to pay them with a kiss. Not even the serving maids of a priestess are purchased at a brothel; before a priestess, men refrain from crude speech. There is a good reason why a lictor[292] attends a priestess: to move prostitutes from her path!

10.12 Valerius Maximus *Memorable Deeds and Sayings* 2.10.8. First half of first century CE. The event Valerius describes took place in 55 BCE. In one of his letters (97.8), the younger Seneca describes these games as a sportive occasion when prostitutes strip naked.

Because Cato[293] was watching the Games of Flora,[294] which the aedile[295] Messius had arranged, the people were ashamed to ask the girls in the mime-show to strip. When Cato was informed of this by Favonius, a close friend seated beside him, he left the theater so that his presence would not prevent the spectacle from proceeding as it usually did. As he was leaving, the crowd honoured his old-fashioned morals with great applause, and then returned its attention to the sport of the stage-show. By doing this, the people showed greater respect for the dignity of this one man than they claimed for themselves as a whole.

10.13 Graffiti from Pompeii. *CIL* 4.2175, 2192–3, 2248, 2259, 3999, 8949. Before 79 CE. Messages written by the city's inhabitants on the walls of local brothels record a variety of sexual acts. The as, a coin mentioned in these inscriptions, was the basic unit of money and could be subdivided into 'small change'. The denarius was worth 16 asses.

2175: Here I fucked many girls.
2192: 17 days before the Kalends of July,[296] Hermerus fucked here with Phileterus and Caphisus.
2193: Here Harpocras had a good fuck with Drauca for a denarius.
2248: Phoebus is good at fucking.
2259: Fortuna sucks.
3999: Glyco licks cunt for two asses.
8949: Maritimus licks cunt for four asses. He accepts virgins.

10.14 Plutarch *Life of Pericles* 24.1–7. Late first century CE. Plutarch's biography of the Athenian statesman Pericles includes a discussion of his relationship with Aspasia, a *hetaira* from Miletus with whom he had a son. Pericles died in 429 BCE and Aspasia around 400 BCE.

After this, when a thirty-year peace had been established between the Athenians and the Lacedaemonians, [Pericles] obtained a vote in favour of a naval expedition against Samos, on the grounds that the Samians did not heed instructions to cease their war against the Milesians.

Now, since it appears that he undertook the expedition against the Samians in order to please Aspasia, this may be the right place to raise the question of the great skill and power possessed by this woman that enabled her to bring the foremost politicians under her sway, and supplied the philosophers with serious and lengthy matter for discussion. It is agreed that she was of a Milesian family, the daughter of Axiochus, and they say that she sought influence over very powerful men by emulating an Ionian woman from ancient times, one Thargelia. A woman of outstanding beauty who combined pleasing manners with sharp wits, this Thargelia cohabited with many Greeks, and she brought all those who slept with her over to the Persian king, sowing the seeds of favouritism toward the Persians among the Greek cities through these great and powerful men. Some say that Aspasia too was highly respected by Pericles on account of her wisdom and political acumen, for Socrates sometimes visited her with his pupils, and Pericles' close friends brought their wives to hear her speak.

They did these things even though she ran a business that was neither decent nor respectable, for she raised young courtesans. Aeschines says that the sheep-dealer Lysicles, a man of ignoble and base origins, became the most important man in Athens through his association with Aspasia after the death of Pericles. And Plato's *Menexenus*, even though the first part was written in a lighthearted style, is factual in its description of the woman's reputation as a teacher of rhetoric among the Athenians. Pericles' affection for Aspasia, however, seems to have been amorous in nature. For his own wife was quite closely related to him, and had been married previously to Hipponicus, to whom she bore Callias, known as 'the Wealthy'.[297] And by Pericles she had Xanthippus and Paralus. Then, since their life together did not please them, he gave her by her own consent to another man, and taking Aspasia to himself he loved her above all others. They say that he kissed her tenderly every day as he left for the city centre, and he greeted her the same way when he returned home.

But in comedies they call her the new Omphale, and Deianira, and Hera.[298] Cratinus openly called her a mistress in this verse:

Lechery bore that shameless mistress, to be his Hera.[299]

And it seems that she bore Pericles a bastard son, about whom Eupolis in his *Demes* makes him ask:

And does my bastard thrive?

To which Pyronides answers:

Yes, and would have been a man long since,
Were his mother not a whore.[300]

So renowned and famous was Aspasia, they say, that even Cyrus, who battled the King of Persia for sovereignty over the Persians, named his favourite concubine Aspasia, the one who before was called Milto. She was born a Phocaean, the daughter of Hermotimus. When Cyrus fell in battle, she became the King's captive and was extremely influential.

10.15 Martial *Epigrams* 1.34. Ca. 86 CE. In the tradition of Catullus and other Roman poets, Martial makes liberal use of obscenity and invective. Here the narrator compares the sexual habits of an acquaintance he calls 'Lesbia' unfavourably with those of prostitutes.

You do the deed, Lesbia, with the doors wide open
And never try to hide what you're up to.

Being watched turns you on more than your lover;
The secret thrill is what pleases you most.
Courtesans repel onlookers with a curtain or bolt;
Summemmius' brothel is closed up tight.
Learn modesty's lesson, if only from Ias or Chione.[301]
Even dirty hookers take cover in tombs.
Does my advice seem too severe? I only meant:
Don't get caught, but do get fucked.

10.16 Juvenal *Satires* 6.115–32. Late first or early second century CE. Juvenal's sixth satire is his longest and is framed as an argument against marriage. Throughout, he catalogues the vices of women. In this vignette, he imagines the empress Messalina sneaking out at night to work as a prostitute.

Consider the rivals of the gods; hear what Claudius
Endured. The minute his spouse heard him snore,
That imperial whore would don her hooded cloak,
Spurning the palace for a cheap mat in a stall,
And hiding her black hair beneath a yellow wig,
She took one servant alone as her companion,
Entered the steaming brothel with its well-used rags,
And reached the stall reserved for her alone.
Then naked, with gilded nipples, she sold herself,
Posting the false name of 'Wolf-girl' on her stall,
Flaunting the womb that bore noble Britannicus.[302]
She wheedled the customers, demanded her fee,
And serviced the rutting crowds flat on her back.
The pimp sends home his girls too soon for her;
She is the last to close shop and sadly depart,
Still on fire, her female parts swollen with lust.
Worn out by the men, yet hardly satisfied,
She leaves filthy, her cheeks grimy from smoke,
And carries home to her bed the stench of the brothel.

10.17 Dio Chrysostom *Orations* 7.133–9. Late first or early second century CE. The widely travelled Stoic philosopher and orator strongly condemned prostitution on moral grounds.

In the matter of brothel-keepers and prostitution, one must not admit any doubts in the matter but instead firmly prohibit the practice as abominable and forbid anyone, whether poor or rich, from plying this trade, a commerce in brutality and unbridled lust that is singled out for condemnation by all the world. Brothel-keepers bring people together for intercourse lacking Aphrodite's charms and the fulfillment of lust without love, all for the sake of profit. They expose to shame the bodies of women or children, taken captive or purchased with money, and exhibit them in filthy booths before the entire city, in the doorways of the magistrates and in the marketplaces, near town halls and temples, in the midst of that which is most hallowed. They ought not to bring under this outrageous constraint either the bodies of barbarians or those of Greeks, formerly free but now subject to an unenviable and complete servitude. They ply a trade far more base and unclean than the breeders of horses and asses, who mate their livestock without compulsion, where both partners are willing and feel no shame; instead they pair human beings, who are unwilling and feel shame, with lecherous libertines in embraces that lead to no fruitful outcome, but tend more to destruction than to procreation. They respect neither humans nor gods, not Zeus who presides over the family, nor Hera goddess of marriage, nor the Fates who bring children to adulthood, nor Artemis who eases childbirth, nor Mother Rhea, nor the Ilithyae who preside over human births, nor Aphrodite, whose name refers to the natural and companionable union between male and female. Such activity for profit must not be permitted or legalised by magistrates or lawgivers, whether in cities with the highest reputation for virtue or those of the second, third, fourth or any other rank, if it is within their power to prevent it. But if cities inherit old and sick customs ingrained over time, they must by no means ignore and leave them unpunished, but consider what can be done to suppress and kerb them in one way or another; for social ills are never content to remain as they are, but always grow active and spread toward greater licentiousness if they meet with no constraints. Therefore we must give our attention to this matter, and not take it lightly that people are being cast violently into dishonour and enslavement, not only because the entire human race has been equally honoured by God, its begetter, with the signs and marks that it deserves honour, namely the capacity for reason and the experience of both right and wrong, but also because of this consideration: that when brutality is fostered in an atmosphere of permissiveness, it becomes difficult to set any limits that it will not dare to transgress. Instead, starting from practices and habits that seem minor and allowable, it gathers uncontrollable strength and force, and stops at nothing. Now we must keep in mind that this manifestly dishonourable form of adultery, accomplished in our midst in a fashion that is far too shameless and unrestrained, is no small contributor to subtle and hidden assaults on respectable women and children, since it is all to easy to boldly attempt such things, when modesty is despised by all. Prostitution was not, as some people suppose, invented in order to put us at a secure and safe remove from these crimes.

10.18 Tacitus *Annals* 2.85. Ca. 117 CE. Tacitus' *Annals* is a history of the four emperors who succeeded Augustus. This episode involving senatorial scrutiny of women's behaviour took place during the reign of Tiberius.

That same year, the Senate took strict action against the lustfulness of women, and prohibited any woman whose grandfather, father, or husband was a Roman knight from seeking profit with her body. One Vistilia, born of a praetorian family, had proclaimed to the aedile her intent to commit fornication,[303] according to the custom of our ancestors, who believed that public acknowledgement of disgrace was a sufficient punishment for unchaste women. Vistilia's husband, Titidius Labeo, was required to explain why he had failed to apply the law's penalty to a wife who was clearly guilty. When he gave as his excuse that the sixty days allowed for deliberation had not passed, this was considered sufficient to establish the case against Vistilia, and she was banished to the island of Seriphos.

10.19 Lucian *Dialogues of the Courtesans* 3. Second century CE. In this dialogue, a mother gives her courtesan daughter advice on how to handle a quarrel with a lover.

Mother:
Did you lose your mind at the party last night, Philinna? Diphilus came to me early this morning in tears and told me what you did to him – how you drank too much and then danced in front of everyone, though he tried to stop you, and then kissed his friend Lamprias. And when he became angry with you, you abandoned Diphilus, walked over to Lamprias and embraced him. He said he was choked with rage while this was happening. And even later, I gather, you did not sleep with him but left him crying while you lay down on a nearby couch singing, much to his grief.

Philinna:
Then he didn't tell you what *he* did, mother, or you would not be pleading the case for someone who behaved outrageously. He left me and started up a conversation with Thaïs, Lamprias' girl, because Lamprias hadn't arrived yet. And when he saw that I was angry and put off by what he was doing, he got hold of the tip of Thaïs's ear, pulled her head back, and planted such a kiss on her that she could scarcely tear her lips away. I started crying, but he laughed, and kept whispering things in Thaïs's ear, obviously directed at me, and Thaïs kept glancing at me and smiling. But when at last they'd noticed Lamprias coming and had enough of kissing each other, I went and lay down next to him anyway, so that he wouldn't be able to complain about it later.

But Thaïs jumped up and was the first to dance, pulling up her dress as if she was the only one with pretty ankles. And when she finished, Lamprias kept quiet and had nothing to say, but Diphilus was overly full of praise for her graceful movement, her costly dress, her skill in keeping time with the lyre, her pretty ankles, and a hundred other things, as though he were applauding the Sosandran Aphrodite of Calamis[304] instead of Thaïs, and you know what she looks like because she goes to the baths with us. But the way she mocked me right after! She said, 'Anyone who isn't ashamed of having skinny legs will get up and dance too.' What could I say, mother? I got up and danced. What was I supposed to do? Sit there and prove that her insult was true, and let Thaïs be the queen of the party?

Mother:
You are too proud, my daughter. You should not have let it bother you. Still, tell me what happened next.

Philinna:
The others praised me, but Diphilus lay on his back and looked up at the ceiling until I got tired and stopped.

Mother:
But is it true that you kissed Lamprias, and then went over and embraced him? Why are you silent? Surely that behaviour was going too far.

Philinna:
I wanted him to feel upset in return.

Mother:
And then afterwards you didn't sleep with him, but sang while he cried? Don't you understand, my daughter, that we are broke? Have you forgotten how much he has done for us, and how we would have spent last winter, if Aphrodite had not sent him to us?

Philinna:
What then? Does that mean I have to put up with such insults from him?

Mother:
Be angry, but avoid insulting him in return. Don't you know that when a lover is insulted, he ceases to love, and begins to question himself? You've always been very hard on this man. Remember the proverb, and make sure we don't strain the cord so tight that it breaks.

10.20 Justin Martyr *Apology* 1.27.1–5. Ca. 155 CE. In this petition to the emperor Antoninus Pius, the Christian leader Justin asks for relief from what he considers unjust prosecutions of Christians.

But as for us, in order that we may avoid doing wrong or acting impiously, we have been taught that it is wicked to expose a newborn child. First, because we see that nearly all are led into prostitution, not only the girls but also the males, and in the same way the ancients are said to have collected herds of grazing cattle, goats, sheep or horses, the people nowadays collect infants in order to use them shamefully. In all the nations, a great number of females as well as effeminate males[305] who do unspeakable things are set up to practice this defilement, and you receive their wages as taxes and levies, when you ought to eradicate them from your realm. And anyone who makes use of them, besides engaging in a godless, impious and self-indulgent sexual act, may in fact be having intercourse with his own child, or relative, or brother. There are those who prostitute even their own children or wives, and some openly castrate themselves in order to become sexual perverts, and they present the mysteries to the mother of the gods. And before everyone a serpent is set up publicly as the symbol and mystery of things that you suppose to be divine. The things you openly practice and honour, acting as though the divine light were trampled over and absent, you ascribe to us. This does not harm us, who are far from doing any of these things, but instead it harms the ones who do such things and bear false witness against us.

10.21 Athenaeus *The Philosophers at Dinner* 13.590d–91d. Early third century CE. Book 13 of Athenaeus' work contains numerous anecdotes about famous courtesans. One of the best known of these was Mnesarete, nicknamed Phryne ('Toad'), who lived during the fourth century BCE.

Now Phryne was from Thespiae. Although Euthias brought her to trial on a capital offense,[306] she was acquitted. As Hermippus says, Euthias was so angered by this that he never argued another case again. When Hyperides was defending Phryne and making no headway, and it seemed likely that the judges would condemn her, he led her to a spot where all could see and tore away her tunic, baring her chest. Then he concluded his speech with such piteous lamentations at the sight of her that he aroused in the judges a superstitious awe of this interpreter and sacred servant of Aphrodite, and indulging themselves in pity, they did not put her to death. After she was let off, they passed a law that no one speaking in another person's defense could make use of lamentation, nor could a judgement be made on the basis of viewing the accused man or woman. As a matter of fact, it was really Phryne's unseen parts that were more beautiful, and it was no easy matter to get a look at her naked. She always wore a tunic that covered her body, and she did not use the public baths. At the great festivals of the Eleusinia and the Poseidonia, in the sight of all the assembled Greeks, she removed her outer garment and let her hair down before stepping into the sea. She was the model for Apelles' painting of 'Aphrodite Rising From the Sea'. Praxiteles the sculptor too, who was in love with her, modelled his Cnidian Aphrodite[307] on her and wrote on the base of his statue of Eros below the stage of the theater,

> Praxiteles brought to perfection the Love he felt,
> Drawing the model from his own heart
> And giving Me to Phryne as My price.
> No longer do I cast My spell with an arrow,
> For all who gaze upon Me fall in Love.

He also gave Phryne a choice of his statues, to see whether she preferred to take the Eros or the Satyr from the Street of the Tripods. She chose the Eros and gave it as a dedication to the god at Thespiae.[308] The people living roundabout commissioned and dedicated at Delphi a golden image of Phryne herself, on a pillar of Pentelic marble, made by Praxiteles. When the Cynic philosopher Crates saw it, he said it was an offering to the Greeks' lack of self-control. This image stands halfway between that of Archedamus, king of the Lacedaemonians, and that of Philip son of Amyntas, and the label says 'Phryne daughter of Epicles, from Thespiae'. That is what Alcetas says in the second book of his work called *On the Offerings at Delphi*. And Apollodorus in his book *On Courtesans* writes that there were two Phrynes, one of whom was nicknamed Tearful Smile, and the other Blackfish. But Herodicus in the sixth book of his *People in the Comedies* says that in the works of the orators, one of the two was called Sifter, because of the way she stripped her clients and separated them from their money, and the other was the one from Thespiae. Now Phryne was very rich, and she used to promise that she would rebuild the wall around Thebes, if the Thebans would put up an inscription saying, 'Alexander tore down the wall, but Phryne the courtesan restored it'. So records Callistratus in his book *On Courtesans*.

Further Reading

For arguments against the historicity of 'sacred prostitution', see Assante 1998, 2003, and Budin 2008. For famous courtesans such as Laïs and Phryne, and for Athenaeus as a source on courtesans, see McClure 2003 and Keesling

2006. For Phryne's relationship with the orator Hyperides, see Cooper 1995. On Neaera, see Hamel 2003. For male prostitution at Athens, see Halperin 1990; for the economics of prostitution at Athens, see Cohen 2006. Economic and social factors affecting prostitution at Rome are covered fully in McGinn 2003 and 2004; see also Flemming 1999. For the relationship between prostitution, social status, and public exhibition of the body in Roman thought, see Edwards 1997. Faraone and McClure (eds) 2006 and Glazebrook and Henry (eds) 2011 gather essays on prostitution in the ancient world

Notes

1   Most recently, see Carne-Ross (2010) and McElduff and Sciarrino (2011).

2   For the *cinaedus* and similar figures see Introduction and 3.13, 3.16, 3.17, 3.18, 9.14.

3   Aegis-bearer Zeus: The aegis was a magical goatskin fringed with snakes and used to frighten enemies in battle.

4   Wife of Ixion…Pirithous: Dia was mother of Pirithous, the king of the Lapiths.

5   Daughter of Phoenix: Europa, whom Zeus in the form of a bull carried off to Crete.

6   Leto: Mother of Apollo and Artemis.

7   Tritogenia: A title of Athena.

8   Themis…the Hours: Themis was a personification of divine law. Her daughters the Horae ('Hours') represented the seasons and the passing of time.

9   Eurynome: An elder goddess, daughter of Oceanus.

10 Mnemosyne: The goddess of memory.

11 Hebe…Ilithyia: Hebe was the personification of youth, Ares of war, and Ilithyia was a goddess of childbirth.

12 Orion: One of several Greek heroes beloved by the goddess Eos (Dawn). In other versions of the myth, he incurs the anger of Artemis either by attacking her or by boasting of his prowess in the hunt.

13 Iasion: A mortal hero, son of Zeus and the Pleiad Electra.

14 The Host of All: Hades, ruler of the dead in the underworld.

15 Phales: A divine personification of the penis.

16 Lamachuses: Lamachus was an Athenian general in the Peloponnesian war.

17 Sabazian rites: the Thraco-Phrygian god Sabazius was worshiped with ecstatic rites similar to those of Dionysus.

18 We should invade Sicily: A reference to the recent and ill-fated Athenian expedition to Sicily (415–13 BCE).

19 And shut out his wife: Praxinoa quotes an unknown saying, perhaps a comical reference to a bridegroom shutting out his wife from the nuptial chamber in favour of the bridesmaids.

20 Honey-sweet goddess: A euphemism for Persephone.

21 Golgi, Idalium and Eryx: Places known for the worship of Aphrodite. Golgi and Idalium were in Cyprus and Eryx in Sicily.

22 Acheron: A river of the Underworld.

23 Cypris child of Dione: Aphrodite, whose mother is Dione according to Homer.

24 Berenice: One of the Ptolemaic queens, deified mother of the reigning queen Arsinoë.

25 Miletus and Samian pastures: Miletus and Samos were renowned for textiles.

26 Agamemnon…Pelasgian race: The list of heroes stretches back from the heroes of the Trojan War to the time of the flood (Deucalion) and the dawn of the human race (the Pelasgians).

27 Gallae: A feminised version of Gallus (plural Galli), the more commonly used title for Cybele's castrated followers.

28 Dindymus' mistress: Cybele was associated with Mount Dindymus in Phrygia. Compare 1.13, 1.15.

29 Lictors: bodyguards who escorted important Roman officials.

30 Stimula: A Roman deity identified with Dionysus' mother Semele.

31 Tanaquil: Wife of the king Tarquinius.

32 Tyrrhenians: The Etruscans.

33 Phidias: A famous Greek sculptor of the fifth century BCE.

34 Let the first syllable… 'Canus': The syllables pe-di-ca-re together form the Latin verb denoting anal penetration.

35 Mother Dindymene: Cybele, who was associated with Mount Dindymus in Phrygia. Compare 1.10 and 1.13.

36 Baubo: An old woman connected with the Demeter myth, and (like her counterpart Iambe in other sources) the personification of scurrilous sexual banter. Her name seems to refer to the female belly or womb.

37 Iacchus: A cult figure associated with the torch-lit procession of the Eleusinian Mysteries, sometimes identified with Dionysus.

38 To go down into Hades: Dionysus wished to travel there in order to rescue his mother Semele from the underworld.

39 Lenaea: A festival held in Athens (where it involved comic performances) and in other parts of the Greek world.

40 Educa and Potina: Each of the functional gods was given a name pertinent to his or her role. For example, Educa is 'She who brings up [a child]' and Potina is 'She of the beverage'.

41 Liber: A Roman wine god who was identified with Greek Bacchus/ Dionysus.

42 Silvanus: A Roman god of woodlands and fields.

43 Priapus: A Greek god identified in later times with the indigenous Italian phallic god Mutinus Titinus.

44 Cora...Pluto: Cora (Kore in the non-Latinised spelling) is the name of Demeter's daughter, and also the Greek word for 'young woman'. Pluto ('Wealthy') is an epithet for the god Hades.

45 Models: The models (*plasmata*) referred to here are probably the dough snakes and genitalia mentioned later in the paragraph.

46 Arrhetophoria: Literally 'the carrying of secret/unnamable objects'.

47 Thesmophoros: Lawgiver.

48 Lacedaemon: The territory of Sparta, home of Helen.

49 Phrygia...Maeonia: Kingdoms in the west central part of Asia Minor near Troy; Maeonia is a synonym for Lydia.

50 Danaans: Greeks.

51 Erebus: A personification of darkness.

52 Erinyes: Avenging spirits.

53 Melian nymphs: Nymphs of the ash trees, which in some sources are connected with human origins.

54 Philommedes: This title means 'genital-loving' and puns on Aphrodite's epithet Philomeides, 'laughter-loving'.

55 Paphian precinct: Aphrodite had a sanctuary at Paphos on Cyprus.

56 Argus-Slayer: The god Hermes, who killed the many-eyed monster Argus.

57 Aeneas: Aphrodite puns on Aeneas' name and the Greek word *ainos*, 'dreadful, dire'.

58 Cydonia: A poetic name for Crete; also a city-state in northwest Crete.

59 Maidens: Nymphs.

60 Hellas: The Greek peoples understood collectively.

61 Alpheus: The river flowing by the sanctuary of Olympia.

62 Pythian house of Apollo: Delphi, a major sanctuary of Apollo.

63 Girl of Oechalia: Iole, whom Heracles loved and took from her father Eurytion by force.

64 Dirce's spring: The name of a Theban heroine and a spring and river nearly synonymous with the town.

65 The mother of twice-born Bacchus: Semele, mother of Dionysus, killed when Zeus appeared to her as the thunderbolt. Zeus sewed the fetus into his thigh until it came to term.

66 Wind-egg: An imperfect or infertile egg.

67 Sorb-apple: The fruit of the service tree (genus *Sorbus*), which is rarely eaten today.

68 Arcadians...Lacedaemonians: The inhabitants of Mantinea in Arcadia were dispersed to separate villages by the Spartans in 385 BCE.

69 Desire to weep: A quotation from Homer, *Iliad* 23.108 on grief for Patroclus, or *Odyssey* 4.183 on the absence of Odysseus.

70 Aeson's son: Jason. Aeson was king of Iolcus in Thessaly.

71 Memmius: Gaius Memmius, a Roman orator, poet and patron of Lucretius. He served as tribune in 66 BCE.

72 Sabellian: Of Umbria or Campania, regions in central and southern Italy.

73 Thyiad: A maenad or ecstatic female worshiper of Dionysus.

74 Mount Cithaeron: A peak on the mountain range dividing Attica and Boeotia in Greece.

75 Tyrians: Dido was queen of Carthage, a Phoenician city colonised from Tyre.

76 Iarbas: An indigenous king who wished to wed Dido.

77 Milanion...heart: Milanion (also known as Melanion or Hippomenes) was the suitor of the fierce huntress Atalanta. In a better-known version of the myth, he wins her hand by beating her in a footrace.

78 Parthenian caves: the rugged landscape of Arcadia in the central Peloponnese. 'Parthenian' suggests the untamed virginity of Atalanta.

79 Hylaeus' branch: Hylaeus was a centaur who tried to rape Atalanta.

80 Cytae's streams: Cytae was the birthplace of the witch Medea.

81 Semiramis: A legendary queen of Assyria.

82 Laïs: A famous Greek courtesan of the fourth century BCE. For more on Laïs, see 10.6, 10.7.

83 Pamphos: Like Orpheus, a mythical poet supposed to be much more ancient than Homer.

84 Lycomidae: A priestly family who supervised a mystery cult at Phlya in Boeotia, and later supplied the Torch Bearer for the famous Eleusinian Mysteries of Athens.

85 For the courtesan Phryne, see 10.21.

86 Gaius the Roman Emperor: Caligula.

87 Livy *History of Rome* 34.3.3.

88 Iapetus' son: Prometheus. Iapetus was a Titan, one of the older generation of gods.

89 Limping God: Hephaestus, the craftsman god, was lame.

90 Epimetheus: 'He who thinks afterward', the brother of Prometheus ('He who thinks ahead').

91 Phaedra: A reference to the stepmother in Euripides' tragedy *Hippolytus*; see 3.4.

92 Maenads: 'Madwomen', the female worshipers of Dionysus.

93 Ino...Actaeon: Agave is Pentheus' mother; Ino and Autonoë are his aunts.

94 Thyrsus: A ritual staff topped with ivy and used in the worship of Dionysus.

95 Zeus Ctesius in Piraeus: Zeus was worshiped under the name Ctesius as a god of families and household property. He had a shrine in Piraeus, the port of Athens.

96 Clytemnestra: In Greek myth, a notorious murderess who killed her husband Agamemnon.

97 Gnaeus Domitius: The magistrate presiding at the trial.

98 Blind Claudius: A renowned Roman politician of the early Republic (ca. 340–273).

99 Claudia Quinta: A Roman matron famed for her virtue.

100 Pyrrhus: King of Epirus and Macedon during the early third century BCE and a strong opponent of Rome.

101 Baiae: A resort town on the Bay of Naples.

102 Brother: Publius Clodius Pulcher, a political opponent of Cicero.

103 Mamurra: A military officer and crony of Julius Caesar. Compare Catullus *Songs* 29.

104 Formiae: Mamurra's hometown, halfway between Rome and Naples.

105 Woman's toga: At Rome, female prostitutes wore the toga.

106 Sesterces: The *sestertius* was a small-denomination silver coin used during the Republican period.

107 Licinian law: This law (367 BCE) limited the amount of public land an individual might hold to 500 *iugera*. A *iugerum* was a unit of land analogous to an acre, but smaller.

108 Cincian law: This law (204 BCE) forbade advocates from accepting gifts or payments from their clients, and had the effect of reducing the indebtedness of the plebs to the senatorial class.

109 Decemviri: The panel of 'Ten Men' chosen to write laws for Rome in 450 BCE. Their work resulted in the law code known as the Twelve Tables.

110 Cannae: The battle (216 BCE) at which the Carthaginian general Hannibal disastrously defeated the Romans.

111 Aufidius: A contemporary jurist, or perhaps a notorious adulterer mentioned by Juvenal (*Satires* 9.25)

112 Panniculus: In a mime show, the more stupid of two characters who always gets a swat on the head from Latinus, the smarter character.

113 Baptae…Cottyto: The Baptae were the worshippers of the Thracian goddess Cottyto, whose rites had a reputation for lascivious behaviour.

114 Otho: A dissolute companion of Nero who briefly ruled as emperor in 69 CE.

115 Galba: A governor in Spain who deposed Nero and became emperor in 69, only to be murdered by Otho.

116 Lopping…Phrygian blades: A reference to the self-castration of the Galli. See 1.10, 1.13, 1.15.

117 Quintilian: A noted rhetorician of the first century CE.

118 Hannibal…Colline tower: A reference to Hannibal's siege of Rome in 211 BCE.

119 Sybaris…Tarentum: Greek city-states throughout the Mediterranean.

120 'Lady lutist'…Anti-Catos: Probably a reference to Publius Clodius Pulcher, who infiltrated the rites of the Bona Dea dressed as a woman in 62 BCE. Caesar's writings attacking his political opponent Cato were notoriously lengthy.

121 Publius…Paulus: The general Scipio Aemilianus, who destroyed Carthage in 146 BCE.

122 *Lampsourē...chphyris*: A magical incantation of unintelligible words, with possible references to the Hebrew divine title Sabaoth, storm winds, and scarab beetles.

123 Isis: A reference to the goddess Isis' use of incantation in the reanimation of her dead husband Osiris for intercourse.

124 'In pain...over you': A paraphrase of *Genesis* 3.16.

125 Tree: The tree of knowledge of good and evil, *Genesis* 3.1–6.

126 Abraham...sister: The story of Abraham and Sarai/Sarah is told in *Genesis* 12.10–13.

127 See Koehl (1997) and Marinatos (2003).

128 During the fifth and fourth centuries, there is evidence in Athenian vase painting for same-sex lovers of roughly equal age: Hupperts (2000) Vol. 1, pp. 181–4. It is not surprising that the reality of erotic relationships included many that did not fit prescribed and traditional patterns.

129 For Aeschylus see frs. 135–37 *TGrF* and Plutarch 8.19 in this volume. On intercrural intercourse see Dover 1989, p. 98.

130 Socrates' admiration for beautiful youths: Plato *Charmides* 154a–155d. For his opposition to sexual relations with youths see e.g. Plato *Symposium* 216c–223d; Xenophon *Memorabilia* 1.3.8–14, 2.1.30, 2.6.28–33.

131 See DeVries (1997).

132 'Dust cloud': the *konisalos*, a lascivious dance that involved display of the genitals.

133 Phrynis: A lyre-player from Mytilene who won a prize at the Panathenaic games in 456 BCE.

134 Civic Zeus...Ox-killing: Unjust Argument refers scornfully to archaic Athenian rituals such as the Dipolieia (festival of Zeus of the City), the Buphonia (Ox-Killing) and to the gold cicada hairpins worn by men in early times.

135 Panathenaea...Lady Tritogenia: The Panathenaea was a festival in honour of Athena, also called Tritogenia.

136 Iapetus: A Titan, one of the older generation of gods.

137 Hippocrates' dullard sons: Hippocrates was an Athenian general.

138 Antimachus: An Athenian citizen elsewhere criticised by Aristophanes for his stinginess (*Acharnians* 1150).

139 Great Panathenaea: The annual Panathenaic festival for Athena was augmented with games every four years to become the 'Great' Panathenaea.

140 Ceramicus: The area surrounding the Dipylon gate at Athens.

141 Leocorium: A shrine for a local hero and his daughters.

142 Ionia...barbarians: Ionia fell under the rule of the Persians after 387 BCE.

143 Aristogiton...Harmodius: These lovers were credited with bringing about the end of the Pisistratid tyranny in Athens; see 4.5.

144 Ganymede: Zeus' abduction of the Trojan youth Ganymede to be his cupbearer was viewed by the Classical Greeks as an archetypal example of pederastic love.

145 For a similar argument about the 'victory over pleasure,' see 6.5.

146 Lycurgus: The legendary lawgiver of Sparta. For Lycurgus see also 5.12, 8.16.

147 Miletus, Boeotia and Thurii: Miletus and Thurii were Greek city-states in Ionia and Italy respectively, and Boeotia was a region in mainland Greece. The Stranger thinks that these places experienced civil unrest because of the custom of having the male citizens dine together. For the relationship between men's dining halls and pederasty, see 4.11.

148 Amphion: One of a pair of brothers who built the walls of Thebes, here referred to as Dirce from the Theban spring of that name.

149 Daphnis: A mythical herdsman of Sicily famed for his beauty.

150 Polybius: A Greek historian whose *Histories* covered the rise of the Roman Republic during the period 220–146 BCE.

151 Quaestor: A Roman official who supervised finances.

152 Horny Thunderer: Jupiter.

153 Tiryns…Hylas: Heracles/Hercules was born at Tiryns in Greece. He had a pederastic love affair with the youth Hylas.

154 Daphne…Spartan lad: The love of Apollo (Phoebus) for Daphne was unrequited; Martial contrasts the god's love for the Spartan youth Hyacinthus.

155 Briseïs…beardless friend: Martial contrasts the concubine of Achilles with his friend Patroclus.

156 Pisistratus: Tyrant of Athens from 546–527/8 BCE.

157 'Still smouldering…fire': A quotation from Euripides (*Bacchae* 8).

158 'Confronting…boxer': A quotation from Sophocles (*Trachiniae* 441–2).

159 Cadmeian citadel: The fortress of Thebes, named for its founder Cadmus.

160 Pammenes: A Theban general of the fourth century BCE.

161 That clan…another: A quotation from Homer (*Iliad* 2.363).

162 Iolaus: The son of Heracles' half-brother Iphicles.

163 Chaeronea: Philip of Macedon unified the Greek states under his rule after defeating Athens and Thebes at Chaeronea in 338 BCE.

164 Parthenopaeus: One of the Seven Against Thebes, a warrior whose Greek name evokes virginal youth.

165 Eurotas…Leda: Eurotas was the river flowing by Sparta, and Leda was a mythic Spartan queen, mother of Castor and Pollux.

166 Elis: The site of the Olympic games.

167 Haemonian friend…pledge: In the original, Statius uses the proper name 'Pylades' as a synonym for friend; Haemonian = Thessalian and this is probably a reference to the friendship and love between Achilles and Patroclus. The 'Athenian pledge' refers to the friendship between the Athenian hero Theseus and his comrade Pirithous.

168 Eumaeus: The loyal slave who assisted Ulysses/Odysseus to slay the suitors.

169 Licinius Calvus: A Roman poet and friend of Catullus who died ca. 47 BCE.

170 Dolabella…Curio: Dolabella was a Roman general and sometime ally of Julius Caesar (died in 43 BCE). For the elder Curio, who objected to his son's relationship with Antony, see also 3.14.

171 Bibulus: Consul with Caesar in 59 BCE.

172 Marcus Brutus: The assassin of Julius Caesar; he died in 42 BCE.

173 Gaius Memmius: A Roman orator, sometime ally of Julius Caesar, and patron of Lucretius (see 2.16).

174 Lacedaemonians: Spartans.

175 For more on Classical depictions of Sappho, see Snyder 1989.

176 See Aristophanes *Wasps* 1346, *Frogs* 1308, *Women at the Assembly* 920.

177 Venetic racehorse: The region of Venetia in northern Italy was known for its fast horses.

178 Colaxes…Ibenian: Colaxes was a Scythian king. Ibenian is a synonym for Lydian. Horses from these areas were famed for speed.

179 Pleiades: A rival chorus at the festival, named for the constellation.

180 Guards me: An alternative reading of the text can be translated 'wears me out (with love)'.

181 Aotis: Perhaps another name for the goddess Orthria.

182 Xanthos river: A river in Asia Minor, either the Lycian river by the city of Xanthos, or the Scamander near Troy.

183 Cinyras: A legendary king of Cyprus, associated with the worship of Aphrodite.

184 The Lydians: During Sappho's lifetime, the nearby kingdom of Lydia in Asia Minor was renowned for its wealth and power.

185 Gapes…a girl: Alternatively, the last lines can be translated 'she gapes eagerly at someone else's hair', possibly a reference to black pubic hair.

186 Dildo: The Greek noun used here, *baubōn*, suggests a 'pacifier', either something that lulls a person to sleep or the comfort provided a baby by a wet-nurse.

187 Erinna…Nossis: Both are names of famous female poets whose work was woman-centred; for Nossis, see 5.4.

188 Adrastea: An epithet of the goddess Nemesis, who punished haughtiness in mortals.

189 Plectrum: A pick used to pluck the strings of a lyre.

190 Bird-thief…lap: This seems to be a wry comment on the eagerness of Coritto's friends to gain possession of the dildo.

191 Daughter of the Sun: Pasiphaë, the wife of Minos, who gave birth to the hybrid Minotaur. For Pasiphaë, see 9.5.

192 Daedalus: The mythical Greek inventor who escaped from the labyrinth on wings also devised the wooden heifer for Pasiphaë's use with the bull.

193 Juno…Hymenaeus: Juno is the Roman goddess of marriage, and Hymenaeus personifies the wedding.

194 Paraetonia, Mareota and Pharos: Places in Egypt in the area of the capital Alexandria.

195 Sistrum: A rattle used in the rituals of Isis.

196 Scaurus: Probably Mamercus Aemilius Scaurus, a rhetorician and poet under the Julio-Claudian emperors.

197 Hybreas: A famous Greek orator of the mid-first century BCE.

198 Women having sex: The Latin word used here for both women is *tribas*.

199 Women who love women: The Latin word used here is *tribas*.

200 Liber: A Roman god identified with Dionysus, god of wine. ·

201 Lucretia: A Roman matron famous for her virtue: see 7.12, 9.12.

202 Sphinx: The mythical monster who strangled passers-by unless they could answer her riddle.

203 Anubis and Hermes: The Egyptian funerary deity Anubis is paired with Hermes, the Greek god thought to escort the dead to the underworld.

204 Whom Helen bore: Both women are identified using their mothers' names, a standard practice in these formulaic magical texts.

205 Lysippus…courtesan: Lysippus, Menestratus and Silanion were sculptors of the fourth century BCE. Praxilla was a lyric poet of the fifth century BCE. Learchis was another woman poet of whom little is known. For Sappho, see 2.4, 5.2.

206 Woman-lover: This word (*hetairistria*) reflects a cultural association between prostitutes and female same-sex love.

207 Tiresias: The Theban prophet was transformed into a woman after witnessing snakes mating in the forest. When seven years had passed he saw the snakes again and again became male.

208 Caecina Severus: A Roman consul who lobbied the Senate (21 CE; Tacitus *Annals* 3.33–4) against permitting freedoms of dress and behaviour to elite women.

209 Without their formal robes: The *stola* was a garment worn by married women that covered the body from neck to ankles.

210 Women who have sex with each other: Latin *frictrīcēs*.

211 A woman who has sex with other women: Latin *frictrix*.

212 A chief Gallus: A self-castrated priest of Cybele. The chief Gallus performed administrative duties for the cult under the Romans.

213 Soranus *Gynecology* 3.12.

214 E.g. Hippocrates *On Generation* 6–7.

215 Athenaeus, *The Philosophers at Dinner* 563e.

216 Sirius: The heliacal rising of Sirius marked the hottest days of summer for the Greeks.

217 Thyestes...sister: Thyestes had sex with his daughter, Oedipus with his mother and Macareus with his sister. All these mythic stories were presented in Greek tragedies.

218 Full of sexual vigour: literally, 'full of semen.'

219 Iccus of Tarentum: An athlete and trainer of wrestlers who focused on the relationship between athletics and health.

220 'Inferior to themselves': This reference to people who are unable to achieve self-discipline is further explained in Plato *Laws* 626e–627a.

221 Same place...emitted from there: Possibly a reference to the clitoris.

222 Wind-egg: An infertile or imperfect egg.

223 Desire for sex: Literally, 'desire for the bed.' Aristotle probably refers to Homer *Iliad* 24.130.

224 Ceres suckling Iacchus: Iacchus was a child-deity related to Dionysus and one of the group of deities worshiped in the Eleusinian Mysteries of Demeter (Ceres to the Romans). For Iacchus and Demeter see 1.16.

225 Silenus: The silens were creatures in Greek mythology, part goat or horse and part man (similar to the satyrs). Silenus was depicted as elderly, with a blunt nose and thick lips.

226 Epididymis: The narrow, coiled tube connecting the testicle to the vas deferens, which contracts during ejaculation to propel the semen.

227 Satraps: Governors of the Persian provinces, who represent wealth and power.

228 Thrasonides: A character in Menander's comedy *Misoumenos* ('The Object of Hate'), the soldier Thrasonides fell in love with his slave captive Cratea, but she despised him.

229 Diogenes: This is likely a reference to Diogenes of Oenoanda, an Epicurean philosopher of the 2nd century CE.

230 Samos: Hera had an important sanctuary on the island of Samos, where the painting in question may have been displayed.

231 Yet youngest...Zeus: Cronus swallowed his children in the order they were born. When Zeus subdued his father, he forced Cronus to disgorge the children, and Hestia emerged last.

232 Dascylus: A Lydian nobleman.

233 Bear-priestess: The bear was important in the myths and cults of Artemis, goddess of wild nature and the hunt.

234 Epaminondas: A leading Theban general and politician of the fourth century BCE who challenged Spartan military power.

235 Cimon: A celebrated Athenian general of the fifth century BCE who fought against the Persians.

236 Inachus' daughter: Io. Inachus was a river god and primordial ruler of Argos in Greece.

237 Capitoline Juno: Juno, goddess of marriage, as worshiped on the Capitoline hill in Rome beside Jupiter and Minerva.

238 Palatine: The site of the original settlement of Rome. The Julio-Claudian and later emperors had their residences there.

239 Marriage bed of Julia: Wife of the emperor Tiberius and daughter of his predecessor Augustus.

240 Decemvir Applius Claudius: Appius Claudius Crassus, a corrupt official of the early Republic who held office in 451 BCE – not to be confused with Appius Claudius Caecus (the Blind) mentioned in 3.12. The Decemviri or 'Ten Men' were magistrates entrusted with the revision of the laws.

241 Pytho: The sanctuary of Apollo at Delphi.

242 Medes: The Persians, who invaded Greece in the 490s BCE.

243 Servius: Servius Tullius, the sixth king of Rome.

244 Bearers of the *fascēs*: The *fascēs* was a bundle of sticks with an axe at the centre, a symbol of Roman officials' authority. When they travelled through the city, important officials were preceded by bodyguards carrying the *fascēs*.

245 Pontifex Maximus: The high priest of the college of priests at ancient Rome.

246 Acheron: A river of the underworld, used poetically later in this passage as an epithet for Hades.

247 Eucrates: An Athenian general suspected of treachery.

248 The Two Goddesses: Demeter and Persephone; women were more likely to invoke goddesses than gods, and the ritual of these goddesses involved sex-talk (1.18).

249 Mount Taygetus: A mountain range with a peak overlooking Sparta, the hometown of Lampito.

250 Poseidon and a boat: A reference to the tragedy *Tyro* by Sophocles, in which Poseidon seduced Tyro and she abandoned the resulting twin sons in a boat.

251 Quintus Hortensius: A renowned orator who competed against Cicero in the law courts. Marcia bore him one child and inherited much of his wealth when he died in 50 BCE; scholars disagree on whether she afterwards remarried Cato.

252 Until he cares…sweet lips: Solon Fr. 25 West.

253 You lacked reverence…kisses: These lines from a lost play (*TrGF* 3, fr. 135) were probably spoken by Achilles to his dead friend Patroclus (Aeschylus portrayed Achilles as lover and Patroclus as beloved).

254 Pindar…charms: Perhaps a mistaken reference to Pindar *Pythian* 2.42 where Centaurus is born when Ixion rapes a simulacrum of Hera.

255 Sappho…charm: Sappho Fr. 49 Lobel-Page.

256 Plato…reproduction: Plato *Phaedrus* 250e.

257 'Full of semen': Plato *Laws* 839b; for this passage see 6.5.

258 Now I delight…merriment to men: Solon Fr. 26 West.

259 Compare Plato's *Symposium*, in which Pausanias argues (2.10) that Heavenly Aphrodite, whom he associates with pederastic love, is older than Common Aphrodite, the ruler of hetersexual love.

260 Herod did in fact kill Mariame's grandfather, though not her father. She suspected his complicity in the drowning death of her brother.

261 The Sintians: A non-Greek tribe on the island of Lemnos in the northern Aegean. They worshiped a god the Greeks identified as Hephaestus.

262 Hasty bitch: The Greeks had a proverbial saying that a hasty bitch gives birth to blind puppies.

263 Oracle...Thesprotia: Thesprotia was a remote district in northwestern Greece. Its association with the underworld and the gods Hades and Persephone was very ancient.

264 Cadmus' daughters: Agave, Ino, and Semele, the mother and aunts of Pentheus.

265 Thesmothetae: Literally 'those who set down the laws', a group of six magistrates who acted as judges at Athens.

266 I render a literal translation of the phrase *apokalypsai aschēmosynēn*, 'uncover the shame of', which is a euphemism for 'have sexual relations with'. The repetition of this phrase most likely sounded as archaic to the Hellenistic readers of the Septuagint as it does to us.

267 Magus: A sorcerer-priest of the Persian religion of Zoroastrianism. The Romans thought that magi were skilled at reading omens and born of incestuous unions.

268 Consualia: A festival that other sources say was in honour of Consus, the god who protected the harvested grain. The games consisted of chariot races.

269 Collatia...Collatinus: Collatinus was the husband of Lucretia. He himself was a member of the royal Tarquin family and took his name from the town of Collatia where he resided.

270 Spurius Lucretius...Lucius Junius Brutus: These four men were the leaders of the revolution that overthrew the Tarquin kingship and established a republic. Spurius Lucretius was Lucretia's father.

271 Phoebe...both: Castor and Pollux carried off their brides, the sisters Phoebe and Hilaera, by force.

272 Tertian fever: a periodic fever that recurs every 48 hours.

273 Satyrion: an aphrodisiac substance.

274 Pervert: I have translated the Latin term *cinaedus* as 'pervert'.

275 Drinking horn: Petronius uses the term *embasicoetas*, which refers to a drinking cup as well as a passive partner in sex.

276 Artemis at Caryae: Caryae was a Peloponnesian city in the territory of the Spartans, famous for its sanctuary of Artemis where the local maidens danced in her honour.

277 With necessity all is good: Compare the remark of Haterius in 7.11 that lack of chastity in slaves was necessary.

278 Aphrodite: As we learn later in this passage, the local name of the goddess in question was Mylitta. The Greeks identified this goddess with Aphrodite.

279 Thesmothetae: Literally 'those who set down the laws'. See also 9.9.

280 Mysteries: The mysteries of Demeter and Persephone celebrated at Eleusis near Athens.

281 Obol: In Classical Athens, the obol was a silver coin of relatively small denomination. Six obols made one drachma.

282 The Paphian: Aphrodite, who had a famous sanctuary at Paphos on Cyprus.

283 Pirene: A spring at Corinth associated with poetic inspiration by the Muses.

284 Tyndareus' daughter: Helen, whose beauty drew many suitors for her hand in marriage.

285 The girl in the toga: Female prostitutes in Rome wore the toga.

286 Lynceus: One of the Argonauts famous for his keen eyesight.

287 Hypsaea: Hypsaea's blindness must have been proverbial, but nothing else is known about her.

288 Catia: A noted adulteress.

289 Hebrus: A river of Thrace, associated with the frozen north.

290 Uprights of the loom: The Greek word used here is *histos*, which refers to masts, the vertical support for looms, or anything standing upright.

291 When her name…the urn had been cleaned out: These sentences cast doubt on the legitimacy of the voting in the girl's acquittal on the charge of murder.

292 Lictor: Bodyguards who attended important officials at Rome carrying the symbol of power called the *fascēs*. Compare 7.13 on the Vestal Virgins.

293 Cato the Younger (95–46 BCE), an orator and statesman known for his moral rigour. On Cato, see also 8.18.

294 Flora: The Roman goddess of flowers and the Spring season. Her festival was held in late April or early May.

295 Aedile: A Roman official responsible for financial matters including organising city festivals.

296 Kalends of July: In the Roman calendar, the term 'kalends' refers to the first day of the month.

297 Hipponicus… 'the Wealthy': Hipponicus and Callias were members of one of the wealthiest noble families in Athens, the Alcmaeonids.

298 Omphale, Deianira, and Hera: Omphale was a Lydian queen to whom Heracles was enslaved. Deianira's jealousy resulted in Heracles' death, and Hera was notorious for her rebelliousness and her jealousy of Zeus' mistresses.

299 Cratinus…to become his Hera: Cratinus *PCG* 4, Fr. 259. Cratinus was an Athenian master of Old Comedy who died in 422 BCE.

300 Eupolis…not a whore: Eupolis *PCG* 5, Fr. 110. With Aristophanes and Cratinus, Eupolis was the third of the three great Athenian poets of Old Comedy. His lost play *Demes* dealt with the political situation of Athens, which was divided into several districts called demes.

301 Ias and Chione: Typical prostitutes' names.

302 Britannicus: The son of Claudius and Messalina, who was passed over for the throne and murdered by his stepbrother Nero in 55 CE.

303 Proclaimed…fornication: In other words, Vistilia registered as a prostitute with the aedile, a Roman official.

304 The Sosandran Aphrodite of Calamis: Calamis was a sculptor of the fifth century BCE. His Aphrodite Sosandra ('Savior of Men') stood on the Athenian Acropolis.

305 Effeminate males: The Greek term used here is *androgunos*, 'man-woman'.

306 Capital offense: Phryne was tried for profaning the Eleusinian Mysteries.

307 Praxiteles…Cnidian Aphrodite: The sculptor Praxiteles' most famous statue was a nude Aphrodite that stood in a round temple at Cnidus in Caria.

308 Thespiae in Boeotia was the site of a sanctuary and festival for the god Eros. See 2.22.

Bibliography

Adams, J. N. (1982), *The Latin Sexual Vocabulary*. Baltimore: Johns Hopkins University Press.

Ancona, R. (2005), '(Un)Constrained male desire: an intertextual reading of Horace Odes 2.8 and Catullus Poem 61', in R. Ancona and E. Greene (eds), *Gendered Dynamics in Latin Love Poetry*, pp. 41–60.

Ancona, R. and Greene, E. (eds), (2005), *Gendered Dynamics in Latin Love Poetry*. Baltimore: Johns Hopkins University Press.

Archer, L. J., Fischler, S. and Wyke, M. (eds), (1994), *Women in Ancient Societies: An Illusion of the Night*. New York: Routledge.

Arieti, James A. (1997), 'Rape and Livy's view of Roman history', in S. Deacy and K. F. Peirce (eds), *Rape in Antiquity*, pp. 209–29.

Assante, J. (1998), 'The kar.kid/harimtu, prostitute or single woman? A reconsideration of the evidence', *UF* 30, pp. 5–96.

—(2003), 'From whores to hierodules: The historiographic invention of Mesopotamian female sex professionals', in A. A. Donohue and M. D. Fullerton (eds), *Ancient Art and its Historiography*. Cambridge and London: Cambridge University Press, pp. 13–47.

Barton, C. A. (1999), 'The Roman blush: The delicate matter of self-control', in J. I. Porter ed., *Constructions of the Classical Body*, pp. 212–34.

Beard, M. (1995), 'Re-reading (Vestal) virginity', in R. Hawley and B. Levick (eds), *Women in Antiquity: New Assessments*. London and New York: Routledge, pp. 166–77.

Blundell, S. and Williamson, M. (eds), (1998), *The Sacred and the Feminine in Ancient Greece*. London: Routledge.

Bolmarcich, S. (2001), '*Homophrosynē* in the *Odyssey*', *CPh* 96 (3), pp. 205–13.

Borgeaud, P. (2004), *Mother of the Gods. From Cybele to the Virgin Mary*. Tr. L. Hochroth. Baltimore and London: Johns Hopkins University Press.

Boswell, J. (1980), *Christianity, Social Tolerance, and Homosexuality: Gay People in Western Europe from the Beginning of the Christian Era to the Fourteenth Century*. Chicago: University of Chicago Press.

Breitenberger, B. (2007), *Aphrodite and Eros. The Development of Erotic Mythology in Early Greek Poetry and Cult*. London and New York: Routledge.

Bremmer, J. N. (1996), 'Magic, martyrdom and women's liberation in the Acts of Paul and Thecla', in J. N. Bremmer ed., *The Apocryphal Acts of Paul and Thecla*, pp. 36–59.

Bremmer, J. N. ed., (1996), *The Apocryphal Acts of Paul and Thecla*. Kampen: Kok Pharos Publishing House.

Brooten, B. J. (1996), *Love Between Women: Early Christian Responses to Female Homoeroticism*. Chicago: University of Chicago Press.

Brouwer, H. H. J. (1989), *Bona Dea: The Sources and a Description of the Cult*. Leiden and New York: Brill.

Brown, P. (1990), 'Bodies and minds: sexuality and renunciation in early Christianity', in D. Halperin, J. Winkler and F. Zeitlin (eds), *Before Sexuality: The Construction of Erotic Experience in the Ancient Greek World*, pp. 479–93.

Brown, R. D. (1987), *Lucretius on Love and Sex: A Commentary on De rerum natura IV, 1030–1287, with Prolegomena, Text, and Translation*. Leiden and New York: Brill.

Brumfield, A. (1996), '*Aporreta*: verbal and ritual obscenity in the cults of ancient women', in Hägg, R. ed., *The Role of Religion in the Early Greek Polis*, pp. 67–74.

Budin, S. (2003), *The Origin of Aphrodite*. Bethesda, MD: CDL Press.

—(2008), The Myth of Sacred Prostitution in Antiquity. Cambridge and London: Cambridge University Press.

Burian, P. ed., (1985), *Directions in Euripidean Criticism. A Collection of Essays*. Durham, NC: Duke University Press.

Cairns, D. L. (1993), *Aidōs. The Psychology and Ethics of Honour and Shame in Ancient Greek Literature*. Oxford: Clarendon Press.

—(1996), 'Off with her AIDŌS: Herodotus 1.8.3–4', *CQ* 46 (1), pp. 78–83.

—(1997), 'The meadow of Artemis and the character of the Euripidean Hippolytus', *QUCC* 57 (3), pp. 51–75.

Calame, C. (1997), *Choruses of Young Women in Ancient Greece: Their Morphology, Religious Role, and Social Function*. Tr. D. Collins and J. Orion. Lanham, MD: Rowman and Littlefield.

—(1999), *The Poetics of Eros in Ancient Greece*. Princeton: Princeton University Press.

Cantarella, E. (1992), *Bisexuality in the Ancient World*. New Haven: Yale University Press.

—(2002), 'Marriage and sexuality in republican Rome: a Roman conjugal love story', in M. C. Nussbaum and J. Sihvola (eds), *The Sleep of Reason: Erotic Experience and Sexual Ethics in Ancient Greece and Rome*, pp. 269–82.

Carey, C. (1995), 'Rape and adultery in Athenian law', *CQ* 45 (2), pp. 407–17.

Carne-Ross, D. S. (2010), *Classics and Translation: Essays*. Edited by K. Haynes. Lewisburg, PA: Bucknell University Press.

Carson, A. (1986), *Eros the Bittersweet: An Essay*. Princeton: Princeton University Press.

—(1990), 'Putting her in her place: woman, dirt and desire', in D. Halperin, J. Winkler and F. Zeitlin (eds), *Before Sexuality: The Construction of Erotic Experience in the Ancient Greek World*, pp. 135–69.

Cartledge, P. (1992), 'The politics of Spartan pederasty', in W. R. Dynes and S. Donaldson (eds), *Homosexuality in the Ancient World*, pp. 75–94.

Chew, K. (2003), 'The chaste and the chased: *sōphrosynē*, female martyrs and novelistic heroines', *SyllClass* 14, p. 205–22.

Chlup, R. (2007), 'The semantics of fertility: levels of meaning in the Thesmophoria', *Kernos* 20, pp. 69–95.

Clark, E. A. (1995), 'Antifamilial tendencies in ancient Christianity', *Journal of the History of Sexuality* 5 (3), pp. 356–80.

Clark, G. (1998), 'The old Adam: the Fathers and the unmaking of masculinity', in L. Foxhall, and J. Salmon (eds), *Thinking Men: Masculinity and its Self-Representation in the Classical Tradition*, pp. 170–82.

Clarke, J. R. (1998), *Looking at Lovemaking. Constructions of Sexuality in Roman Art.* Berkeley: University of California Press.
—(2003), *Roman Sex, 100 BC-AD 250.* New York: Harry N. Abrams.
Clarke, W. M. (1992), 'Achilles and Patroclus in Love', in W. R. Dynes and S. Donaldson (eds), *Homosexuality in the Ancient World*, pp. 95–110.
Clayton, B. (1999), 'Lucretius' erotic mother: maternity as a poetic construct in *De rerum natura*', *Helios* 26 (1), pp. 69–84.
Cohen, B. ed., (1995), *The Distaff Side: Representing the Female in Homer's Odyssey.* New York: Oxford University Press
Cohen, D. (1991a), *Law, Sexuality and Society: The Enforcement of Morals in Classical Athens.* Cambridge and New York: Cambridge University Press.
—(1991b), 'The Augustan law on adultery: The social and cultural context', in D. I. Kertzer and R. P. Saller (eds), *The Family in Italy from Antiquity to the Present*, pp. 109–26.
—(1993), 'Consent and sexual relations in classical Athens', in A. E. Laiou ed., *Consent and Coercion to Sex and Marriage in Ancient and Medieval Societies*, pp. 5–16.
Cohen, E. (2006), 'Free and unfree sexual work: an economic analysis of Athenian prostitution', in C. Faraone and L. K. McClure (eds), *Prostitutes and Courtesans in the Ancient World*, pp. 95–124.
Connell, S. M. (2000), 'Aristotle and Galen on sex difference and reproduction: a new approach to an ancient rivalry', *Studies in History and Philosophy of Science* 31 (3), pp. 405–27.
Conybeare, C. (2007), 'Tertullian on flesh, spirit, and wives', in S. C. R. Swain, S. J. Harrison, and J. Elsner (eds), *Severan Culture*, pp. 430–9.
Cooper, C. (1995), 'Hyperides and the trial of Phryne', *Phoenix* 49 (4), pp. 303–18.
Corbeill, A. (1996), *Controlling Laughter: Political Humour in the Late Roman Republic.* Princeton: Princeton University Press.
Csapo, E. (1997), 'Riding the phallus for Dionysus: Iconology, ritual and gender-role de/construction', *Phoenix* 51 (3–4), pp. 253–95.
Curran, L. C. (1984), 'Rape and rape victims in the *Metamorphoses*', in J. Peradotto and J. P. Sullivan (eds), *Women in the Ancient World: The Arethusa Papers*, pp. 263–86.
Cyrino, M. (1995), *In Pandora's Jar: Lovesickness in Early Greek poetry.* Lanham, MD: University Press of America.
Deacy, S. and Peirce, K. F. (1997), *Rape in Antiquity.* London and Swansea: Duckworth in association with The Classical Press of Wales.
Dean-Jones, L. (1994), *Women's bodies in classical Greek science.* Oxford: Clarendon Press; New York: Oxford University Press.
Detienne, M. (1994), *The Gardens of Adonis: Spices in Greek Mythology.* Tr. J. Lloyd. Princeton: Princeton University Press.
Devries, K. (1997), 'The frigid *eromenoi* and their wooers revisited. A closer look at Greek homosexuality in vase painting', in M. Duberman ed., *Queer Representations: Reading Lives, Reading Cultures*, pp. 14–24.
Dodd, D. B. and Faraone, C. A. (eds), (2003), *Initiation in Ancient Greek Rituals and Narratives.* New York and London: Routledge.
Doherty, L. ed., (2009), *Homer's Odyssey.* Oxford and New York: Oxford University Press.

Donohue, A. A. and Fullerton, M. D. (eds), (2003), *Ancient Art and its Historiography*. Cambridge and London: Cambridge University Press.

Dover, K. J. (1989), *Greek Homosexuality*. Second Edition. Cambridge, MA: Harvard University Press.

Duberman, M. ed., (1997), *Queer Representations: Reading Lives, Reading Cultures*. New York: New York University Press.

DuBois, P. (1992), 'Eros and the woman', *Ramus* 21, pp. 97–116.

Dynes, W. R. and Donaldson, S. (eds) (1992), *Homosexuality in the Ancient World*. New York: Garland.

Edmunds L. (1981), 'The cults and the legend of Oedipus', *HSPh* 85, pp. 221–38.

Edwards, C. (1997), 'Unspeakable professions: public performance and prostitution in ancient Rome', in J. P. Hallett and M. B. Skinner (eds), *Roman Sexualities*, pp. 66–95.

Emlyn-Jones, C. (2009), 'The reunion of Penelope and Odysseus', in L. Doherty ed., *Homer's Odyssey*, pp. 208–30.

Fantham, Elaine. (1991), 'Stuprum. public attitudes and offenses for sexual penalties in republican Rome', *EMC* 35, pp. 267–91.

Faraone, C. (2011), 'Magical and medical approaches to the wandering womb in the ancient Greek world', *ClAnt* 30 (1), pp. 1–32.

Faraone, C. and McClure, L. K. (eds), (2006), *Prostitutes and Courtesans in the Ancient World*. Madison, WI: University of Wisconsin Press.

Finnegan, R. J. (1992), 'Women in Herodian mime', *Hermathena* 152, pp. 21–37.

Flemming, R. (1999), '*Quae corpore quaestum facit*: the sexual economy of female prostitution in the Roman Empire', *JRS* 89, pp. 38–61.

Flemming, R. and Hanson, A. E. (eds), (1998), 'Hippocrates' *Peri Parthenion* (*Diseases of Young Girls*): text and translation', *Early Science and Medicine* 3 (3), pp. 241–52.

Flower, H. I. (2002), 'Rereading the Senatus Consultum de Bacchanalibus of 186 BC: gender roles in the Roman Middle Republic', in V. B. Gorman and E. W. Robinson (eds), *Oikistes: Studies in Constitutions, Colonies and Military Power in the Ancient World*, pp. 79–98.

Foley, H. P. (2001), *Female Acts in Greek Tragedy*. Princeton: Princeton University Press.

—ed., (1981), *Reflections of Women in Antiquity*. New York: Gordon and Breach Science Publishers.

Foxhall, L. and Salmon, J. (eds), (1998), *Thinking Men: Masculinity and its Self-Representation in the Classical Tradition*. London and New York: Routledge.

Gaca, K. L. (2003), *The Making of Fornication: Eros, Ethics, and Political Reform in Greek Philosophy and Early Christianity*. Berkeley: University of California Press.

Gilhuly, K. (2006), 'The phallic lesbian: philosophy, comedy and social inversion in Lucian's *Dialogues of the Courtesans*', in C. Faraone and L. K. McClure (eds), *Prostitutes and Courtesans in the Ancient World*, pp. 274–91.

Glazebrook, A. and Henry, M. (eds), (2011), *Greek Prostitutes in the Ancient Mediterranean, 800 BCE-200 CE*. Madison WI: University of Wisconsin.

Gleason, M. (1995), *Making Men: Sophists and Self-Presentation in Ancient Rome*. Princeton: Princeton University Press.

Goff, B. (2004), *Citizen Bacchae: Women's Ritual Practice in Ancient Greece*. Berkeley: University of California Press.

Goldhill, S. (1995), *Foucault's Virginity: Ancient Erotic Fiction and the History of Sexuality*. Cambridge: Cambridge University Press.

Gorman, V. B. and Robinson, E. W. (eds), (2002), *Oikistes: Studies in Constitutions, Colonies and Military Power in the Ancient World*. Leiden: Brill.

Greene, E. ed., (1996), *Reading Sappho: Contemporary Approaches*. Berkeley: University of California Press.

—(1998), *The Erotics of Domination: Male Desire and the Mistress in Latin Love Poetry*. Baltimore: Johns Hopkins University Press.

—(2005), 'Impossible lesbians in Ovid's *Metamorphoses*', in R. Ancona and E. Greene (eds), *Gendered Dynamics in Latin Love Poetry*, pp. 79–110.

Gunderson, E. (2000), *Staging Masculinity: The Rhetoric of Performance in the Roman World*. Ann Arbor, MI: University of Michigan Press.

Gutting, E. (2006), 'Marriage in the *Aeneid*: Venus, Vulcan, and Dido', *CPh* 101 (3), pp. 263–79.

Gutzwiller, K. (1998), *Poetic Garlands: Hellenistic Epigrams in Context*. Berkeley: University of California Press.

—(2004), 'Gender and inscribed epigram: Herennia Procula and the Thespian Eros', *TAPhA* 134 (2), pp. 383–418.

Hägg, R. ed., (1996), *The Role of Religion in the Early Greek Polis*. Stockholm and Göteborg: Swedish Institute at Athens.

Haley, S. (2002), 'Lucian's 'Leaena and Clonarium': voyeurism or a challenge to assumptions?' in N. S. Rabinowitz and L. Auanger (eds), *Among Women: From the Homosocial to the Homoerotic in the Ancient World*, pp. 286–303.

Hallett, J. P. (1997), 'Female homoeroticism and the denial of Roman reality in Latin literature', in J. P. Hallett and M. B. Skinner (eds), *Roman Sexualities*, pp. 255–73.

Hallett, J. P. and Skinner, M. B. (eds), (1997), *Roman Sexualities*. Princeton: Princeton University Press.

Halperin, D. (1990), 'The democratic body: prostitution and citizenship in Classical Athens', in D. Konstan and M. Nussbaum (eds), *Sexuality in Greek and Roman Society. Differences: A Journal of Feminist Cultural Studies*, Vol. 2, pp. 1–28.

Halperin, D., Winkler, J. and Zeitlin, F. (eds), (1990), *Before Sexuality: The Construction of Erotic Experience in the Ancient Greek World*. Princeton: Princeton University Press.

Hamel, D. (2003), *Trying Neaira: The True Story of a Courtesan's Scandalous Life in Ancient Greece*. New Haven: Yale University Press.

Hanson, A. (1990), 'The medical writers' woman', in D. Halperin, J. Winkler and F. Zeitlin (eds), *Before Sexuality: The Construction of Erotic Experience in the Ancient Greek World*, pp. 309–38.

Hanson, A. H and Green, M. H. (1994), 'Soranus of Ephesus: methodicorum princeps', in W. Haase ed., *Aufstieg und Niedergang der römischen Welt* II, 37, 2, pp. 968–1075. Berlin and New York: de Gruyter.

Hawley, R. and Levick, B. (eds), (1995), *Women in Antiquity: New Assessments*. London and New York: Routledge.

Henderson, J. (1991), *The Maculate Muse. Obscene Language in Aristophanic Comedy*. Second edition. London and New York: Oxford University Press.

Houser, J. S., (2002), 'Eros and *aphrodisia* in Dio Chrysostom', in M. C. Nussbaum and J. Sihvola (eds), *The Sleep of Reason: Erotic Experience and Sexual Ethics in Ancient Greece and Rome*, pp. 327–53.

Hubbard, T. K. ed., (2000), *Greek Love Reconsidered*. New York: W. Hamilton Press.
—ed., (2003), *Homosexuality in Greece and Rome: A Sourcebook of Basic Documents*. Berkeley: University of California Press.
Hupperts, C. (2000), *Eros Dikaios*. 2 Vols. Diss. Amsterdam. [in Dutch.]
Irwin, E. (2007), 'The invention of virginity on Olympus', in B. MacLachlan and J. Fletcher, J. (eds), *Virginity Revisited: Configurations of the Unpossessed Body*, pp. 13–23.
Johns, C. (1982), *Sex or Symbol. Erotic Images of Greece and Rome*. Austin: University of Texas Press.
Joshel S. R. (1992), 'The body female and the body politic: Livy's Lucretia and Verginia', in A. Richlin (ed.), *Pornography and Representation in Greece and Rome*, pp. 112–130.
—(1997), 'Female desire and the discourse of empire: Tacitus' Messalina', in J. P. Hallett and M. B. Skinner (eds), *Roman Sexualities*, pp. 221–54.
Kaimio, M. (2002), 'Erotic experience in the conjugal bed: good wives in Greek tragedy', in M. C. Nussbaum and J. Sihvola (eds), *The Sleep of Reason: Erotic Experience and Sexual Ethics in Ancient Greece and Rome*, pp. 95–119.
Keesling, C. (2006), 'Heavenly bodies: monuments to prostitutes in Greek sanctuaries', in C. Faraone and L. K. McClure (eds), *Prostitutes and Courtesans in the Ancient World*, pp. 59–76.
King, H. (1994), 'Producing woman: Hippocratic gynaecology', in L. J. Archer, S. Fischler and M. Wyke (eds), *Women in Ancient Societies: An Illusion of the Night*, pp. 102–114.
Koehl, R. (1997), 'Ephoros and ritualized homosexuality in Bronze Age Crete', in M. Duberman ed., *Queer Representations: Reading Lives, Reading Cultures*, pp. 7–13.
Konstan, D. (1994), *Sexual Symmetry: Love in the Ancient Novel and Related Genres*. Princeton: Princeton University Press.
—(2002), 'Women, boys, and the paradigm of Athenian pederasty', *Differences: A Journal of Feminist Cultural Studies*. 13 (2), pp. 35–56.
Laiou, A. E. ed., (1993), *Consent and Coercion to Sex and Marriage in Ancient and Medieval Societies*. Washington, DC: Dumbarton Oaks Research Library and Collection.
Langlands, R. (2006), *Sexual Morality in Ancient Rome*. Cambridge: Cambridge University Press.
Lape, S. (2006), 'The psychology of prostitution in Aeschines' speech against Timarchus', in C. Faraone and L. K. McClure (eds), *Prostitutes and Courtesans in the Ancient World*, pp. 139–60.
Laqueur, T. (1990), *Making Sex: Body and Gender From the Greeks to Freud*. Cambridge, MA: Harvard University Press.
Larmour, D., Miller, P. and Platter, C. (eds), (1998), *Rethinking Sexuality: Foucault and Classical Antiquity*. Princeton: Princeton University Press.
Lear, A. and Cantarella, E., (2008), *Images of Ancient Greek Pederasty: Boys Were Their Gods*. London and New York: Routledge.
Lefkowitz, M. R. (1993), 'Seduction and rape in Greek myth', in A. E. Laiou ed., *Consent and Coercion to Sex and Marriage in Ancient and Medieval Societies*, pp. 17–37.
Leitao, D. (2002), 'The legend of the Sacred Band', in M. C. Nussbaum and J. Sihvola (eds), *The Sleep of Reason: Erotic Experience and Sexual Ethics in Ancient Greece and Rome*, pp. 143–69.

Lincoln, B. (1979), 'The rape of Persephone. A Greek scenario of women's initiation', *HThR* 72, pp. 223–35.

Llewellyn-Jones, L. (2003), *Aphrodite's Tortoise: The Veiled Woman in Ancient Greece*. Swansea, Wales: The Classical Press of Wales.

—(2007), 'House and veil in ancient Greece', in R. Westgate, N. Fisher and J. Whitley (eds), *Building Communities: House, Settlement and Society in the Aegean and Beyond*. British School at Athens Studies, 15, pp. 251–8.

Loreaux, N., Nagy, G. and Slatkin, L. (eds), (2001), *Antiquities*. New York: The New Press.

Lowe, N. J. (1998), 'Thesmophoria and Haloa: myth, physics and mysteries', in S. Blundell and M. Williamson (eds), *The Sacred and the Feminine in Ancient Greece*, pp. 149–73.

MacLachlan, B. and Fletcher, J. (eds), (2007), *Virginity Revisited: Configurations of the Unpossessed Body*. Toronto: University of Toronto Press.

Marinatos, N. (2003), 'Striding across boundaries: Hermes and Aphrodite as gods of initiation', in D. B. Dodd and C. A. Faraone (eds), *Initiation in Ancient Greek Rituals and Narratives*, pp. 130–51.

McClure, L. K. ed., (2002), *Sexuality and Gender in the Classical World : Readings and Sources*. Oxford and Malden, MA: Blackwell.

—(2003), *Courtesans at Table: Gender and Greek Literary Culture in Athenaeus*. New York: Routledge.

McElduff, S. and Sciarrino, E. (eds), (2011), *Complicating the History of Western Translation: The Ancient Mediterranean in Perspective*. Manchester: St Jerome.

McGinn, T. A. J. (2003), *Prostitution, Sexuality, and the Law in Ancient Rome*. New York: Oxford University Press.

—(2004), *The Economy of Prostitution in the Roman World: A Study of Social History and the Brothel*. Ann Arbor, MI: University of Michigan Press.

Moreau, P. (2002), *Incestus et prohibitae nuptiae: conception romaine de l'inceste et histoire des prohibitions matrimoniales pour cause de parenté dans la Rome antique*. Paris: Belles Letters.

Moses, D. C. (1993), 'Livy's Lucretia and the validity of coerced consent in Roman law', in A. E. Laiou ed., *Consent and Coercion to Sex and Marriage in Ancient and Medieval Societies*, pp. 39–81.

Nussbaum, M. C. (1994), *The Therapy of Desire: Theory and Practice in Hellenistic Ethics*. Princeton: Princeton University Press.

—(2002), 'The incomplete feminism of Musonius Rufus, Platonist, Stoic, and Roman', in M. C. Nussbaum and J. Sihvola (eds), *The Sleep of Reason: Erotic Experience and Sexual Ethics in Ancient Greece and Rome*, pp. 283–326.

Nussbaum, M. C. and Sihvola, J. (eds), (2002), *The Sleep of Reason: Erotic Experience and Sexual Ethics in Ancient Greece and Rome*. Chicago: University of Chicago Press.

Ogden, D. (1997), 'Rape, adultery and the protection of bloodlines in classical Athens', in S. Deacy and K. F. Peirce (eds), *Rape in Antiquity*, pp. 25–41.

—ed., (2007), *The Blackwell Companion to Greek Religion*. London and New York: Blackwell.

Olender, M. (1990), 'Aspects of Baubo: ancient texts and contexts', in D. Halperin, J. Winkler and F. Zeitlin (eds), *Before Sexuality: The Construction of Erotic Experience in the Ancient Greek World*, pp. 83–113.

—(2001), 'Misshapen Priapos', in N. Loreaux, G. Nagy and L. Slatkin (eds), *Antiquities*, pp. 283–91.

Palmer, R. E. A. (1974), *Roman Religion and Roman Empire: Five Essays*. Philadelphia: University of Pennsylvania Press.

Parker, H. (1997), 'The teratogenic grid', in J. P. Hallett and M. B. Skinner (eds), *Roman Sexualities*, pp. 47–65.

—(1998), 'Sex, tyranny, and Hippias' incest dream: (Herodotos 6.107)', *GRBS* 39 (3), pp. 221–41.

—(2004), 'Why were the Vestals virgins? Or, the chastity of women and the safety of the Roman state', *AJPh* 12 (4), pp. 563–601.

Peradotto, J.and Sullivan, J. P. (eds), (1984), *Women in the Ancient World: The Arethusa Papers*. Albany: State University of New York Press.

Pierce, K. F. (1997), 'The portrayal of rape in New Comedy', in S. Deacy and K. F. Peirce (eds), *Rape in Antiquity*, pp. 163–84.

Pintabone, D. (2002), 'Ovid's Iphis and Ianthe: when girls won't be girls', in N. S. Rabinowitz and L. Auanger (eds), *Among Women: From the Homosocial to the Homoerotic in the Ancient World*, pp. 256–85.

Pirenne Delforge, V. (1994), *L'Aphrodite grecque*. Athens and Liège: Centre International d'Étude de la religion grecque antique.

—(2007), 'Something to do with Aphrodite: *Ta aphrodisia* and the sacred', in D. Ogden ed., *The Blackwell Companion to Greek Religion*, pp. 311–23.

Porter, J. I. ed., (1999), *Constructions of the Classical Body*. Ann Arbor, MI: University of Michigan Press.

Rabinowitz, N. S. (2002), 'Excavating women's homoeroticism in ancient Greece: the evidence from Attic vase painting', in N. S. Rabinowitz and L. Auanger (eds), *Among Women: From the Homosocial to the Homoerotic in the Ancient World*, pp. 106–66.

Rabinowitz, N. S. and Auanger, L. (eds), (2002), *Among Women: From the Homosocial to the Homoerotic in the Ancient World*. Austin: University of Texas Press.

Redfield, J. (2003), *The Locrian Maidens: Love and Death in Greek Italy*. Princeton: Princeton University Press.

Reed, J. D. (1995), 'The sexuality of Adonis', *ClAnt* 14 (2), pp. 317–47.

Reeder, E. D. ed., (1995), *Pandora: Women in Classical Greece*. Princeton: Princeton University Press.

Rehm, R. (1994), *Marriage to Death: The Conflation of Wedding and Funeral Rituals in Greek Tragedy*. Princeton: Princeton University Press.

Richardson, P. (1996), *Herod: King of the Jews and Friend of the Romans*. Columbia: University of South Carolina Press.

Richlin A. (1981), 'Approaches to the sources on adultery at Rome', in H. P. Foley ed. *Reflections of Women in Antiquity*, pp. 379–404.

—(1983), *The Garden of Priapus: Sexuality and Aggression in Roman Humour*. New Haven: Yale University Press.

—ed., (1992), *Pornography and Representation in Greece and Rome*. New York: Oxford University Press.

Rist, J. M. (2001), 'Plutarch's *Amatorius*: A commentary on Plato's theories of love?' *CQ* 51 (2), pp. 557–75.

Roller, L. (1999), *In Search of God the Mother: The Cult of Anatolian Cybele*. Berkeley: University of California Press.

Rosenzweig, R. (2004), *Worshipping Aphrodite: Art and Cult in Classical Athens*. Ann Arbor, MI: University of Michigan Press.

Rousselle, A. (1993), *Porneia: On Desire and the Body in Antiquity*. Tr. F. Pheasant, Cambridge, MA: Blackwell.

Scaife, A. R. (1994–5), 'Ritual and persuasion in the house of Ischomachus', *CJ* 90 (3), pp. 225–32.

Sergent, B. (1986), *Homosexuality in Greek Myth*, Tr. A. Goldhammer. Boston: Beacon Press.

Sissa, G. (1990), *Greek Virginity*. Tr. A. Goldhammer. Cambridge MA: Harvard University Press.

Skinner, M. (2002), 'Aphrodite Garlanded: Eros and Poetic Creativity in Sappho and Nossis', in N. S. Rabinowitz and L. Auanger (eds), *Among Women: From the Homosocial to the Homoerotic in the Ancient World*, pp. 60–81.

—(2005), *Sexuality in Greek and Roman Culture*. Malden, MA and Oxford: Blackwell.

—(2011), *Clodia Metelli: The Tribune's Sister*. Oxford and New York: Oxford University Press.

Smith, W. S. (2005a), 'Advice on sex by the self-defeating satirists: Horace *Sermones* 1.2, Juvenal *Satire* 6, and Roman satiric writing', in W. Smith ed., *Satiric Advice on Women and Marriage: From Plautus to Chaucer*, pp. 111–28.

—(2005b), 'The cold cares of Venus: Lucretius and anti-marriage literature', in W. S. Smith ed., *Satiric Advice on Women and Marriage*, pp 71–91.

—ed., (2005c), *Satiric Advice on Women and Marriage: From Plautus to Chaucer*. Ann Arbor, MI: University of Michigan Press.

Snyder, J. (1989), *The Woman and the Lyre: Women Writers in Classical Greece and Rome*. Carbondale and Edwardsville: Southern Illinois University Press.

—(1997), *Lesbian Desire in the Lyrics of Sappho*. New York: Columbia University Press.

Sommerstein, A. (1998), 'Rape and young manhood in Athenian comedy', in L. Foxhall and J. Salmon (eds), *Thinking Men: Masculinity and its Self-Representation in the Classical Tradition*, pp. 100–14.

Staples, A. (1998), *From Good Goddess to Vestal Virgins: Sex and Category in Roman Religion*. London and New York: Routledge.

Stehle, E. (1989), 'Venus, Cybele and the Sabine women', *Helios* 16 (2), pp. 143–64.

—(1990), 'Sappho's gaze: fantasies of a goddess and young man', in D. Konstan and M. Nussbaum (eds), *Sexuality in Greek and Roman Society. Differences: A Journal of Feminist Cultural Studies*, Vol. 2, pp. 88–125.

Swain, S. C. R., Harrison, S. J. and Elsner J. (eds), *Severan Culture*. Cambridge and New York: Cambridge University Press.

Thomsen, O. (2002), 'An introduction to the study of Catullus' wedding poems: the ritual drama of Catullus 62', *C&M* 53, pp. 255–88.

Walcot, P. (1998), 'Plutarch on sex', *G&R* 45 (2), pp. 166–87.

Watson, L. C. (2006), 'Catullus and the poetics of incest', *Antichthon* 40, pp. 35–48.

Westgate, R., Fisher N. and Whitley, J. (eds), (2007), *Building Communities: House, Settlement and Society in the Aegean and Beyond*. British School at Athens Studies 15. London: British School at Athens.

Williams, C. A. (2010), *Roman Homosexuality*. Second Edition. London and New York: Oxford University Press.

Williamson, M. (1998), 'Eros the blacksmith: performing masculinity in Anakreon's love lyrics', in L. Foxhall and J. Salmon (eds), *Thinking Men: Masculinity and its Self-Representation in the Classical Tradition*, pp. 71–82.

Zeitlin F. (1982), 'Cultic models of the female. Rites of Dionysus and Demeter', *Arethusa* 15, pp. 129–57.

—(1985), 'The power of Aphrodite. Eros and the boundaries of the self in the Hippolytus', in P. Burian ed., *Directions in Euripidean Criticism. A Collection of Essays*, pp. 52–111.

—(1995a), 'Figuring fidelity in Homer's Odyssey', in B. Cohen ed., *The Distaff Side: Representing the Female in Homer's Odyssey*, pp. 117–52.

—(1995b), 'The economics of Hesiod's Pandora', in E. Reeder ed. *Pandora: Women in Classical Greece*, pp. 49–56.

—(1999), 'Reflections on erotic desire in Archaic and Classical Greece', in J. I. Porter ed., *Constructions of the Classical Body*, pp. 50–76.

Index of Sources

Index

The index includes all Greek and Latin words. Roman men and women are indexed by the name of the *gens* unless another name is familiar and more commonly used (e.g. Cicero, Caligula).

abduction, of Bacchon 230; of brides 224–5; and brothels 277; of Ganymede 294n. 144; of girls at Caryae 261; and pederasty 122; of Persephone of 24, 236; of Sabine women 237
Abraham 104, 293n. 126
abstinence, and Christianity 185–6, 206; in comedy 216–19; in marriage 223–4; and men 177; and religion 12, 38, 183–4; and women 158, 198; and virtue 9–10, 166
Acheron 35, 206, 211, 244, 298nn. 246, 246
Achilles, among the maidens 153; and Patroclus 108, 127, 129, 131, 294nn. 155, 167, 298n. 253
Actaeon 89, 291n. 93
active sex role 7, 136, 191
Adam 230
Adonis 48; and Sappho 134; sexual attractiveness of 27, 33–6
adulter 14
adultery, of Aphrodite and Ares 235, 240–2; of Caesar 95–6; and *cinaedus* 82; of Clodia 93–5; comic treatment of 87–8; and complacent husbands 99; cultural views of 236, 237, 238; definition of 135, 235; and female homosexual behavior 135, 148, 149; of Helen and

Paris 210, 235, 239–40; in ideal state 164, 167, 181; and Jewish law 251; and Lucretia 254–5; and pagan law 235–6, 249, 262–3, 265; origin of 66; and Phales 32; prostitution as 282; and Spartan women 226; terminology for 14; unlawfulness of 175
aegis 27, 30, 31, 57, 84, 187, 288n. 3
Aeneas 50, 51–2, 58, 72–3, 290n. 57
affection, of animals 166; of courtesans 38, 228; and *erōs* 181; and family 118, 181, 227; in marriage 164, 200, 207–8, 220, 221, 224, 225, 226, 231–2, 254; and pederasty 8, 67, 108–9, 116, 117, 120, 128, 129; of Pericles for Aspasia 280; terminology for 4–6
Agamemnon 36, 289n. 26; 291n. 96
Agathon 68, 115
Agave 89, 247, 291n. 93, 299n. 264
Agdistis *see* Cybele
Agido 133, 136–8
Agrippina *see* empress(es)
aidoia 11
aidōs 11, 203 *see also* shame
ainos 290n. 57
aischra 11 *see also* shame
aischrologia 23–4, 48, 298n. 248
aischunē 11 *see also* shame
akolasia 9 *see also* self-discipline
akolastos 9
akrateia 9
Alexander *see* Paris
Alexander the Great 286
Alexandria 135, 176, 194; and Adonis 27, 33–6
amāre 5
ambrosia 27–8, 35, 55, 76, 137, 242

201–2; in third century CE
185–6 *see also* Vestal Virgins,
virgin(s)
virtue, celibacy as 185; of cities
282; familial 94, 227; male
38, 194; of matrons 94, 292n.
99, 296n. 201; of Metellus 94;
philosophical 159, 229; physical
172; and prosperity 252; of
Scipio Aemilianus 103; sexual
9–10 see also *aidōs*, chastity,
castitas, *enkrateia*, moderation,
pudicitia, *sōphrosynē*,
self-control, temperantia
vīs 13
Vistilia 283, 301n. 303
vital spirit *see pneuma*
vow(s), for birth of a child 145; for
health 38, 126; of Hestia 187;
of Iphis 148; of Minos 245; of
Xenophon 266, 268
voyeurism 188–9, 237, 246, 249, 260,
280–1
Vulcan 41

war 202, 288n. 11; and Athena 187;
against Love 228; civil 197, 231;
in early Rome 252; Mithridatic
197; and rape 237; of Samians
and Milesians 279; and Spartans
208, 225 *see also* Persian Wars,
Peloponnesian War, Trojan War
warrior(s), arming of 24; beauty of 134;
education of 107, 121–2; Hector
as 235; Parthenopaeus as 294n.
164; and pederasty 107, 121–2,
128–9
weaving 34, 83, 137, 139, 222, 271
wedding(s), celibacy and 201; erotic
aspects of 205; of Evadne and
Capaneus 213–14; feasting at
56; gifts for 210, 224; of Helen
and Menelaus 215; of Iphis
and Ianthe 146, 147, 148; of
Ismenodora and Bacchon 230;
of Nero and Sporus 261; song
for 43, 184, 192, 211, 234;
rituals of 205; of Sabine women
253; women's dress at 80 *see*

also dowry, Hymenaeus, Juno,
marriage, sacred marriage
wet dream 161
widows, dream augury and 150; health
of 199; poverty of 99; ritual
duties of 197; social norms for
194, 224, 227–8; wealthy 208
wife *see* wives
wig 153, 281
wine 150, 228, and Bona Dea 100;
color of 89; and Demeter 44;
and Etruscans 190; Falernian
258; of gods 58, 220; and
lasciviousness 37, 45, 88, 102,
103, 235, 259–60; new 47;
poured on flame 161; as release
from pain 89; summer 160;
tasting of 168; unmixed 101 *see
also* Dionysus, Liber
witch(es) 81, 85, 174, 291n. 80 *see
also* magic
wives, community of 180, 181, 190,
208, 225–6, 226–7; dignity of
224; duties of 205, 221–2, 223,
235; ideal qualities of 206–7;
jealousy of 123, 127; lack of 252;
privileges of 194; role of 222;
sexual behavior of 224; training
of 221–2 *see also* adultery,
marriage, wedding(s)
wolf 17, 55, 281
womb *see* uterus
women, and abstinence 185; advice
to 255; citizen 33, 222, 237, 265,
273; enjoyment of sex by 120,
135, 206, 216–19; household
quarters of 194; physical
weakness of 257; subordination
of 79; suspicion of 33, 79–81,
238–9 *see also* courtesan(s),
daughter(s), empress(es),
priestess(es), prostitute(s),
widow(s), wives, mistress(es)
wrestling 128, 150, 165, 228, 230,
297n. 219

Xenophon of Corinth 266, 268

Zeno of Citium 158–9, 181–2

Zeus 214; and Agdistis 43; and
Aphrodite 49–50, 54, 240, 241;
and Athena 187; Civic 112, 293n.
134; as cosmic mind 176; and
creation of humans 66, 85;
and Cronus 53–4, 58, 187, 188,
297n. 231; Ctesius 291n. 95;
and Dione 49, 64; of the family
282; and Electra 288n. 13; and
Europa 288n. 5; and Ganymede
118, 121, 293n. 144; and Helen
210, 215; and Hera 4, 5, 23, 24,
27–9, 81, 159, 181–2, 300n.
298; and Leda 215; as lover
25, 29–30; and mortal women
25, 188; in oaths 217, 229; and
Pandora 82–4; and Persephone
24; procreative power of 24; as
rapist 236; sacrifice to 90, 122;
and Semele 63, 89, 290n. 65;
thunderbolt of 31, 63, 66, 128,
159, 188, 213, 290n. 65; will of
31; and Wisdom 29 *see also*
aegis, Jupiter